Wittgenstein

For Ruth

Wittgenstein

The Way Out of the Fly-Bottle

Severin Schroeder

polity

Copyright © Severin Schroeder 2006

The right of Severin Schroeder to be identified as Author of this Work has been asserted in accordance with the UK Copyright, Designs and Patents Act 1988.

First published in 2006 by Polity Press

Polity Press
65 Bridge Street
Cambridge CB2 1UR, UK

Polity Press
350 Main Street
Malden, MA 02148, USA

All rights reserved. Except for the quotation of short passages for the purpose of criticism and review, no part of this publication may be reproduced, stored in a retrieval system, or transmitted, in any form or by any means, electronic, mechanical, photocopying, recording or otherwise, without the prior permission of the publisher.

ISBN: 0-7456-2615-7
ISBN: 0-7456-2616-5 (pb)
ISBN-13
ISBN: 978-0-7456-2615-7
ISBN: 978-0-7456-2616-1(pb)

A catalogue record for this book is available from the British Library.

Typeset in 10 on 11.5 pt Palatino
by SNP Best-set Typesetter Ltd, Hong Kong
Printed and bound in Great Britain by MPG Books Ltd, Bodmin, Cornwall

Every effort has been made to trace all copyright holders, but if any have been inadvertently overlooked the publishers will be pleased to include any necessary credits in any subsequent reprint or edition.

For further information on Polity, visit our website: *www.polity.co.uk*

Contents

Acknowledgements viii
Abbreviations ix

1 Between Vienna and Cambridge 1
   1.1 The Wittgensteins 2
   1.2 Vienna 5
   1.3 Moral Solipsism 10
   1.4 Aviator or Philosopher 14
   1.5 Logic 16
   1.6 Norway and the War 21

2 *Tractatus Logico-Philosophicus* 23
   2.1 Logic and Sins 23
   2.2 Foundations: Referentialism, Analysis, Determinacy and Bipolarity 30
   2.3 Logical Atomism 38
   2.4 Pictures: Language and Thought 52
   2.5 Logic 62
   2.6 Whereof One Cannot Speak 88
      (a) Sense, logical syntax, internal properties and formal concepts 88
      (b) The logical form of reality 91
      (c) Solipsism 92
      (d) Ethics 99
      (e) The *Tractatus* paradox 104

3	Schoolmaster, Architect and Professor of Philosophy		113
4	*Philosophical Investigations*		121
	4.1	Only an Album	121
	4.2	The Dissolution of Logical Atomism	128
		(a) Referentialism	128
		(b) Determinacy of sense	134
		(c) Logical analysis	136
		(d) Bipolarity	138
		(e) Essentialism	139
		(f) Meaning through meaning	145
	4.3	The Nature of Philosophy	151
	4.4	Meaning and Use	168
	4.5	The Philosophical Problem about Mental Processes and States	181
	4.6	Understanding and Meaning	185
		An instructive misinterpretation	197
	4.7	The Inner-Object Conception of Sensations	201
		(a) The Ascribability Argument	202
		(b) The Idle-Wheel Argument	206
		(c) Knowledge of other minds	208
		(d) The No-Criterion Argument	210
		(e) An understandable use	215
		(f) The grammar of a sensation word	216
	4.8	Actions and Reasons	219
		(a) Voluntary action	219
		(b) Acting for reasons	227
5	The Final Years		234
6	After Wittgenstein		237
	6.1	Oxford Philosophy and American Philosophy	237
	6.2	Challenges to Wittgenstein's Philosophy	240
		(a) Attacks on the distinction between conceptual and empirical statements	240

(b)	Attacks on the common-sense view of linguistic meaning	247
(c)	Putnam's criticism of 'logical behaviourism'	251

Further Reading 255
Bibliography 257
Index 265

Acknowledgements

Parts of sections 4.0, 4.6 and 4.7 are based on sections of four previously published papers of mine: 'Private Language and Private Experience', in H.-J. Glock (ed.), *Wittgenstein: A Critical Reader* (Oxford: Blackwell, 2001), 174–98; 'The Concept of Trying', *Philosophical Investigations*, 24, 3 (July 2001), 213–27; 'Are Reasons Causes? A Wittgensteinian Response to Davidson', in S. Schroeder (ed.), *Wittgenstein and Contemporary Philosophy of Mind* (Basingstoke: Palgrave, 2001), 150–70; 'The Demand for Synoptic Representations and the Private Language Discussion – *PI* 243–315', in E. Ammereller and E. Fischer (eds), *Wittgenstein at Work: Method in the 'Philosophical Investigations'* (London: Routledge, 2004), 147–69. I thank the publishers for permission to use this material.

I am grateful to Erich Ammereller, Daniel Came, Dorothea Debus, Belinda Jack, Benedikt Ledebur, David Maw, Michael Vogt and Robert Williams for reading parts of the book and giving me valuable comments. My greatest debts are to David Dolby and to the two anonymous readers for Polity, whose criticisms and suggestions were most helpful.

Abbreviations

AL   *Wittgenstein's Lectures, Cambridge, 1932–1935*, ed. A. Ambrose. Oxford: Blackwell, 1979.
B   *Briefe: Briefwechsel mit B. Russell, G. E. Moore, J. M. Keynes, F. P. Ramsey, W. Eccles, P. Engelmann und L. von Ficker*. Frankfurt/Main: Suhrkamp, 1980.
BB   *The Blue and Brown Books*. Oxford: Blackwell, 1958.
BT   *The Big Typescript* = TS 213, published as *WA*, vol. 11; ch. 'Philosophie', 405–35. Published and tr. in *PO*, 160–99.
CL   *Cambridge Letters: Correspondence with Russell, Keynes, Moore, Ramsey and Sraffa*, ed. B. McGuinness and G. H. von Wright. Oxford: Blackwell, 1995.
CV   *Culture and Value*, rev. edn, ed. G. H. von Wright; tr. P. Winch. Oxford: Blackwell, 1998.
D   *Denkbewegungen: Tagebücher 1930–32, 1936–37 (MS 183)*, ed. Ilse Somavilla. Innsbruck: Haymon Verlag, 1997. [Quoted by MS page numbers.]
E   'Letters from Wittgenstein' to Paul Engelmann. Tr. in Engelmann 1967, 1–59 [originals in *B*].
EPB   *Eine philosophische Betrachtung*. In *Werkausgabe Band*, 5, Frankfurt/Main: Suhrkamp, 1984, 117–282.
FB   *Wittgenstein: Familienbriefe*, ed. B. McGuinness, M. C. Ascher, O. Pfersmann. Vienna: Hölder-Pichler-Tempsky, 1996.
FF   '*Frühfassung*': an early version of *PI*: MSS 225, 220, 221. In *PU*, 203–446.
LE   'A Lecture on Ethics'. In *PO*, 37–44.
LF   'Letters to Ludwig von Ficker', tr. B. Gillette. In Luckhardt 1979, 82–98 [originals in *B*].
LFM   *Wittgenstein's Lectures on the Foundations of Mathematics, Cambridge, 1939*, ed. C. Diamond. Hassocks, Sussex: Harvester Press, 1976.

Abbreviations

LL	*Wittgenstein's Lectures, Cambridge, 1930–1932*, ed. D. Lee. Oxford: Blackwell, 1980.
LM	'Wittgenstein's letters to Norman Malcolm'. In Malcolm 1984, 85–134.
LO	*Letters to C. K. Ogden*, ed. G. H. von Wright. Oxford: Blackwell, 1973.
LPP	*Lectures on Philosophical Psychology 1946–47*, notes by P. T. Geach, K. J. Shah and A. C. Jackson; ed. P. T. Geach. Hemel Hempstead: Harvester Wheatsheaf, 1988.
LW I	*Last Writings on the Philosophy of Psychology*, Vol. 1: ed. G. H. von Wright and H. Nyman; tr. C. G. Luckhardt and M. A. E. Aue. Oxford: Blackwell, 1982.
LW II	*Last Writings on the Philosophy of Psychology. Vol. 2: The Inner and the Outer, 1949–1951*, ed. G. H. von Wright and H. Nyman; tr. C. G. Luckhardt and M. A. E. Aue. Oxford: Blackwell, 1992.
ML	'Wittgenstein's Lectures in 1930–33', notes by G. E. Moore. In his *Philosophical Papers*, London: Allen & Unwin, 1959, 252–324.
MS	Unpublished manuscript, numbered in accordance with von Wright's catalogue (1982).
NB	*Notebooks 1914–1916*, ed. G. H. von Wright and G. E. M. Anscombe; tr. G. E. M. Anscombe, rev. ed. Oxford: Blackwell, 1979.
NfL	*Notes for Lectures on "Private Experience" and "Sense Data"* (1934–36). In *PO*, 202–88.
OC	*On Certainty*, ed. G. E. M. Anscombe and G. H. von Wright, tr. D. Paul and G. E. M. Anscombe. Oxford: Blackwell, 1961.
PG	*Philosophical Grammar*, ed. R. Rhees, tr. A. J. P. Kenny. Oxford: Blackwell, 1974.
PI	*Philosophical Investigations*, ed. G. E. M. Anscombe and R. Rhees, tr. G. E. M. Anscombe. Oxford: Blackwell, 1953.
PO	*Philosophical Occasions, 1912–1951*, ed. J. Klagge and A. Nordmann. Indianapolis: Hackett, 1993.
PR	*Philosophical Remarks*, ed. R. Rhees, tr. R. Hargreaves and R. White. Oxford: Blackwell, 1975.
PTLP	*Prototractatus*. London: Routledge & Kegan Paul, 1971.
PU	*Philosophische Untersuchungen: kritisch-genetische Edition*, ed. J. Schulte, Frankfurt/Main: Suhrkamp, 2001. [Contains four earlier versions of *PI*: 'Urfassung', 'Frühfassung', 'Bearbeitete Frühfassung', 'Zwischenfassung'.]
RFM	*Remarks on the Foundations of Mathematics*, ed. G. H. von Wright, R. Rhees and G. E. M. Anscombe; tr. G. E. M. Anscombe, rev. edn. Oxford: Blackwell, 1978.

	Abbreviations
RLF	'Some Remarks on Logical Form' (1929). In *PO*, 29–35.
RPP	*Remarks on the Philosophy of Psychology*, 2 vols, ed. G. E. M. Anscombe, G. H. von Wright and H. Nyman; tr. G. E. M. Anscombe, C. V. Luckhardt and M. A. E. Aue. Oxford: Blackwell, 1980.
TLP	*Tractatus Logico-Philosophicus*, tr. D. F. Pears and B. F. McGuinness. London: Routledge & Kegan Paul, 1961.
TS	Unpublished typescript, numbered in accordance with von Wright's catalogue (1982).
VW	*The Voices of Wittgenstein: The Vienna Circle*, by Ludwig Wittgenstein and Friedrich Waismann, ed. G. Baker. London: Routledge, 2003.
WA	*Wiener Ausgabe*, ed. Michael Nedo. Vienna: Springer, 1993– .
WVC	*Ludwig Wittgenstein and the Vienna Circle: Conversations Recorded by Friedrich Waismann*, ed. B. McGuinness, tr. J. Schulte and B. McGuinness. Oxford: Blackwell, 1979.
Z	*Zettel*, ed. G. E. M. Anscombe and G. H. von Wright, tr. G. E. M. Anscombe. Oxford: Blackwell, 1967.

Longer quotations from the *Tractatus Logico-Philosophicus* are marked by the number of the proposition at the beginning (e.g. 1, 1.1); longer quotations from the *Philosophical Investigations* are indicated by a section number, followed by a full stop (e.g. 1.). Occasionally I make slight changes to the published translations, which are indicated by an asterisk after the section number.

What is your aim in philosophy? –
To shew the fly the way out of the fly-bottle.

PI §309

1
Between Vienna and Cambridge

On 18 October 1911 Bertrand Russell was having tea with his friend Ogden, in his rooms in Trinity College, Cambridge, when (as he wrote in a letter to Lady Ottoline Morrell):

> an unknown German appeared, speaking very little English but refusing to speak German. He turned out to be a man who had learned engineering at [Berlin] Charlottenburg, but during his course had acquired by himself, a passion for the philosophy of mathematics and has now come to Cambridge on purpose to hear me.

The next day:

> My German friend threatens to be an infliction, he came back with me after my lecture and argued till dinner-time – obstinate & perverse, but I think not stupid.

On 25 October 1911:

> My German, who seems to be rather good, was very argumentative.

On 1 November:

> My German engineer very argumentative & tiresome. He wouldn't admit that it was certain that there was not a rhinoceros in the room ... [He] came back & argued all the time I was dressing.

On 2 November:

> My German engineer, I think, is a fool. He thinks nothing empirical is knowable – I asked him to admit that there was not a rhinoceros in the room, but he wouldn't. (McGuinness 1988, 88f; Monk 1990, 38f)

And so on for the following weeks. The German, it turned out, was an Austrian by the name of Ludwig Wittgenstein.

1.1 The Wittgensteins

Ludwig Wittgenstein was born in Vienna on 26 April 1889, the youngest of five brothers and three sisters. His paternal grandfather, Hermann Christian Wittgenstein, was a German Jew who had converted to Protestantism and moved to Vienna about 1850. The most remarkable of his eleven children was Karl Wittgenstein, Ludwig's father. 'My father was a business man,' Ludwig Wittgenstein once said, 'and I am a business man: I want my philosophy to be businesslike, to get something done, to get something settled' (Drury 1984, 110). Karl Wittgenstein was a man of outstanding practical intelligence and independence of mind, which soon brought him into conflict with his old-fashioned environment. In his final year at school he was expelled for writing an essay denying the immortality of the soul. Shortly afterwards he ran away from home and lived in New York for two years. He worked there as a waiter, a violinist, a helmsman on a canal boat, a bar-tender, and as a teacher of the violin, the horn, mathematics, Latin, Greek and mathematical drawing. At last he returned home to Vienna, well dressed, with some money, but in low spirits. He then studied engineering at the Technical High School for a year, completed his training by taking on a number of posts as technical draughtsman or engineer with various firms, and began an extraordinarily swift rise to wealth and power. In 1877 he became managing director of the Teplitz Rolling Mill, and within the next ten years, due to his enormous energy, astuteness and daring, he brought the whole Bohemian iron industry under his control. By the time his youngest son was born, Karl Wittgenstein had become one of the Empire's leading industrialists, comparable to Krupp in Germany and Carnegie in the United States. Karl Kraus, a regular critic of Wittgenstein's aggressive, American style of business, remarked in 1899: 'the Vienna Stock Exchange stands in fear of God, Taussig, Wittgenstein and nothing else in the world' (*Die Fackel* 17, 10). However, in 1898, when he was only 51 years old, Karl Wittgenstein suddenly resigned from all company boards, transferred his investments into property and foreign equities, and retired into the private life of a connoisseur and generous patron of the arts.

In 1873 Karl Wittgenstein had married Leopoldine Kalmus, whose father was also of Jewish descent, but the family had become Catholic. Leopoldine was a quiet woman who lived entirely in the shadow of her strong-willed and jovial husband. She seems to have been a devoted wife, but given to nervousness and not quite equal to the task of overseeing the large Wittgenstein household, with eight children and an army of cooks, maids, gardeners, footmen, nurses, private tutors and other servants. Her eldest daughter, Hermine, would later remember various occasions when, due to incompetent employees whom her mother was unable to control, the care of the children had been neglected. Altogether, Hermine recalled, her parents' household was characterized by 'a peculiar excitedness', 'a lack of ease' (Nedo and Ranchetti 1983, 27). But what Leopoldine Wittgenstein was mainly remembered for was her exceptionally accomplished piano playing.

The children of Karl and Leopoldine Wittgenstein were brought up in the Catholic faith, and although fully aware of their Jewish ancestry, did not regard themselves as Jewish.[1] All the Wittgenstein children had extraordinary talents and character. The eldest son, Hans, was a musical prodigy who at the age of 4 played the piano and the violin, and began to compose his own music. His precocious gifts seemed comparable to Mozart's, and he might well have become a renowned composer or at any rate a world-class performer. But his father had already decided that his sons were to follow in his own footsteps and pursue a career in engineering and industry. Hans was taught mathematics and Latin at home, and was later sent to work in various enterprises in Bohemia, Germany and England to acquire whatever else was necessary for his career. In 1902 he ran away to America (as his father had done before) and, probably, committed suicide. So did his brothers Rudolf, in 1904, and Kurt, in 1918. Quite unlike Karl Wittgenstein, all his sons suffered from depression, a 'lack of vitality and will to live', as their sister Hermine put it (Nedo and Ranchetti 1983, 27). The remaining sons, Paul and especially Ludwig, seem to have been more than once on the brink of suicide (which in Austria in those days was widely regarded as an acceptable and often honourable way out of insoluble problems). Their sister thought it was only due to fortunate circumstances that they did not share the fate of their elder brothers. But they were also put under less pressure from their father. They were sent to school, and Paul was even allowed to train as a pianist. He gave his first concert in 1913. But in 1914, soon after the war had begun, he was severely injured at the Eastern front and lost his right arm. When Ludwig heard of his brother's misfortune he expected him to commit suicide (MS 101, 51); but Paul proved to be of a different mettle. Not only did he go on living; he continued both as a soldier, having arranged as soon as possible to be sent back to the front, and as a concert pianist, teaching himself to play with only one hand. He commissioned pieces for the left hand from Britten, Hindemith, Prokofiev, Richard Strauss and Ravel (of which Ravel's *Concerto pour la main gauche* is probably the best known), and in spite of his handicap became a very successful

---

[1] See Prokop 2003, 99f, 221; McGuinness 1999, 30; FB 166; MS 101, 48; cf. Monk 1990, 5.

performer, and later a professor of music in New York. His own family, however, extremely fastidious in their musical taste, did not greatly admire the style of his playing.

Ludwig seemed to be the only one of the brothers inclined and suited to follow the career plan laid out by his father. He was also, in his childhood, regarded as the least gifted. His mind developed rather slowly; he learned to speak only when he was 4. He seemed generally bad at learning according to conventional methods, as if he were reluctant to accumulate knowledge without yet understanding its purpose. He preferred to teach himself when he felt the need, and then he would learn with ease. From early on he showed practical inclinations, rather than artistic or intellectual ones. He had a considerable interest in mechanisms and machines, and displayed some remarkable manual skills. Thus at the age of 10, after a careful study of the sewing machine in the house, he was able with wood and wire to construct a functioning replica of it. Until he was 14 he was taught at home by private tutors, apparently without too much success. Then for three years he was sent to a *Realschule* in Linz: that is, a school with a more technical and less academic syllabus than a gymnasium (such as his brother Paul attended). In particular, at a *Realschule* Ludwig did not have to study Latin or Greek. In 1906 he took his final exams, called *Matura*, with very unimpressive results. Only in Religious Studies did he obtain a first, in English the second highest grade ('laudable'), while in all other subjects he got merely 'satisfactory' or 'sufficient'.

As a schoolboy Ludwig seems to have lost the religious faith of his childhood, and about the same time he read and to some extent adopted Schopenhauer's emphatically atheistic philosophy. An influence of Schopenhauer's idealism, the view that the world exists only in our minds, is still clearly noticeable in the *Tractatus* (see sect. 2.5c).

It is remarkable that in his childhood Wittgenstein showed no signs of his later strength of character. On the contrary, he was a weakly child, in both body and mind, eager to please and 'afraid of the bad opinion of those around [him]' (autobiographical notes quoted in McGuinness 1988, 47f). Nor did he show any particular musical talent; at least not by his family's high standards. He did not learn to play any instrument as a child, though of course he experienced the intense musical life that played such an important role in the house, where Brahms was a frequent guest and the finest performers, such as the violinist Joseph Joachim, played. He absorbed his elders' sensitivity and taste, and later in life people were impressed by his musical understanding and authority as a musical critic. On one occasion his brother Paul was practising the piano when Ludwig was in another room of the house. Then 'the music suddenly stopped and his brother burst into the room saying, "I can't play when you are in the house. I feel your scepticism seeping under the door"' (Drury 1984, 135f). And in 1949, after writing the

Philosophical Investigations, he expressed regret at not being able to say in his book one word about all that music had meant in his life. 'How then can I hope to be understood?' (Drury 1984, 160).

Classical German and Austrian literature formed another important part of the life in the Alleegasse 16, the Wittgensteins' palatial house in Vienna, and the Hochreith, their country estate. All through his life Wittgenstein would return to Goethe's and Mörike's poetry, to Schiller's and Grillparzer's plays, and to Keller's and Hebel's stories. He admired naturalness and clarity in style, and had no time for anything mannered or pretentious. In this respect aesthetic value was inseparably linked with moral qualities. Moreover, literature for the Wittgensteins was a constant stimulus for discussions of moral issues.

Wittgenstein's taste in literature was as conservative as it was in music (where he always stuck to the Viennese classics from Haydn to Brahms). His cultural ideal, he once noted, if not that of the first half of the nineteenth century, was a continuation of that ideal (*CV* 4). In many ways he felt he belonged to an earlier epoch, as did the city in which he was at home.

1.2 Vienna

Vienna was the capital of the Habsburg Empire of Austria-Hungary, the second largest state in Europe, but it was not an exciting hub of political life or social development. Its atmosphere was one of stagnation: 'Nothing moves, nothing can happen' (Steed 1913, 204). There was a feeling that history had come to an end with the battle of Königgrätz, in 1866, when Austrian troops were beaten decisively by the Prussians. The House of Habsburg had lost its position of primacy in the German lands and – especially after the foundation of the German Reich in 1871 – had ceased to be a leading player in European politics. There was also not much change or excitement to be expected in home affairs. For one thing, the country was ruled by a tenacious monarch who never abandoned his belief in the divine right of kings and did his best to keep democratic participation to a minimum. 'There was a Parliament, which asserted its freedom so forcefully that it was usually kept shut; there was also an Emergency Powers Act that enabled the government to get along without Parliament, but then, when everyone had happily settled for absolutism, the Crown decreed that it was time to go back to parliamentary rule' (Musil 1931, 29 (1.1.8)). In any case, the government was not elected by Parliament, but appointed by the Emperor, who also maintained his full authority in foreign and military affairs. Moreover, public life was impeded by censorship and a notoriously foot-dragging bureaucracy. For another thing, what room for public politics the monarchy vouchsafed its subjects was largely taken up by never-ending and insoluble quarrels among the numerous nationalities. For example, with eighty-seven representatives in the 1907 *Reichsrat* the Social Democrats should have been a considerable parliamentary force – had it not been for their internal ethnic differences: they were fifty Germans, twenty-three Czechs, seven Poles, five Italians and two Ruthenes (Timms 1986, 406). If a particular national group was dissatisfied with a decision, it would often effectively obstruct parliamentary procedures with endless speeches, or even with the noise of drums and bugles. That was the forceful way in which Parliament 'asserted its freedom', so that occasionally it had to be closed down.

There was a sense of political stagnation, but there was also a sense of security (Zweig 1941, ch. 1), especially among the professional middle classes; and not only in Austria. 'In the later nineteenth century, it looked as if this world would go on for ever. Money not only kept its value; it increased in value as prices gently fell' (Stone 1999, 22). Violent upheavals seemed impossible in this age of reason and technological progress, particularly in Vienna: a society both pedantically policed and carelessly easy-going; a state of 'absolutism mitigated by *Schlamperei* [slackness]' (Johnston 1972, 50). This security was personified magnificently by the man who held together the huge multinational empire: His Majesty the Emperor Franz Joseph, Apostolic King of Hungary, King of Bohemia, Dalmatia, Croatia, Slavonia, Galicia, Lodomeria, Illyria, Jerusalem, Archduke of Austria, Grand Prince of Transylvania, Grand Duke of Tuscany and Krakow, Duke of Lorraine, Salzburg, Styria, Carinthia and Carniola. A soldier by upbringing, he had a well-regulated, austere and diligent life-style, was averse to any innovation, and demanded a strict observance of the most archaic forms of court ceremonial and etiquette. Imperial pomp and circumstance gave an impression of dynastic power and splendour, many centuries old and by all appearances likely to continue unchanged for ever. And Franz Joseph's sheer longevity; the continuous presence of that steadfast old man (– whose portrait was to be seen everywhere: a fatherly appearance, bald, a white bushy moustache forming a line with his mutton-chop side-whiskers, in a white uniform embellished by half a dozen medals –) seemed almost to guarantee political stability. When Wittgenstein was born in 1889, Franz Joseph had already been on the throne for forty years, and he was to reign for another twenty-seven years, almost to the end of the monarchy.

The Viennese enjoyed the magnificence of Imperial display in compensation for their lack of political influence. 'No European capital has so Imperial an air,' an English observer wrote, 'none finer boulevards, none a more magnificent park at its gates or more delightful surroundings' (Steed 1913, 202). There was an army of picturesquely attired members of the Court in daily evidence; there were regularly great pageants through streets whose grand architecture was itself part of the city's Imperial decoration. From 1860 onwards the old city ramparts had been abolished, and a grand boulevard, the *Ringstraße*, put in its place. Its monumental buildings were in a variety of historical styles: for example, the Town Hall in massive Gothic, the *Burgtheater* in early Baroque, the University in Renaissance, the Parliament in classical Greek style. 'Ringstraßenstil' soon became a general term of opprobrium for an architecture designed to demonstrate magnificence that had no style of its own, but eclectically borrowed from the past (see Schorske 1981, ch. 2). The Emperor's beloved military gave a picturesque note to the townscape. There were frequent military parades and bands, and officers dressed routinely like operetta heroes (in blue or green tunics over white trousers with anachronistic dress swords), adding some colour to the elegant urban crowds (in high starched collars, top hats or whalebone corsets). Military ideas of conduct and honour were more old-fashioned in Austria than in other European countries: a telling example is that in 1915 Wittgenstein, as a recruit, after some unpleasant scenes with an officer, seriously considered that it might be necessary for them to fight a duel (MS 102, 59). The theatre should also be mentioned as, to some extent, part of the Imperial display in Vienna. Indeed, it has been aptly said that the theatre was an epitome of fin-de-siècle Vienna and the baroque manner in which life was centred on the Court of its absolutist ruler (Broch 1955, sect. I. 4) Theatre and opera were art forms that thrived under special Imperial patronage. Singers at the Opera and actors at the *Burgtheater* were annually received in audience by the Emperor. They had Imperial equipages at their disposal to take them to work and home again. All theatres had to keep a box ready at all times for the Emperor (just as major railway stations needed to have an extra waiting room reserved for royalty). So in a way all dramatic entertainment was addressed primarily to the Court, somewhat like public fireworks on a royal birthday. At the same time, generously endowed theatres appeared as part of 'the constant effort of the authorities to turn attention away from public affairs and towards amusement' (Steed 1913, 202). And, on the whole, the Viennese public, genial, fun-loving and fond of make-belief, liked it that way. Their outlook was, simply, 'to avoid unpleasantness, to take life easily, sceptically, and to get out of it as much thoughtless enjoyment as possible' (ibid.). They were known for their long and intense carnival season, light opera, waltz and opulent pastry, and of course for their coffee-houses. In Vienna everybody seemed to be able to spend hours each day sitting in a coffee-house reading the papers, playing chess or in leisurely conversation (which was cultivated as an art form), conducted in a softly accented local dialect that was laced with old-fashioned formulas of politeness. The coffee-house was a perfect expression of the city's contemplative and politically inactive way of life. Even those who preached political change seemed unlikely ever to get round to doing anything about it, because of their addiction to an indolent coffee-house life. (When in 1914 Count Berchtold, the Foreign Minister, was warned that war with Russia might provoke a revolution there, he replied mockingly: 'And who is supposed to make that revolution? Perhaps Herr Bronstein from the Café Central?' Bronstein was an elegantly dressed Russian immigrant with Marxist ideas, often seen at a chess-board in his habitual haunt. Later, however, he was to become known in a different capacity, under the name of Trotsky.) Associated with the institution of the coffee-house was another Viennese speciality: the journalistic-literary genre of the *feuilleton*, a light and chatty, impressionistic essay written in the same spirit as the coffee-house conversation. The subjective response of the writer was more important than matters of fact. Objective analysis was replaced by personal feeling (see the example given on p. 10). This was symptomatic of the tendency in Viennese culture to turn inward in response to an unpleasant political reality and individual political impotence (Schorske 1981, ch. i). It has been said that the Viennese always liked to impose a joke between themselves and the harsh realities of life. (Towards the end of the First World War in Berlin the situation was described as 'serious, but not hopeless'; in Vienna they called it 'hopeless, but not serious'.) While their attitude towards politics often seemed indifferent or frivolous – to some extent, no doubt, because they were prevented from playing a part in it – and moral questions were treated with nonchalance, the theatre and music were taken perhaps more seriously than anywhere else, practised according to the highest standards, and subjected to the most rigorous and fastidious criticism. The Wittgensteins well exemplified this attitude towards music. They were also typical of the Vienna higher middle classes and *nouveaux riches* in the generous patronage they bestowed on music and the arts.

The theatre was not only a popular amusement, it was also a school of manners, for style in Vienna was more important than substance. In the theatre, the local journalist Hermann Bahr wrote:

> the Viennese wants to find out how to behave. This goes for the common man as for the elevated. The one learns from Fichtner or Sonnenthal [two actors] how to move in a drawing-room, how to wear his hat and hold his cane; Vienna's elegance is always derived from the Burgtheater. The other listens to discover how to feel with distinction. The Viennese always needs an example. For this he visits the theatre. It is no image of life. Life is its image. (Spiel 1987, 122f)

The burghers of Vienna were famous for their theatrical politeness: every social encounter, every business transaction, was played like a scene on the stage. Life was varnished with a pleasant untruthfulness, which was not really insincerity, as it was not meant to be taken at face value.

However, the untruthfulness or inauthenticity of *Ringstraßen* Vienna – of grand eclectic façades, extravagant ornamentation, conventional make-belief and clichés – found some eloquent Viennese critics, notably two, whom Wittgenstein came to admire (*CV* 16) and later met: the architect Adolf Loos and the writer Karl Kraus.

Adolf Loos (1870–1933) had been to the USA and England in the 1890s and was impressed by the functional architecture he had seen there, especially the skyscrapers of the Chicago School. Back in Vienna he became a fierce critic of all ornamental architecture and the fashionable fusion of craft and art in interior design. He poured scorn both on the historicism of the *Ringstraße* and on the exuberantly decorated furniture of *art nouveau*. His own style of practical efficiency without any frills became famous through some controversial buildings like the Café Museum (1899) and especially the house on the Michaelerplatz (1911), conspicuous by the lack of pediment or ornamental moulding on its windows. As the title of his provocative pamphlet *Ornament and Crime* (1908) suggests, Loos condemned ornament on moral grounds. Aesthetics, for him, was largely a matter of ethics. Ornament was wrong, because in the modern era it was a form of dishonesty. The façades of the *Ringstraße* were attempts to disguise modern apartment houses as Renaissance palaces. What looked like Baroque stucco was in fact made of cement; and what pretended to be the dwellings of aristocrats were in fact inhabited by the *nouveaux riches*. More generally, it was insincere to pass off as art what essentially could only be craft: functional objects like bicycles, bathtubs and houses. 'Architecture,' Loos wrote, 'is not to be counted as an art form' (Loos 1931, 101).

In the name of truthfulness, of cultural and moral hygiene, Loos insisted on a clean separation of art and craft; of autonomous virtuosity and matter-of-fact functionality. Karl Kraus (1874–1936), cultural critic, satirical moralist, and one of the most brilliant writers of German prose, had exactly the same programme in the sphere of language:

> Adolf Loos and I – he in fact, I in language – have done nothing more than show that there is a difference between an urn and a chamber pot and that it is only due to this difference that culture has sufficient elbow room. The others, however, the positive ones, are divided into those who use the urn as a chamber pot and those who use the chamber pot as an urn. (Kraus 1913: 389–90, 37)

His periodical *Die Fackel* (The Torch) appeared from 1899 to 1936, and from 1911 onwards he was the only contributor. Through the years he attacked the injustice of the courts, the prevalent sexual morality, the corruption of the press, war profiteering, public hypocrisy and so on. But his immediate target was always the debasement or shameless use of language, stylistic humbug, in which he found the reflection of moral depravity. He was a master of the unmasking quotation: citing and bandying about a phrase or a few sentences that most effectively betrayed a person's vulgarity or pretentiousness. Like Loos, he was inclined to believe that 'Ethics and aesthetics are one' – as Wittgenstein was to put it, tersely, in his first book (*TLP* 6.421). At least there was 'a pre-established harmony between language and the spheres' (Kraus 1920: 546–50, 50); between stylistic and moral defects. So it was by attempting to 'drain the vast swamp of clichés' (1899: 1, 2) that Kraus fought his crusade against wickedness.

What in architecture was inauthentic ornamentation, in language and thought were cliché and claptrap, especially as they were used in the Viennese *feuilleton*: to decorate serious information with belletristic sentimentality. This 'aestheticising rage,' wrote Kraus in 1909, 'is the curse of our days' (279–80, 8). For Vienna's press there was 'no nothing without emotional disturbance' and 'no event without poetry' (1912: 363–5, 8). Here is one of the numerous examples he quoted, from a war correspondent reporting on a battle between Bulgarian and Turkish troops in 1912:

Battle at Adrianople

For two whole days now I have been feasting my eyes on the spectacle of the fortress of Adrianople emerging in the distance from the silver light of the morning and stretching its glittering shape along the winding banks of the Maritza, with its ramparts and its towers . . . Early in the day the city is wrapped in fluttering mists, later in the smoke of gunpowder, just like delicate veils around the face of a beautiful woman . . . one feels oneself drawn towards this city by some secret, unfathomable longing, one wants to hasten towards her, to conquer her oneself as it were, to take possession of her. (Kraus 1912: 360–2, 47; tr. in Timms 1986, 155)

Kraus remarked that 'Austria was represented on the Balkan by impressionists'; and that the wounded in this war were 'ambushed and attacked with poetry' (1912: 360–2, 39). Such journalistic blend of serious information and cheap literary decoration was a frivolous exploitation of human suffering. Moreover, it was likely in the long run to ruin the reader's imagination and spoil his sensitivity to real literature (1912: 363–5, 4).

1.3 Moral Solipsism

Between his eighteenth and his twenty-fourth year, when he finally became determined to pursue philosophy, Wittgenstein lived through a particularly difficult and unhappy time. This was partly because he was unclear about his vocation: torn between, on the one hand, an undeniable aptitude for engineering and his father's wish that he apply himself in that direction, and on the other hand, doubts about such a career and a growing interest in philosophical questions. But there occurred also in these years a thorough change in his moral character that must have been a slow and painful process. This change, the way he turned against his earlier self, bears a remarkable similarity to the way Adolf Loos and Karl Kraus turned against *Ringstraßen* Vienna, the city of baroque façades and charming untruthfulness. He used to be a shy and docile child, eager to please and constantly worrying about the impression he would make on others. In fact, that worry would never leave him entirely (e.g. *D* 148 (1937)), but at some point in his life he decided to fight against it and at least not to be influenced by it in his behaviour any more. Any concern for appearances and others' opinions of himself he came to regard as unacceptable vanity. Henceforth his ideal was authenticity: to be true to his own self (cf. *D* 194). He would no longer tolerate any affectation, pretentiousness or polite insincerity, in himself or in others.

In this austere moral outlook Wittgenstein was influenced not only by Loos and Kraus, but most of all by another Viennese writer: Otto Weininger (1880–1903). Weininger achieved fame, or notoriety, through the publication of his doctoral dissertation under the title *Geschlecht und Charakter* (*Sex and Character*) (1903), which offered a theory about the nature of man and woman, conceived as archetypes, only impurely realized in actual men and women. His views were vehemently misogynistic, and the book was made even more unpalatable through an added chapter in which Jews were claimed to suffer from similar moral shortcomings as women. (Weininger was Jewish himself and, on his own theory, a particularly feminine type of man. He committed suicide soon after the publication of his book.) However, it was not on account of those infamous doctrines that Wittgenstein was attracted to Weininger.[2] In fact, there is reason to believe that Wittgenstein derived his inspiration less from Weininger's main work than from a posthumously published collection of essays and aphorisms, entitled *Über die letzten Dinge* (1904), which is virtually free from misogyny and anti-

---

[2] Wittgenstein may not have been averse to the idea of archetypal male and female characters, but he had no sympathy for Weininger's misogynistic evaluations (Drury 1984, 91). As regards the character traits Weininger describes in his chapter on Jewishness – above all a frivolous lack of piety, of seriousness and of true commitment (1903, 430–3) – Wittgenstein felt an equal dislike of them, but he would not have regarded them as particularly Jewish. Only for a short period, in 1931, did he use the word 'Jewish' when describing his own, and others', intellectual capacities and limitations: a mind more analytical and elaborative than creative; but then those characteristics were not something he wished to disparage or overcome (*CV* 16f; cf. McGuinness 1999).

Semitism, and contains a long essay on Ibsen's *Peer Gynt* that must have greatly appealed to Wittgenstein (cf. *FB* 30; E 46). Ethics, for Weininger, is akin to logic in that ultimately its only concern is truth (1903, 207; 1904, 24). And truth and untruth, the deepest ethical problem, is the theme of *Peer Gynt*. The play tells the story of the hero's struggle to free himself from the untruthfulness of his life (*Lebenslüge*). At the outset he is a braggart and a confidence trickster. This is the 'vain attempt to enhance one's own value through others' admiration' (Weininger 1904, 24). But 'all vanity in front of others, all primary regard for others is the result of abandoning one's own self and the value one has in one's own eyes' (1904, 41). Man's moral imperative is: 'Be yourself!' – as opposed to the motto of the trolls that try to drag Peer Gynt into their society: 'Be complacent and satisfied with yourself!' At the end Peer Gynt meets the fatal Button Moulder, who accuses him of having failed to be himself: to develop his own personality or soul. Therefore, like a bad button he is to be thrown back into the melting pot. – In his dissertation Weininger presents the moral outlook of Ibsen's play as a consequence of a Kantian approach to ethics. All heteronomy is rejected: I am responsible neither to God nor to anybody else, only to my own self as the source of the moral law. As a moral agent, 'man is alone in the universe in eternal, immense loneliness' (1903, 210): 'Truth, purity, faithfulness, sincerity towards oneself: that is the only conceivable ethics. . . . Duty exists only towards oneself' (Weininger 1903, 206, 208). This is *moral solipsism* (from Latin: *'solus'* – *'ipse'*: 'only' – 'self'); which, however, is not supposed to be as ruthlessly egoistic as one might suspect. For Weininger, to be moral towards oneself entails being likewise moral towards others (1903, 227). The assumption is that the self one is trying to develop and be true to is essentially decent and benevolent. According to Russell, this was indeed so with Wittgenstein: 'His nature is good through and through; that is why he doesn't see the need of morals', that is to say: conventional moral principles (Monk 1990, 52). Wittgenstein's moral solipsism was expressed in his advice to friends: 'Just improve yourself, that is all you can do to improve the world' (Monk 1990, 17f).

His moral solipsism was reinforced by an unsatisfied religious temperament. From early on his moral thinking was shaped by religious categories, like sin, guilt or losing one's soul (McGuinness 1988, 43). That tendency was further strengthened when as a soldier in the First World War, in the town of Tarnov in Galicia, he came upon a bookshop with a curiously small stock:

> [It] seemed to contain nothing but picture postcards. However, he went inside and found that it contained just one book: Tolstoy on the Gospels. He bought it merely because there was no other. He read and re-read it, and thenceforth had it always with him, under fire and at all times. (Russell in *CL* 140; cf. MS 101, 12ff and 39)

He became known among his comrades as 'the man with the gospels' (Monk 1990, 116). Later he said that it was Tolstoy's book that had kept him alive in those difficult days (LF 91). In 1917 he explained to his sister Margaret that 'religion and ethics are utterly inseparable' (Prokop 2003, 94). And in 1929 he wrote that his ethics could be summed up by the sentence: 'What is Good is Divine too' (*CV* 5). Later in life he gave this characterization of a religious temperament: 'Anyone who is half-way decent will think himself utterly imperfect, but the religious person thinks himself *wretched*' (*CV* 51). In that sense Wittgenstein was certainly a religious person for most of his life. Time and again he was, as Russell described him in 1912, 'not far removed from suicide, feeling himself a miserable creature, full of sin' (Monk 1990, 64). He was what William James called a 'sick soul', in need of 'redemption through faith' (*CV* 32) – but unable to obtain it. 'I cannot utter the word "Lord" meaningfully,' he wrote in 1937, '*Because I do not believe* that he will come to judge me; because *that* says nothing to me' (*CV* 38; cf. 63; *D* 193). Ideally, for Wittgenstein, morality should be a matter between oneself and God – being responsible to God, one need no longer worry about one's relationship to other people (cf. McGuinness 1988, 114; *CL* 14; *D* 154); but since he couldn't believe in God, he felt thrown back on his lonely self, as described by Weininger.

Two more aspects of Wittgenstein's moral views are worth noting. First, *non-cognitivism*: Weininger held that morality, by its very nature, could not be explained or given a rational foundation (1903, 228). Modifying a saying of Schopenhauer's,[3] Wittgenstein echoed Weininger's view: 'To preach morality is difficult, to give reasons for morality is impossible' (*WVC* 118; cf. *CV* 23; *D* 75).

Secondly, *individualism*: Morality is not based on reasons, but ought to be rooted in a person's character; consequently, different characters will and ought to have different moral attitudes. In conversations with a friend, 'Wittgenstein would emphasize that one man's nature and another's are not the same, and that what is right (or imperative) for one man may not be right for another' (Rhees 1984, 187).[4] For example, it was imperative for *him* after the war to give away his money and live without luxury off his own earnings, but he wouldn't have dreamt of asking or expecting the same of any other member of the family;

---

[3] Namely: 'To preach morality is easy, to give reasons for morality is difficult' (Schopenhauer 1840, 1).

[4] Wittgenstein would have agreed with St Augustine's maxim: '*Dilige et quod vis fac* – if you but love, you may do as you incline' (quoted in William James's *Varieties of Religious Experience* (1902), 80, a book which Wittgenstein read in 1912 (*CL* 14)).

indeed, he wanted them to take his money. It was his view that any attempt to emulate other people's admirable behaviour was likely to go wrong: where one's own nature was different, it would result only in untruthfulness, the ultimate sin (cf. *CV* 47). Wittgenstein was always prepared to agree to differ about moral issues as long as he was convinced that the other person was serious and sincere in his disagreement. At a time when he tried to follow Tolstoy's version of the Gospels, he was still able to admire Nietzsche's vitriolic attacks on Christianity (in *The Anti-Christ*); for Nietzsche too was serious in his moral views (MS 102, 40f). To Russell, Wittgenstein conceded: 'that your value-judgements are just as good and just as deep-seated in you as mine in me, and that I have no right to catechize you' (*CL* 74; Feb. 1914). When on one occasion in 1929 F. R. Leavis, thinking that Wittgenstein had been rude to someone, stormed after him and angrily told him off, he responded with sympathy. Putting his hand on Leavis's shoulder, he said: 'We must know one another' (Leavis 1973, 53). 'He allowed one to have strong feelings,' his Russian teacher remembered, 'and would accept things said in a temper' (Pascal 1973, 22). An outburst of strong feeling, whatever the feeling, would command Wittgenstein's respect, since it evinced seriousness and sincerity.

Wittgenstein's moral individualism explains why ethics is almost absent from his philosophical writings.[5] Since morality has to be an expression of one's natural character, a profitable discussion of moral questions requires that one know each other well. 'An ethical proposition is a personal act' (*D* 76), and, like religious views, rather 'too intimate for print' (as Wittgenstein protested to Russell after having read his article 'The Essence of Religion' (McGuinness 1988, 109)).[6]

1.4 Aviator or Philosopher

Wittgenstein finished school in 1906 and went to the *Technische Hochschule* in Berlin Charlottenburg to study mechanical engineering for three semesters. It seems that his plan was to go into aeronautics: to construct and fly an aeroplane. In that, he was possibly inspired by the Viennese physicist Ludwig Boltzmann (1844–1906), whose writings

---

[5] Apart from a few sentences in the *Tractatus*, which will be discussed in sect. 2.6 below.

[6] In 1930 Wittgenstein suggested: 'Russell's books should be bound in two colours: those dealing with mathematical logic in red – and all students of philosophy should read them; those dealing with ethics and politics in blue – and no one should be allowed to read them' (Drury 1984, 112).

he admired,[7] and who had predicted (in 1894) that the future of aeronautics lay not in dirigible airships, but in aeroplanes propelled by airscrews. To overcome the enormous technical difficulties in developing a serviceable aeroplane was, Boltzmann thought, a task for a genius who, having to improve his constructions by trial and error, should at the same time be a hero (McGuinness 1988, 69). Perhaps Wittgenstein meant to take up that challenge.

After having received his leaving certificate in May 1908, Wittgenstein, following his father's advice, moved to England for further studies. He matriculated as a research student at the College of Technology in Manchester, and for the first few months experimented with kites at the Kite Flying Upper Atmosphere Station, near Glossop, in Derbyshire. Then his interest shifted to the construction of an engine suitable for aeroplanes. He developed a propeller that was powered by hot gases channelled from a combustion chamber through reaction jets at the tips of the blades (somewhat like a rotating lawn-sprinkler). A laboratory assistant in Manchester remembered Wittgenstein's nervous temperament: when anything went wrong during their experiments with the combustion chamber, which often occurred, he would 'stamp, throw his arms about, and swear volubly in German' (Mays 1967, 87). However, before much experimental work had been done with the combustion chamber, Wittgenstein became more interested in the design of the propeller, which was essentially a mathematical task. From that he moved on to the study of pure mathematics, until finally he was drawn into the philosophical discussion of the foundations of mathematics; so his engineering work and aeronautical ambitions were abandoned. The Manchester philosopher Samuel Alexander referred Wittgenstein to Gottlob Frege in Jena, who advised him to study with Russell in Cambridge. Wittgenstein moved to Cambridge, and after his first term there, still unsure whether his taste for philosophy was accompanied by sufficient talent, he asked Russell: 'Will you please tell me whether I am a complete idiot or not?' Russell replied: 'My dear fellow, I don't know. Why are you asking me?' Wittgenstein said: 'Because, if I am a complete idiot, I shall become an aeronaut; but, if not, I shall become a philosopher.'

---

[7] Wittgenstein was even thinking of studying physics in Vienna under Boltzmann, when the latter's suicide in 1906 put paid to that idea. Boltzmann's views – like those of another physicist, Heinrich Hertz – had a considerable influence both on Wittgenstein's account of science in the *Tractatus* (*TLP* 6.3s) and, more importantly, on his conception of philosophy. They anticipated the idea that lack of conceptual clarity can be the source of essentially nonsensical philosophical questions (cf. Hacker 1986, 2–5; McGuinness 2002, 163f; Graßhoff 2004).

> I told him [Russell continued] to write me something during the vacation on some philosophical subject and I would then tell him whether he was a complete idiot or not. At the beginning of the following term he brought me the fulfilment of this suggestion. After reading only one sentence, I said to him: 'No, you must not become an aeronaut.' And he didn't. (Russell 1956b, 26f)

Russell's encouragement came as a great relief to Wittgenstein, putting an end to a particularly bad stretch of depression and paralysing self-doubt. At last he had found his real vocation and could with a clear conscience give up his half-hearted work in engineering. From now on he would focus all his energies on what truly fascinated him: mathematical logic. Russell soon realized the extraordinary qualities of his new pupil. He later called him

> the most perfect example I have ever known of genius as traditionally conceived; passionate, profound, intense and dominating. He had a kind of purity which I have never known equalled except by G. E. Moore. I remember taking him once to the Aristotelian Society, at which there were various fools whom I treated politely. When we came away he raged and stormed against my moral degradation in not telling these men what fools they were. His life was turbulent and troubled, and his personal force was extraordinary. He lived on milk and vegetables, and I used to feel as Mrs Patrick Campbell did about Shaw: 'God help us if he should ever eat a beefsteak.' (Russell 1968, 98f)

After just one term Russell felt that he had taught his new pupil all he had to teach. And soon afterwards he gracefully accepted that henceforth the leading force in the analysis of mathematical logic was Wittgenstein. When Ludwig's sister Hermine came to visit Cambridge in July 1912, she was amazed to be told by Russell: 'We expect the next big step in philosophy to be taken by your brother' (Hermine Wittgenstein 1949, 2). And when, a few months later, Wittgenstein had discovered inaccuracies in some of the proofs in Russell's and Whitehead's *Principia Mathematica*, Russell remarked in a letter: 'fortunately it is his business to put them right, not mine' (Monk 1990, 72).

1.5 Logic

Towards the end of the nineteenth century it was felt that mathematics was in need of some theoretical foundation that would explain the status of mathematical propositions and justify their claim to certainty. One promising approach was the attempt to show that mathematics, or at least arithmetic, was just a branch of logic: that from a set of purely logical axioms and rules one could derive any truth of arithmetic. This approach – which attracted Wittgenstein's attention soon after his arrival in Manchester – was called 'logicism', and its foremost proponents were the German mathematician Gottlob Frege (1848–1925) and, a little later, Bertrand Russell (1872–1970) in collaboration with A. N. Whitehead (1861–1947). Obviously, the first requirement for carrying through the programme of logicism was a sufficiently rigorous and general system of formal logic. This was invented by Frege in his book *Begriffsschrift* (*Conceptual Notation*), published in 1879, which, although hardly noticed at the time, is now generally regarded as having revolutionized the subject. Frege's new mathematical logic was a major contribution to a development that eventually led to the construction of modern computers.

Frege's conceptual notation is a symbolism designed to render conspicuous the logical relations implicit in our natural languages. In order to work out whether a given statement logically entails another, or whether two statements are logically incompatible, they are *formalized*: that is, translated into an artificial notation in which logical relations can be demonstrated with more ease and precision. Frege's method of symbolization has become today's standard formal logic, although the actual symbols used in his writings have generally been replaced by Russell and Whitehead's typographically more convenient notation, or a variant thereof. Here is a brief outline of the elements of logical notation. (Readers already familiar with the basics of formal logic can omit this section.)

Introduction to Logical Formalization
First of all, we have to distinguish names and predicates. A name picks out one individual person or object; a predicate is an expression used to say something about some person or object: that it has a certain property, or belongs to a certain class, or acts in a certain way. Logicians abbreviate names by small letters from the beginning of the alphabet (a, b, c, etc.), and predicates are usually symbolized by the capital letters 'F', 'G', 'H', etc.[8] In logical notation the order of proper name and predicate is reversed: the predicate comes before the name. Consider the following simple declarative sentences:
(1) Fiddleworth is petulant.
(2) Fiddleworth is a bore.
(3) Fiddleworth plays the trombone.

---

[8] In the *TLP* predicates too are symbolized by small letters: f, g, etc.

To formalize them, we first write down an interpretation or key to our symbols:
a: Fiddleworth
Fx: x is petulant
Gx: x is a bore
Hx: x plays the trombone

The letter 'x' after the predicate letters indicates a slot for a name (letter). It is called a variable. Given this interpretation we can formalize as follows:

(1') Fa
(2') Ga
(3') Ha

So much for simple declarative sentences consisting only of a name and a predicate. Now consider more complex statements, such as:

(4) Fiddleworth is not petulant.
(5) Fiddleworth is a bore and plays the trombone.
(6) If Fiddleworth plays the trombone, he is a bore.
(7) Fiddleworth is a bore, or he plays the trombone.

To deal with those, we introduce symbols that correspond (roughly) to the English expressions in:

It is not the case that φ   ~φ
φ and ψ   φ ⊃ ψ
If φ then ψ   φ . ψ
φ or ψ   φ ∨ ψ

The Greek letters 'φ' (phi) and 'ψ' (psi) are placeholders for complete declarative sentences or their abbreviations ('p', 'q', 'r'). Thus we can formalize:

(4') ~Fa
(5') Ga . Ha
(6') Ha ⊃ Ga
(7') Ga ∨ Ha

The next extension of our logical vocabulary is to cover general statements (e.g., 'All bores play the trombone') and statements about unnamed people or objects (e.g., 'Someone plays the trombone'). Logicians use two symbols called the *universal quantifier* and the *existential quantifier*. They allow us to say respectively that *everything* is so-and-so, or that *at least one thing* is so-and-so, e.g.:

(x) Fx   For every object x: it is the case that x is petulant.
In short: Everything is petulant.
(∃x) Fx   For at least one object x: it is the case that x is petulant.
In short: Something is petulant.

Of course, one rarely has occasion to say that everything in the universe has a certain property. Normally, our general statements are

restricted to only a certain class of objects. In order to say that only a certain subclass of things falls under a certain predicate, we make a conditional general claim: Everything is so-and-so *if it is such-and-such*. E.g.:
(8) All bores play the trombone.
– appears as a generalized conditional:
(8′) (x) (Gx ⊃ Hx);
i.e., it is true of everything: that if it is a bore, then it plays the trombone.
Finally, we add to our stock of symbols the identity sign '='. 'a = b' reads: a is the same object (or person) as b.

Frege's greatest achievement in his *Begriffsschrift* was the introduction of quantifiers. Now for the first time formal logic was able to handle inferences involving 'multiple quantification': that is, different combinations of expressions like 'all' (or 'every') and 'some' (or 'a') in one sentence (for example: 'Every number has a successor').

In his next books, *Grundlagen* [*Foundations*] *der Arithmetik* (1884) and *Grundgesetze* [*Basic Laws*] *der Arithmetik* (1893–1903), Frege set out to apply his new logical devices to the task of a logicist reconstruction of arithmetic. He began by defining cardinal numbers as classes of equivalent classes, i.e. classes with the same number of objects. Zero was defined as the class of all classes equivalent to the class of objects which are not identical with themselves, i.e., the empty class. Then the number 1 was defined as the class of classes equivalent to the class of empty classes (as there is only one empty class). Next, he took the class containing the numbers 0 and 1, and defined the number 2 as the class of classes equivalent to that class. The number 3 was defined as the class of classes equivalent to the class containing 0, 1 and 2 – and so on and so forth.

Unfortunately, as Russell discovered in 1903, this procedure was flawed. It is essential to Frege's definitions that classes can themselves be members of classes. But then it must be licit to ask whether a given class is a member of itself, and you can define

R: the class of all classes which are not members of themselves.

But if you consider whether this class, R, is a member of itself, you get the following contradiction, known as *Russell's paradox*:

R is a member of R   if & only if   R is *not* a member of R.
(p if & only if ~p)

(By way of illustration, suppose that a village barber shaves all and only the men in the village who do not shave themselves. Does the barber shave himself? If he does, it follows that he is a man who does *not* shave himself; but if he does not shave himself, it follows that he does!)

Thus, Frege's axiomatic system which was meant to give a firm logical foundation to arithmetic is flawed, as it allows the proof of a contradiction (and from a contradiction you can deduce anything whatsoever). It was imperative to find a way of avoiding Russell's paradox, or the programme of providing a logical foundation to arithmetic had to be given up.

It appears that just as Wittgenstein was drawn into engineering by the challenge to construct and fly an aeroplane, so he was drawn into philosophy by the challenge to find a solution to Russell's paradox. Already in 1909, when still experimenting with his propeller engine, he had had a go at it and sent his attempted, yet unsuccessful, solution to the mathematician Philip Jourdain, a friend of Russell's.

Russell's own attempt at avoiding his paradox, in *Principia Mathematica* (1910–13), was his theory of types, which prohibited the formation of classes that contain themselves as an element, and a modification of the definition of numbers as classes. Rather than defining numbers as classes of equivalent classes of other *classes* (as Frege had done), Russell defined numbers as classes of equivalent classes of *objects*. That meant, however, that an infinity of numbers required an infinity of objects. So Russell had to rely on an axiom of infinity, stating that the number of objects in the world was not finite. Wittgenstein had good reason to be dissatisfied with this solution, for even if the axiom of infinity were true, it would certainly not be a truth of logic, and so its inclusion in *Principia Mathematica* defeated the book's ambition of providing a purely logical foundation to arithmetic. Wittgenstein thought that Russell's theory of types should be 'rendered superfluous by a proper theory of the symbolism' (*CL* 24; see sect. 2.6 below); but more dramatically, while holding on to the logicist view of mathematics as 'a logical method' (*TLP* 6.2), he was going to reject the Frege–Russell approach of taking the theory of classes as the foundation of arithmetic (*TLP* 6.031). In the account of arithmetic given in his first book, the *Tractatus Logico-Philosophicus*, the notion of a class is replaced by that of a logical operation. Numbers are construed as the numbers of applications of a symbolic procedure (*TLP* 6.02).[9] However, the logical reconstruction of mathematics is given very little space in the *Tractatus*. It seems that when Wittgenstein arrived in Cambridge, his main interest had already shifted from the logical nature of mathematics to the nature of logic itself.

---

[9] For a general account of Wittgenstein's philosophy of mathematics, both in the *Tractatus* and later, see Frascolla 2001.

1.6 Norway and the War

In 1913, when on holiday in Norway with his friend David Pinsent, Wittgenstein decided that Cambridge, with its many distractions and antipathetic people, was not a suitable environment for finishing his work on logic. Russell described (in a letter) how he heard of Wittgenstein's plan:

> Then my Austrian, Wittgenstein, burst in like a whirlwind, just back from Norway, and determined to return there at once to live in complete solitude until he has solved *all* the problems of logic. I said it would be dark, and he said he hated daylight. I said it would be lonely, and he said he prostituted his mind talking to intelligent people. I said he was mad, and he said God preserve him from sanity. (God certainly will.) (McGuinness 1988, 184)

Having left Russell with a dictation of his ideas on logic, as far as they had evolved by then (now published as 'Notes on Logic'), he moved to a Norwegian village called Skjolden, near Bergen, and stayed there in the postmaster's house from October 1913 till June 1914, with the exception only of a short visit to Vienna over Christmas. He built himself a little house on a slope overlooking the Sognefjord, but he wasn't able to live there until his next visit in 1921. The summer 1914 he spent in Austria, in order to avoid any tourists that might find their way to Skjolden. Through the death of his father early in the previous year, he had come into a large fortune, and now, back in Vienna, he made a donation of 100,000 crowns (then equivalent to £4,000) to be distributed among Austrian artists and writers by Ludwig von Ficker, a writer and editor who had been commended by Karl Kraus. Among the beneficiaries were Rainer Maria Rilke, Georg Trakl, Oskar Kokoschka and Adolf Loos.

Following the assassination of the Austrian Crown Prince Franz Ferdinand in Sarajevo, on 28 July, Austria declared war on Serbia. Wittgenstein enlisted on 7 August. For three months he served on a patrol boat on the River Vistula, then in artillery workshops at Cracow and Lemberg. In 1916, at his own request, he was transferred to a howitzer regiment on the Galician front. Later that year his service on the Eastern Front was interrupted by an officer training course in Olmütz, in Moravia. In March 1918, after Russia had withdrawn from the war, Wittgenstein was transferred to the Southern Front, where in November, on the collapse of the Austrian army, he was taken prisoner by the Italians. By the end of the war he had risen to the rank of lieutenant, and had received five decorations for 'exceptionally courageous behaviour'.

Throughout the war Wittgenstein had worked on his book. (As Russell remarked: 'He was the kind of man who would never have noticed such small matters as bursting shells when he was thinking about logic' (1968, 99).) And when he was taken prisoner, he carried the finished manuscript in his rucksack. From a prison camp in Monte Casino, where he spent eight months, he managed to send copies to Russell and Frege. After his release in August 1919, the manuscript, entitled *Logisch-philosophische Abhandlung*, was offered to several publishers: Jahoda & Siegel and Braumüller, both in Vienna, von Ficker's journal *Der Brenner*, Insel Verlag and Reclam, both in Leipzig, Otto Reichl in Darmstadt, and also Cambridge University Press. They all turned it down. Of course, Wittgenstein could easily have published the book by bearing the printing costs himself, but he thought it indecent to force his work upon the world in such a way (LF 93). Eventually it appeared in 1921 in Wilhelm Ostwald's *Annalen der Naturphilosophie*, and a bilingual edition, with an English translation by C. K. Ogden, was published in 1922 by Kegan Paul in London, under the title *Tractatus Logico-Philosophicus*.

2
Tractatus Logico-Philosophicus

2.1 Logic and Sins

Of all the canonical philosophical texts, Wittgenstein's *Tractatus Logico-Philosophicus* is perhaps the most inaccessible, the most difficult to understand without any introductory commentary: not so much because it is concerned with some intricate issues in formal logic, but mostly due to its highly compressed style of presentation, which makes it also one of the shortest of the outstanding books in the history of the subject: a mere eighty pages of text. The author was well aware that he had not made things easy for his readers. The Preface begins with a frank admission that the book is unlikely to be understood by anyone who has not himself already had the thoughts expressed in it. One hurdle is that it presupposes familiarity with the works of Frege and Russell, especially the latter, with whom Wittgenstein had discussed logic for about two years and from whom he had derived many of the problems he set out to solve. But apparently even Frege and Russell were not equal to the hermeneutic challenge. In a letter to Russell, Wittgenstein reported that he had sent the manuscript of the book to Frege, from whose reply he could gather 'that he doesn't understand a word of it all' (*CL* 124). And even Russell was warned: 'In fact you would not understand it without a previous explanation as it's written in quite short remarks. (This of course means that *nobody* will understand it; although I believe, it's all as clear as crystal . . .)' (*CL* 111). Already during their time together in Cambridge, Russell had complained about Wittgenstein's reluctance to spell out his arguments in sufficient detail, for fear of spoiling the beauty of his presentation (McGuinness 1988, 104). Later, in 1949, Wittgenstein would admit that his book was unduly syncopated:[1] 'Every sentence in the *Tractatus* should be seen as the heading of a chapter, needing further exposition' (Drury 1984, 159).

The impression that the *Tractatus* is merely an extensive table of contents is reinforced by the fact that all its remarks are numbered. Due to the numbering system the progression is not linear, but moves in two dimensions: not only forward, but also sideways, as it were, into notes on preceding remarks and notes on those notes, and even third-, fourth- and fifth-order notes. Thus there are six levels: the main text, consisting of a mere seven propositions, numbered 1 to 7; first-order notes commenting on those seven propositions (e.g., 1.1, 1.2, 2.1); notes on those notes (e.g., 1.11, 1.12); and so on till the lowest level indicated by six digits (e.g., 2.15121). Thus the opening remarks, for instance, could be more perspicuously presented in the following two-dimensional manner:

I	II	III	level
1	→ 1.1 →	1.11	
		1.12	
		1.13	
	1.2 →	1.21	
2			

Whenever a longer number is followed by a shorter one (e.g., 1.13, 1.2) there is a break: the end of a sequence of notes and a return to a higher level of text. Occasionally that is important to bear in mind to avoid misunderstandings. Thus the anaphoric pronoun 'this' in remark 4.02 'We can see this from the fact that . . .' does not refer back to the immediately preceding remark 4.016, but to 4.01 on the previous page. Apart from the ordering, the numbers are, as Wittgenstein says in a footnote, also meant to indicate the logical importance of each remark: the more digits a proposition has, the less important it is. However, the system does not seem to be applied very rigorously and consistently. What Wittgenstein calls his 'fundamental idea', for instance, is hidden away as the second paragraph of proposition 4.0312. And occasionally explanatory notes seem to precede a main proposition instead of

---

[1] As the Cambridge philosopher C. D. Broad had called it in his ironical remark: 'I shall watch with a fatherly eye the philosophical gambols of my younger friends as they dance to the highly syncopated pipings of Herr Wittgenstein's flute' (Broad 1925, p. vii).

following it (as in the case of 7, which is elucidated by the propositions 6.5 to 6.54).

The seven main propositions present the major topics of the book in this order:

The world
Thought
Language
Logic
The ineffable

A more detailed table of contents looks like this:

1–2.0	World
2.1–2.2	Pictures
3.0	Thinking
3.1	Propositions
3.2	Names
3.3	Sign & symbol
3.4	Logical space
4.0	Propositions as pictures
4.11	Philosophy (also 4.003)
4.12	Logical form
4.2	Elementary proposition
4.3–5.14	Logic: truth-functional combination
5.15	Probability
5.2–5.3	Operations
5.4	Logic: its nature
5.5	Negation
5.52	Generality
5.53	Identity
5.54	Propositional attitudes
5.55	Logic: a priori
5.6	Solipsism
6.0	General form of truth function
6.02	Numbers
6.1	Logic: tautologies
6.2	Mathematics
6.3	Science
6.4–6.52	Ethics, value, the mystical
6.53–7	Philosophy

During his first terms in Cambridge, Wittgenstein would call on Russell almost every evening at midnight, and 'pace up and down the room like a wild beast for three hours in agitated silence'. Russell recounts how he once asked him what he was thinking about: logic or his sins? Wittgenstein replied: 'Both,' and continued his pacing (Russell 1968, 99).[2] Both logic and ethics are major concerns of the *Tractatus*. What holds them together in the book is that they fall on the same sides of two crucial distinctions. According to the Preface, Wittgenstein's overall aim in the *Tractatus* is to demarcate the bounds of sense. He endeavours 'to draw a limit... to the expression of thoughts... and what lies on the other side of the limit will simply be nonsense'. A related, but slightly different, distinction is that between what can be said and what can only be shown. In a letter to Russell, Wittgenstein called this distinction 'the main point of his theory' and 'the cardinal problem of philosophy' (*CL* 124).[3] The former distinction divides the realm of sentences, whereas the latter is concerned with what they can or cannot express, but what can in any case be somehow comprehended. The two distinctions run parallel, except that the class of nonsense contains more than the failed attempts to say what can only be shown. Thus, according to the *Tractatus*, both

> 6.44 It is not *how* things are in the world that is mystical, but *that* it exists.

and

> 0.0 Too never or or.

– are pieces of nonsense, yet only (6.44) is an attempt to say something that shows itself (*TLP* 6.522).

As both the *Tractatus* doctrines of logic and language and talk about ethics (or the mystical) are failed attempts to say what can only show itself, and therefore nonsense, they are subject to the book's final injunction:

> 7 Whereof one cannot speak, thereof one must be silent.

As far as ethics is concerned, Wittgenstein comes close to practising what he preaches: apart from the negative point that ethics cannot be put into words, the book contains merely a few terse and gnomic remarks on the subject. Its importance is conveyed only negatively by

---

[2] Russell adds: 'I did not like to suggest that it was time for bed, as it seemed probable both to him and me that on leaving me he would commit suicide' (1968, 99).

[3] Of late an interpretation has become popular according to which Wittgenstein never seriously intended this second distinction. I shall discuss this interpretation in sect. 2.6e below.

indicating the limitations of meaningful – scientific – discourse (*TLP* 6.52). As Wittgenstein put it in a letter to Ludwig von Ficker:

> [The book] consists of two parts: of the one which is here, and of everything which I have *not* written. And precisely this second part is the important one. For the Ethical is delimited from within ... by my book; and I am convinced that, *strictly* speaking, it can ONLY be delimited in this way. (LF 94f)

Logic and language, by contrast, are evidently the book's main subjects, and are dealt with in great detail. This is a curious inconsistency: Wittgenstein presents a treatise on logic and language, assures the reader in the Preface that the *truth* of his thoughts is unassailable and definite, and that he has solved all the problems – yet at the end the reader is invited to dismiss the whole book as nonsense (*TLP* 6.54)! This paradoxical exit, and Wittgenstein's reason for it, will be discussed in due course (in sect. 2.6e). At this point, I will merely draw attention to something related to that paradox: namely, the development of Wittgenstein's conception of philosophy between 1913 and 1918. Three stages can be distinguished.

(i) In 1913, in his 'Notes on Logic', Wittgenstein characterized philosophy as a regular academic doctrine: 'the doctrine of the logical form of scientific propositions' (*NB* 106). Not a science (to that he will always stick), but at least comparable to the sciences in the way our understanding of its subject matter: logic has progressed (*PO* 3). Apart from logic, philosophy is also said to consist of metaphysics, based on logic (*NB* 106).

(ii) In the early *Tractatus* period (i.e., *Tractatus* remarks written before 1916), metaphysics is no longer regarded as a legitimate discipline: there are said to be no philosophical propositions (*TLP* 4.112). Most philosophical propositions and questions are dismissed as nonsense (*TLP* 4.003), but not all of them. Presumably, those that make no substantial claims, but limit themselves to the elucidation of scientific propositions, are deemed acceptable (*TLP* 4.112). And Wittgenstein has no qualms about envisaging a *'theory'* of knowledge' (*TLP* 4.1121; emphasis added).

(iii) At the end of the *Tractatus*, in a remark written only on 2 Dec. 1916 (*NB*), and not included in the first draft of the book (which was probably finished by March 1916; cf. McGuinness 2002, 262ff), Wittgenstein says:

> 6.53 The correct method in philosophy would really be the following: to say nothing except what can be said, i.e. propositions of natural science – i.e. something that has nothing to do with philosophy – and then, whenever someone else wanted to say something metaphysical, to demonstrate to him that he had failed to give a meaning

to certain signs in his sentences. Although it would not be satisfying to the other person – he would not have the feeling that we were teaching him philosophy – *this* method would be the only strictly correct one.

At this stage even the philosophical elucidation of scientific propositions appears to have become improper. Instead, philosophers should merely lay in wait, quietly, for other philosophers to say something metaphysical and then complain about its incomprehensibility. It is clear that this is not the philosophical method practised in the *Tractatus*: not only does the book contain a fair amount of metaphysics, but the counterfactual wording of 6.53 (*wäre eigentlich*) implies that the author is fully aware of not having lived up to this *ideal* of a philosophical method (cf. *WVC* 183). But also the earlier *Tractatus* account of philosophy (ii) is not an entirely correct description of what is practised in the book. For one thing, science is treated only in the most general terms; there is no elucidation and clarification of any particular scientific propositions, as apparently envisaged in 4.112.[4] For another thing, too much in the *Tractatus* is undeniably what is proscribed here: a 'doctrine', and not just the 'activity' of clarifying scientific statements (*TLP* 4.112). The most accurate description of the nature of the *Tractatus* is Wittgenstein's earliest account of philosophy (i): the book is mainly concerned to present 'the doctrine of the logical form of scientific propositions' (*NB* 106), which is formulated in the penultimate first-level proposition:

6 The general form of a truth function is $[\bar{p}, \bar{\xi}, N(\bar{\xi})]$.
   This is the general form of a proposition.

Again, true to the notes of 1913, from his theory of logic and language Wittgenstein derives a metaphysics: a theory of the world as consisting of indestructible atoms. Note also that even in 1919, after having finished the book, Wittgenstein is still prepared to call its contents a 'theory' (*CL* 124), in spite of his latest conception of philosophy as an activity. The *Tractatus* philosophy is not what, according to the *Tractatus*, philosophy should be. The book failed to keep up with the changes in its author's views on philosophy. Not surprisingly, for ultimately no philosophical book would have been compatible with those views. On

---

[4] What he had in mind here is probably what in 1929 he described thus: 'It is the task of the theory of knowledge to find [the elementary propositions] and to understand their construction out of the words or symbols. This task is very difficult, and Philosophy has hardly yet begun to tackle it at some points' (*RLF* 29).

the other hand (as will be shown in the following chapters), those views on philosophy were not at all arbitrary, but seemed to follow inexorably from the *Tractatus* theory of language.

Another tension appears to be between the predominantly logical contents of the *Tractatus* and Wittgenstein's often quoted announcement to von Ficker that 'the point of the book is ethical' (LF 94). Of course, that did not mean that the book was mainly about ethics. On the contrary, as quoted above, ethics was supposed to be conspicuous by its absence. The ethical point that the book is making is exactly the negative one, that what really matters, 'the problems of life', cannot be discussed in meaningful (scientific) language (*TLP* 6.52), and so one should not even try to do so (*TLP* 7). But is that really the main point of the book? It is its final conclusion, and it is what, after its completion, Wittgenstein thought most important about it; but it is far from obvious that this aspect of the *Tractatus* should be seen as its main achievement, or even, objectively, its main concern. After all, for the most part the book presents an account of logic and language that can be assessed and appreciated quite independently of any considerations of ethics, and what is more, the book was largely written without any such considerations in mind. In 1911 Wittgenstein moved to Cambridge in order to investigate the nature of logic. An explanation of logical propositions required an understanding of non-logical propositions, of language in general (1914), which in turn led to certain ontological assumptions (1915). His diaries show that it was only in June 1916 that he began to regard his thoughts about ethics and the meaning of life as part of his philosophical project. Suddenly among his discussions of logic occurs the question: 'What do I know about God and the purpose of life?' (*NB*, 11 June 1916). Understandably, at first he was struggling to find any connection between such questions and his work on logic, but he was determined to establish one:

6. 7. 16
Colossal strains in the last month. Have thought a lot about all sorts of things, but oddly enough I cannot establish the connection with my mathematical lines of thought.

7. 7. 16
But the connection shall be established!
(MS 103, 15f)

The 'colossal strains' were due to the beginning of the Brusilov Offensive in June: a Russian counter-attack which involved some of the heaviest fighting of the war and inflicted enormous casualties on Wittgenstein's regiment, the Austrian Eleventh Army (McGuinness 1988, 241–5). It is not surprising that under such circumstances

Wittgenstein should have assigned particular importance to ethical and quasi-religious questions, and that he should have tried to find a place for them in the book that was meant to be his life-work. And it is understandable that from that time on he would also be inclined to view his earlier thoughts as far as possible from that angle: as negatively demarcating the ineffable area of ethics or the mystical.

As noted earlier, Wittgenstein's philosophical starting point was the study of Frege's and Russell's formal logic. This attempt to understand the nature of logical propositions led to considerations of their opposite, empirical propositions, and thus of the nature of language in general. The essential features of language Wittgenstein thought to reflect some very general features of the world. Thus the *Tractatus* ontology (*TLP* 1–2.0s) is a product of the book's philosophy of logic and language, and not (as the order of presentation might suggest) a foundation of the *Tractatus* system. Read for the first time and without any knowledge of the later parts of the book, the opening pages of the *Tractatus* will appear pointlessly abstract, speculative and dogmatic. Only when reconsidered in the light of some of Wittgenstein's views on logic and language do those ontological pronouncements gain some plausibility. Therefore, in section 2.2, I shall begin with an outline of some fundamental assumptions and ideas about language on which the whole of the *Tractatus* – and not least its first propositions – is built.

2.2 Foundations: Referentialism, Analysis, Determinacy and Bipolarity

It is quite natural to regard linguistic significance as essentially a matter of reference. Thus Russell wrote in 1903: 'Words all have meaning in the simple sense that they are symbols that stand for something other than themselves' (Russell 1903, 47). This view that the meaning of a word has to be explained in terms of what it stands for, its reference, I shall call *referentialism*. The most straightforward form of referentialism simply identifies the meaning with the reference, the object denoted. A more refined version holds that a word's meaning is not the object denoted, but the way in which the object is referred to. For referentialism, the paradigm of a word is a proper name, like 'Plato' or 'Birmingham'. With proper names it is not altogether implausible to suggest that all that matters to their understanding is their reference. If you know which person 'Plato' refers to and which city the word 'Birmingham' stands for, then you seem to know all you have to know about these words. So in the case of proper names one may well be inclined to say that meaning is simply reference. Referentialism generalizes this view, holding that all, or most, words function like that: all, or most,

Tractatus Logico-Philosophicus

words are essentially names whose meaning is (or is explicable in terms of) their reference. This position is held in the *Tractatus*. All the words out of which elementary propositions are constructed are names (*TLP* 4.22). And:

> 3.203 A name means an object. The object is its meaning.

Referentialism was a common view when the *Tractatus* was written. Wittgenstein inherited it from the two philosophers who had the greatest influence on his early thinking: Frege and Russell.

The extent to which referentialism was a matter of course for Frege is manifest in his use of the word *Bedeutung*, German for 'meaning', in the sense of 'reference'. Frege was happy to say that the meaning of the term 'Morning Star' is a planet, Venus. But then he enriched his account, adding that beside a 'meaning' (i.e., a reference), words also have a sense. The sense of an expression is defined as the way in which its reference is presented (Frege 1892, 57). The expression 'Morning Star', for instance, presents its reference, the planet Venus, in a certain way: namely, as a star that is visible in the morning. The name 'Evening Star', although referring to the same object, Venus, presents it rather differently: as a star of the evening. So the two names have the same 'meaning' (reference), but differ in sense. With his distinction between sense and reference, Frege does not hold a crude or simple version of referentialism. Still, a form of referentialism it is, for the notion of reference retains its crucial position in this account of linguistic understanding. Meaning (at any rate, word meaning), for Frege *is* reference, while sense is defined in terms of reference.

Wittgenstein did not adopt Frege's dual account of meaning and sense. According to the *Tractatus*, a name has a meaning – i.e., a reference – but no sense. In this, Wittgenstein followed Russell. Russell's philosophy of language can, to a large extent, be seen as a response to problems incurred by his referentialist assumptions. In retrospect, in 1956, Russell gave the following slightly ironic account of his struggles with the consequences of referentialism:

> I thought that every word that can be used significantly must signify something, and I took this to mean that it must signify some *thing*. But the words that most interest logicians are difficult from this point of view. They are such words as 'if' and 'or' and 'not'. I tried to believe that in some logicians' limbo there are things that these words mean, and that perhaps virtuous logicians may meet them hereafter in a more logical cosmos. I felt fairly satisfied about 'or' and 'if' and 'not', but I hesitated about such words as 'nevertheless'. My queer zoo contained some very odd monsters, such as the golden mountain and the present King of France – monsters which, although they roamed my zoo at will, had the odd property of non-existence. (Russell 1956b, 43)

Here Russell mentions two problems with referentialism. First, there are words, such as 'if', 'or' and 'not', that do not look at all like names of objects. We shall come back to this point later. Secondly, there are compound expressions, like 'the present king of France', that might well have had a reference, an object to stand for, but as it happens they haven't. There is neither a present King of France, nor a golden mountain. Hence, these expressions have no denotation; no reference. But if the meaning of an expression is identical with its reference; if having a meaning is the same as having a denotation – as Russell wanted to say – then those expressions must be meaningless. But are they meaningless? Does a name lose its meaning the moment its bearer ceases to exist? Is the expression 'Soviet Union' devoid of meaning since the Soviet Union has disintegrated? That would be extremely awkward for historians. Not only could one not give any historical accounts of objects that no longer exist, one could not even *say* that they don't exist! The statement that the Soviet Union doesn't exist any more would be meaningless. But of course it isn't. It's perfectly intelligible, and even true.

Another objection to unqualified referentialism is that it cannot account for the fact that identity statements can be illuminating. The expressions 'Scott' and 'the author of *Waverley*', for example, denote one and the same person. But if denotation is all there is to the meaning of an expression, then these two expressions, having the same denotation, must have the same meaning. Hence one would expect the identity statement

(SW)   Scott = the author of *Waverley*

to be just as trivial as:

(S)   Scott = Scott.

But in fact, (SW) – unlike (S) – conveys a useful piece of information about Scott (Russell 1905, 47f).

Frege took similar observations (about the identity of Morning Star and Evening Star) as grounds for distinguishing between sense and reference. (SW), he would say, is illuminating, unlike (S), because although both expressions have the same reference (what Frege calls 'meaning'), they differ in sense. But Russell would have none of this distinction. He held on to his view that meaning can be accounted for in terms of reference alone, and tried to overcome those problems in a different way.

Russell's pivotal idea was that one should distinguish between the *grammatical form* of an English sentence and the *logical form* of the proposition it expresses. How things appear on the linguistic surface may not be as they are from a logical point of view. Compare the following two arguments:

(A) Smith is the winner of the race.
The winner of the race is received with applause.
Therefore, Smith is received with applause.

(B) My new car is green.
Green is a colour.
Therefore, my new car is a colour.

Argument (A) is perfectly valid, whereas (B) is not. The conclusion of (B) is nonsense. But both arguments seem to be of the same form:

A is B.
B is C.
Therefore, A is C.

So how can we account for the failure of (B)? – We have to distinguish between the grammatical form, on the surface, and the logical form, which may sometimes be hidden underneath. Although (A) and (B) have the same grammatical form, their logical form is different. What in this case disguises the difference in logical form is an ambiguity in the use of the copula, 'is': It may mean 'is identical with' (as in 'Smith is the winner of the race'), or it may not: 'My new car is green' does not mean 'My new car *is identical with* green'. And therefore I cannot go on to say of my new car what is true of green. Whereas, since 'Smith is the winner of the race' means 'Smith *is identical with* the winner of the race', I *can* go on to say of Smith what is true of the winner of the race.

In order to bring such logical differences to light, Russell proposed that one translate English sentences into a logically perfect language, a language that will do what English sometimes fails to do: namely, mirror the logical form of the proposition. Such a translation should prevent us from logical errors, such as the one illustrated in (B), for it makes absolutely transparent what follows from what.[5] Just by mechan-

---

[5] Using Russell's notation (introduced in sect. 1.5 above), argument (A) can be formalized thus:
a = b
Fa
Therefore, Fb.
Not so argument (B), which will come out as:
Fa
Gb
Therefore, Ga.

ically applying the rules of formal logic, we should then be able to check whether an argument is valid or not, whereas application of such rules of inference to arguments couched in natural language may lead astray. Moreover, natural languages contain ambiguities and vagueness, which in a logically perfect language would be removed.

But if the appearance of an English sentence may be logically deceptive; if it isn't really an adequate expression of the proposition it is meant to convey, then perhaps a referentialist needn't be too worried about the fact that such sentences don't seem to fulfil the requirements of referentialist semantics. The apparent counter-examples to referentialism that Russell was concerned with were what he called 'denoting phrases': for example, 'the present King of France'. Under the title *Theory of Descriptions*, Russell offered a logical analysis of sentences containing such phrases (e.g., 'The present King of France is bald') to show how we can take such sentences as meaningful without having to ascribe a meaning (i.e., a reference) to the denoting phrase in question (Russell 1905). He argued that once the proposition is fully and properly expressed – in its logical form, and not in its misleading colloquial English formulation – then the denoting phrase will be gone (Russell 1905, 51). On the grammatical surface,

(K) The present King of France is bald

has a straightforward subject–predicate form. So it would appear that it should be formalized as 'Fa'. But appearances are deceptive. From a logical point of view, the grammatical subject, 'the present King of France', is not a name (here Russell disagreed with Frege); it is a denoting phrase that is dissolved in analysis. (K) should be spelt out as a conjunction of three distinct claims:

(K1) There exists at least one present King of France.
(K2) There exists at most one present King of France.
(K3) All present Kings of France are bald.

In logical notation (Fx: x is a present King of France; Gx: x is bald):

(K1') $(\exists x)\ Fx$
(K2') $(x)\ (y)\ ((Fx \cdot Fy) \supset x = y)$

Read: take anything x and anything y: if x is a present King of France and y is a present King of France, then x and y are the same (person). In other words, there aren't two different present kings of France.

(K3') $(x)\ (Fx \supset Gx)$

Conjoining the three claims we can write:

(K') $(\exists x)\ ((Fx \cdot (y)\ (Fy \supset y = x)) \cdot Gx)$

Read: there's at least one present King of France, and every present King of France is identical with him (i.e., there's no other present King of France), and he is bald. (K') is false – for its implication (K1') is false – but there's no reason to doubt that it's perfectly meaningful.

Moreover, the Theory of Descriptions yielded a solution to the puzzle of informative identity statements. It appeared that referentialism could not account for informative identity statements; statements of the form 'a = b'. For if 'a = b' is true, both names must have the same meaning (on this theory); hence it must be trivial. But it is hard to deny that (SW) 'Scott = the author of *Waverley*', for example, is informative. Now, on Russell's analysis (SW) turns out not to be an identity statement after all, and so the problem is resolved. The logical form of (SW) is not 'a = b', but (Wx: x wrote *Waverley*; a: Scott):

(SW') (∃x) ((Wx . (y) (Wy ⊃ y = x)) . x = a)

Read: there is at least one author of *Waverley*, and every author of *Waverley* is identical with him (i.e., there is no other author of *Waverley*) and he is identical with Scott. Unlike 'a = b', (SW') contains only *one* name (or singular term), not two supposedly synonymous ones. As 'the author of *Waverley*' is not another *name* of Scott, there is no reason why it should have the same meaning.

Referentialism and the method of logical analysis (developed at least partly in order to defend referentialism) were the mainstays of Russell's philosophy when Wittgenstein entered the scene. Wittgenstein adopted them both to play major roles in his first philosophy. However, there are important differences even with respect to those points of agreement. As for referentialism, Wittgenstein subscribed to a more limited version of it than Russell (or Frege). He emphatically refrained from applying it to logical symbols (*TLP* 4.0312; see sect. 2.5 below); and he resisted the temptation to treat sentences also as names (*TLP* 3.143; see sect. 2.4 below). As regards analysis, Wittgenstein expected even greater things from it than Russell, because he had a higher opinion of everyday language. Russell was convinced that common English parlance, like any other natural language, was hopelessly defective, full of ambiguity and vagueness, probably containing numerous meaningless expressions (1919a, 172; 1920, p. x; 1959, 241f). The logical calculus he devised in *Principia Mathematica* was intended as an ideal language to replace English for scientific or philosophical purposes, where precision is of the essence.[6] Hence the applicability of logical analysis to everyday language was limited. In some cases English statements are sufficiently precise, but their precise meaning is not obvious. Then logical analysis can bring it to light. But where an English expression

---

[6] Frege had similar ideas about *his* logical system in *Begriffsschrift* (1879).

is simply ambiguous or vague, no amount of logical analysis can make it determinate and exact. After all, analysis is not supposed to produce anything new, but merely to dig out what is implicitly already there in the unanalysed expression. Wittgenstein, by contrast, believed that 'all the propositions of our everyday language, just as they stand, are in perfect logical order' (*TLP* 5.5563), appearances to the contrary notwithstanding. In their colloquial expression propositions may appear vague or ambiguous, but closer scrutiny will reveal that the expressed thought is perfectly exact. Here, then, is another field for analysis, not envisaged by Russell: to excavate the exactness, the *determinacy of sense*, that lies hidden even in our most colloquial and lax utterances. Logical symbolism, as introduced by Frege and Russell and further refined by Wittgenstein himself, was not regarded by him as a new *language* to say things that could not fully be said in English, but merely as a new *notation* to express exactly the same thoughts, just more lucidly (*TLP* 3.325). The requirement that sense be determinate can be traced back to Frege, who held that for something to qualify as a concept it must have sharp boundaries. Its definition must 'unambiguously determine, for any object, whether or not it falls under the concept' (Frege 1903, §§56–64). But this was meant as a desideratum for an ideal language, not as Wittgenstein took it, as an actual feature of any language.

The fundamental ideas which Wittgenstein developed on the background of Russell's legacy concerned the nature of logic. An explanation of logical truth was not only, historically, the starting point of Wittgenstein's philosophical work; it lies at the heart of the *Tractatus* system. The following remark gives a summary of Wittgenstein's position:

> 6.113 It is the peculiar mark of logical propositions that one can recognize that they are true from the symbol alone, and this fact contains in itself the whole philosophy of logic. And so too it is a very important fact that the truth or falsity of non-logical propositions *cannot* be recognized from the propositions alone.

Consider the proposition:

(E) Pandas eat fish.

If you can read English, you understand what (E) means. But a perfect linguistic understanding of the proposition (E) does not give you any knowledge as to whether (E) is true or false. To find out whether pandas do eat fish, you have to observe pandas; you cannot ascertain it from the proposition alone. That is the situation with every empirical proposition, with every proposition that makes a substantive claim about the world. A linguistic understanding of a proposition leaves it still open whether that proposition is true or false. Either is possible.

For this essential feature of empirical propositions Wittgenstein in his early writings introduced the term *'bipolarity'* (*NB* 94–9, 104, 113). The principle of bipolarity demands that every empirical proposition is capable of being true and capable of being false.

In contrast, consider:

(L) If pandas eat fish, then pandas eat fish.

You don't have to observe any pandas to know that (L) is true. The moment you understand (L), you know *eo ipso* that it is true. This truth is independent of how things are in the world; it is entirely due to the logical form of (L), that is 'p ⊃ p'. One could also say that logical propositions are *necessarily* true; they are true come what may.

How is it possible for a proposition to be true under all possible circumstances and wear its truth on its sleeve like that? The price for such a self-evidently guaranteed truth is complete lack of content. (L) cannot say anything wrong about pandas, because it doesn't *say* anything about pandas. It says the same thing as all propositions of logic say – 'to wit nothing' (*TLP* 5.43).

The view that logical propositions have no content was developed in opposition to Russell's logical Platonism: that is, the view that logical propositions are statements about logical objects. Logical objects, logical forms and 'indefinable logical constants' are, for Russell, the subject matter of symbolic logic (Russell 1903, 11; 1913, 97). We cannot define those objects, we must become acquainted with them in 'logical experience' (Russell 1913, 97). Thus, following Russell, there does not seem to be a sharp distinction between the logical and the empirical realm. Logical propositions would appear to be just a subset of empirical propositions, reporting a specific kind of experience.

There are two serious problems with that position. First, the notion of a logical experience is rather mysterious, to say the least. Russell himself seemed unable to give any further description of such an experience. He simply based this claim on his general referentialist assumption that all meaningful words that cannot be removed by analysis must stand for objects. Obviously we understand logical symbols; so they too must stand for objects (Russell 1913, 97, 99). A second problem, which Wittgenstein thought fatal, is that an experiential account of logical propositions, in terms of acquaintance with logical objects, cannot provide a satisfactory explanation of logical necessity. Where something can only be learnt through experience, it is always conceivable that it might have been otherwise. Experience teaches us how things happen to be, but it can never show us that things *must* be as they are. It doesn't yield any necessary truths; but that is exactly what logical truths are. Therefore – and this is the core of the *Tractatus* – Wittgenstein insists against Russell on a sharp distinction between logical and empirical propositions, and a characterization of the former as necessarily true, but vacuous, and of the latter as essentially true *or* false.

In this section I presented four fundamental ideas underlying the *Tractatus*. They are:

1 *Referentialism*: words stand for objects.
2 *Logical analysis*: the logical form of a proposition may be different from its apparent form.
3 *Determinacy of sense*: every proposition must have a definite sense.
4 *Bipolarity*: empirical propositions are essentially true *or* false, whereas logical propositions are necessarily true but vacuous.

(1) and (2) Wittgenstein inherited from Russell and Frege; (3) and (4), though developed in dialogue with those philosophers, are original and can be regarded as the core doctrines of the *Tractatus*.

In the next section I shall investigate how Wittgenstein's logical atomism is informed by the requirement of determinacy of sense (3). In the following chapters the principle of bipolarity (4) will be seen to have shaped both the picture theory and the *Tractatus* philosophy of logic.

2.3 Logical Atomism

'What is the case – a fact – is the existence of states of affairs' (*TLP* 2). Note the plural: states of affairs. *One* fact is the existence, or obtaining, of a *set* of states of affairs. This is logical analysis as already encountered in Russell. It is a fact that Scott was the author of *Waverley*. The proposition that expresses this fact can be analysed into a conjunction of three more basic propositions: At *least* one person wrote *Waverley*; at *most* one person wrote *Waverley*; whoever wrote *Waverley* was Scott. Wittgenstein was full of praise for Russell's Theory of Descriptions, which he thought demonstrated 'that the apparent logical form of a proposition need not be its real one' (*TLP* 4.0031). Later he was to remark that what he had in mind when in the *Tractatus* he postulated a complete analysis was something like Russell's Theory of Descriptions (*PG* 211). If you carry on such logical analysis as far as possible, you will eventually get down to propositions which can no longer be broken up into more basic propositions. These are what Wittgenstein calls *elementary propositions*. A normal or complex proposition, if it is true, describes a fact, whereas an elementary proposition describes a state of affairs (*TLP* 4.21). Thus, as in language a complex proposition can be analysed into elementary propositions, so a fact can be analysed into states of affairs.

'A state of affairs is a combination of objects (things)' (*TLP* 2.01). This, again, is mirrored in language: an elementary proposition is composed of names, the verbal representatives of objects (*TLP* 3.22). That objects can occur in states of affairs is not a coincidence or a merely contingent matter, it is part of their nature (*TLP* 2.011, 2.0123). An object must occur in states of affairs or not at all: it *cannot* occur on its own, outside any state of affairs (*TLP* 2.0121a, 2.0122, 2.0131). A chair, for example, can be in various locations; and (if it exists) it must be in *some* location: it cannot be outside space. An object can occur in *various* states of affairs. As a matter of fact, it occurs in one state of affairs, S_1; but it would have been logically possible for it to occur in countless other states of affairs: S_2, S_3, S_4, etc.; – which, as it happens, are not existing states of affairs. Similarly, this chair happens to be in this room, but (as far as logic is concerned) it might have been next door or in the garden. However, this chair could not possibly be within a pencil, much smaller than itself. Likewise, a *Tractatus* object can occur in certain states of affairs, but cannot occur in others. This definite range of combinatorial possibilities that an object has Wittgenstein calls its *internal properties* (*TLP* 2.01231), or its *form* (*TLP* 2.0141). And the totality of objects, with their fixed forms, Wittgenstein calls the *substance of the world* (*TLP* 2.021), or the *fixed form of the world* (*TLP* 2.023, 2.026f).

So much for the terminology and general outline of the *Tractatus* ontology. On this background Wittgenstein advances the following fundamental propositions:

1.1   The world is the totality of facts, not of things.
2.02, 2.0271   Objects are simple [...] unalterable and subsistent (enduring).
2.061   States of affairs are independent of each other.

I shall look at them in turn.

Facts, not things   Why should the world not be regarded as the totality of objects? Because the world is more than just a collection of objects; it is objects *in particular arrangements*. If you know of all the objects in the world, have a complete inventory of everything there is – you still have only a very inadequate idea of what the world is like. A satisfactory account of the world would have to contain not only a list of all the objects, but also descriptions of where they are and in what relations they stand to each other. For instance, an adequate account of the world would tell you not only that the world contains the Eiffel Tower, but also that it is in Paris. Hence, the world is more than the totality of things, it is the totality of facts. This becomes even more obvious if you take into account that the world is not static, but has a history. That Charles Dickens wrote *Bleak House* and that William Hague lost the

General Election in 2001 are features of this world: but they are not objects, they are facts.

Simple objects   'Logical atomism' is the title Russell gave to the philosophy he developed around his method of logical analysis, because logical analysis was supposed to construe propositions as consisting of simple parts, atoms of language, so to speak. And those atoms of language were supposed to denote simple things with which we are immediately acquainted, mostly sense-data. In fact this construal remained a mere programme. No such complete analysis of a sentence of ordinary language has ever been achieved. We are shown how to break down complex sentences containing definite descriptions into a set of sentences containing predicates, variables and quantifiers. But it remains utterly obscure how that kind of analysis should be continued, and how it could ever reduce our talk of a Scottish novelist, say, to talk about mere sense-data. There is a yawning gap in Russell's logical atomism between the first steps of analysis and its intended terminus. But at least that terminus is moderately clear, and its existence seems fairly likely. After all, we seem to be well acquainted with simple sense-data (this spot of red in my visual field, that little noise just now), and there is no reason to doubt that we could have atomic propositions about them.

Wittgenstein adopted Russell's ideas about logical analysis, and thus the *Tractatus* also presents a version of logical atomism. Analysis is to uncover the atoms of language, simple signs or names (*TLP* 3.202), which stand for simple objects (*TLP* 2.02, 3.203). But Wittgenstein did not adopt Russell's empiricism about those simples. Although he was inclined to believe that sense-data are examples of simple objects (*NB*, 6 May 1915; cf. *TLP* 2.0131), he did not seem fully decided on that point (cf. Malcolm 1984, 70). No examples of simple signs or objects are given in the *Tractatus*. Wittgenstein's belief that there are such things did not rest on any empirical evidence; he postulated them for *a priori* reasons alone. Three arguments as to why there have to be simple objects are suggested.

(i) *Analysis must come to an end*. In his *Notebooks* Wittgenstein writes:

> It seems that the idea of the SIMPLE is already to be found contained in that of the complex and in the idea of analysis, and in such a way that we come to this idea quite apart from any examples of simple objects, or of propositions which mention them, and we realize the existence of the simple object – *a priori* – as a logical necessity. (*NB*, 14 June 1915; cf. *TLP* 4.221)

An analysis of single words or expressions (as opposed to full propositions) is a definition (*TLP* 3.24, 3.261). Thus, the term 'vixen' can be analysed by the definition 'vixen = def. female fox'. Definitions are substitution rules. The one I just gave allows you to substitute the expression 'female fox' for any occurrence of the word 'vixen' you may come across, thereby making more explicit what is meant by the propositions in question. Perhaps the words 'female' and 'fox' can in turn be substituted according to their dictionary definitions. But of course this process of clarification by substitution of more explicit terms cannot go on forever (*NB*, 9 May 1915). For one thing, if our understanding of a word always consisted in the understanding of some other words, we would not really understand any of them. To know that 'red' means the same as *'rouge'*, and that that means the same as *'rot'*, and that that means the same as *'rosso'*, etc., etc. is not enough for an understanding of any of these words. At some point words must be explained and understood not merely in terms of other words, but by reference to something outside language. For another thing, our expressions are not infinitely complex. The number of different ideas implicit in them that can be spelled out by analysis is limited. Eventually, we must reach a paraphrase that makes explicit everything that was contained in the original expression (*PTLP* 3.20102).

These considerations are persuasive, but they do not establish that there must be simple *objects*. There must be semantic simplicity, expressions that cannot be analysed further, or expressions whose meaning can be understood without further analysis. But it does not follow that what such expressions denote must itself be simple. Why should there not be a simple sign denoting a complex object, say, a tree?

(ii) *Autonomy of sense*. Wittgenstein held that questions of sense must be decidable independently of what happens to be the case. This leads to the most explicit justification in the *Tractatus* for the claim that there are simple objects:

2.021   Objects make up the substance of the world. That is why they cannot be composite.

The substance of the world cannot be composite, because whatever is composite could conceivably be decomposed: destroyed. But of the substance of the world it is required that it 'subsists independently of what is the case' (*TLP* 2.024). Thus, even if it were the case that everything destructible was destroyed, there must be substance. Hence, substance cannot be destructible, or decomposable. It must not be composite, but absolutely simple. But granted that anything that is to qualify as substance must be simple, the question remains: Why do we need a substance? Wittgenstein's answer is:

2.0211   If the world had no substance, then whether a proposition had sense would depend on whether another proposition was true.

2.0212   In that case we could not sketch out any picture of the world (true or false).

Both statements call for explanation. Why would the complexity of objects make sense dependent on truth? And why should that have the consequence that we could not describe the world?

Ad 2.0211   The worry expressed here is dependent on a referentialist assumption. The meaning of a name is the object it denotes. Hence, if there is no such object, the name will be meaningless, and the sentence in which it occurs will have no sense. But if a name is supposed to stand for a complex object, the decomposition or non-existence of that complex is a real possibility. So to ascertain that the original proposition does have a sense, one would have to check whether the complex in question did in fact exist, i.e., whether another proposition describing that complex was true (cf. *WVC* 252f).

Note that the case envisaged here (of a *name* denoting a complex) must not be confused with the perfectly straightforward case of a *description* denoting a complex. That case was satisfactorily dealt with by Russell's Theory of Descriptions. If a proposition refers to a complex by a description, and the complex does not exist, the proposition will not be nonsensical but simply false (*TLP* 3.24). Consider:

(D)   My invalid *friend* asked me to call on him.

If the underlined expression has no reference, it would appear, from a referentialist point of view, that (D) must be nonsensical. But that conclusion can be avoided, since, according to Russell's analysis, (D) can be spelt out in a way that removes that underlined, and apparently meaningless, expression:

(D')   I have at least one invalid friend,
& I have at most one invalid friend,
& whoever is an invalid friend of mine asked me to call on him.

Now the proposition that says that the complex in question (my invalid friend) exists turns out to be itself part of proposition (D). And if such a complex does not exist, the first conjunct, and hence the whole proposition (D), will be false. But, as argued under (i) above, analysis must come to an end at some point. Eventually we must reach propositions that cannot be broken up any further: propositions that do not contain analysable descriptions, but only indissoluble names. Suppose 'Bunbury' were such an unanalysable name. What if it was meant to refer to something complex, such as a man? (This is exactly what argument (i) could not rule out.)

(N) Bunbury asked me to call on him.

If, *ex hypothesi*, (N) cannot be further analysed, there is no escape from the demands of referentialism: For (N) to have sense, the name 'Bunbury' must have a reference. In other words, the sense of (N) depends on the truth of another proposition: namely, that there exists a man that is Bunbury.

Ad 2.0212 It remains to be seen why Wittgenstein thought that with such dependence of sense on empirical truth 'no description at all would be possible' (*WVC* 253). Max Black offers the following explanation:

> If a proposition had no final analysis, there would be an infinite (and vicious) regress. In order for p to have sense we should first have to determine by experience that some other proposition q was true (2.0211). But before doing so, we should have to know that q made sense, i.e. we should have first to verify some *other* proposition r, etc. (Black 1964, 62)

This is perhaps what Wittgenstein had in mind; but the argument is flawed. Even if in order for a proposition p to have sense, another proposition q must be true (*TLP* 2.0211), it does not follow that in order to state that p, one first has to *determine by experience* that q is true. Suppose I introduce the term 'dow' to denote a given drop of water, which is composed of a certain number of H_2O molecules. Then, according to Wittgenstein's referentialist assumptions, the proposition 'Dow is on the table' has a sense only if what I named 'dow' does actually exist. But that condition can be fulfilled even if I do not *know* that it is fulfilled. So, contrary to Black's explanation, there is no need for me to determine by experience whether the condition is fulfilled; hence I am not launched on an infinite regress that would prevent me from making a statement in the first place.

Of course I would like to know that my proposition has a sense. So I investigate if what I named 'dow' exists. Does that mean that I have to find out whether that drop of water consists of certain H_2O molecules, $x, y, z, \ldots$? That is rather implausible. I did not introduce the term 'dow' as denoting a specific combination of particular H_2O molecules; rather, I conferred it on what I saw: a drop of water. Provided that I did indeed pick out something while introducing the term 'dow', it must at least initially have had a reference, and thus a meaning. But to be aware of that reference, I did not have to know anything about its molecular composition. And even when re-identifying the drop later, it is not obvious that its molecular composition must remain exactly the same. As John Locke argued convincingly, the identity of a thing over time does not always require the numerical identity of all of its particles; machines and animals are clear counter-examples (Locke 1689, 2.27).

44   *Tractatus Logico-Philosophicus*

The dependence of one proposition's sense on another proposition's truth envisaged in *TLP* 2.0211 does not lead to a vicious regress, and so the claim of *TLP* 2.0212 does not seem to follow: it would *not* be impossible to sketch out any picture of the world.

A different elaboration of the argument sketched in *Tractatus* 2.021ff can be drawn from Wittgenstein's later critical discussion of logical atomism in the *Philosophical Investigations*, where he characterizes something like his earlier position as follows:

> 55. "What the names in language signify must be indestructible; for it must be possible to describe the state of affairs in which everything destructible is destroyed. And this description will contain words; and what corresponds to these cannot then be destroyed, for otherwise the words would have no meaning." I must not saw off the branch on which I am sitting.

The argument can be spelt out as follows:

1 Description presupposes objects (as word meanings).   [*premiss* (*referentialism*)]
2 It is possible to describe the state of affairs in which everything destructible is destroyed.   [*premiss*]
3 There are objects that are not destroyed when everything destructible is destroyed, i.e., indestructible objects.   [*from (1) & (2)*]
4 What is composite is not indestructible.   [*premiss*]
5 There are simple objects.   [*from (3) & (4)*]

The argument is valid, but are all its premisses true? (4) sounds plausible enough, but what about (1) and (2)? There is an ambiguity in (2), the claim that description is possible even when everything destructible is destroyed. We may well want to say that every possible state of affairs is in principle describable. Read in that way, (2) seems acceptable – but then it does not follow that there are indestructible objects (3). To reach that consequence, we need a stronger reading of (2): namely, that a description could be given not just *of* any possible situation, but even *in* that situation. But a moment's reflection shows that taken in that stronger sense required for the argument, (2) is false. We can, for example, describe the state when the entropy of the universe has reached its final maximum, when there is no more life and hence no more intelligent being that could give any description (cf. *PI* §55b).

Is it perhaps possible to develop the argument in *TLP* 2.021–2.0212 in a different way that avoids the problematic premiss (2) of the reconstruction above (which after all is not mentioned in the *Tractatus*)? The *Philosophical Investigations* contains yet another pertinent and illuminating passage:

39.   ... one is tempted to [say]: *a name ought really to signify a simple*. And for this one might perhaps give the following reasons: The word "Excalibur", say, is a proper name in the ordinary sense. The sword Excalibur consists of parts combined in a particular way. If they are combined differently Excalibur does not exist. But it is clear that the sentence "Excalibur has a sharp blade" makes *sense* whether Excalibur is still whole or is broken up. But if "Excalibur" is the name of an object, this object no longer exists when Excalibur is broken in pieces; and as no object would then correspond to the name it would have no meaning. But then the sentence "Excalibur has a sharp blade" would contain a word that had no meaning, and hence the sentence would be nonsense. But it does make sense; so there must always be something corresponding to the words of which it consists. So the word "Excalibur" must disappear when the sense is analysed and its place be taken by words which name simples. It will be reasonable to call these words the real names.

In this passage no use is made of the problematic premiss (2) above. Instead, there is a very sensible observation: Even a proposition in which a complex seems to be named rather than described does not lose its sense with the destruction of that complex. This might be taken as a straight refutation of referentialism. It appears to show that even the meaning of a proper name (like 'Excalibur' or 'Bunbury') can survive the demise of its reference and cannot, therefore, be identical with it. Russell and the early Wittgenstein, however, did not see it like that. Rather, they contended that what is commonly regarded as a proper name is not really a proper name from a logical point of view. In general, no expression that refers to a complex can really be a name. 'A complex can be given only by its description' (*TLP* 3.24). Now the *Tractatus* argument can be reconstructed as follows:

1   For a proposition to have sense, the names it contains must refer to existing objects.   [*premiss (referentialism)*]
2   A proposition does not lose its sense when a complex that *seems* to be named in it is destroyed.   [*premiss (observation)*]
3   Where a complex seems to be named in a proposition, it is not in fact named but described.   [*from (1) & (2)*]
4   The (real) names in a proposition refer to simple objects.   [*from (3), hence from (1) & (2)*]

This version avoids the false second premiss in our previous attempt. The argument seems valid, and the only dubious premiss it contains is (1): the doctrine of referentialism. Thus the core idea of logical atomism has been shown to follow from referentialism, – which will be discussed later, in section 4.2, when we turn to Wittgenstein's criticisms of his earlier views.

(iii) *Determinacy of sense*. Finally, Wittgenstein offers this laconic remark in support of his logical atomism:

> 3.23 The demand that simple signs be possible is the demand that sense be determinate.

A simple sign is not only a fully analysed sign, which has no significant parts, it is by definition the linguistic correlate to a simple object (*TLP* 3.2, 3.201, 2.02). Hence the demand that simple signs be possible implies the demand that simple objects exist. And that is how Wittgenstein put it in his *Notebooks*: 'The demand for simple things *is* the demand that sense be determinate' (*NB*, 18 June 1915). As noted above (sect. 2.2), Frege demanded of an ideal language that sense be determinate, that every concept be defined with perfect precision; Wittgenstein believed this demand to be already met by our ordinary language (*TLP* 5.5563). The propositions of everyday life 'are not in any way... less exact... than propositions written down, say, in Russell's symbolism or any other "Begriffsschrift". (Only it is easier for us to gather their logical form when they are expressed in an appropriate symbolism.)' (*LO* 50). But granted that sense must be determinate, why should that require the existence of simple objects?

We must turn to Wittgenstein's *Notebooks* for further remarks on this point, from which an argument of sorts can be reconstructed. Wittgenstein considers as an example the proposition 'The book is on the table' (*NB*, 20 June 1915). Does this really have a completely clear sense? Would I be able under all possible circumstances to say whether it was true or false (cf. *TLP* 4.023)? No, one can easily imagine a borderline case in which one would not be sure whether to call the proposition true or false. For example, if part of the book touched the table while another part rested on the window sill; or if the book lay on a chair that was placed on the table. But Wittgenstein holds on to his intuition that sense must be exact. To overcome the objection he suggests: 'that I am using the words, e.g., "lying on", with a *special* meaning (*Bedeutung*) here, and that elsewhere they have another meaning. What I mean (*meine*) by the verb is perhaps a quite special relation which the book now actually has to the table' (*NB*, 20 June 1915). The meaning of a word or sentence in general may be quite indefinite. An expression may be used in a variety of ways, and it is not always clear whether a possible application is still acceptable. Nevertheless, Wittgenstein insists, what is said on a particular occasion has a precise sense. For the sense of a proposition on a particular occasion of use is determined not just by the words – taken in isolation, they may indeed be somewhat vague (*NB*, 22 June 1915) – but by what I mean by them in that situation. And it 'seems clear that what we MEAN must always be "*sharp*"' (*NB*, 20 June 1915). So sense is made determinate by what is 'added in thought' to the proposition (NB, 21 June 1915).[7] But what exactly is added? What precisely does Wittgenstein mean (by the expression 'is on') when he says 'The book is on the table'? His answer is: 'I should say: "I *know* what I mean; I mean just THIS", pointing to the appropriate complex with my finger' (NB, 22 June 1915). So in a particular utterance the meaning (*Bedeutung*) of an expression (e.g., 'lying on') is determined by what the speaker means (*meint*) by it. And he means by it what he uses it to refer to: the complex he is talking about. After all, the meaning of a word *is* its reference (TLP 3.203). Propositions have a sense, but the parts of a proposition which are not themselves propositions have none: their semantic role is exhausted by their standing for things in the world (unless they are logical symbols). But if the sense of a proposition depends on the meanings of its parts, and those meanings are (at a first stage of analysis) complex things referred to by the speaker, then ultimately the sense of a proposition will have only as definite an analysis as those complexes. That is to say: for the sense of a proposition to be fully determinate, it must be possible to give a complete analysis of the complexes involved. But such an analysis, it would appear, can be completed only if it gets down to absolutely simple objects: atoms. If, on the other hand, a complex were divisible *indefinitely*, the meaning of some part of the proposition, and hence the sense of the proposition, would be equally indefinite.

The crucial idea in this argument is that the actual composition of a complex determines the meaning of an expression referring to that complex (*even if the speaker is ignorant of that composition*), and thus it determines the sense of the proposition in which that expression occurs. 'When I say this watch is shiny, and what I mean by "this watch" alters its composition in the smallest particular, then ... *what I am saying about this watch* straightway alters its sense' (NB, 16 June 1915). The thought is not as clearly expressed in the *Tractatus*, but it is implicit in the following terse remark:

> 3.24   A proposition about a complex stands in an internal relation to a proposition about a constituent of the complex.

An internal relation is a necessary relation, one that could not possibly fail to hold (TLP 4.123). And the necessary relation that Wittgenstein has in mind here is that of logical entailment. If C is a complex and a is one of its constituents, then the proposition 'C is in the drawer' logically entails 'a is in the drawer'. That is because the constitution of the complex C is reflected in the meaning of the linguistic expression 'C', which could be analysed as, say, 'the combination of a, b, c & d', or

---

[7] Cf. LL 7: 'in the process of analysing a proposition ... we get the imagination into the symbol.'

for short, 'a-b-c-d'.[8] Consequently, 'to say that one thing is part of another is always a tautology' (*NB*, 17 June 1915). Thus, to say that *a* is part of *C* is a logical truth, as becomes obvious once 'C' is analysed into 'a-b-c-d', which makes it clear that 'C is in the drawer' logically entails 'a is in the drawer'.

One way of putting the demand that a proposition's sense be determinate is that 'it must be completely settled what propositions follow from it' (*PTLP* 3.20103; = *NB*, 18 June 1915). But this would not be the case if, rather than consisting of a fixed number of simple objects, a complex were indefinitely divisible. The complex would have indefinitely many parts, and thus the list of propositions following from it would be open-ended.

This third argument for logical atomism depends on a corollary of Wittgenstein's version of referentialism: namely, the doctrine that meaning, being nothing but reference, includes *all* the essential features of the objects referred to, even features we are not aware of. Thus the contents of meaning and sense can outstrip what competent speakers know, indeed even what they are able to find out. We shall postpone critical discussion of this presupposition till we reach the recurrence of these issues in Wittgenstein's later philosophy. However, even apart from this problematic presupposition, the argument is flawed. It rests on a dichotomy of finite divisibility, leading to simple objects, and indefinite, open-ended divisibility, with unpredictable results. But there is the third possibility of an infinite divisibility that is regular and predictable. Suppose a particle can be split into halves, and the results halved again, and so forth, *ad infinitum*. Then there is nothing indeterminate about the particle's composition; it *is* completely settled what propositions follow from the statement that this particle is at a certain place, even though there is an infinite number of such implications. The possible divisions of the particle are as definitely fixed as the series of natural numbers, and yet there is no complete decomposition: no absolutely simple objects (cf. *PTLP* 5.4103; *WA* 1, 52:4 and 8f).

Independent states of affairs   The last of the fundamental ontological claims listed above was that states of affairs are independent of each other (*TLP* 2.061). That means:

> 2.062   From the existence or non-existence of one state of affairs it is impossible to infer the existence or non-existence of another.

---

[8] On the other hand, while 'C' is left unanalysed, there is (or appears to be) an indeterminacy in the proposition 'C is in the drawer' (*TLP* 3.24c). It is not yet clear what exactly it says.

This too is supposed to be a consequence of the idea of a complete analysis. A complex proposition is composed of other propositions, which therefore can follow from it (as 'p' follows from 'p.q') or be incompatible with it (as 'p' is incompatible with '~p.q'). So it might be thought that with fully analysed elementary propositions, none of which contain any other propositions, no such logical relations obtain:[9]

> 5.134 One elementary proposition cannot be deduced from another.
>
> 4.211 It is a sign of a proposition's being elementary that there can be no elementary proposition contradicting it.

Therefore, what correspond to elementary propositions in reality, states of affairs (*TLP* 4.21), must be independent of each other.

At this point it may be helpful to consider a model to illustrate the *Tractatus* ontology. Anthony Kenny suggested the possible positions of pieces on a chess-board (1973, 74): The objects of this model world are the chess-pieces and the squares of the chess-board. The relations between the pieces and the squares are states of affairs. It may, for instance, be an obtaining state of affairs that there is a white pawn on square a2. The world, all that is the case, will be the position on the board at any given time.

However, as Kenny himself goes on to remark, this analogy is deficient in at least two respects. First, the objects are not as enduring as demanded in the *Tractatus*: chess-pieces can be taken, and new pieces can come into play when a pawn gets promoted. But that can easily be remedied. We just have to imagine the rules of chess altered a little: so that it is no longer permitted to take pieces or to promote pawns. The second disanalogy is more serious. States of affairs on the chess-board are *not* independent of each other. From the fact that there is a white pawn on square a2, you can infer that there is not a black bishop on a2. For two pieces cannot be on the same square simultaneously. Again, from the fact that the white king is on square e1, it follows that the white king is *not* on square a7. For one piece cannot be on two squares simultaneously. Contrary to *TLP* 2.062, from the existence or non-existence of one state of affairs we *can* infer the existence or non-existence of another. The problem can be generalized. Any concrete object will occupy a particular place. And from the fact that it occupies one given location, it will always follow that it does not occupy another

---

[9] As we shall see in sect. 2.5, the truth-functional logical analysis that Wittgenstein defended provided him with another motive for regarding elementary propositions, and hence states of affairs, as logically independent of each other.

location. Hence, as long as we are dealing with concrete particulars, there will always be states of affairs that infringe Wittgenstein's independence requirement, *TLP* 2.061. An object's being in one place will not be logically independent of its being (or non-being) in another place. It follows, then, that the *Tractatus* objects cannot be concrete particulars.[10]

Wittgenstein himself had only a vague idea of simple objects. But among the things that occurred to him were points in visual space and properties such as colours.[11] Not a particular coloured spot, but *a* colour: something that can be simultaneously in different places. So let us take up these examples and try to construct a more adequate model of the *Tractatus* world. Our objects are two properties: *blue* and *hot*, and the nine squares of a diminutive chess-board. As it is, this world contains five states of affairs, which may be expressed by the following elementary propositions:

a3: hot
c1: blue
c2: blue
c3: blue
c3: hot

Alternatively, we can depict this model world diagrammatically:

	a	b	c
1			B
2			B
3	H		B,H

---

[10] For a further discussion of this issue see Glock 1996a, 103–7.
[11] In his *Notebooks* he wrote: 'Relations and properties, etc. are *objects* too' (*NB*, 15 June 1915; cf. *WA* 1, 6; 49:5; 51:2). And in conversations with Desmond Lee in 1930/1 he is recorded as having explained the *Tractatus* notion of an object as follows: 'Objects . . . is here used for such things as a colour, a point in visual space etc. . . . "Objects" also include relations' (*LL* 120).

The object blue (B) occurs three times: in three states of affairs. It might have occurred in nine states of affairs; or it might have occurred not at all.[12] But it might not have occurred on its own, outside any state of affairs. That is the form of this object *blue*: that it can occur in exactly nine different states of affairs: on nine different squares.

Here, then, we have the required independence of states of affairs that was missing in Kenny's chess model. That c3 is blue does not allow us to infer whether c1 is blue or not (unlike a chess-piece, the object blue can occur simultaneously in different places). And that c3 is blue does not allow us to infer whether c3 is hot or not (unlike two chess-pieces, the two objects blue and hot *can* occur simultaneously on the same square).

Our objects, the nine squares and the qualities blue and hot make up the substance of this model world, subsisting eternally and independently of what happens to be the case (*TLP* 2.021, 2.024). The substance is 'form and content' (*TLP* 2.025). This means that those objects are what one can encounter in this world, the world's content, but they also determine what states of affairs are possible. To know an object is to know its combinatorial possibilities (*TLP* 2.0123). Thus if you know the square a1, you know that it can be linked with blue or hot to form a state of affairs, whereas it is impossible for a1 to combine with c1 or any other square.

So far, so good. But what if we tried to make our model a little more like the real world by adding the further qualities *red* and *cold*? Then it would no longer satisfy Wittgenstein's demands, for now states of affairs are not entirely independent of each other. If square a1 is blue, it cannot at the same time be red, and if it is hot, it cannot be cold. Wittgenstein was well aware that 'the simultaneous presence of two colours at the same place is impossible' (*TLP* 6.3751). So obviously, 'Point *a* is red' and 'Point *a* is blue' cannot be mutually independent elementary propositions. The author of the *Tractatus* had hoped that somehow physics might enable us to give an analysis of colour predicates that would solve this problem. But, as he realized in 1929 (*RLF* 32f), that was a vain hope. Physics accounts for colours in terms of electromagnetic radiation of different wavelengths. But different wavelengths are just as mutually exclusive as are different colours: What is 700 nm long cannot be 450 nm long. To avoid this problem, one would have to be able to give a complete description of the world without predicating any qualities that make up a range of incompatible speci-

---

[12] This might appear to conflict with the demand that objects be subsistent (*TLP* 2.0271), but it seems to be required by *TLP* 2.013: '[The] space of possible states of affairs . . . I can imagine empty.' We are probably meant to distinguish between the sempiternal subsistence of the quality blue and its contingent instantiation in particular states of affairs (cf. *PI* §57).

fications, different degrees on the same scale (like colour, temperature, weight, pitch, length or velocity). Alternatively, one could give up the requirement that states of affairs must be mutually independent. That was what Wittgenstein would advocate in 1929.

2.4 Pictures: Language and Thought

In 1913 and 1914, when Europe was sliding into the First World War, Wittgenstein pondered three philosophical puzzles, two of which where engendered by his referentialist presupposition.

(i) Given that language is essentially a matter of signs standing for things (referentialism), how can there be false propositions: i.e., propositions that are meaningful although there is no actual fact represented by them (cf. *NB*, 30 Sept. 1914)?
(ii) How is it possible with a limited number of different signs to describe any of an infinite number of possible states of affairs (cf. *NB* 98)?
(iii) Words are essentially names, standing for objects (referentialism). A sequence of names ('Tom Dick Harry') is not a statement (cf. *NB* 96, 105). How, then, is it possible for a proposition to be more than just a sequence of names and to make a statement about the world?

The first two of those puzzles led Wittgenstein to a recognition of the essential difference between names and propositions. Initially he had followed Frege and Russell in treating propositions like names, as standing for some kind of object. Taking that line, one might be inclined to say that, for instance, the proposition:

(P) The Elgin Marbles are in the Louvre

stands for, or refers to, the complex formed by the Elgin Marbles being in the Louvre. Unfortunately, no such complex exists (for the Elgin Marbles are in the British Museum). So it would appear, on such a referentialist account, that without a reference, proposition (P) must be meaningless. But of course it is perfectly understandable. Very similar considerations, though about thoughts rather than statements, occupied Plato in his dialogue *Theaetetus*:

> SOCRATES: And if someone thinks mustn't he think *something*?
> THEAETETUS: Yes, he must.
> SOCRATES: And if he thinks something, mustn't it be something real?
> THEAETETUS: Apparently.

SOCRATES: Hence if someone thinks what is not, he thinks nothing.
THEAETETUS: So it seems.
SOCRATES: But if someone thinks nothing, he surely doesn't think at all.
THEAETETUS: Obviously. (189a; cf. *PG* 137; *PI* §518)

It would appear that one cannot have false thoughts, or make false statements! Of course one can: A meaningful proposition may be true, but it can also be false. This is what Wittgenstein called the principle of bipolarity. Any satisfactory theory of language must take it into account.

In 1914 Wittgenstein held that: 'The *Bedeutung* [meaning] of a proposition is the fact that corresponds to it, e.g., if our proposition be "aRb", if it's true, the corresponding fact would be the fact aRb, if false, the fact ~aRb' (*NB* 112). On this account, 'The Elgin Marbles are in the Louvre' is not meaningless, but its meaning is, paradoxically, the fact that the Elgin Marbles are *not* in the Louvre (cf. Russell 1919b, 314): Knowledge of the meaning of the proposition is, then, the knowledge that it is false. But knowledge of the meaning of an expression – that is, understanding – needs to be distinguished from the knowledge of truth or falsity. For one can perfectly well understand the proposition 'The Elgin Marbles are in the Louvre' without knowing whether it is true or false (*TLP* 4.024b). Therefore Wittgenstein soon abandoned this explanation of the meaning of a proposition. Indeed, he came to think that it was altogether wrong to ascribe a 'meaning', that is a reference, to propositions. The semantic role of propositions is very different from that of names, and so, Wittgenstein concluded, referentialism must be restricted to the latter. Only names have meaning, that is, reference (*TLP* 3.203; *NB*, 2 Nov. 1914). A proposition is a combination of names (*TLP* 4.22), but it is not itself a name (*TLP* 3.143). So it need not refer to, or describe, an actually existing state of affairs in order to be intelligible, provided its constituent names refer to existing objects. We require a fixed one-to-one correlation between language and world not at the complex level of propositions, but only at the level of the simple parts of a proposition. With the capacity for being true *or* false, propositions have essentially a two-way relationship to reality. To extend the application of the term 'meaning' to the reality that happens to correspond to a proposition is only misleading, in that it makes propositions appear more similar to names than they are (cf. *TLP* 3.143; *NB* 97).

The relation between a word and the object it stands for is very different from that between a proposition and the corresponding fact. For each name we have a convention that determines its reference. Thus linguistic convention alone makes the name 'London' stand for the capital of Great Britain. But the relation between a proposition, like (P), 'The Elgin Marbles are in the Louvre', and the corresponding part of reality is quite different. There are two possible states of affairs that *could* correspond to (P): that the Elgin Marbles are in the Louvre and that the Elgin Marbles are not in the Louvre. Hence for (P) there are two possible relations to reality: it could describe things either correctly or incorrectly. And which of these two relations to reality (P) has is not just a matter of linguistic convention (*TLP* 2.223–2.225). Only experience can tell us which existing state of affairs corresponds to a proposition: the one that it describes (i.e., the one that makes it true) or its contradictory (the one that makes it false).

Occasionally philosophers overlook this crucial distinction between words and propositions and come to alarming conclusions. Friedrich Nietzsche, in an early essay that has often been credited with debunking truth as a mere illusion, is a case in point. With respect to stipulations of word meaning, Nietzsche writes:

> That which is to count as 'truth' . . . becomes fixed, i.e., a way of designating things is invented that has the same validity and force everywhere . . . [W]hat is the status of those conventions of language? Are they perhaps products of knowledge, of the sense of truth? Is there a perfect match between things and their designations? Is language the full and adequate expression of all realities? . . . When different languages are set alongside one another it becomes clear that, where words are concerned, what matters is never truth; never the full and adequate expression; otherwise there would not be so many languages. (Nietzsche 1873, 143f)

'Where words are concerned, what matters is never truth' – correct. But from the observation that conventions about *word* meaning are not based on truth, Nietzsche jumps to the (self-refuting!) conclusion that *language* cannot really express any truths: a simple failure to distinguish between words and propositions.

The distinction between names and propositions also provides a solution to puzzle (ii). We understand only those names whose meanings have been explained to us (*TLP* 4.026). Hence, if states of affairs were to be referred to by names, we could not talk about any new and unforeseen state of affairs that has not yet been given a name. But that is not the case, for instead of *naming* states of affairs, we talk about them by forming propositions. And we can understand propositions that we have never heard before and that have never been explained to us, provided only that we are familiar with all their constituent words and the rules of syntax (*TLP* 4.02, 4.03). Likewise, once we know the meanings of the relevant names and the licit ways of combining them to form sentences, we can express an endless number of new propositions. In this respect our languages compare very favourably with some other systems of communication where, for each message, one has to learn a new sign (e.g., the non-alphabetical use of naval signal flags).

With such a system one can send and understand only a very limited number of different messages, since one can learn and remember only a very limited number of different signs.

The crucial difference between names and propositions Wittgenstein sums up with a simile: 'Names are like points; propositions like arrows – they have sense' (*TLP* 3.144). Both the German word *Sinn* and its English equivalent 'sense' can also mean direction (as in 'sense of rotation'[13]). That makes it natural to associate sense with an arrow, pointing in one direction. Arrows have opposites: for any arrow, you can draw another one pointing in the opposite direction; just as for any proposition 'p' there is another proposition '~p' that has the opposite sense (*TLP* 4.0621). As Wittgenstein explains in a manuscript from 1913:

> A proposition is a standard to which facts behave[14] [stand in a certain way], with names it is otherwise; it is thus bi-polarity and sense comes in; just as one arrow behaves [stands] to another by being in the same sense or the opposite, so a fact behaves [stands] to a proposition. (*NB* 95)

Thus the sense of proposition (P) above and the facts about the Elgin Marbles' current location may, as it were, run parallel or in opposite directions (cf. *TLP* 4.2).

The sense of a proposition is what it represents (*TLP* 2.221), a situation that may or may not obtain (*TLP* 4.031). Proposition (P) represents the possible situation of the Elgin Marbles' being in the Louvre. That situation is the sense of (P), independently of whether it actually exists (*TLP* 4.061).

There remains puzzle (iii): given that all the words of a fully analysed sentence are names (*TLP* 3.202, 4.22), it is unclear how such a string of names could express anything. If it were merely a medley of names, it surely could not; but, according to Wittgenstein, a sentence is more than this (*TLP* 3.141). A sentence is composed not only of its ingredient names, but also of their particular configuration. The same names occurring in a different order might convey a different sense. 'Jones sues Smith' does not say the same as 'Smith sues Jones'. Hence, a sentence is a fact (*TLP* 3.14); it is the fact that certain names are arranged in a particular order (*TLP* 3.1432).

> 3.14 What constitutes a propositional sign is that in it its elements (the words) stand in a determinate relation to one another.

---

[13] Cf. Russell 1912, 126.

[14] A Germanism in Wittgenstein's English: a literal translation of *sich verhalten*.

This idea is developed in what has become known as Wittgenstein's Picture Theory of Language –:

At the beginning of the First World War, when Wittgenstein was serving on a patrol boat on the River Vistula, he read a newspaper report about a lawsuit in Paris concerning a car accident. In court, instead of a merely verbal description of the event, dolls and miniature cars were used to represent the relative positions and movements of the people and vehicles involved (*NB*, 29 Sept. 1914; *WA* 2, 279). A model played the role of a proposition. But if a proposition's job can be done by a model, Wittgenstein thought, the two must essentially function in the same way (*WVC* 185). A proposition too must be a kind of model. Thus the picture theory of language was born. Names stand for objects, and a certain syntactic arrangement of those names represents a certain arrangement of those objects. For instance, the arrangement of the expressions 'London', 'Southampton' and 'is north of' in the sentence 'London is north of Southampton' represents the geographical situation of London *vis-à-vis* Southampton. Thus a sentence is a representation, a picture of reality.

It has often been said that in the *Tractatus* the term 'picture' is used in a broader sense than usual. One should say, rather, that the term is used in a quite different sense. For most of the things we normally call pictures are not pictures according to the *Tractatus*. The elements in a *Tractatus* picture can be arranged differently to depict a different situation. In ordinary pictures that is hardly possible, due to perspective and occlusion. Consider a painting of a cart drawn by two horses, seen from the rear (as in Constable's *Hay Wain*). Certain sections of the canvas depict the cart, and other sections depict the horses. But you could not arrange them differently to represent a different situation, for a different situation, a different spatial arrangement of cart and horses, would require entirely new bits of painting. For example, if the horses were to be on this side of the cart, the sections depicting them would have to be larger (perspective), and you would have to add something for those parts of their bodies that in the actual painting seem hidden behind the cart. This explains why in *TLP* 4.0311 Wittgenstein compares a proposition not to a normal picture, but to a living picture, a *tableau vivant*. Living pictures were a popular pastime in eighteenth- and early nineteenth-century good society. People would don costumes and posture in static representations of scenes from fiction, mythology or history.[15] After a while the participants in a *tableau vivant* would change their positions and represent a slightly different scene, just as the miniature vehicles and dolls in a court room traffic model (or a model

---

[15] Cf. Goethe's novel *Selective Affinities* (*Die Wahlverwandtschaften*), part 2, chs 5–6.

railway) can be shifted around freely to represent different situations. So the term 'picture' in the *Tractatus* should be taken to mean model (*TLP* 2.12).

Consider again the Paris court room model. Suppose it consisted of a toy omnibus and a doll: these, the elements of the model (or 'picture') stand, or deputize, for objects (*TLP* 2.131). Let us say that the doll stands for a certain Jean Dupont who was hit by a bus, which is symbolized by the toy bus. This correlation of the model's elements with things is called the *pictorial relationship* (*TLP* 2.1514). But for something to be a 'picture' (i.e., a model), its elements must not only be related to real objects, they must also be related to one another in a determinate way (*TLP* 2.14). And these relations among the model's elements Wittgenstein calls its *structure* (*TLP* 2.15). Wittgenstein emphasizes that the model itself is a fact (*TLP* 2.141): It is the fact that it has a certain structure, which means that its elements are related to one another in a certain way (*TLP* 2.15). This fact (that a model has a certain structure) represents a certain state of affairs. So in our example, the fact that the toy car touches the doll in a certain way represents the possible situation of the bus hitting Monsieur Dupont.

Next Wittgenstein introduces the term 'pictorial form'. The model's elements are related to one another in a determinate way (the model's structure), but they could have been related to one another in various different ways. That is to say, the model could have had a different structure. And the potential for all its possible structures is the model's pictorial form (*TLP* 2.15f). The pictorial form of a model consisting of a toy car and a doll is that these two elements can be in all sorts of *spatial* relations to one another: the doll can be on top of the car, or in front of the car, or underneath the car, and so on and so forth. And in each case the model would represent a certain situation involving a real car and a real pedestrian. As both the elements in the model and the corresponding objects are three-dimensional material objects, they can both be variously arranged in space: that is what they have in common: the possible arrangements of their elements: their form (*TLP* 2.16–2.171).

Because a traffic model is a three-dimensional spatial picture (like a *tableau vivant*), it can obviously represent the spatial situations on a road. In a different model, the fact that an object *a* is red and another object *b* is blue may be represented by writing 'a' in red ink and 'b' in blue ink. This, then, is a coloured picture, as the traffic model is a spatial picture. That is their pictorial form: what they have in common with what they depict; but not all pictures represent by straightforward resemblance. A sonata may be depicted by a musical score, but temporal succession of notes in the sonata is not represented by temporal succession among the elements of the picture; instead, it is represented by the fact that the signs are ordered in rows from left to right, or, if they are simultaneous they are written above each other. Or, consider the representation of a particular position in a game of chess: Such a representation is often given by a diagram, a stylized drawing; but one could also give a purely verbal description of the position: e.g.

(D)   White: Ka2, Bb3, Pa3, Pb4, Ph7.
       Black: Kg5, Nh1, Pa7, Pb7, Pc7.

Unlike a diagram, this verbal picture (D) does not share the two-dimensional form of what it depicts. Still, it has some kind of form (its pictorial form) in common with the position depicted. That form is the possibility that the elements in (D) combine in a way that is analogous to the combinatorial possibilities of the pieces on the chess-board. That is to say, just as any of the sixty-four squares can be occupied by a piece, so in the picture (D) any of the sixty-four co-ordinates a1 to h8 can be linked with a capital letter naming a certain piece. So, the pictorial form that a model shares with what it depicts need not be the same possibilities of spatial, temporal or colour arrangements; but to such arrangements in reality there must correspond arrangements of elements. The combinatorial possibilities that world and picture must have in common Wittgenstein calls *logical form* (*TLP* 2.18).

Logical form not only allows certain combinations, but also excludes others. Just as in chess a square cannot be on top of another square, so it must be impossible for the sign 'a1' to combine with 'c3': 'a1c3' is not a picture of a state of affairs on the chess-board. For the logical form of chess – which any picture must share in order to be a picture of a position in chess – disallows that combination.

Every picture is a logical one (*TLP* 2.182). That is to say, in every picture the combinatorial possibilities of its elements must match the combinatorial possibilities of the corresponding objects, 'the form of reality' (*TLP* 2.18). That makes it difficult to present convincing examples of pictures in the *Tractatus* sense. The Paris traffic model for one is ruled out, for the representing toys have obviously not the same logical multiplicity as the objects represented. The real bus might, for example, have run out of petrol, and Monsieur Dupont might have 500 francs in his pocket, but nothing in the configuration of the toy models would represent these states of affairs. To represent the scene according to *Tractatus* standards, the toys would need the same complexity as the objects they stand for: the toy omnibus would need something like a fuel tank, and the doll would need something like pockets in its trousers, and so for any other feature of the original objects (cf. *NB*, 4 Sept. 1914 d). Here we re-encounter Wittgenstein's demand for complete analysability of both world and picture. For every atom in the depicted scene, there must be a corresponding atom in the model depicting it. And if no such atomic structure meets the eye, it must be assumed that analysis could bring it to light: an assumption that could evidently not be upheld in the case of the traffic model used in a Paris law court.

To summarize Wittgenstein's general account of the picture theory: What constitutes a picture in the *Tractatus* sense (a model) is that its elements are related to one another in a certain way. And the fact that these elements are related to each other in this way represents the possibility that the objects for which the elements stand are related to each other correspondingly. For a picture to depict, there does not have to be a fact corresponding to it (the picture need not be true); but there must be objects corresponding to the simple elements of the picture. This is a necessary precondition of depiction. Moreover, objects and pictorial elements must have their logical form in common; that is to say, they must have the same combinatorial possibilities. Finally, each pictorial element must somehow be connected with an object. That connection is the pictorial relationship, which 'makes a picture into a picture' (*TLP* 2.1513).

What turns a string of words into a sentence is that the words stand in a determinate relation to one another (*TLP* 3.14). And that means that a sentence is a 'picture', for 'What constitutes a picture is that its elements stand in a determinate relation to one another' (*TLP* 2.14). Once we recognize propositions as models, it becomes immediately clear how propositions can be true or false. The principle of bipolarity is implicit in, and elucidated by, the picture theory (*TLP* 4.06). Propositions are true or false inasmuch as the combinations of their words match or fail to match the combinations of the corresponding objects. Again, the very idea of a model is that its elements can be arranged in different ways to represent different situations. Once we have understood how a model works, new combinations of its elements can present us with new situations. Hence the fact that a proposition can communicate a new sense to us (*TLP* 4.027) – that we can understand propositions that we have never come across before – can be explained by regarding propositions as models (*TLP* 4.02). Being a model, a proposition *shows* its sense (*TLP* 4.022). Just as an arrangement of toys can show the relative positions of a pedestrian and a vehicle, so the order of the words 'Smith', 'Jones' and 'sues' in the proposition 'Smith sues Jones' shows who sues whom, according to this proposition (*TLP* 3.1432). The proposition does not need any further explanation. It represents the situation 'off its own bat' (*NB*, 5 Nov. 1914).

However, there is an obvious difference between a traffic model or a living picture, on the one hand, and a verbal representation, on the other. In the former case, the pictorial relationship is based on resemblance, but in the latter case it is quite arbitrary. The toy bus resembles the bus it stands for, but the elements of a verbal representation do not normally resemble the objects denoted.[16] How, then, in the case of verbal representation is the pictorial relationship brought about? How does one manage to make names *stand for* objects?

> 3.11 We use the perceptible sign of a proposition (spoken or written, etc.) as a projection of a possible situation.
> The method of projection is to think out the sense of the proposition.
>
> 3.12 I call the sign with which we express a thought a propositional sign. – And a proposition is a propositional sign in its projective relation to the world.

Wittgenstein distinguishes between a propositional sign and a proposition (*TLP* 3.12). A *propositional sign* is a declarative sentence. A *proposition* is not an entity distinct from the propositional sign: rather, it is the propositional sign plus something else that makes it meaningful: namely, a mental act of thinking, or meaning.

As explained above, for something to be a picture, its elements must be connected with objects. Thus, for a proposition to be a picture – and so to have sense – its simple signs, or names, must mean objects. Only then does the propositional sign stand in a projective relation to the world. But this connection with objects is not *intrinsic* in words. By themselves they are just noises or marks on a piece of paper. It is the mind that endows words with significance, that connects them with objects in the world (cf. *BB* 3f). This is done by the mental act of meaning something by a word (cf. *NB*, 20 June 1915), or 'thinking out' the sense of a proposition (*TLP* 3.11), and thus setting up a 'projective relation' between the propositional sign and the world (*TLP* 3.12). Thus a sentence is infused with a sense and becomes an expressed thought (*TLP* 3.5). And an expressed thought is a proposition (*TLP* 4, 3.1).

It is *thinking* that, by expressing itself in words, enables those words to depict the world. Thoughts, unlike conventional noises or signs, are intrinsically models of the world. Linguistic signs become models of the world only by courtesy of the thoughts that express themselves in them. For this reason, Wittgenstein, after giving a general exposition of the picture theory, applies it first not to language, but to thoughts (*TLP* 3–3.05). 'A logical picture of facts,' Wittgenstein writes, 'is a thought' (*TLP* 3); *every* picture is also a logical picture (*TLP* 2.182): every picture is or expresses a thought. Thought is, as it were, the

---

[16] The same applies to the picture's structure, which can be iconographic or conventional.

lowest common denominator of all different kinds of pictures (painting, construction drawing, verbal description, musical score or wordless pondering). Through signs a thought becomes public: the picture can now be perceived by the senses (*TLP* 3.1). What the English sentence 'It's raining' and the French sentence 'Il pleut' have in common is that they can be used to express the same thought, by means of different linguistic conventions. Like these statements, the thought expressed is also a picture of a situation in which it is raining, but it is independent of any linguistic stipulations. It is depiction pure and simple.

What exactly is a thought? It is supposed to be a picture: not a verbal or spatial picture, but a mental picture. As a picture it must be composite (*TLP* 4.032). It must consist of elements combined in a certain way. But what are these elements? Russell put this question to Wittgenstein, who replied:

> I don't know *what* the constituents of a thought are but I know *that* it must have such constituents which correspond to the words of Language.... the kind of relation of the constituents of thought and of the pictured fact is irrelevant. It would be a matter of psychology to find out. (*CL* 125)

Russell suggested that perhaps thinking too goes on in words (as when we quietly speak to ourselves). Wittgenstein denied that: '– Does a Gedanke [a thought] consist of words? No! But of psychical constituents that have the same sort of relation to reality as words. What those constituents are I don't know' (*CL* 125). So there is in our minds something like a language (cf. *NB*, 12 Sept. 1916), but not a real language. For the constituents of thoughts are not words; on that point Wittgenstein is decided. That is because words have their pictorial relation to objects not intrinsically, but only through an act of thinking. Hence, if the elements of a thought were words, it would require some further thought to make *them* stand for objects. And if that further thought were again composed of words, we would need yet another thought to bestow meaning on them, and so on and so forth. We would be launched on an infinite regress. If linguistic meaning is only derivative – derived from the meaning of elements of thought – then the elements of thought must not themselves be linguistic entities. They had better relate to objects intrinsically. But how do they do it? We don't really know. But then, mental capacities just are wonderful ... – This problem will be reconsidered in section 4.2f below.[17]

---

[17] For more on Wittgenstein's views on intentionality (as the capacity of language and thought to be *about* something is often called) see Ammereller 2001.

2.5 Logic

To utter: 'either it's raining or it's not raining' is not to *say* anything (cf. *TLP* 4.461e). In this not uncommon sense of the expression, 'to say something' means: to be (possibly) informative, to convey something that might be new to a hearer. That is the sense in which Wittgenstein uses the word 'say' in the *Tractatus*. A proposition can *say* only what does not go without saying: what might be or might have been otherwise (*TLP* 5.634): what one could conceivably be mistaken about. That is, again, the principle of bipolarity: for a proposition to say something (i.e., to have a sense) it must have both possibilities: truth and falsity. And that is what the picture theory has elaborated in further detail. For a proposition to have a sense, it must represent a situation that may or may not obtain (*TLP* 4.031). 'A proposition is a picture of reality' (*TLP* 4.01), but in order 'to tell whether a picture is true or false we must compare it with reality' (*TLP* 2.223). 'There are no pictures that are true *a priori*' (*TLP* 2.225). Hence any expression of what is logically necessary is not a proposition with a sense. If something is a matter of logic, it cannot be said. What, then, is to become of the subject of logic, being thus pushed beyond the bounds of meaningful discourse? 'Logic must take care of itself' (*TLP* 5.473). This means that logical (or 'internal') relations, since they cannot be described in meaningful propositions, must *show themselves* (*TLP* 4.121ff). They must be made self-evident by analysis and an appropriate notation. To this task we must now turn.

A complete analysis of ordinary propositions is supposed to result in elementary propositions. No actual analysis of that kind is provided by Wittgenstein. What he had in mind is something roughly along the lines of Russell's analysis of definite descriptions (*PG* 211). But from the results of that kind of analysis it is still a long way down to elementary propositions. More light is shed on Wittgenstein's conception of analysis by beginning at the bottom end to see how elementary propositions are supposed to combine to form more complex ones. There is only one mode of combination: elementary propositions are combined in so-called *truth-functions* (*TLP* 5).

If a number of propositions are combined in a truth-function, then the truth or falsity (the truth-value) of the combination is determined completely by the respective truth or falsity of the propositions thus combined. Consider the conjunction of two propositions: 'p.q' ['p and q']. Whether this complex proposition is true or false depends entirely on the truth-values of the ingredient propositions 'p' and 'q'. If both 'p' and 'q' are true, their conjunction 'p.q' is true too. If either or both of 'p' and 'q' are false, 'p.q' is false too. A convenient representation of the matter is a so-called *truth-table*:

p	q	p.q
T	T	T
F	T	F
T	F	F
F	F	F

In modern logic truth-tables are commonly used to give definitions of logical connectives. To add a couple of examples, conditional ['if p then q'] and negation ['it is not the case that p'] are defined thus:

p	q	p⊃q
T	T	T
F	T	T
T	F	F
F	F	T

p	~p
T	F
F	T

'p⊃q' ['if p then q'] is defined to be false only in case 'p' is true and 'q' is false. Unlike conjunction and conditional, negation is a truth-function based on only one proposition. Consequently, its truth-table lists only two possibilities: the ingredient proposition 'p' (called the *argument* of the truth-function (*TLP* 5.02)) can either be true or false. And the truth-function '~p' ('it is not the case that p') always takes the opposite truth-value to 'p'.

An elementary proposition 'p' can be either true or false: these are its two possible truth-values, or *truth-possibilities* (*TLP* 4.31). So a truth-function based on only one elementary proposition (like '~p') is represented by a truth-table with two lines. A pair of elementary propositions has four truth-possibilities (TT, FT, TF, FF), and three elementary propositions have eight truth-possibilities (TTT, FTT, TFT, FFT, TTF, FTF, TFF, FFF). In general, for n states of affairs there are 2^n possibilities of existence or non-existence; so for n elementary propositions there are 2^n truth-possibilities, or lines in a truth-table (*TLP* 4.27).[18] Note, however, that this presupposes the logical independence of all the ingredient propositions. Otherwise, not all those truth-possibilities would exist. If, for example, for 'p' we took 'Smith is a bachelor' and for 'q' 'Smith is married', then it would be logically impossible for both to be true. So the first line of the truth-table (TT) would have to be left out. Complete truth-tables can be guaranteed only if the arguments of the truth-functions are *elementary* propositions, which are understood to be logically independent, like the states of affairs they describe (*TLP* 2.061, 4.211, 5.134).

---

[18] 2^n is what Wittgenstein's formula in *TLP* 4.27 amounts to: $K_n = \sum_{v=0}^{n} \binom{n}{v}$.

Given a certain number of elementary propositions, we can also calculate the number of different truth-functions that can be based on them. An elementary proposition can be the sole argument of four different truth-functions, as there can be four different columns of truth-values expressing agreement or disagreement with the truth-values of 'p' (TLP 4.4):

	1	2	3	4
p		p	~p	
T	T	T	F	F
F	T	F	T	F

Those four columns Wittgenstein calls expressions of the *truth-conditions* of the truth-functions thus defined (TLP 4.431). Column 3 gives the truth-conditions of '~p'; column 2 gives the truth-conditions of 'p' itself. For completeness' sake, an elementary proposition is regarded as a truth-function of itself (TLP 5). The remaining two columns exemplify the limiting cases of truth-functions:

> 4.46 ... In one of these cases the proposition is true for all the truth-possibilities of the elementary propositions. ... In the second case the proposition is false for all the truth possibilities ...
> In the first case we call the proposition a tautology; in the second, a contradiction.

In Russell's notation, we could write on top of column 1 the tautology: 'pv~p', and on top of column 4 the contradiction: 'p.~p'.

Both tautology and contradiction lack sense (TLP 4.461). For what enables a proposition to have sense is that it represents a situation (TLP 4.031); that it is a picture of a situation. But a picture must have both possibilities: truth and falsity. There are no pictures that are true *a priori* (TLP 2.225); nor could a picture be false *a priori*. Bipolarity is essential to pictures, and hence 'tautologies and contradictions are not pictures of reality' (TLP 4.462).

In fact, if propositions are essentially pictures, it would follow that tautologies and contradictions are not even propositions. On the other hand, a proposition is a truth-function of elementary propositions (TLP 5); and tautology and contradiction are that, all right. From a logical point of view, they just come together with all the other possible results of truth-operations, and so it would seem artificial to exclude them. Therefore, Wittgenstein compromises between the demands of the picture theory (which would rule out tautologies and contradictions) and the method of truth-functional composition (which would include them). The compromise is to say that they are propositions, but not regular propositions. They lack sense, are senseless (*sinnlos*), but they are not nonsensical (*unsinnig*). For they are part of the logical symbolism, just as '0' is part of the symbolism of arithmetic (*TLP* 4.4611). They are the limiting cases of the combination of signs (*TLP* 4.466).

A single elementary proposition has two truth-possibilities and can be the basis of four different truth-functions. In general, n elementary propositions have 2^n truth-possibilities and yield 2^{2^n} different truth-functions.[19] Thus there are $2^{2^2} = 16$ two-place or binary truth-functions; according to the 16 possible permutations of Ts and Fs in a column of four. Wittgenstein gives the complete list at *TLP* 5.101.

So far I have presented truth-tables the way they appear in logic books today: as definitions of logical connectives. However, that is not how Wittgenstein introduced them in the *Tractatus*. For Wittgenstein, a truth-table does not just provide a definition of a truth-function; rather, a truth-table is itself the most appropriate expression of a truth-function. In Wittgenstein's notation, the propositional sign 'p⊃q' is replaced by a truth-table. Instead of 'p⊃q' one writes:

p	q	
T	T	T
F	T	T
T	F	F
F	F	T

This can be abbreviated: once the order of the truth-possibilities is conventionally fixed,[20] one only needs to write down the final column, followed by the sentence letters involved: '(TTFT) (p,q)' (*TLP* 4.442). What is the point of this notation?

Again, we have to turn to the issue of referentialism. We saw in the previous section that Wittgenstein resisted the temptation to treat propositions as names of objects. Here we encounter another crucial restriction on referentialism. Logical connectives must be exempt from that doctrine:

> 4.0312 ... My fundamental idea is that the 'logical constants' are not representatives.

---

[19] Wittgenstein writes: $\sum_{x=0}^{K_n} \binom{K_n}{x} = L_n$ (*TLP* 4.42).

[20] First column: alternating TF..., second column: alternating TTFF..., third column: alternating TTTTFFFF... etc. (There is a misprint in *TLP* 4.31: lines 4 and 5 of the first table should swap places.)

Words like 'and', 'not' or 'if' (or their equivalents in a formal notation) do not represent any objects in the world. In the case of 'and', that stands to reason. Compare:

(A) The cat is on the mat. The dog is in the garden.
(B) The cat is on the mat and the dog is in the garden.

Is (B) in any way more informative than (A)? Clearly not. In particular, (B) does not mention any new object not mentioned in (A). So it cannot be the function of the word 'and' to denote an object (cf. *TLP* 4.441). Wittgenstein makes a related point with respect to negation:

> 5.44 ... The proposition '~~p' is not about negation, as if negation were an object ... if there were an object called '~', it would follow that '~~p' said something different from what 'p' said, just because the one proposition would then be about [the object] ~ and the other would not.

But of course 'p' and '~~p' are synonymous. 'It's not true that it's not raining' simply means 'It's raining'. Hence the negation sign does not represent an object.

This conclusion can also be reached from the principle of bipolarity. Any elementary proposition 'p' implies the possibility of '~p'. Understanding 'p' brings with it understanding of negation (and disjunction), which therefore cannot involve reference to new objects.

Wittgenstein offers two further arguments for his 'fundamental idea'. First:

> 4.0621 But it is important that the signs 'p' and '~p' *can* say the same thing. For it shows that nothing in reality corresponds to the sign '~'. ...

There could be a language in which negation was not symbolized by the use of a sign like 'not' or '~', but by the *absence* of a certain sign, whereas the presence of that sign indicated affirmation. In short, whereas we have a negation sign, such a language would employ an affirmation sign. If as affirmation sign that language used our negation sign 'not', while otherwise the two languages were identical, we could give the following translations:

It's raining.   = *It's not raining.*
It's not raining. = *It's raining.*

So far so good. But it does not follow, as Wittgenstein claims, that unlike most other words the negation sign does not stand for an object. For a similar scenario can also be imagined for a proper name. There might be a variant of English in which the word 'Paris' meant nowhere, while reference to the French capital was made by the word 'nowhere', which in English is obviously *not* the name of any place. Thus we can translate:

Unicorns are nowhere. = *Unicorns are in Paris.*
Unicorns are in Paris. = *Unicorns are nowhere.*

Clearly, this possibility, that the word 'Paris' *might* be used not to refer to anything, does not show that *in English* it is not a proper name, referring to a particular place.[21]

A more convincing argument derives from the observation that logical connectives are interdefinable (*TLP* 5.42), so that any one of them is dispensable. The conjunction 'p.q', for example, can be defined in terms of negation and disjunction ['p v q': 'p or q']. 'It's raining *and* the grass is green' can be expressed thus: 'It's *not* the case that it's *not* raining *or* that grass is *not* green.' A truth-table renders this synonymy perspicuous:

1	2	3	4	5	6	7	8
p	q	pvq	~p	~q	~pv~q	~(~pv~q)	p.q
T	T	T	F	F	F	T	T
F	T	T	T	F	T	F	F
T	F	T	F	T	T	F	F
F	F	F	T	T	T	F	F

Column 3 gives the truth-conditions of disjunction: a disjunction is true if either or both of its disjuncts are true; it is false if they are both false. As we saw above, negation turns a truth-value into its opposite: True into False, and False into True. So column 4 is the inverse of column 1, and column 5 is the inverse of column 2. Column 6 combines negation and disjunction. As shown in column 3, disjunction works like this: TT yields T, TF yields T, FT yields T, FF yields F. Now in column 6, what are conjoined in disjunction are not 'p' and 'q', but '~p' and '~q'. Hence the basis for '~pv~q' are the truth-values given in columns 4 and 5: FF, TF, FT, TT. But disjunction leads from FF to F, and to T from all other combinations. So in column 6 we get FTTT. Column 7 presents the negation of column 6, hence each truth-value is turned into its opposite:

---

[21] Cf. Black 1964, 181.

TFFF. But these are exactly the truth-conditions of conjunction ['p . q']: columns 7 and 8 are identical.

Thus we have shown that 'p.q' and '~(~pv~q)' have the same truth-table. They are true under exactly the same conditions. So conjunction can be defined in terms of negation and disjunction, which means that conjunction is dispensable. Everything that can be said using the connective '.' can also be said without it, using '~' and 'v' instead. But these connectives are equally dispensable. Disjunction can be defined in terms of conjunction and negation:

p	q	p.q	~p	~q	~p.~q	~(~p.~q)	pvq
T	T	T	F	F	F	**T**	**T**
F	T	F	T	F	F	**T**	**T**
T	F	F	F	T	F	**T**	**T**
F	F	F	T	T	T	**F**	**F**

And introducing a new connective 'p|q' ('neither p, nor q', called joint negation), we can use this to define and replace negation:

p	q	p|q	p	~p	p|p
T	T	F	T	F	F
F	T	F	F	T	T
T	F	F			
F	F	T			

But, to close the circle, joint negation is itself definable in terms of negation and conjunction:

p	q	~p.~q	p|q
T	T	F	F
F	T	F	F
T	F	F	F
F	F	T	T

So each logical connective can be defined in terms of other logical connectives. That suffices to show that they are not names in the *Tractatus* sense, according to which 'a name cannot be dissected any further: it is a primitive sign' (*TLP* 3.26). Concatenations of such primitive signs standing for objects are supposed to be the absolute terminus of analysis: where no further analysis is possible. It follows that logical connectives, analysable into other connectives, are no such primitive signs (*TLP* 5.42).

This point can be combined with the observation above that, according to the principle of bipolarity, an understanding of negation and disjunction is already implied in understanding 'p'. Not only '~' and 'v' are already given with any elementary proposition (and hence are not names of further objects), but also those logical connectives that can be defined in terms of '~' and 'v': namely, *all* of them (as will be shown below: n. 25) (*TLP* 3.3441, 5.442).

To remove any temptation to mistake logical connectives for names, Wittgenstein proposes his truth-table notation of truth-functions. Propositions like 'pvq', in Russell's notation, look deceptively as if they stated a relation between two things (like 'a is on the left of b').[22] Such a false impression can be dispelled by writing '(TTTF)(p,q)' instead. For it should be obvious 'that a complex of the signs "F" and "T" has no object (or complex of objects) corresponding to it, just as there is none corresponding to . . . the brackets' (*TLP* 4.441). Moreover, there is the evident advantage of Wittgenstein's notation that for each truth-function there is one and only one expression, whereas the conventional notation allows each truth-function to be expressed in infinitely many ways, which are not always immediately recognizable as equivalent.

A further justification of the view that logical symbols do not name any objects was already mentioned in section 2.2. If they did, it would be difficult to explain the necessity of logical truths. Consider the tautology '~(p.~p)'. What makes this proposition a logical truth is not the content of 'p'; the truth of '~(p.~p)' is independent of what proposition we take 'p' to stand for. By contrast, the meaning of the logical constants '~' and '.' is absolutely crucial to the truth of '~(p.~p)'. Now if, as Russell believed, logical constants stood for logical objects (1903, p. xv; 1913, 99), the truth of such a tautology would depend on the nature of the logical objects referred to; and our knowledge of logical truths would be derived from experience: namely, our 'acquaintance with logical objects' (1913, 97). (Russell was indeed prepared to compare the allegedly required experience of logical objects with that of 'redness or the taste of pineapple' (1903, p. xv).) But it is difficult to understand how empirical knowledge could ever attain the necessity we ascribe

---

[22] Note incidentally how Wittgenstein's two crucial restrictions on referentialism are connected. If propositions do not name objects, then the symbols connecting propositions cannot stand for relations between such objects.

to logical truth. For it seems that where experience teaches us that something is the case, it is always conceivable that experience might have taught us otherwise (*TLP* 5.634). But what is logically true is exactly what one could not conceive to be otherwise (cf. *TLP* 6.1222).

Wittgenstein distinguishes truth-functions both from operations (*TLP* 5.25) and from material functions (*TLP* 5.44). His terminology requires some explanation. Use of the mathematical term 'function' in this area goes back to Frege (as Wittgenstein acknowledges at *TLP* 3.318), but – confusingly – Wittgenstein uses the word in a markedly different way. For Frege, a function is a rule that provides a correlation of freely chosen objects as *arguments* with certain objects as *values* of the function for those arguments. Thus x^2 is a function that provides the following correlations:

Argument	Value
1	1
2	4
3	9
etc.	

One of Frege's great innovations was to apply this mathematical concept of a function to the logical analysis of propositions, replacing the traditional analysis in terms of subject and predicate. The proposition 'Paris is the capital of France', for instance, Frege would break up into the expressions 'Paris', 'France' and 'x is the capital of y', the latter being the name of a function, comparable to 'x^2'. Replacing the variable 'x' in 'x^2' by the numeral '2' yields the expression '2^2'. But '2^2' denotes the number 4. So the function x^2 maps the number 2 on to the number 4. Frege is very careful to distinguish between words and what they stand for. 'x is the capital of France' is not a function; it is the name of a function. Likewise, 'Paris' and 'France' are not arguments of the function, but names of arguments. Hence, if the variables in 'x is the capital of y' are replaced by the names 'Paris' and 'France', the result 'Paris is the capital of France' is not the value of the function for those arguments, but the *name* of the value. (Just as, above, the sign '2^2' is not the value, but the *name* of the value 2^2, which equals 4.) Now Frege regarded propositions as names of truth-values. The object denoted by a true proposition is the True, while a false proposition stands for the False. So the function named by the expression 'x is the capital of y' provides the following correlations of objects:

Arguments	Value
Paris, France	True
Paris, Italy	False
Rome, Italy	True
Didcot, Russia	False
etc.	

This account Wittgenstein could not accept, for, as expounded in the previous section, he was strongly opposed to the view that propositions are names. His remark:

3.318   Like Frege and Russell I construe a proposition as a function of the expressions contained in it

is quite inaccurate. Of course, he adopted Frege's and Russell's basic idea that, for instance, 'Socrates is a man' should be analysed into 'x is a man' and 'Socrates', and that their combination could somehow be described in terms of function and argument. But for Frege a proposition was not itself a function, but the name of the value of a function. And Russell, too, distinguished between a proposition (like 'Socrates is a man') and a propositional function ('x is a man') (Russell 1903, §22).

In Wittgenstein's terminology, 'x is a man' is called an *expression* (*Ausdruck*). It is common and essential to a certain class of propositions (e.g., 'Socrates is a man', 'Aristotle is a man') (*TLP* 3.31).[23] Then, an expression like 'x is a man' is also called a *variable*, or a *propositional variable* (*TLP* 3.313).[24] A *function* for Wittgenstein is an elementary proposition (*TLP* 4.24): that is, the result of replacing all the variable letters 'x', 'y' etc. in a propositional variable by names, which are the function's *arguments*. Similarly, a truth-function is the *result* of applying, say, negation to a particular elementary proposition. Thus '~p' is a truth-function, whose argument is 'p' (*TLP* 5.02), whereas negation, in general, Wittgenstein calls an *operation*. While a truth-function contains actual elementary propositions, an operation (like an 'expression' – e.g., 'Fx') manifests itself in a variable (*TLP* 5.24). To sum matters up:

---

[23] To simplify matters, I treat 'Socrates is a man' etc. here as if it were an elementary proposition.

[24] Which is a little unfortunate, as the term 'variable' is also used by Wittgenstein in a more conventional way for the letters in such an expression that are to be replaced by names: e.g., 'x' in 'x is a man'. Then for '(propositional) variable' he uses the term 'variable proposition' (*TLP* 3.315).

Fx
Propositional variable

Fa
Function: elementary proposition

~ɸ [negation]
Operation

~p
Truth-function: proposition

Once it is understood that a truth-function is a proposition resulting from the application of a truth-operation (*TLP* 5.324, 5.3), the difference between a truth-operation and a truth-function should be obvious – as obvious as, in arithmetic, the difference between the operation of squaring (x^2) and the number 4, which results from squaring 2. An operation can take one of its own results as its base, whereas a function cannot be its own argument (*TLP* 5.251). The number 4 can be squared again, but of course the 'function' (in Wittgenstein's sense) 2^2 cannot be its own argument: for its argument is 2, and if its argument were 2^2, it would no longer be the same function. Instead of being the result of squaring 2, it would be the result of squaring 2^2. Similarly, the result of negating 'p' can be negated again, but '~p' cannot be the argument of itself, for its argument is 'p', and if you change it to '~p', you get a different truth-function: '~~p' (cf. *TLP* 3.333). In the realm of material functions it is even more obvious that a function cannot be its own argument. For if in 'Socrates is a man' you replace the argument 'Socrates' by the function itself, you get 'Socrates is a man is a man', which is nonsense. Furthermore, operations can cancel one another (*TLP* 5.353). By applying the same operation twice, you can get back to your original base, as in the case of negation. But it doesn't even make sense to speak of applying '~p' to '~p'.

The remark that 'truth-functions are not material functions' (*TLP* 5.44) is merely a paraphrase of the point that logical connectives do not represent things in the world. For the expressions that occur in a proper or material function do represent things in the world. They are predicates that make an essential contribution to a proposition's sense. To the sense of the truth-function, however, it is not essential that it is expressed by means of any particular connectives (as the result of any particular truth-operation) (*TLP* 5.25). As demonstrated above, it could also be expressed without that connective. The truth-function '~~p', for instance, can also be written 'p'. So the symbol '~' makes no essential contribution to its sense. It is not essential to the sense of this proposition that it can be produced by the operation of negation (for that is true of every proposition).

From a pair of elementary propositions one can produce sixteen different truth-functions (cf. *TLP* 5.101), and each truth-function is the result of a particular operation applied to those two elementary propositions. However, not all those sixteen operations are needed to

Tractatus Logico-Philosophicus 73

produce the complete list of truth-functions. Above, I demonstrated how 'pvq' can be defined in terms of negation and conjunction: as '~(~p.~q)'. In other words, to produce the truth-function '(TTTF)(p,q)' it is not necessary to have the operation of disjunction at one's disposal; one can use negation and conjunction instead. (Apply negation to both 'p' and 'q' respectively, then apply conjunction to the results, producing '(FFFT)(p,q)'; and finally apply negation to that.) It can be shown that all sixteen binary truth-functions – indeed, all truth-functions from any number of elementary propositions – can be produced applying only the operations of negation and conjunction.[25] After all, 'the world is

---

[25] Consider the list of all sixteen binary truth-functions at *TLP* 5.101. Apart from the first, all of them have at least one 'F' in their final column (the first parenthesis in Wittgenstein's abbreviated notation). The second truth-function (FTTT)(p, q) has an 'F' in the first line, which means that it is false if both 'p' and 'q' are true. Remember, the full table is this:

p	q	
T	T	F
F	T	T
T	F	T
F	F	T

But a truth-function that is *false if both 'p' and 'q' are true* can be expressed by the words: 'it's not the case that p and q', or the formula: ~(p.q). And in this manner all truth-functions that contain at least one 'F' in their final column can be expressed in terms of negation and conjunction. For every line that has an 'F' in the final column, we write down a negation sign and brackets:

~( ).

If there are two or more 'F's, we write two or more such negated brackets joined in conjunction:

~( ) . ~( ). . . .

The contents of those brackets depends on the position of the corresponding 'F'. For an 'F' in line 1, where both 'p' and 'q' are true, we write inside the brackets the conjunction of 'p' and 'q':

~(p.q).

For an 'F' in line 4, where both 'p' and 'q' are false, we write the conjunction of '~p' and '~q':

~(~p.~q).

And for an 'F' in line 2 or 3, where one of the sentence letters has a 'T' and the other one an 'F', we write a mixed conjunction of one sentence letter (the one with a 'T') and the negation of the other one (the one with the 'F'). Thus the truth-function (TFFT)(p,q) can be rendered:

completely described by giving all elementary propositions, and adding which of them are true and which false' (*TLP* 4.26). So any state of the world could be described by an extremely long proposition of the form: '(~)p.(~)q.(~)r.(~)s. . . .', where all elementary propositions are, either positive or negated, linked by conjunction. Hence everything can be said by using only elementary propositions and the two operations of negation and conjunction. But one can be even more economical. The single operation of joint negation (which applied to 'p' and 'q' yields '(FFFT)(p,q)') is enough to produce any truth-function.[26] I have already shown that negation can be replaced by joint negation ('~φ' is equivalent to 'φ | φ'), and so can conjunction: 'φ.χ' is equivalent to '(φ | φ) | (χ | χ)'. That is to say, the truth-function '(TFFF)(p,q)' can be produced, instead of by conjunction, by first applying joint negation to 'p,p', then to 'q,q', and finally to the results of those applications:

p	q	p | q	p | p	q | q	(p | p) | (q | q)	(p.q)
T	T	F	F	F	T	T
F	T	F	T	F	F	F
T	F	F	F	T	F	F
F	F	T	T	T	F	F

Thus, since any truth-function can be produced by conjunction and negation, and conjunction and negation can both be replaced by joint negation, the operation of joint negation alone is sufficient to generate any truth-function. And since all propositions are truth-functions of

---

~(~p.q) . ~(p.~q).

Now we have a mechanical procedure for expressing all binary truth-functions in terms of negation and conjunction – with the exception of the tautology (TTTT)(p,q), for which we write:

~(p.~p) . ~(q.~q).

Thus we have demonstrated that all binary truth-functions can be expressed in terms of negation and conjunction alone. And the procedure can easily be extended to cover also truth-functions of three or more places. Furthermore, using that result, it can easily be shown that negation and disjunction are also jointly sufficient to express any truth-function (*TLP* 3.3441), for any conjunction can be expressed in terms of negation and disjunction, as 'p.q' is equivalent to '~(~pv~q)'.

[26] And so is the operation corresponding to the truth-function '(FTTT)(p,q)'. That either of those two operations is sufficient to express all truth-functions was first shown by H. Sheffer.

elementary propositions (*TLP* 5), it follows that every proposition is a result of successive applications to elementary propositions of the operation of joint negation. That is 'the general form of a proposition' (*TLP* 5.5, 6, 6.001).[27]

Is it really? Is Wittgenstein right in holding that *every* proposition is susceptible of a truth-functional analysis? Before examining a few possible counter-examples, we need to say a little more about the pivotal role that truth-functional analysis plays in the system of the *Tractatus*. For one thing, the possibility of a complete truth-functional analysis is a corollary of Wittgenstein's logical atomism, with its conception of an elementary proposition. That 'the world is completely described by giving all elementary propositions, and adding which of them are true and which false' (*TLP* 4.26), means that everything can be said by a truth-function of the elementary propositions (here presented in terms of conjunction and negation). But for another thing, truth-functional analysis, in Wittgenstein's notation, is singularly suited to meet the requirement drawn from the principle of bipolarity (unfolded in the picture theory): that 'logic must take care of itself' (*TLP* 5.473).

The principle of bipolarity requires that every meaningful proposition has the possibilities of being true and of being false. For Wittgenstein, the sense of a proposition is what it depicts: a *possible* situation (*TLP* 2.221, 4.031), something that could be the case, but could also not be the case (*TLP* 5.634). It follows that no proposition with a sense can be *a priori*, or necessarily true (or necessarily false) (*TLP* 2.224f). There are only empirical, or contingent, propositions. But, as already noted above, that conclusion leaves the discipline of logic in an awkward position. For logic treats of precisely those matters that are *not* contin-

---

[27] Here are some further technical details of Wittgenstein's specification of the general form of a proposition. First, Wittgenstein formulates the operation of joint negation (he just calls it 'negation') to apply to truth-functions involving not just two, but any number of elementary propositions:

5.5 Every truth-function is a result of successive applications to elementary propositions of the operation
'(------T)(ξ, ...)'.
This operation negates all the propositions in the right-hand pair of brackets, and I call it the negation of those propositions.

Compare this with the binary truth-function produced by joint negation (the fifth from the bottom of the list in *TLP* 5.101): '(FFFT)(p,q)'. Here we have two elementary propositions and four truth-conditions. The Greek letter 'ξ' (*xi*) in *TLP* 5.5 stands for any elementary proposition; and the following dots indicate that there may be any number of them. And that number will determine the number of truth-conditions in the first pair of brackets (as specified by the formula given in *TLP* 4.27). The last combination

gent or empirical. What is logically true is necessarily true, independently of experience. So, for Wittgenstein, there can be no meaningful propositions stating what is logically true, or what is entirely down to the meanings of words – reflecting the logical form of the world – and thus a non-empirical matter. For example, that a certain combination of words has one sense, rather than another, and that a certain other combination of words makes no sense at all – such matters, of what Wittgenstein calls 'internal' properties or relations, must somehow become clear without being said. They must *show themselves* (*TLP* 4.122). This is the famous distinction between saying and showing. 'What expresses *itself* in language, *we* cannot express by means of language' (*TLP* 4.121). All we can do is present language in a more perspicuous notation, so that such indescribable features show themselves more distinctly (*TLP* 3.325).

Language shows the internal features both of the world and of language itself (its logical form reflecting that of the world). Logic is primarily concerned with the latter: the internal features of language. These ineffable matters of logic include (1) logical truth and (2) entailment –:

(1) Since it cannot be *said* that something is a logical truth (for that is not a matter of contingent fact), it must show itself. And that would indeed seem possible if Wittgenstein were right in his claim that all logical relations can be captured by truth-functional analysis and that, consequently, all logical truths are tautologies (i.e., truth-functions

---

of truth-values among the elementary propositions, where all elementary propositions are false, is assigned the value T. And that is the only 'T' in that group of truth-conditions, as the preceding dashes indicate (sometimes Wittgenstein puts an 'F' for 'false', sometimes he just leaves a gap, or puts a dash; cf. *TLP* 4.442).

A bit further down Wittgenstein introduces an abbreviation for the formula of *TLP* 5.5:

5.502   ... instead of '(------T)(ξ, ...)', I write 'N($\bar{\xi}$)'.
N($\bar{\xi}$) is the negation of all the values of the propositional variable ξ.

This ξ-with-a-bar convention is illustrated thus:

5.501   ... '$\bar{\xi}$' is a variable whose values are terms of the bracketed expression and the bar over the variable indicates that it is the representative of all its values in the brackets.
(E.g. if ξ has the three values P, Q, R, then
($\bar{\xi}$) = (P, Q, R).)

Further:

5.2521   If an operation is applied repeatedly to its own results, I speak of successive applications of it. . . .

that come out true under all circumstances). For 'every tautology itself shows that it is a tautology' (*TLP* 6.127). In the official *Tractatus* notation, a truth-function is represented by its truth-table (*TLP* 4.44). Thus the tautology 'p⊃q .⊃ p :⊃: p' is written:

p	q	
T	T	T
F	T	T
T	F	T
F	F	T

And the unbroken column of Ts on the right makes it perfectly obvious that this is a tautology. However, the truth-table notation (unlike Russell's) does not distinguish between different tautologies. Not only 'p⊃q .⊃ p :⊃: p' is symbolized by the above truth-table, but also 'p.q .⊃ p', or 'p ⊃ .q⊃p', or any other tautology involving 'p' and 'q'. And that is as it should be, for all those tautologies say exactly the same thing – namely, nothing (*TLP* 6.11); so there is, in a sense, only one tautology (*LO* 30). In the *Tractatus* logic, the difference between two tautologous formulae, say 'p⊃q .⊃ p :⊃: p' and 'p.q .⊃ p', is not one between two different propositions, but one between two different ways of producing the same – senseless – proposition, expressed by the tautologous truth-table above. That is to say, a tautology can be produced by first applying the operation '⊃' to 'p' and 'q', then apply-

---

And a symbol for such a successive application is introduced in the next section:

> 5.2522 Accordingly I use the sign '[a, x, O'x]' for the general term of the series of forms a, O'a, O'O'a, ... This bracketed expression is a variable: the first term of the bracketed expression [viz. 'a'] is the beginning of the series of forms, the second is the form of a term x arbitrarily selected from the series, and the third is the form that immediately follows x in the series.

So that bracketed expression is a variable that can take as a value either *a*, the basis of any operation, or the result of applying the operation O' any number of times to *a*.

Putting all this together, we are finally in a position to decipher what Wittgenstein presents in *TLP* 6 as the general form of a proposition:

> 6   The general form of a truth-function is $[\bar{p}, \bar{\xi}, N(\bar{\xi})]$.
> This is the general form of a proposition.

ing it to the result of the first operation and 'p', and finally applying it to the result of the second operation and 'p'; or it can be produced by first applying the operation of conjunction to 'p' and 'q', and then applying the operation of conditional to the result of the first operation and 'p'; or in countless other ways. But whether or not a succession of operations yields a tautology can be made obvious by step-by-step drawings of truth-tables, using the final column(s) of the last one(s) as basis for the next one (as already demonstrated above). Thus the first line of the truth-table symbolizing 'p⊃q .⊃ p :⊃: p' is produced in three steps:

(i) | p q | p⊃q .⊃ p :⊃: p |
     | T F | T F F | ['⊃' applied to T and F yields F]

(ii) | p q | p⊃q .⊃ p :⊃: p |
     | T F | F **T** T | ['⊃' applied to F and T yields T]

(iii)| p q | p⊃q .⊃ p :⊃: p |
     | T F | T **T** T | ['⊃' applied to T and T yields T]

And likewise for the remaining three lines (cf. *TLP* 6.1203).[28] In other words, Wittgenstein has a decision procedure for truth-functional logic (what today is called the propositional calculus): a mechanical method by which for any truth-function it can be ascertained, and made manifest, whether it is a logical truth or not.

(2) It cannot meaningfully be stated that a set of propositions entails a proposition. Hence in Wittgenstein's logic there cannot be laws of inference, as in the works of Frege and Russell (*TLP* 5.132), for laws of inference would be attempts to state and justify what cannot be said: that, for example, the premises 'p' and 'p⊃q' entail the conclusion 'q'

In other words: take any number of elementary propositions as bases; then any proposition is the result of applying the operation of joint negation to that basis, or to its own results, any number of times. As Wittgenstein explains in the next section:

    6.001   What this says is just that every proposition is a result of successive applications to elementary propositions of the operation N($\bar{\xi}$). [i.e. joint negation]

[28] Wittgenstein's procedure in *TLP* 6.1203 is in principle the same as this one, only written a little differently.

(a form of argument that is called *modus ponens*). Instead logical entailment shows itself, in two ways.

First, we saw above that tautologies are easily recognizable as such; yet every correct logical inference (in truth-functional logic) can be translated into a tautologous conditional, with the (conjunction of the) premisse(s) as antecedent and the conclusion as consequent. Thus:

> 6.1221 ... For example, ... it is ... possible to show [that 'q' follows from 'p⊃q . p'] in *this* way: we combine them to form 'p⊃q . p :⊃: q', and then show that this is a tautology.

Secondly, even this method is not strictly necessary in order to recognize valid inferences:

> 6.122 ... we can actually do without logical propositions [i.e., tautologies]; for in a suitable notation we can in fact recognize the formal properties of propositions by mere inspection of the propositions themselves.

A suitable notation is of course the one in which a proposition is written as a truth-table. And the kind of inspection that is required for noticing logical relations between propositions is explained in sections 5.101ff: First, Wittgenstein introduces the notion of *truth-grounds*:

> 5.101 ... I will give the name *truth-grounds* of a proposition to those truth-possibilities of its truth-arguments that make it true.

Take the proposition 'p.q', written thus:

p	q	
T	T	T
F	T	F
T	F	F
F	F	F

A set of two elementary propositions has four truth-possibilities (the truth-table has four lines). But only the first of those four possibilities makes 'p.q' true. So only the first truth-possibility (TT) is a truth-ground of 'p.q'.

> 5.12 ... the truth of a proposition 'p' follows from the truth of another proposition 'q' if all the truth-grounds of the latter are truth-grounds of the former.

5.121 The truth-grounds of the one are contained in those of the other: p follows from q.

Take another proposition, the disjunction 'pvq', written:

p	q	
T	T	T
F	T	T
T	F	T
F	F	F

The truth-grounds of 'pvq' are the first three possibilities. The truth-grounds of the conjunction (TT) are contained in the truth-grounds of the disjunction (TT, FT, TF). Therefore the conjunction entails the disjunction. For what makes the conjunction true, will also make the disjunction true.

Thus, even without the method sketched in *TLP* 6.1221, merely by inspecting propositional signs, written in truth-table notation, we can see whether one proposition follows from another (*TLP* 5.13, 5.131). It shows itself; we do not have to spell it out. Thus, if logic is amenable to truth-functional analysis – it can take care of itself.

Having cast some light on Wittgenstein's motivation for his claim that all propositions are truth-functions of elementary propositions (*TLP* 5), we must now consider some difficulties or possible objections to it.

(i) General propositions How is a general proposition, like 'All swans are white' or 'There are no unicorns', to be given a truth-functional analysis? Wittgenstein introduces the topic in *TLP* 5.52:

5.52 If ξ has as its values all the values of a function fx for all values x, then $N(\bar{\xi}) = \sim(\exists x).fx$.

Taking 'fx' to mean 'x is a unicorn', we can construct the general proposition that there are no unicorns – '$\sim(\exists x).fx$' – by applying joint negation to all propositions of the form 'x is a unicorn', i.e.: 'Tom is a unicorn', 'Harry is a unicorn', and so on for all proper names that could be substituted for 'x'. In other words, all propositions of the form 'x is a unicorn' are said to be false ('Neither Tom is a unicorn, nor Harry is a unicorn, nor . . .'). Negating that complex proposition – by another application of the operator N – yields the proposition that something is a unicorn – '$(\exists x).fx$' – that is: $NN(\overline{fx})$.

Wittgenstein does not explain how a universal statement, like 'Everything is a unicorn': '(x)fx', could be expressed in his joint negation notation. One would need to apply joint negation to all propositions of the form '~fx'. That could be written:

$N(\overline{N(fx)})$,[29]

and spelt out like this:

N(N(fa), N(fb), N(fc), N(fd), . . .).

I.e.: 'Neither is Tom not a unicorn, nor is Harry not a unicorn, nor . . .';[30] which of course is synonymous with: 'Tom is a unicorn, & Harry is a unicorn, etc.'. In short, setting the official presentation in terms of joint negation aside for the moment, Wittgenstein regards universal statements as conjunctions and existential statements as disjunctions. However, the conjuncts and disjuncts of these are not listed individually (cf. *PG* 268). Rather, they are determined as the values of a given propositional variable (such as 'fx').

Later, in the 1930s, Wittgenstein was to criticize this account of generality on the ground that it is applicable only to a finite domain of objects. 'The shop is open on all days of the week' is indeed a conjunction, for it is possible to write down all its conjuncts. But that is not the case with 'All men die before they are 200 years old' (*PG* 268f).

Another problem is that general logical truths, even though they are truth-functions of elementary propositions, do not meet the requirement which the *Tractatus* lays down for logical propositions: 'that one can recognize that they are true from the symbol alone' (*TLP* 6.113). As explained above, they need to *show* that they are logical truths (*TLP* 6.127b), since it is impossible to *say* it. And they show it in truth-table notation by an unbroken final column of Ts. However, as Wittgenstein

---

[29] Alternatively, one could write: 'N(x: N(fx))', indicating that joint negation is to be applied to the class of propositions obtained by substituting actual names for the variable 'x' in the variable proposition 'N(fx)' (Geach 1981; cf. Fogelin 1987, 78–82). This way of developing the joint negation notation makes it possible to represent also multiply general formulae, such as '(x)(∃y)Rxy', which could be rendered: N(x: N(y: (Rxy))).

[30] Fogelin remarks that this might involve an infinite number of applications of joint negation, which he claims contradicts *TLP* 5.32: 'All truth-functions are the result of successive applications to elementary propositions of a finite number of truth-operations' (Fogelin 1987, 80). It does not, for what that passage requires to be finite is the number of truth-operations, not the number of their applications. (That Wittgenstein was indeed careful to distinguish between the number of operations and the number of their applications is clear from *TLP* 5.2521.)

noted himself, the truth-table notation is not applicable to propositions that contain a generality sign (*TLP* 6.1203). Hence, for instance:

(Q) (∃x)(y)Gxy ⊃ (y)(∃x)Gxy

is a logical truth, just as:

(P) p⊃q.p :⊃: q.

But unlike (P), (Q) cannot be written in a way that its being a logical truth becomes self-evident. The truth-table notation provides a decision procedure for the propositional calculus. But for the predicate calculus, which involves generality signs (today called 'quantifiers'), there is no decision procedure. We may succeed in finding a proof that (Q) is a logical truth, but – contrary to *TLP* 6.113 – there is no method to guarantee that we will.

(ii) Identity Another device of Frege's and Russell's logic that does not fit into Wittgenstein's account of a purely truth-functional logic is the identity sign '='. The meaning of a name is its bearer (*TLP* 3.203). In order to understand a proposition, one has to know the meanings of the names involved. In order to understand 'a = b', one has to know what the names 'a' and 'b' stand for, in particular whether they both stand for the same object (*TLP* 6.2322). This means that an understanding of an identity statement involves a recognition of its truth or falsity; and if an identity statement is true, it is a necessary truth: For given that 'a' and 'b' stand for the same object (their meaning), 'a = b' could not possibly be false. Not being a contingent matter, the identity of *a* and *b* cannot be meaningfully stated: 'to say of *one* thing that it is identical with itself is to say nothing at all' (*TLP* 5.5303).

Necessities should become self-evident in an appropriate notation. But no truth-table notation could help us here; 'a = b', even if necessarily true, cannot be constructed as a tautology. Nor is there any other way in which a scrutiny of two different names (say, 'Eric Blair' and 'George Orwell') could bring to light that they stand for the same object (or person). The only solution is not to allow any object to have two different names. Then all *true* identity statements would be of the form 'a = a', and hence obviously pointless attempts at stating what is self-evident. So there is no more need for the identity sign:

> 5.53 Identity of object I express by identity of sign, and not by using a sign for identity. Difference of objects I express by difference of signs.

However, the use to which Frege and Russell put the identity sign is not limited to cases covered by this remark. The sign '=' seems to play an important role in statements about numbers of things, where it is flanked by variables rather than proper names. For example, Russell expresses the proposition 'There are at least two chairs in the room' like this [Fx: x is a chair in the room]:

(∃x)(∃y): Fx.Fy . ~x=y

To dispose of the identity sign also in this kind of case, Wittgenstein stipulates that different variables indicate different objects (*TLP* 5.532). So instead of Russell's formula, he would write:[31]

(∃x)(∃y): Fx.Fy

The identity sign is altogether dispensable (*TLP* 5.533).

By banning the identity sign from his official notation, Wittgenstein also disposes of a type of statement that his logical atomism forces him to reject as nonsense. Since objects are sempiternal, and their existence is not a contingent matter (only their combination is), to say that there exist at least three objects would (if true) be a necessary truth, hence not a meaningful statement (*TLP* 4.1272). In Russell's notation such a nonsensical statement can be expressed thus:

(∃x)(∃y)(∃z): ~x=y. ~x=z. ~y=z

But with the abolition of the identity sign in the *Tractatus*, such a pseudo-proposition cannot even be written down. At most one can formulate tautologies that, saying nothing, *show* the existence of three objects by containing three different names or three different variables bound by existential quantifiers:

fa v ~fa . fb v ~fb . fc v ~fc
(∃x)(∃y)(∃z): fx v ~fx . fy v ~fy . fz v ~fz

That is as it should be: Logical propositions do not say anything (they are senseless), but they mirror the necessary features of language and the world (*TLP* 6.12).

(iii) Propositional attitudes Wittgenstein himself brings up an apparent counter-example to the claim that all complex propositions are truth-functions of elementary ones:

---

[31] Strictly speaking, he would want to write the given formula's equivalent in joint negation notation, which could be done thus: NN(xy: N(N(fx), N(fy))) (cf. n. 29 above).

5.541 At first sight it looks as if it were possible for one proposition to occur in another in a different way [i.e., not as the base of truth-operations].

    Particularly with certain forms of proposition in psychology, such as 'A believes that *p* is the case' and 'A has the thought *p'*, etc.

    For if these are considered superficially, it looks as if the proposition *p* stood in some kind of relation to an object A.

Wittgenstein adds that such a position had been put forward by Russell. But Russell had soon changed his mind, as he explained in his article 'On the Nature of Truth and Falsehood':

> if I judge that A loves B, that is not a relation of me to 'A's love for B' ... If it were a relation of me to 'A's love for B' it would be impossible unless there were such a thing as 'A's love for B', i.e. unless A loved B, i.e. unless the judgement were true; but in fact false judgements are possible. (Russell 1910, 155)

The argument shows that my judgement that A loves B cannot be construed as a relation between myself and the *fact* that A loves B (which Russell called the proposition 'A loves B'). But why not regard it as a relation between myself and the *thought* that A loves B? The thought is a mental picture, and thus also a fact, but one that obtains independently of whether A does love B or not.

In Russell's subsequent account, my judgement that A loves B is analysed as 'a relation between me and A and love and B' (ibid.). But again, Wittgenstein disagrees:

5.5422 The correct explanation of the form of the proposition, 'A makes the judgement *p*', must show that it is impossible for a judgement to be a piece of nonsense. (Russell's theory does not satisfy this requirement.)

There is nothing in Russell's new account, Wittgenstein thought, to prevent one from standing in a relation of judgement to any unsuitable string of entities. There is nothing to prevent one from judging such nonsense as 'this table penholders the book' (*NB* 103).

What, then, did Wittgenstein himself suggest? His solution is laconic and puzzling:

5.542 It is clear, however, that 'A believes that *p'*, 'A has the thought that *p'*. and 'A says *p*' are of the form '"*p*" says *p*': and this does not involve a correlation of a fact with an object, but rather the correlation of facts by means of the correlation of their objects.

When I believe or judge that Romeo loves Juliet, I construct a mental picture of that state of affairs. Therefore, saying that I judge that Romeo loves Juliet simply amounts to saying that: the thought 'Romeo loves Juliet', which I framed in my mind, says that Romeo loves Juliet. So Wittgenstein's analysis involves neither a person nor a soul. The latter point is emphasized in the following remark: 'there is no such thing as the soul – the subject, etc. – as it is conceived in the superficial psychology of the present day' (*TLP* 5.5421). Instead of the soul, or mind, there are just mental representations of what is judged or thought.[32]

However, it is obvious that 'I judge that Romeo loves Juliet' means something different from, or at any rate more than, ' "Romeo loves Juliet" says that Romeo loves Juliet'. After all, 'I judge that Romeo loves Juliet' is a *contingent* proposition. I might just as well have judged something else or nothing at all. ' "Romeo loves Juliet" says that Romeo loves Juliet', by contrast (given the conventional meanings of the words) is a necessary truth, and thus only a pseudo-proposition. For it tries to say what can only be shown: that a proposition 'p' has the sense that p (*TLP* 4.022). Wittgenstein's solution could at most be the second half of a more satisfactory account: '*A* judges that *p*' means 'The thought "*p*" occurs in *A*'s mind, and "*p*" says that *p*'. Yet this second half is unsayable and superfluous, for what it tries to say shows itself. What remains, however, is exactly of the form Wittgenstein rejected: the thought expressed by the proposition 'p' stands in a relation to a subject *A*. We may agree with Wittgenstein that neither the person nor his mind is a simple object. Hence, if, as Wittgenstein believed, a soul cannot be composite (*TLP* 5.5421b), the analysis will not involve a soul. Nevertheless, it seems unavoidable in an analysis of '*A* judges that *p*' to relate the thought expressed by '*p*' to a person *A*. But it is not obvious that such an analysis would go beyond Wittgenstein's truth-functional logic. A thought, or a mental picture, can presumably be described just as any other picture. It is a certain combination of certain elements occurring in someone's mind at a certain time.

Above I presented some support for the claim that logical signs are exempt from referentialism (*TLP* 4.0312). It is not clear, however, why Wittgenstein should call this claim his 'fundamental thought'. After all, its import seems entirely negative. Perhaps it would have been more

---

[32] This is reminiscent of a famous passage from Hume: 'For my part, when I enter most intimately into what I call *myself*, I always stumble on some particular perception or other, . . . I never can catch *myself* at any time without a perception, and never can observe anything but the perception' (Hume 1739, 252). Hume concluded that the mind was merely a bundle of thoughts and feelings ('perceptions').

accurate to call it a 'ground-clearing' thought. Rather than laying the foundation of Wittgenstein's own philosophy of logic, it disposes of alternative views held by Frege and Russell.[33] However, the negative impact of this ground-clearing thought is not limited to theories of Wittgenstein's philosophical predecessors; it seems also to get into conflict with the picture theory, or at any rate to limit its scope.

The sense of a proposition is the situation that the proposition represents, a situation that may or may not obtain (*TLP* 2.221, 4.031). So the sense of the proposition 'The cat is on the mat' is the situation that the cat is on the mat. Now what is the sense of 'The cat is *not* on the mat'? Here the *Tractatus* points us in two opposite directions. On the one hand, we are told that a proposition 'p' and its negation '~p' have opposite senses (*TLP* 4.0621). On the other hand, it seems that the picture theory and Wittgenstein's 'fundamental thought' force us to attribute the same sense to 'p' and '~p'. For if linguistic pictures are configurations of names representing configurations of objects (*TLP* 3.21), yet logical constants are not names of objects (*TLP* 4.0312), then logical constants cannot themselves be part of a linguistic picture. Which situation is represented by a verbal picture depends entirely on the configuration of its names. Hence a sign that is not a name, nor analysable into names, cannot have any influence on which situation a verbal picture represents. So 'p' and '~p' must represent the same situation. And indeed, which other configuration of objects could be said to be represented by 'The cat is not on the mat'? The cat's *not* being on the mat is not itself a configuration of objects, but the non-existence of a configuration. So it is not something that a picture could represent. At most, a picture could represent some other, incompatible configuration. A picture that shows the cat sitting beside the mat conveys of course that the cat is not on the mat. But that is clearly not the sort of picture involved in 'The cat is not on the mat', which does not represent the cat as being in any particular location. The only picture that can plausibly be said to be involved in 'The cat is not on the mat' is the picture of the situation that the proposition asserts *not* to obtain: the picture of the cat being on the mat. This position Wittgenstein explicitly adopted in his *Notebooks*:

> If a picture presents what-is-not-the-case . . . this only happens through its presenting *that* which *is* not the case.
> For the picture says, as it were: "*This* is how it is *not*". (*NB*, 3 Nov. 1914)[34]

So 'p' and '~p' present the same picture, but in different ways. Implicit in 'p' is the added assertion: 'This is how it is', whereas the negation

---
[33] See Hacker 1986, sect. II.2.
[34] Cf. *NB*, 30, 31 Oct. 1914; 1, 5–6, 9, 12, 14 Nov. 1914; *TLP* 4.0641.

sign adds to the picture: 'This is how it is not'. Of course, it does make a big difference whether one says the one or the other, a difference that is well described by saying that they have opposite senses (*TLP* 4.0621), even though the situation they represent is the same. But then we cannot agree with Wittgenstein that the sense of a proposition is simply the situation it represents (*TLP* 2.221, 4.031). We need a broader concept of sense, which leaves room for the contribution of logical symbols which, not being names, are not strictly part of the verbal pictures. In other words, the picture theory, although intended to cover all meaningful language, certainly all propositions (*TLP* 4.03d), applies only to elementary propositions (*NB*, 31 Oct. 14). The semantics of truth-functions involves more than is explained by the picture theory.

How then do logical symbols work? The *Notebooks* contain these remarks:

> The logical constants of the proposition are the conditions of its truth. (*NB*, 7 Dec. 1914)

> It is as if the logical constants projected the picture of the proposition on to reality – which may then accord or not accord with this projection. (*NB*, 12 Nov. 1914)

In the official *Tractatus* notation logical constants are indeed written as truth-conditions. Thus the truth-function '~p' is rendered '(FT)(p)', indicating that the proposition is false if 'p' is true, and true if 'p' is false. That is the specific way in which negation projects the picture 'p' on to reality. That is the meaning of the negation sign. Likewise the meanings of other logical constants are given by their truth-table, which amounts to a conjunction of conditions spelling out when the truth-function in question is true and when it is false.

There seems nothing wrong with this, but it raises a worry. If logical symbols have to be acknowledged as exceptions from the sweeping claims made on behalf of the picture theory of meaning, how can we be sure that there are not more exceptions, limiting the scope of that theory even further? The *Tractatus* account of logical connectives demonstrates how words can convey very abstract ideas (such as being true only under certain conditions) without functioning as (or being analysable into) names of objects. Why should that not also be the case with lots of other abstract terms, outside logic? Consider, for example, the words 'justice', 'change' or 'evidence'. How could one even begin to analyse them (or propositions containing them) in a way that was likely to lead to names of simple objects, as postulated by the picture theory?[35]

---

[35] Such criticisms will be developed further in sect. 4.2.

2.6 Whereof One Cannot Speak

In the preceding section I explained how the principle of bipolarity committed Wittgenstein to the extreme view that one could not meaningfully say that a proposition is a logical truth or that one proposition is logically entailed by another. These matters cannot be said; they must show themselves. And there are yet other kinds of pseudo-propositions that, trying to say what can only be shown, fall foul of the principle of bipolarity: (a) explications of sense and nonsense, and of categorial features of language; (b) descriptions of the logical form of reality; (c) the doctrine of solipsism; (d) ethics and other value judgements; and hence, generally, (e) the *Tractatus* propositions themselves. As Russell remarked in his Introduction to the book: 'Mr Wittgenstein manages to say a good deal about what cannot be said' (1920, p. xxi).

(a) Sense, logical syntax, internal properties and formal concepts

One cannot say what sense a proposition has. If we were to say what sense, for instance, the proposition 'Smith is at home' has, that is to say, state which possible situation it represents, it would come down to something like this: The proposition 'Smith is at home' represents the possibility that Smith is at home. Evidently not a substantial statement, but a (trivial) logical necessity: a proposition says what it says. And that, according to the principle of bipolarity, is not something that can be said. It can only be shown: 'A proposition *shows* its sense' (*TLP* 4.022; cf. 4.1212).

One cannot say that a would-be proposition is nonsense; that too must show itself. In insisting that nonsense must be self-evident as such, Wittgenstein rejects Russell's theory of types. To avoid Russell's paradox – the inconsistency implied in the notion of the class of all classes which are not members of themselves (see Sect. 1.5 above) – Russell proposed that objects and classes be ordered in a hierarchy of types:

Type 0 are individual objects;
Type 1 are classes of objects;
Type 2 are classes of type 1 classes;
Type 3 are classes of type 2 classes; etc.

And the formation of classes was to be restricted such that the members of a class must always be of a lower type than the class itself. Thus the possibility of a class's being its own member is ruled out, and hence Russell's paradox can no longer arise.

The theory of types is a set of syntactical rules. It lays down that certain sentences or formulae are not well formed. It demands, for instance, that the predicate 'x is a member of the class of flowers' (i.e., 'x is a flower') can only be a applied to type 0 entities: that is, to individual objects. So you may say: 'This table is a member of the class of flowers (i.e., is a flower)', which of course is false, but not ruled out as nonsense by the theory of types. Whereas if you say: 'The class of flowers is a member of the class of flowers (i.e., is a flower)', you do infringe the theory of types, for you speak of a type 1 class that contains another type 1 class as its member, which is not allowed. So the theory of types rules that the sentence 'The class of flowers is a flower' is nonsense.

Wittgenstein did not disagree with this result, but thought that such a syntactical rule could not be formulated. For, again, what it is trying to say is something that, given the meanings of our words, is *necessarily* true. If our words mean what they do mean, then it follows with necessity that that sentence is nonsense. But what is necessarily so cannot meaningfully be stated: – it must show itself. Therefore, Wittgenstein wrote to Russell (in January 1913):

> All theories of types must be done away with by a theory of symbolism showing that what seem to be *different kinds of things* are symbolised by different kinds of symbols which *cannot* possibly be substituted in one another's place. (*CL* 25)

And more generally he says in the *Tractatus*:

> 3.334   The rules of logical syntax must be obvious, once we know how each individual sign signifies.

Rules of logical syntax – allowing some combinations and prohibiting others – cannot be stated explicitly. 'Logical form', which determines what does and what does not make sense, 'cannot be represented in propositions: it is mirrored in them. What expresses *itself* in language, *we* cannot express by means of language' (*TLP* 4.121). So it must simply be obvious whether a given combination yields sense or not. Logical form or syntax must be self-evident. This is another sense in which 'logic must take care of itself' (*TLP* 5.473).

How, in particular, does the impossibility of forming the propositions that create Russell's paradox show itself? The answer is given, in *Tractatus* style, in one sentence:

> 3.332   No proposition can make a statement about itself, because a propositional sign cannot be contained in itself (that is the whole of the 'theory of types').

Russell's paradox requires that one could ask whether or not a class is contained in itself. But that is equivalent to the question whether or not a predicate can be correctly applied to itself. A class, the class of flowers for example, can be represented by a predicate: e.g., 'x is a flower'. Thus, in considering whether the class of flowers is a member of itself (i.e., a flower), we should ask whether the predicate 'x is a flower' can be applied to itself. The result would be: '(x is a flower) is a flower'. This is not only patent nonsense, but more importantly, Wittgenstein argues, it cannot possibly be the statement one would need in order to formulate Russell's paradox. That is to say, it cannot be a statement in which a predicate is applied to itself, for the two occurrences of 'is a flower' have different forms and so cannot be the same predicate. One appears to have the form 'fx', and the other one 'F(fx)'. But if we assume that in fact the first one too has the more complex form 'F(fx)' – taking a predicate as its argument – then we find that the other one (in order to have the first as its argument) must be of the yet more complex form: 'ϕ(F(fx))'. Either way, the outer predicate needs to have a more complex form than the inner predicate; and so they cannot be the same predicate; hence it is impossible to apply a predicate to itself. Hence you cannot ask whether a predicate applies to itself. And that makes the formulation of Russell's paradox impossible (*TLP* 3.333).

An *internal property* is a property of which it is inconceivable that its object should not possess it (*TLP* 4.123). Consequently, one cannot *say* which internal properties an object has, or in which internal relations it stands to other objects; this must show itself in meaningful propositions about the objects in question (*TLP* 4.122). That, for instance, a certain shade of blue (say Oxford blue) is darker than another one (Cambridge blue) is not a contingent matter, but an internal relation (*TLP* 4.123), which cannot be expressed in a meaningful proposition. It shows itself – quite literally: one can see it when looking at those colours in juxtaposition; but it is, presumably, also 'shown' by the fact that whenever an object a is Oxford blue and an object b is Cambridge blue, it is correct to say that a is darker than b.

Internal properties are also called 'formal properties' (*TLP* 4.122); and Wittgenstein uses the term '*formal concept*' accordingly (*TLP* 4.126). Examples of formal concepts are 'object', 'fact' and 'number' (*TLP* 4.1272). '1 is a number' is not a contingent statement, and hence nonsense. And given that 'a' is the name of an object, it is nonsense to say that a is an object – for what else could it be? The only correct use of a formal concept is such that it can be expressed by a bound variable. Thus it is licit to say, 'There are at least two objects on the table', which can be rendered: '($\exists x,y$): x is on the table . y is on the table'. Here the bound variables 'x' and 'y' are signs of formal concepts (*TLP* 4.1271). However, one cannot say, 'There are at least two objects', or 'There are $\aleph_0$ objects'[36]

---

[36] This statement means that there exists an infinity of objects. Under the title 'axiom of infinity' it plays an important role in Russell's mathematical logic. '$\aleph_0$' (pronounced: aleph-zero) signifies the infinity of natural numbers.

(*TLP* 4.1272). In Russell's logic, statements about the number of existing objects would be expressed using the identity sign (e.g., '(∃x)(∃y): ~x=y', for 'There are at least two objects'). Wittgenstein's abolition of the identity sign (see sect. 2.5 above) makes it impossible to form such propositions. One cannot enumerate objects without using a proper concept (e.g., 'object on the table'), as opposed to a formal or pseudo-concept like 'object' (*TLP* 4.1272). That there are two, or infinitely many, objects in the world cannot be said; it shows itself through the use of two, or infinitely many, names with different meanings (*TLP* 5.535).

But why *should* it be impossible to state how many objects there are? After all, unlike all the other cases of things that cannot be said, the number of objects in the world appears to be a contingent matter. Such a statement would not violate the principle of bipolarity. Still, it is incompatible with the way the principle is established in the *Tractatus*: namely, as a consequence of the picture theory. For the picture theory allows only propositions that represent a particular configuration of objects, not the existence of objects, which must already be presupposed for names to have any meaning.

(b) *The logical form of reality*

Language reflects the logical form of the world: that is, the possible ways in which objects can combine to form states of affairs. For the possible combinations of objects are mirrored by the possible combinations of their names (*TLP* 2.18, 4.04). However, those possibilities cannot be stated:

4.12 Propositions . . . cannot represent what they must have in common with reality in order to be able to represent it – logical form.
 In order to be able to represent logical form, we should have to be able to station ourselves with propositions somewhere outside logic, that is to say outside the world.
4.121 Propositions cannot represent logical form: it is mirrored in them.

The same point is elaborated in notes Wittgenstein dictated to G. E. Moore in Norway in 1914:

It is impossible to *say* what [the logical] properties [of the Universe] are, because in order to do so, you would need a language, which hadn't got the properties in question, and it is impossible that this should be a *proper* language. Impossible to construct [an] illogical language. . . . An illogical language would be one in which, e.g., you could put an *event* into a hole. (*NB* 108)

The force of this argument is not obvious. Why would we need, in order to say what those properties are, a language which hadn't got those properties? After all, it is perfectly possible to describe some grammatical features of English (say word order) in English, a language that has those very features. – Again, we need to invoke the principle of bipolarity, as a hidden premiss. Suppose an object *a* could be conjoined with an object *b*, but not with a third one *c*. That is *a*'s logical form. Why can that not be said? Because for it to be possible to *say* that *a* cannot be conjoined with *c*, it would have to be a contingent matter and the opposite be possible as well. That is to say, the language in which one could say that *a* cannot be conjoined with *c* would have to be one in which the opposite statement, '*a* can be conjoined with *c*', also makes sense. But since that combination is logically impossible, it would take an illogical language to say such a thing – 'e.g. one in which an event can be put into a hole'. – Thus the impossibility of describing the logical form of the world is the ontological correlate of the impossibility of stating that something is nonsense (cf. (a) above). Not only can one not say that 'The event dropped into a hole' is nonsense (as this would presuppose that it could have made sense), but it is equally out of bounds to say that events cannot drop into holes (as this would presuppose the opposite possibility). Logical form cannot be described, it can only manifest itself in well-formed propositions (*TLP* 2.172, 4.121). Thus ordinary propositions like 'The event took place last week', or 'A pebble fell into the hole', *show* how the words 'event' and 'hole' can be used, and, indirectly, which combinations are impossible.

Wittgenstein also says that logical form is shown by tautologies, and in a more systematic way (*NB* 108):

> 6.124 The propositions of logic describe the scaffolding of the world, or rather they represent it. . . . They presuppose that names have meaning and elementary propositions sense; and that is their connexion with the world. It is clear that something about the world must be indicated by the fact that certain combinations of symbols – which essentially have a definite character – are tautologies. . . . in logic the nature of the essentially necessary signs speaks for itself.
>
> 6.13 Logic is not a body of doctrine, but a mirror-image of the world.

Perhaps what Wittgenstein has in mind is this: That '*fa* v ~*fa*', for example, is a tautology shows that '*fa*' is a meaningful proposition, which makes it clear that there is an object *a* that can form a state of affairs in combination with a property *f* (which ultimately has to be analysed in terms of simple objects).

(c) Solipsism

> *At death the world does not alter, but comes to an end.*
> TLP 6.431

Tractatus Logico-Philosophicus

> *Good creatures, do you love your lives?*
> *and have you ears for sense?*
> *Here is a knife like other knives,*
> *that cost me eighteenpence.*
> *I need but stick it in my heart*
> *and down will come the sky.*
> *And earth's foundations will depart*
> *and all you folk will die.*
>
> A. E. Housman[37]

A solipsist (in the general, not only the moral sense of the word) is someone who holds the strange view that nobody else exists. Roughly speaking, the world is seen as nothing more than a long dream in the solipsist's mind. None of the people and things occurring in that dream have an independent existence outside the solipsist's mind. This extreme position has rarely been defended; it is typically presented only as a sceptical worry that seems hard to refute. One does not seriously believe that there are no other minds, but one wonders whether one can really be certain that there are. All the more surprising, then, that the author of the *Tractatus* presents solipsism as another item on the list of unsayable *truths*: admittedly what the solipsist means cannot be stated, as it is not a contingent matter, but it is 'quite correct' and 'shows itself' (*TLP* 5.62).[38]

Wittgenstein declares:

5.6 *The limits of my language* mean the limits of my world.
[cf. 5.62c: . . . the limits of *language* (of that language which alone I understand) mean the limits of *my* world.]

---

[37] For more examples of solipsism in literature see Cioffi 1998, ch. 9. – Housman, incidentally, was later to be Wittgenstein's neighbour in Trinity College, Cambridge. Unlike Wittgenstein, he had his own bathroom, but would not share it with the philosopher (McGuinness 2002, 19).

[38] Some commentators found it so incredible that Wittgenstein should have held as absurd a doctrine as solipsism that they tried to read him as saying merely that solipsism is in some ways tempting, but ultimately nonsense (Black 1964, 309; Pears 1987, 188). But that is not a plausible interpretation. For one thing, it is contradicted by *TLP* 5.62, where solipsism is implicitly called 'a truth' and explicitly described as something that is 'entirely correct' and 'shows itself'. For another thing, the fact that by *Tractatus* standards any formulation of the doctrine must indeed be dismissed as 'nonsense' does not, for Wittgenstein, preclude the doctrine from being true – as according to its author the whole of the *Tractatus* is in the same situation: its sentences are nonsense (*TLP* 6.54), yet the truth of the thoughts they express is 'unassailable and definitive' (*TLP*, *Preface*, h).

5.61 Logic pervades the world: the limits of the world are also its limits. . . .

What does he mean by '*my* language'? Is the language whose limits are in question an essentially private one, a language that only *I* can understand? The parenthesis in 5.62c could be interpreted that way (see Anscombe 1959, 167) – but such a reading would not go well with the fact that in elucidating 5.6 Wittgenstein switches from 'the limits of my language' to 'the limits of logic' (in *TLP* 5.61); for it is unlikely that he should have thought logic to be an essentially private matter. Furthermore, that interpretation is ruled out by a correction Wittgenstein made in the English translation of the *Tractatus*, indicating clearly that the word 'alone' (*allein*) was meant to refer to 'language', rather than 'I' (Lewy 1967, 419; cf. McGuinness 2002, 137f). This different reading of the parenthesis in 5.62c provides a better explanation of the possessive pronoun in 'my language'. My language is the type of language that it is at all possible for me to understand. What kind of language does that exclude? For one thing, the change from 'language' to 'logic' in 5.61 suggests that a (would-be) language that was not in accordance with logic would be disqualified: 'what we cannot think we cannot *say* either' (*TLP* 5.61d; cf. *NB*, 15 Oct. 1916). For another thing, for language to be meaningful, its names must be correlated with objects; hence, if an object is entirely inaccessible to me, I cannot give it a name, and so cannot talk about it. So a language containing names of objects beyond my ken would be incomprehensible to me. *My* language includes only names I can understand, and that, according to 5.6, means that my world contains only objects I am or can be acquainted with. In fact 5.6 has been read as saying that my world 'is a function of the objects that I have encountered in my lifetime' (Pears 1987, 156). But that seems rather unlikely, for it would make the boundaries of my world a contingent and empirical matter. Depending on whether I had happened to encounter a given object or not – a purely contingent matter – it would or would not belong to my world. It seems clear, however, that the limits that Wittgenstein is concerned about are not contingent, but necessary ones, which for that reason cannot be stated and must show themselves (*TLP* 5.62). Remember also that, as a matter of fact, none of us can produce or name any simple object; we just assume that analysis could in principle bring them to light. But if acquaintance with *Tractatus* names and objects needs to be taken as a postulated possibility rather than an actuality, one should not expect Wittgenstein to be concerned about any purely incidental limitations of his actual vocabulary.[39]

---

[39] For further discussion, from a different perspective, see Sullivan 1996, 204–7.

Be that as it may, 5.6 certainly means that *what is absolutely inaccessible to me, what I could not possibly experience, is not part of my world, and so I cannot represent it in language*. Obviously the term 'world' must be understood differently here from its occurrence at the beginning of the book. The world whose boundaries are indicated by the limits of my language is not 'the totality of facts' (*TLP* 1.1); for clearly my language goes beyond 'what is the case' with every false, yet meaningful proposition. 'The world' in 5.6ff refers to all that *could be* the case; the possible configurations of the objects in my world (cf. *TLP* 5.5561).

The crucial, and not at all transparent, step in these passages is the one from 5.6 to an endorsement of solipsism:

5.62 This remark provides the key to the problem, how much truth there is in solipsism.[40]
For what the solipsist *means* is quite correct; only it cannot be *said*, but shows itself.
The world is *my* world: this shows itself in that the limits of *language* (of that language which alone I understand) mean the limits of *my* world.[41]

Why should solipsism be thought to follow from, or at any rate be indicated by, the observation that the limits of my language mean the limits of my world?

Two issues need to be distinguished, as solipsism is the rejection of two different positions. First, the solipsist denies that there is a material world, existing independently of his mind. In other words, solipsism implies idealism. But it goes beyond idealism, which, as propounded by Berkeley and Schopenhauer, does not rule out the existence of other minds. This is the second issue: the solipsist denies that there are other minds.

In the *Tractatus* discussion of solipsism Wittgenstein is mostly concerned with the second point, the dismissal of other minds. Idealism – expressed in *TLP* 5.621: 'The world and life are one'[42] – is taken for granted, rather than argued for; as it was largely taken for granted by Schopenhauer, who claimed that 'no truth is more certain, more independent of all others, and less in need of proof than this' (1859, vol. 1, §1; p. 3). Schopenhauer's influence on Wittgenstein at this point is undeniable (cf. Hacker 1986, ch. 4). However, it should not be over-

---

[40] As the numbering system makes 5.62 an elucidation of 5.6, that is what 'this remark' is likely to refer to.

[41] The published translations have 'the fact that the limits &c', which sounds more idiomatic, but conflicts with Wittgenstein's use of the term 'fact' as applicable only to what is *contingently* the case.

[42] Cf. 'the subject is not a part of the world but a presupposition of its existence' (*NB*, 2 Aug. 1916).

estimated. For one thing, Schopenhauer provides no source for the *Tractatus* solipsism, the denial of other minds, a position that Schopenhauer dismissed as madness (1859, vol. 1, §19; p. 104). Admittedly, for an idealist the sceptical threat of solipsism may be, or should have been, a particularly serious concern; but Wittgenstein's arguments for a non-contingent solipsism are quite independent of the issues of idealism and scepticism. They apply to any dualist position (that sets the mind sharply apart from the body), no matter whether bodies are regarded as material objects or not. – For another thing, neither the *Tractatus* nor the *Notebooks* show any signs of Schopenhauer's *transcendental* idealism. Transcendental idealism is based on the distinction between things as they are in themselves and as they appear to us. In itself the world exists independently of us, but the way it appears to us is determined by our cognitive faculties: notably, that all objects are experienced in space and time and according to causal laws is not due to their independent nature, but is imposed on the world by the perceiving subject. This doctrine, originating with Kant and adopted by Schopenhauer, is absent from the *Tractatus*. Wittgenstein's most explicit solipsist pronouncements contradict the independence that transcendental idealism accords to the world in itself. For instance, 'My world is the first and only one' (*NB*, 2 Sept. 1916); 'at death the world does not alter, but comes to an end' (*TLP* 6.431). And although it has occasionally been suggested that logic, in the *Tractatus*, has the transcendental status that space, time and causality have in Kant and Schopenhauer, that is not so. In the relation between logic and the world it is not logic, but the world, that wears the trousers. Logic is not said to *shape* the world, but merely to *pervade* it (*TLP* 5.61a), which suggests that the world has a certain extension independently of logic. Again, Wittgenstein does not say that 'the limits of logic are (i.e., determine) the limits of the world'; he puts it the other way round: 'the limits of the world are also its [i.e., logic's] limits'. Thirdly, note that (both in 5.6 and 5.62c) the limits of language are not said to *be* the limits of my world, but to *mean* or *indicate* them (*bedeuten*). Logic and language *reflect* the form of the world; they do not produce it (cf. *TLP* 5.511 and 6.13, where logic is said to mirror the world). Anyway, Wittgenstein nowhere entertains the idea that logic might be subjective in a transcendental sense: imposed upon the world by us.

Back to the solipsistic denial of other minds. Wittgenstein's idea is that the apparently common-sense view that others have experiences like myself cannot really be imagined or expressed in language. Language does not allow of the ascription of mental life to others; and since the boundaries of language reflect the boundaries of the world (*TLP* 5.6), others cannot have a mental life. It remains to be seen why, according to the *Tractatus*, one cannot make sense of another person's experiences.

The argument proceeds in two steps only the first of which is (fairly) explicit in the *Tractatus*. It takes up 5.63s, being a commentary on 5.63: 'I am my world'. The preceding remark, 5.621, identifies the world with life. That is to say, the world is only the world one experiences in life: objects and events exist only as part of a person's experiences. So 5.63 means: 'I am the world of my experiences', and the stress falls on 'am': Not, as one might expect, 'I *have* (or experience) the world of my experiences', but 'I *am* that world'. Why? Because, as the next two sections explain, the I, the subject, is not an object in the world. If I wrote a book called *The World as I Found It*, the subject could not be mentioned in it (*TLP* 5.631). Although we know *a priori* that we have a subject – it is a logical truth that without a subject there could not be any experience – that subject cannot be encountered in experience. It is not an object (*NB*, 7 Aug. 1916) that could stand in a possessive relation to its experiences. Therefore the subject must be identified with its experiences: I *am* my world. Alternatively, the subject could be regarded as an outer boundary of the world (*TLP* 5.632). Wittgenstein's positive characterization of the metaphysical subject vacillates between these two metaphors for what is strictly speaking unsayable. What matters, however, is the negative point that the subject does not belong to the world (*TLP* 5.632).

How can one make out that the subject is not an object in the world? First, it appears that the real subject of experience cannot be one's physical body or a part of it (*AL* 23). The argument is this. The fact that my perceptions and thoughts are lodged in this particular body is merely contingent. Tomorrow I could find myself looking at the world from a different body while still being myself. Hence my self is not identical with my body. To put the same point in a slightly different way: if 'I' meant 'this body that has such-&-such characteristics', I might be mistaken in claiming that, say, I am in pain. Perhaps my body no longer has any of those characteristics. But, surely, I cannot be wrong in thinking that *I* am in pain. So by 'I' I must mean something that is quite independent of any of my bodily features (cf. *BB* 66f). Then, having distinguished the self from one's body, one is inclined to look for it in one's mind or consciousness. But, as Hume was the first to discover, introspection, close attention to one's feelings and perceptions fails to reveal anything one might call the self. As Wittgenstein puts it: 'The experience of feeling pain is not that a person 'I' has something. I distinguish an intensity, a location, etc. in the pain, but not an owner' (*PR* 94, §65). So, nowhere in the world, neither in the physical nor in the mental realm, do I encounter a subject (*TLP* 5.633). In fact, it is not just an empirical datum that the subject is not to be found in the world, it could not be otherwise. For that all experience must depend on a subject is an *a priori* truth. But an *a priori* truth can (as such) never be learnt from experience. For 'no part of our experience is at the same time *a priori*. Whatever we see could be other than it is' (*TLP* 5.634). In order to see that my experience was had by a subject, it would have to be possible likewise to see that it was *not* had by a subject (the bipolarity principle); yet that is impossible.

Now if the subject is not part of the world, a proposition like 'I see a tree' would appear to transgress the bounds of sense. For, contrary to the requirements of the *Tractatus* semantics, the word 'I' does not stand for anything in the world. Thus it should not appear in a logically more appropriate notation (cf. *TLP* 4.002). Analysis must transform the proposition into one that no longer contains the objectionable word 'I'. All that can be meant by 'I see a tree' is 'A tree is seen' (cf. ML 309). But with the removal of the term that apparently denoted a subject, we have removed the mark that distinguishes between propositions reporting *different* people's experiences, for instance, 'I see a tree' and 'You see a tree', or 'Smith sees a tree'. So 'what the solipsist means is quite correct': *we cannot make sense of the idea that there might be different people having experiences*. There is only *this* experience ⇨ – and here I focus on whatever may be in my field of vision and hearing at the time. As Wittgenstein was to put it later in some lecture notes: 'what I now see, this room, plays a unique role, it is the visual world!' (*NfL* 258; cf. *PI* §398).

Here one might object that even if the self dissolves, in Humean fashion, into a bundle of experiences, it does not seem to follow that there could not be a multiplicity of such bundles. Experience may only allow me to say 'A tree is seen', but could I not easily imagine that at the same time somewhere else a house is seen, a rose is smelt and church bells are heard, each such experiential complex forming another person's world? This objection is not discussed in the *Tractatus*, but Wittgenstein provides a reply to it in *Philosophical Remarks*:

> The two hypotheses, that others have pain, and that they don't and merely behave as I do when I have, must have identical senses if every *possible* experience confirming the one confirms the other as well. In other words, if a decision between them on the basis of experience is inconceivable. (*PR* 94f, §65)

The difference between the view that others have experiences like me and the view that they behave exactly as if they had such experiences without having them is that the former hypothesis goes beyond the latter in assuming the existence of certain entities: others' experiences on top of their behaviour. But such entities are necessarily inaccessible to me. I could not possibly encounter them – I cannot experience what is not experienced by me. Hence I cannot name them or talk about them either. So the first hypothesis inasmuch as it goes beyond the second makes no sense to me.

Shall we then call it an unnecessary hypothesis that anyone else has personal experiences? – But is it an hypothesis at all? For how can I even make the hypothesis if it transcends all possible experience? How could such a hypothesis be backed by meaning? (*BB* 48)

This position, implicit in the *Tractatus* and spelled out in Wittgenstein's later writings, can be called *semi-behaviourism*. Behaviourism tries to reduce all psychological states to dispositions to show certain patterns of behaviour. Thus having a headache, for example, boils down to nothing more than a tendency to moan, complain, rub one's forehead, avoid vigorous movements, take an aspirin, etc., etc. Wittgenstein's semi-behaviourism maintains this only about *other* people's psychological states. And isn't that exactly the way we experience things? In my case, to be sure, pain is not just a tendency to behave in certain ways: it is really felt (and very unpleasant); as regards others, I do not actually experience any pain: what I mean when I say they are in pain is that they are inclined to behave in a certain way. 'Here it can be seen that solipsism, when its implications are followed out strictly, coincides with pure realism' (*TLP* 5.64). It is an accurate account of the world as it actually presents itself in a person's experience: only some pains are really felt (viz. one's own), all others occur only as observed behaviour.

However, solipsism cannot be stated in meaningful language. It is correct, but since it is not just contingently correct, it falls prey – like all other doctrines of the book – to the *Tractatus*'s heroic injunction against all necessary truth. What the solipsist means 'cannot be *said*, but shows itself' (*TLP* 5.62).

(d) Ethics

Although Wittgenstein has written very little on ethics, it is probably true to say that no philosopher of the twentieth century was so constantly and seriously concerned with moral issues as he was. All through his adult life he was deeply troubled and often in downright despair about the things that struck him as morally bad or imperfect in his life and character. Unsurprisingly, there are only glimpses of this concern in the *Tractatus*. From the earlier parts of the book it follows that ethics cannot be put into words (*TLP* 6.421), for matters of moral value are not merely contingent (*TLP* 6.41). One would not say that murder or gratuitous cruelty, for instance, just happen to be bad, but might have been good had things turned out differently. Thus moral (and aesthetic) value judgements violate the bipolarity requirement for meaningful propositions. Moreover, the *Tractatus* allows only *de*scriptive language, but moral judgements are irreducibly *pre*scriptive. They are essentially of the form 'You ought to . . .' (*TLP* 6.422). In some cases this imperative form is only apparent, and the statement is really a conditional. For instance, the injunction 'You should give up smoking' is normally conditional on the addressee's interest in remaining in good health. So roughly the same thought could be expressed in descriptive language: 'If you continue smoking, you are likely to damage your health.' However, moral injunctions are not like that. 'You ought not to steal' is not merely conditional on one's interest in avoiding the unpleasant consequences of theft. It is what Kant called a 'categorical imperative' (as opposed to a 'hypothetical' one): 'No matter what the consequences, you ought not to do it!' (*TLP* 6.422; cf. LE 39). Such categorical imperatives cannot be analysed into *Tractatus* propositions: pictures of possible states of affairs.

Meaningful propositions can only describe what happens and is the case in the world: what is merely accidental. Moral value 'must lie outside the world' (*TLP* 6.41). Wittgenstein locates it in the will, as 'the bearer of the ethical' (*TLP* 6.423), of 'good and evil' (*NB*, 21 July 1916). This is reminiscent of Kant's famous claim that the only thing that is intrinsically good is a good will (1785, 393). But why should the good (or bad) will be outside the world? One possible *Tractatus* reply to this is that 'the world is independent of my will' (*TLP* 6.373), because there is no *logical* connection between my acts of will and what happens (*TLP* 6.374); it is always conceivable that things may happen contrary to my will. In this, Wittgenstein takes a Humean line. Hume described the will as a mental faculty of issuing orders ('volitions') to the world, but to what extent these orders will be carried out is beyond my control and strictly speaking unpredictable (1748, 7.1). The opposition of world and will in *TLP* 6.373 suggests that the will is outside the world, which would fit well with the claim that it is the bearer of value, also outside the world. But is this location of the will plausible? Are acts of will not facts perfectly describable at least in one's own case? Wittgenstein himself seems to think so, as he mentions 'the will as a phenomenon' studied in psychology, which he explicitly distinguishes from the will as the bearer of the ethical (*TLP* 6.423). In his *Notebooks* he wrote:

> Good and evil only enter through the *subject*. And the subject is not part of the world, but a boundary of the world.
> It would be possible to say (à la Schopenhauer): It is not the world of representation that is either good or evil; but the willing subject. (*NB*, 2. Aug. 1916)

This suggests that the will as the bearer of the ethical is identical with the self of solipsism: which is also characterized as 'a boundary of the world', not itself part of it (*TLP* 5.632, 5.641), and hence not a phenomenon studied by psychology (*TLP* 5.641). This is also borne out by the reference to Schopenhauer, for whom it was a metaphysical axiom that the willing subject and the representing subject are identical (1859, vol. 1 §18, p. 102; §51, pp. 250f). (Note that 'the representing subject (*das vorstellende Subjekt*)' in 5.631 is a Schopenhauerian term of art.)

In the discussion of solipsism the metaphysical self is said to be outside the world; then good and evil are located outside the world; so it was only natural for Wittgenstein to combine the two: to make the metaphysical self of solipsism the bearer of good and evil. But this is not just a matter of compositional convenience. In a deeper sense the young Wittgenstein can be described as a moral solipsist. However, his moral views are not fully explained in the *Tractatus*. There are just a few more, rather obscure remarks. He declares that ethics and aesthetics are one and the same (*TLP* 6.421), and that good or bad willing does not change the facts (*TLP* 6.43a). He hints that happiness is relevant to ethics (*TLP* 6.43c), and that one should live in the present (*TLP* 6.4311b). These remarks (which were not part of the earliest version of the book that was completed by March 1916), like the ones about the will presented above, are best understood against the background of Wittgenstein's private moral thinking before and during the First World War. For, as he remarked in 1930, in ethics all one can do is 'step forth as an individual and speak in the first person' (*WVC* 117).

In section 1.3 I tried to give a sketch of Wittgenstein's moral character, his extreme self-consciousness and obsessive concern for his personal integrity, which was in particular a constant struggle against what he regarded as vanity and a striving for perfect truthfulness. It seems that it was a hopeless struggle: he had set himself moral standards impossible to live up to. Apart from the fact that even things that most people would never think of as in any way reprehensible incurred Wittgenstein's reprobation – on one occasion, in the 1930s, he accused himself of vanity for having tried to entertain his academic audience by inserting some jocular remarks in his lectures (*D* 13, 91f) – there even seemed to be some inconsistency in his ideals. On the one hand, truthfulness and freedom from all vanity would mean being guided entirely by one's own natural impulses, unaffected by any worry as to what others might think about one. This is Peer Gynt's ideal of being true only to oneself, free from the self-consciousness and affectations that result from any attempt to conform to others' moral rules and models. On the other hand, truthfulness for Wittgenstein meant also scrutinizing one's own character, relentlessly uncovering all one's sins and weaknesses (*D* 97, 102, 108f). But of course a constant scrutiny of one's own motives and inclinations is hardly compatible with being entirely natural and not self-conscious. And as for the desire to be entirely free from vanity, with as pure a soul as a saint – is this concern with one's own moral character not also a form of vanity? (cf. *D* 130). In any case, one cannot change one's nature. Wittgenstein could not help admitting to himself that, for example, he was – understandably – proud of his intellectual capacities (*D* 56; MS 158, 36r), as manifested in his philosophical work. To that extent he was not free from vanity; but there was nothing he could do about it. His ideal of truthfulness in the sense of following one's own nature would have forced him to accept it, yet it was contrary to his ideal of truthfulness as freedom from vanity.

Wittgenstein's inability to live up to his own exalted moral standards put him in a state of nervous irritability, and often despair. He experienced the wretchedness of a religious temperament feeling the need of redemption from his sinfulness through faith; yet he had no faith. On 31 October 1912 Russell wrote in a letter to Ottoline Morrell that 'Wittgenstein is on the verge of a nervous breakdown, not far removed from suicide, feeling himself a miserable creature, full of sin' (McGuinness 1988, 154). To his friend David Pinsent, Wittgenstein confessed that there was rarely a day when he did not consider suicide (McGuinness 1988, 157). From his hermitage in Norway he wrote to Russell in January 1914:

> [T]hings have gone terribly badly for me in the last weeks . . . Every day I was tormented by a frightful *Angst* and by depression in turns and even in the intervals I was so exhausted that I wasn't able to think of doing a bit of work. It's terrifying beyond all description the kind of mental torment that there can be! It wasn't until two days ago that I could hear the voice of reason over the howls of the damned and I began to work again. . . . But I *never* knew what it meant to feel only *one* step away from madness. (CL 69)

The outbreak of war in August 1914 afforded him a drastic medicine against his mental agonies. Mortal danger and real physical hardship might drive away the ghosts of his tormented conscience and cure him from that constant petty self-conscious worrying for which he despised himself so much. And if that did not work, the war would at least give him an opportunity to get rid of his intolerable life in an honourable manner.

Keeping quiet about his hernia, Wittgenstein enlisted, and on 14 August he was ordered to join the crew of a patrol boat on the River Vistula. They soon entered Russian territory, and he encountered the hardship and danger he had expected: it was his job to operate the searchlight at night, which made him an obvious target for enemy fire. But what he suffered from most was the complete loss of privacy on board, the constant contact with unsympathetic fellow human beings, their 'incredible rudeness, stupidity and wickedness' (MS 101, 4). Moreover, as a soldier, he was evidently not the master of his own fate: he might or might not be shot, as decreed by the gods – or depending on the orders of his superior officers. Wittgenstein's moral thinking during the war was largely shaped in response to these four afflictions: hardship, danger, bad company and the loss of freedom. These were 'the facts setting the problem' for him (cf. *TLP* 6.4321). He had to come to terms with suffering (physical hardship, fear, disgust) while being quite unable to *do* anything about his situation. Hence his ethics needed to be doubly independent of the world: the good life had to be independent both of what happened to him and of what he managed to do. So the good life had to be an inner life, separated from the physical world of facts beyond his control.

This is the biographical underpinning of his claim that the will as the bearer of ethics lies outside the world and is unable to change the facts (*TLP* 6.43). But then what are the effects of a good will?

> 6.43   . . . In short the effect must be that it becomes an altogether different world. It must, so to speak, wax and wane as a whole.
> The world of the happy man is a different one from that of the unhappy man.

The idea seems to be that the same facts can be experienced differently, depending on one's moral attitude. And the last sentence suggests that the right moral attitude goes together with happiness. A notebook entry elaborates:

> I keep on coming back to this: that simply the happy life is good, the unhappy bad. And if I *now* ask myself: But why should I live *happily*, then this of itself seems to me to be a tautological question; the happy life seems to be justified, of itself, it seems that it *is* the only right life.
> . . . The happy life seems to be in some sense more *harmonious* than the unhappy. (*NB*, 30 July 1916)

At the time Wittgenstein was deeply unhappy. He was often despondent, depressed, afraid, and permanently disgusted and annoyed with his comrades-in-arms; and such misery he regarded as a moral failing, as an indication of a wrong attitude (MS 103, 19f and 22f). In particular he thought that 'fear in face of death is the best sign of a false, i.e. a bad, life' (*NB*, 8 July 1916). That is the other respect in which the good life had to be independent of the world of facts: not only would it not change the facts, but it would also not be affected by adverse circumstances. It would be happy come what may. The ideal which Wittgenstein developed at the front was that of stoic equanimity and content. Apart from a firm religious faith, which Wittgenstein felt unable to obtain, stoicism appeared to be the only ethical view that would provide an answer to his miserable situation.[43] Stoic ethics emphasizes the distinction between what depends on us and what

---

[43] Wittgenstein would have come across an account of stoic ethics in Schopenhauer 1859, vol. 1, §16.

does not, and counsels us not to count on the latter at all. That way we will never suffer from having our desires thwarted. In the same spirit Wittgenstein notes:

> I cannot bend the happenings of the world to my will: I am completely powerless. [Cf. *TLP* 6.373]
> I can only make myself independent of the world – and so in a certain sense master it – by renouncing any influence on happenings. (*NB*, 11 June 1916)

The stoic attains a serene happiness by ceasing to worry about what might happen to him. He is no longer concerned about future events; in particular, not about his own death: he 'lives not in time but in the present', and 'for life in the present there is no death' (*NB*, 8 July 1916; cf. *TLP* 6.4311).[44]

Finally, Wittgenstein's laconic identification of ethics and aesthetics (*TLP* 6.421) calls out for an explanation. As remarked in section 1.3, this slogan serves well to characterize the views of Adolf Loos and Karl Kraus. That he may have had their ideas in mind when he wrote that proposition appears likely in view of the fact that later he would list them as major influences on his thinking, immediately after Frege and Russell in what appears to be a chronological order (*CV* 16). However, a more specific commentary can be found in the notebooks: 'The work of art is the object seen *sub specie aeternitatis*; and the good life is the world seen *sub specie aeternitatis*. This is the connexion between art and ethics' (*NB*, 7 Oct. 1916). Schopenhauer characterizes aesthetic contemplation as '*sub specie aeternitatis*', that is, 'from the standpoint of eternity' (1859, vol. 1, §34; the expression is drawn from Spinoza), meaning that one leaves behind all one's personal circumstances and particular interests. Wittgenstein's idea is that the right moral standpoint of stoic equanimity sees the world in an equally disinterested way, without any personal worries. The stoic sage lives in the present; and as 'eternal life belongs to those who live in the present' (*TLP* 6.4311), he will see the world 'from the standpoint of eternity'. Such a disinterested perspective is, as Schopenhauer emphasized, a truly happy one (cf. *NB*, 20 Oct. 1916), as happy as the stoic's good life.

(e) The Tractatus *paradox*

Towards the end of the book Wittgenstein makes an extraordinary recommendation:

---

[44] *TLP* 6.4311 is reminiscent of Marcus Aurelius's remark that we possess only the present moment, and therefore the length of our life is entirely irrelevant (*Meditations*, book 2, §14).

6.53 The correct method in philosophy would really be the following: to say nothing except what can be said, i.e. propositions of natural science – i.e. something that has nothing to do with philosophy – and then, whenever someone else wanted to say something metaphysical, to demonstrate to him that he had failed to give a meaning to certain signs in his proposition.

Evidently, this is not the method that he himself pursued in the book, which after all does not contain any propositions of natural science, but remarks on metaphysics, logic, sense and nonsense, what a language must look like to make sense, solipsism, ethics, and some other equally non-contingent matters that I have not discussed, such as the nature of mathematics and scientific explanation. All of this, as explained in the foregoing sections, falls foul of the principle of bipolarity implicit in the picture theory, according to which linguistic sense is a possible state of affairs represented by the combination of names in a way that corresponds to a possible combination of objects in the world. So only possible, contingent states of affairs can be meaningfully spoken of, whereas any necessary truth would lack sense. Tautologies are still granted a certain borderline status and called 'senseless'; every other non-contingent claim is classified as 'nonsense'. Since philosophy – certainly the *Tractatus* philosophy – is entirely *a priori*, not concerned with any contingent statements, the *Tractatus* must be nonsense too. And Wittgenstein admits as much in the book's famous coda:

6.54 My propositions serve as elucidations in the following way: anyone who understands me eventually recognizes them as nonsensical, when he has used them – as steps – to climb up beyond them. (He must, so to speak, throw away the ladder after he has climbed up it.)
   He must transcend these propositions, and then he will see the world aright.
7   What we cannot speak about we must pass over in silence.

On the one hand, the *Tractatus* propositions are supposed to be dismissed as nonsense; on the other hand, they are meant to give us a correct account of the world. What are we to make of this paradox?

There are two possible responses. *Either* we take the nonsense verdict of 6.54 at face value, accepting that most of the book is indeed intended to be sheer nonsense, not containing any intelligible doctrines (let us call this the 'Nonsense Interpretation'); then it becomes difficult to see how Wittgenstein could have thought those eighty pages of nonsense worth publishing. Of course, an author's intentions are important only to the extent that they are realized in the work; so the Nonsense Interpretation is likely to go together with the view that the book *is* indeed largely nonsense. That, of course, flatly contradicts, and is contradicted by, everything that has been said in this chapter in an attempt to make sense of the *Tractatus*. Alternatively, we can assume that Wittgenstein was somehow under the impression that an intelligible doctrine could be expressed by something that was strictly speaking 'nonsense'. In that case, we need not agree with 6.54 that the book *is* nonsensical; we need only explain why Wittgenstein felt compelled to call it 'nonsensical'. Let us first consider the Nonsense Interpretation, which in recent years has become extremely popular, especially among American academics.[45]

The Nonsense Interpretation purports that in the *Tractatus* Wittgenstein propounds no philosophical doctrines. Apart from the Preface, the final remarks (and possibly just a few others),[46] the book contains only *plain* nonsense that, contrary to what one might be inclined to believe, is *not* meant to convey or draw our attention to anything that cannot be put into words. The very idea that there are such ineffable truths is to be dismissed as an illusion. The main selling point of this interpretation is that it promises for the first time to take fully seriously the nonsense verdict of *Tractatus* 6.54 (albeit at the price of taking seriously virtually nothing else in the book).[47] The only value of the *Tractatus*, on this reading, is therapeutic: the perceptive reader is led to realize that what he took initially to be metaphysical doctrines is nothing but nonsense.

As regards textual evidence, the Nonsense Interpretation appears rather like a post-modernist joke, and has already been thoroughly discredited by more conscientious scholars (Hacker 2000, 2003; Proops 2001). It is flatly contradicted by a large number of remarks in the *Tractatus*. That of course does not impress its proponents, as their very point is that the book is largely nonsense. However, even the few passages that they do accept and refer to as sober expressions of Wittgenstein's views are not compatible with the Nonsense Interpretation. The Preface, allegedly part of the meaningful 'frame' instructing the reader about how the rest is to be read, declares repeatedly that the book expresses *thoughts*, and it claims emphatically that they are *true*. – Another island of sense in a sea of nonsense are supposed to be some remarks on philosophy: 4.111 and, especially,

---

[45] The main proponents of the Nonsense Interpretation are Cora Diamond, who first suggested it in her article 'Throwing Away the Ladder' (1988), and James Conant. See Crary and Read (2000), hyped as *The New Wittgenstein*.

[46] New Wittgensteinians are curiously undecided on what exactly makes sense in the *Tractatus* (see Proops 2001, 381f and 397). The main principle appears to be that what does not fit the Nonsense Interpretation must be dismissed as nonsense.

[47] Those who failed to take *Tractatus* 6.54 at face value were rebuked by Cora Diamond for 'chickening out' (1988, 181, 194), an expression that subsequently seems

4.112 Philosophy aims at the logical clarification of thoughts.
Philosophy is not a body of doctrine but an activity.
A philosophical work consists essentially of elucidations.
Philosophy does not result in 'philosophical propositions', but rather in the clarification of propositions.
Without philosophy thoughts are, as it were, cloudy and indistinct: its task is to make them clear and to give them sharp boundaries.

A lot has been made of this remark by a prominent champion of the 'New Wittgenstein',[48] who failed to notice that it is patently incompatible with the Nonsense Interpretation, according to which *Tractatus* philosophy should aim at the unmasking of nonsensical pseudo-sentences, to show that they do *not* in fact express any thoughts. Here, however, Wittgenstein states, on the contrary, that philosophy aims at the clarification of *thoughts*; and its result is that *propositions* (the opposite of nonsense) become clear.[49] – In fact, not even the ladder metaphor of 5.64 fits the Nonsense Interpretation. If the *Tractatus* sentences were *really* nonsense (and not just 'nonsense' by some unduly restrictive criterion of sense), one could hardly use them to climb up anywhere to achieve a better understanding of the world. The ladder, on that view, would be rotten: it would perhaps *appear* useful from a distance, but collapse the moment one tried to use it. And recognizing it as rotten would give us a better view not of the world – but merely of a rotten ladder. Wittgenstein's ladder, by contrast, is a useful instrument: in spite of the ultimate injunction to throw it away, the fact remains that it is supposed to work: one *can* climb up it and thus achieve a correct view of the world (and not only of an old ladder). Thus, even the famous metaphor of 6.54 cautions us *not* to take the nonsense verdict at face value. True, by *Tractatus* standards there is something wrong about the book's own propositions (therefore, *eventually* they should be thrown away), but Wittgenstein himself has to admit that, for the time being, he cannot do without them (*first* they must be used to gain a correct understanding of the world). Clearly, what Wittgenstein feels compelled to call 'nonsense' here is, by his own admission, far too useful and indispensable to deserve that opprobrious title in common parlance.

---

to have become something like the war-cry of the Nonsense campaign. Its proponents like to describe themselves as 'resolute' and 'austere' in their intrepid acceptance of 6.54.

[48] Conant 2000, 175 and 197. Note that this passage of remarks on philosophy continues till 4.116; but Conant is careful to draw the line after 4.112 (2000, 216), as 4.115 makes the awkward point that philosophical elucidations are a means of 'signifying the unsayable'.

[49] Another telling example of Conant's scholarship occurs at the beginning of the same article (2000, 175). He believes that certain views often attributed to Wittgenstein

Furthermore on the question of textual evidence, P. M. S. Hacker (2000, 2003) and Ian Proops (2001) have shown in great detail that the Nonsense Interpretation is flatly contradicted by virtually all of Wittgenstein's extant comments on the *Tractatus* in other writings, lectures and conversations. And there are a considerable number of such remarks.

Turning now from exegetical to philosophical considerations, the question must be raised as to how the Nonsense Interpretation stands up to the difficulty, mentioned above, of accounting for the book's value. The idea is that the book serves to enlighten us that various things we might be inclined to say are nonsense. This is a good deal less than we might have hoped for. It is not the correct view of 'the world' that we are promised in 6.54. And as the *Tractatus* pronouncements are for the most part rather peculiar, far from commonplace, the value of being cured from an inclination to utter *them* would for most people appear to be quite negligible (Hacker 2000, 126). – Anyway, how is that cure to be achieved? If anyone is under the illusion that some piece of philosophical nonsense is true, it is clearly not enough simply to present the sentences in question and then add that they are nonsense. Some argument seems needed. And how can an argument convince if it does not make sense? One could of course imagine that a sentence that *seems* to make sense, but contains some hidden inconsistency, is transformed by a number of self-evident steps into some obvious piece of nonsense – for example, a straightforward contradiction. That would indeed be a way for debunking nonsense without the need for any meaningful commentary. I doubt if any of the more interesting and controversial philosophical confusions can be disentangled in such a simple and straightforward manner; but be that as it may, this is clearly not what is going on in the *Tractatus*. There is nowhere a clear logical progression to sentences that are *obviously* nonsense. Even if you

---

were in fact not held by Wittgenstein, but only by Rudolf Carnap, a member of the Vienna Circle (on this idea see Hacker 2003). And he claims that 'Wittgenstein says of Carnap that he failed to understand this passage [*TLP* 5.64] and *therefore* failed to understand "the fundamental conception of the whole book"' (Conant 2000, 175). He supports this claim by reference to a letter from Wittgenstein to Moritz Schlick (8 Aug. 1932). But in that letter Wittgenstein says exactly the opposite. The letter is a complaint that Carnap was guilty of plagiarism. Surely, Wittgenstein writes, Carnap must have been aware that certain ideas he published had already been expressed in the *Tractatus*. 'I cannot imagine that Carnap could have completely misunderstood the final sentences of the *Tractatus*' (Nedo and Ranchetti 1983, 255).

could not make sense of some of the more oracular sayings about solipsism or the mystical, that would not demonstrate that the *Tractatus* account of logic and language might not be by and large tenable (that, for example, was the view of members of the Vienna Circle).

Since it is not obvious that the *Tractatus* is nonsense, why should we adopt this view at all? Cora Diamond explains:

> Take a sentence like "A is an object." ... In so far as we take ourselves to understand it, we take its truth and its falsity *both* to be graspable. ... we think of it as itself *the case*; our thought contrasts it with as it were a different set of necessities. ... From the perspective we now seem to ourselves to occupy, the logical rules governing ordinary sentences ... will be thought of as needing to match, to be determined by, which necessities *do* hold. – From the perspective we now seem to occupy; but Wittgenstein's aim is to let us recognize it to be only the illusion of a perspective. (Diamond 1988, 195f)

Now, the idea that a necessary truth (say, 'Yellow is a colour') is really only contingently true (– that yellow might *not* have been a colour) is indeed nonsense. But the claim that when we think that we understand such a necessary truth, we perversely construe it as a contingent matter is patently false (Hacker 2000, 114f). If a child asked you 'What is magenta?', you would probably say: 'Magenta is a colour'. Suppose that at that moment a philosopher interposes: 'So you think that magenta might *not* have been a colour?' Of course not. Why should you want to say *that*?! 'Magenta is a colour', you might say, is an analytic statement: true in virtue of the meanings of the words. So its negation is inconsistent – nonsense.

Diamond's reason for dismissing the *Tractatus* as nonsense is quite implausible. But it looks less odd when seen against the background of Wittgenstein's own reason. *If* one accepts the *Tractatus* doctrine that only bipolar, contingent propositions are meaningful, then the claim that necessary truths, like 'Yellow is a colour', are meaningful would indeed appear to imply that in some sense they are only contingent after all. Thus Diamond's reason seems to be based on the principle of bipolarity, which indeed is Wittgenstein's ultimate justification of the nonsense verdict in 6.54. However, once we accept the bipolarity principle as the basis of 6.54, the Nonsense Interpretation collapses.

First, the distinction between a nonsensical 'body' of text and a perfectly meaningful 'frame', consisting of at least the Preface and the two final remarks, cannot be upheld. It is not a contingent matter whether a (would-be) proposition makes sense or not (see section (a) above). So remark 6.54 is no less 'nonsense' than any other remark in the book. Consequently, any article propounding in earnest the doctrine of 6.54 must, equally, be 'plain nonsense'.

Secondly, the reason for dismissing the *Tractatus* sentences as 'nonsense' is of course itself 'nonsense', as it is not an empirical matter. So if we accept it, we must also accept the view that 'nonsense' can be true, or better: that something can be true and provide a good reason, even though any attempt to state it expressly must be called 'nonsense'. In that case one can hardly avoid the concession that the word 'nonsense' is used with less than its usual pejorative force, somewhat like a technical term. There is plenty of evidence that this is how Wittgenstein himself saw it. He states in no uncertain terms that 'there are, indeed, things that cannot be put into words' (*TLP* 6.522). The final injunction is not just to be silent, but to be silent *about* (*darüber*) what cannot be put into words (*TLP* 7). And, as noted above, 6.54 makes it clear that 'nonsense' – a disposable ladder – is supposed to be the means of conveying what philosophy aims to convey, which involves 'signifying what cannot be said' (*TLP* 4.115). If, none the less, one refuses to attribute to Wittgenstein the view that 'nonsense' can somehow convey truths like the picture theory and its corollary 6.54, it becomes entirely incomprehensible why he should have believed that his propositions were 'nonsense'.

One may well find the idea of a truth that cannot be stated unintelligible. Then the bipolarity principle must be dismissed as self-refuting: for if it were true, it could not be stated. Wittgenstein, however, would argue from the other end: 'The bipolarity principle is true. Hence it cannot be stated. Hence there are truths that cannot be stated.' That is to say, once you have accepted the bipolarity principle, the existence of truths that cannot be stated seems, on the contrary, an unavoidable consequence. Let us try then to assess the bipolarity principle on independent grounds, and consider whether we might not disagree with 6.54. As noted above, that would provide an obvious alternative to the Nonsense Interpretation.

Wittgenstein himself acknowledges that a sentence that has no 'sense', according to the picture theory (*TLP* 4.031), can still have a legitimate use. Tautologies and mathematical equations are cases in point. They are not dismissed as nonsense; but even the somewhat less opprobrious label 'senseless' applied to tautologies is still inappropriate.[50] The original German word *sinnlos* means 'pointless', 'futile' – which (as Wittgenstein grants) neither tautologies nor equations are. It is obvious that tautologies can be used to justify the transition from one empirical statement (e.g. 'p⊃q. p') to another ('q') (*TLP* 6.1221); and the same is true of equations (*TLP* 6.211). Thus the equation '$7 \times 5 = 35$'

---

[50] It is not quite clear whether equations are to be regarded as senseless or as nonsensical. They are called 'pseudo-propositions' (*Scheinsätze*), a term that elsewhere is applied to instances of nonsense (*TLP* 4.1272, 5.534); and as the *Tractatus* does not acknowledge any meaningful identity statements, equations could not be seen, like tautologies, as limiting

justifies the move from 'I have seven bags of five apples' to 'I have 35 apples'. But once it has been granted that lack of 'sense' (as defined by the picture theory) does not rule out linguistic legitimacy, the case against what the *Tractatus* dismisses as 'nonsense' begins to look dubious. Other types of non-contingent propositions may also have a perfectly respectable use. Consider:

N1   Magenta is a colour.
N2   Black is darker than white.
N3   'Socrates is identical' is nonsense.
N4   Suicide is wrong.

As Wittgenstein himself came to realize in later years, the first two can be used as partial explanations of a word's meaning, as 'grammatical propositions' (Waismann 1965 ch. 3; *PI* §251; *BB* 30d): With (N1) one explains that 'magenta' is a colour word and not, say, the proper name of a person. (N2) might be uttered to teach a child the use of the word 'darker'. It may also function like a tautology in licensing the transition from one empirical sentence (e.g., 'This wall is black, while the other one is white') to another one ('This wall is darker than the other one'). As far as empirical (non-linguistic) matters are concerned, such analytic statements are of course uninformative, vacuous, but they do carry some information about the correct use of our language. And so does (N3), which can be used to point out that the word 'identical' has no meaning as a one-place predicate in English (*TLP* 5.4733). (N4) of course is not about language, but it goes without saying that such a sentence has an understandable use in moral discourse: to disapprove of, and discourage, suicide.

Necessary *truths* (tautologies, equations, analytic statements) have their uses; and anyway, admitting them to be true is hardly compatible with dismissing them as nonsense. But the opposite flouting of the bipolarity principle, necessary *falsehood*, is a different matter. Necessary falsehoods are (or appear to be) necessarily false because they contain an inconsistency: they implicitly contradict themselves. And self-contradiction – saying and denying something at the same time – is a paradigm of not making sense. Non-literal figures of speech apart, we have no use for obviously inconsistent statements. It is a little different with *latent* inconsistencies. We would be puzzled if someone seriously asserted:

---

cases of meaningful propositions. On the other hand, equations are like tautologies in showing the logic of the world (*TLP* 6.22), and the symbolism of arithmetic seems to be accepted as respectable (*TLP* 4.4611).

(N5) $2 + 2 = 5$.

Such an assertion would betoken some misunderstanding, for once you fully understand the way the symbols '2', '5', '+' and '=' are used, you *ipso facto* know that 2 + 2 equals 4, not 5. Not so with:

(N6) $735 \times 217 = 159{,}395$.

Even a competent mathematician needs to calculate, in a number of steps, whether (N6) is correct or not, and could easily on occasion make a mistake in the process. Hence it is perfectly understandable for someone to ask whether (N6) is true, or even to assert that it is (though one may say that in that case one has not fully understood its implications; cf. *TLP* 6.232 and 6.2322). So, latent inconsistencies are not nonsense in quite the same way as patent ones. Still, it is reasonable to maintain that ultimately they do not make sense, and hence that, in any case, the negation of a necessary truth should not strictly be regarded as a falsehood, but as nonsense. Thus to the extent that the *a priori* accounts of logic, language, the world or solipsism in the *Tractatus* contain mistakes, considerable parts of the book may after all (like most other philosophical works) be dismissed as nonsense. Yet that verdict would clearly be contrary to the author's intentions at the time, when he regarded the truth of his thoughts as 'unassailable and definite' (*TLP*, Preface).

In conclusion, Wittgenstein intended the *Tractatus* propositions to be 'nonsense' on the grounds that they were to be necessarily true. As this amounts to a misuse of the word 'nonsense', we should not agree with his verdict, nor accept the bipolarity principle underlying it. The currently fashionable Nonsense Interpretation – that is, the view that Wittgenstein intended his book to contain nonsense in a more proper sense of the word: inconsistencies – must be dismissed as itself inconsistent and exegetically fanciful.

3
Schoolmaster, Architect and Professor of Philosophy

On 25 August 1919 Wittgenstein was back in Vienna, and soon began writing letters to find a publisher for his book. During those first few years after the war he was, once more, intensely unhappy: 'I've been extremely wretched these days,' he wrote to his friend Engelmann. 'I have continually thought of taking my own life, and even now the idea still haunts me. *I have sunk to the lowest point*' (E 33; cf. 29, 41). There were a number of reasons for his depression. The general mood, of course, was gloomy. Austria lay in ruins, and with the collapse of the Empire, Wittgenstein lost a good deal of his cultural identity. But more preoccupying for him were presumably the consequences of having completed his masterpiece. As announced in the Preface, he was convinced that he had solved the problems of philosophy and thus finished with the subject. There was for him nothing more to be done in philosophy. The rest was to be silence. So he had lost his vocation and aim in life, and was plunged back into the miserable state of disorientation from which Russell's encouragement in 1912 had rescued him. Moreover, nobody seemed prepared to publish his book, and even the leading experts in the field were unable to appreciate it fully. Even after numerous additional explanations, Russell seemed to misunderstand many crucial points, and Frege just couldn't make head or tail of it. On top of those external grounds for discontent, he was, as so often, dissatisfied with his own moral character. It was probably the very fact that he was dejected by those external circumstances that made him despise himself and become even more depressed. After all, why should he be so unhappy about the unfavourable reception of his work: wasn't that just his deplorable vanity? Wasn't this unhappiness again a sure sign of a bad life (cf. *NB*, 30 July 16)?

On his return to Vienna, Wittgenstein was still a millionaire, but within the next month he committed, as the notary put it, 'financial suicide' (Rhees 1984, 215), by giving all his money to his surviving brother and his sisters. He had decided to earn his living as a primary schoolteacher. After a year's teacher training course in Vienna, he taught from September 1920 until April 1926 in elementary schools in the small villages of Trattenbach, Haßbach, Puchberg and Otterthal, in Lower Austria. He was an uncommonly dedicated teacher, but – not surprisingly – extremely demanding, and he would perhaps too easily lose his temper. In 1926 one of his outbursts led to a formal inquiry. Although acquitted of the suspicion of misconduct, yet frustrated by the growing animosity of his pupils' parents, Wittgenstein resigned. He then worked for five months as an assistant gardener in a monastery in Hütteldorf, until eventually another challenge appeared on the horizon. His sister Margaret, married to the American Jerome Stonborough, decided to have a house built for her in Vienna. Originally the commission had been given to Wittgenstein's friend Paul Engelmann, a former student of Adolf Loos; –

> Then Ludwig arrived on the scene, became interested in his intense way in the models and plans, began to modify them, and became more and more obsessed with the project until eventually he took it over completely. Engelmann had to give way to the much stronger personality, and the house was then built under Ludwig's supervision and following Ludwig's modified version of the plans down to the last detail. Ludwig designed every window and door, every window-lock and radiator, with as much care and attention to detail as if they were precision instruments, and on a most elegant scale. And then, with his uncompromising energy, he ensured that everything was carried out with the same meticulous care. I can still hear the locksmith asking him, in connection with a keyhole, 'Tell me, Herr Ingenieur, does a millimetre here or there really matter so much to you?' Even before he had finished speaking, Ludwig replied with such a loud, forceful 'Yes!' that the man almost jumped with fright. (Hermine Wittgenstein 1949, 6f)

And he meant it: when the house was practically finished, and it was almost time to start cleaning up, he had the ceiling of one large room, which was about four metres high, raised by three centimetres in order to get the proportions exactly right (ibid., 8). The house, completed in autumn 1928, is even more austere than anything built by Loos: an asymmetric arrangement of cubic masses in bare greyish-white plaster, without any ornamentation.[1] Hermine Wittgenstein described it as 'logic become house (*hausgewordene Logik*)'.

Wittgenstein had left philosophy alone in 1918, but philosophy would not leave him alone. In 1923, and again in 1924, the young Cambridge philosopher of mathematics Frank Ramsey had sought him out

---

[1] For a detailed description see Wijdeveld 1993.

in the village of Puchberg and made him explain passages of the *Tractatus* to him (of which Ramsey then published an insightful review in *Mind*). Later, Moritz Schlick, Friedrich Waismann and other members of the Vienna Circle, who greatly admired the *Tractatus*, got in contact with its author. In March 1928 he was persuaded to attend a lecture by the Dutch mathematician L. E. J. Brouwer; and later that year, when his architectural work was finished, he felt able to do some more work in philosophy. In January 1929 he was back in Cambridge.

He registered as a research student at Trinity College and, a little later, submitted the *Tractatus* as a Ph.D. thesis, mainly in order to enhance his chances of receiving a grant. The examiners at his viva were G. E. Moore and Russell. After some discussion of the *Tractatus* conception of philosophy, it was Wittgenstein who unexpectedly ended the proceedings by getting up, slapping each of his examiners on the shoulder and exclaiming: 'Don't worry, I know you'll *never* understand it' (Clark 1975, 438). He duly received both his degree and a research grant of £100 from Trinity College, and later, in December 1930, he was made a Research Fellow of the college for five years.

His thoughts in 1929 were to a large extent concerned with the representation of visual space, which naturally involved considerations of colour (MS 105). He returned to the colour exclusion problem and found his earlier treatment of it unsatisfactory. The *Tractatus* position was that as

(R)   Point a is red at time t

and

(B)   Point a is blue at time t

are mutually exclusive, they cannot be elementary propositions. He had hoped that with the help of physics it would be possible to provide a further analysis of colour statements so that such incompatibilities would prove to involve contradictions, of the form 'p.~p', the only form of incompatibility the *Tractatus* allowed (*TLP* 6.3751; cf. sect. 2.3 above). He now convinced himself that this was impossible and retracted a central claim of his atomism: namely, that elementary propositions cannot exclude one another (*RLF* 33). Some elementary propositions, like (R) and (B), cannot meaningfully be asserted together. The conjunction '[R].[B]' cannot be shown to be a contradiction; it must be excluded as nonsense by rules of syntax. The rules of syntax that determine which elementary propositions are compatible and which are not cannot be stated *a priori*, but await the ultimate analysis of physical phenomena (*RLF* 35). This was the position that Wittgenstein expounded in a paper written for the Joint Session of the Mind Association and the

Aristotelian Society in July 1929: 'Some Remarks on Logical Form'. But the paper was disowned even before the conference (at which he gave a talk on infinity in mathematics instead). He was beginning to realize that his earlier position might require not just some technical patch-ups, but a thorough revision.

Such a thorough revision of his thinking was helped by regular discussions with Frank Ramsey, and even more by the refreshingly radical comments he received in conversations with the Italian economist Piero Sraffa. One day when Wittgenstein was defending the picture theory of the *Tractatus*, and in particular the view that a proposition must have the same logical form as the reality it describes, Sraffa made a Neapolitan gesture of contempt: brushing the underneath of his chin with an outward sweep of the finger-tips, and asked: 'What is the logical form of *that*?' This, Wittgenstein later told a student, 'broke the hold on him of the conception that a proposition must literally be a "picture" of the reality it describes' (Malcolm 1984, 58). Sraffa's comments reminded him of what he had neglected in the *Tractatus*: the way in which language is embedded in our lives and, far from just presenting a picture of the world, has a multiplicity of uses (cf. *PI* §§23, 108).

Following his return to Cambridge, Wittgenstein worked on what was to become a new book. Its final version was composed in 1945/6 and published in 1953, two years after Wittgenstein's death, as *Philosophische Untersuchungen* (*Philosophical Investigations*) Part I. Since then a number of earlier drafts, documenting the stages through which his philosophy developed have also been published. They are:

Philosophical Remarks (TS 209)	1929/30
The Big Typescript (TS 213)	1933
Philosophical Grammar	1933/4
The Blue Book	1933/4
The Brown Book	1934/5
Eine philosophische Betrachtung	1936
Urfassung (MS 142)	1936/7
Early Version (TSS 225, 220, 221)	1936–9
Revised Early Version (TS 239, *RFM* I)	1942/3
Intermediate Version	1944/5

The compilation of the typescript *Philosophical Remarks* was largely due to the need to submit some work with the application for a Research Fellowship. Like all his writings, with the exception of some dictations to students, it is in German. It contains many of his earlier views in unstable combination with new ideas, among them the claim that the meaning of a proposition is the method by which it can be verified (*PR* 200). There are also discussions of intention and expectation; the geometry of visual space; colours; generality and infinity in mathematics;

and the nature of a mathematical proof. Although the philosophy of mathematics is absent from the final version of *Philosophical Investigations* (and will not be discussed in this book), it takes up considerable space in earlier typescripts, notably in the *Revised Early Version*, parts of which have been published under the title *Remarks on the Foundations of Mathematics* (Part I). For about seven years, from 1937 to 1944, questions in the philosophy of mathematics were Wittgenstein's main concern, and it seems that he was planning to publish the results of that work in a second volume of *Philosophical Investigations* (von Wright 1979, 156f).

By 1933 Wittgenstein's thinking had undergone a dramatic change. The so-called *Big Typescript* presents a markedly new approach to philosophy. It is easily recognizable as an early version of the philosophy of the *Investigations*; indeed, a considerable number of remarks from the *Big Typescript* have found their way into the *Investigations*. It is, however, more systematic and conventional in its form than later typescripts, consisting of chapters and sections, with chapter and section headings and an analytic table of contents. Soon after the completion of the *Big Typescript*, Wittgenstein started revising it. This, unfinished revision, together with parts of the original typescript, has been published under the title *Philosophical Grammar*.

Another systematic account of Wittgenstein's views at about this time is due to his collaboration with Friedrich Waismann of the Vienna Circle. From 1928 to 1934 they had regular meetings (Wittgenstein spent most of the summer vacations in Vienna), and it was agreed that on the basis of dictations, discussion notes and Wittgenstein's current typescripts, Waismann was to produce a systematic presentation of Wittgenstein's philosophy. By 1935, however, Wittgenstein seems to have become dissatisfied with the project, and their collaboration came to an end. Waismann finished the book anyway, and eventually it was published under his name alone, in an English translation entitled *The Principles of Linguistic Philosophy* (1965).

The Blue Book Wittgenstein dictated in English to his students. As the text is not broken up into short and condensed remarks, as nearly all Wittgenstein's writings are, and the style is like that of a lecture, it is quite suitable as an introduction to Wittgenstein's later philosophy. *The Brown Book* was dictated in the following year. Subsequently Wittgenstein started to work on a revised version of it in German, *Eine philosophische Betrachtung*, but this was left unfinished. The next attempt was a manuscript begun in 1936, the so-called *Urfassung*, which is the first version of what we now know as the *Philosophical Investigations*, containing the first 188 sections of that book. Together with the subsequent stages of revision and extension leading to the final version, it has recently been published as part of a critical edition of the *Philosophical Investigations*. –

From January 1930 until his retirement in 1947 Wittgenstein gave lectures, or seminars, in Cambridge, usually in his own sparsely furnished and unornamented room.

> When you entered his room for a lecture you found some fifteen or twenty wooden chairs and one deck chair facing the fireplace, before which stood a black iron anthracite stove. . . . Wittgenstein stood waiting, occasionally glancing at a watch which he pulled out of his breast pocket. A short, slightly built man in grey trousers, open-necked shirt and suede golfing jacket. His face was ruddy and very deeply lined . . . (Gasking and Jackson 1951, 50)
>
> . . . with curly hair, extremely piercing and deep-set blue eyes and fine features. He spoke very quickly and had incorporated into his vocabulary a good deal of rather schoolboyish English slang. He had a most engaging smile. (Britton 1955, 57)
>
> It is hardly correct to speak of these meetings as 'lectures', although this is what Wittgenstein called them. For one thing, he was carrying on original research in these meetings. He was thinking about certain problems in a way that he could have done had he been alone. For another thing, the meetings were largely conversation. Wittgenstein commonly directed questions at various people present and reacted to their replies. Often the meeting consisted mainly of dialogue. Sometimes, however, when he was trying to draw a thought out of himself, he would prohibit, with a peremptory motion of the hand, any questions or remarks. There were frequent and prolonged periods of silence, with only an occasional mutter from Wittgenstein, and the stillest attention from the others. (Malcolm 1984, 25)
>
> At first one didn't see where all the talk was leading to. One didn't see, or saw only very vaguely, the point of the numerous examples. And then, sometimes, one did, suddenly. All at once, sometimes, the solution to one's problem became clear and everything fell into place. . . . The solution, once seen, seemed so simple and obvious, such an inevitable and simple key to unlock so many doors so long battered against in vain. One wondered how one could possibly fail to see it. But if one tried to explain it to someone else who had not seen it one couldn't get it across without going through the whole long, long story. (Gasking and Jackson 1951, 52)

After his classes, Wittgenstein would be utterly exhausted and dissatisfied with himself, and would feel the need to clear his mind by going to the cinema to watch an American film. As another light relief from the intensity and seriousness of his character, he developed a great fondness of detective magazines. And he also liked to have some non-intellectual friend with whom he could relax by talking a lot of nonsense. In Vienna that need was met by his sister Helene, in England by Gilbert Pattison, a man with whom he had struck up an acquaintance on a train journey. Wittgenstein enjoyed sending silly picture postcards to Pattison, and in his letters often inserted absurd observations: for example, 'Somehow or other one instinctively feels that Two Steeples No. 83 Quality Sock is a real man's sock. It's a sock of taste – dressy, fashionable, comfortable' (Monk 1990, 266f).

Wittgenstein's attitude towards philosophy and philosophy books was as unconventional as his 'lectures'. For an academic he had read extremely little in the subject. He even warned his students against reading philosophical books. If they took a book seriously, he would say, it ought to puzzle them so much that they would throw it across the room and think about the problem for themselves (Britton 1955, 60, 58). Far from trying to interest people in the subject and to persuade the undecided that it was worthwhile, he tried to dissuade them from coming to his classes if he was not convinced of their seriousness (Mays 1967, 80). And those of his students who intended to pursue philosophy as a profession he tried seriously to talk out of it, suggesting rather some honest manual work (Malcolm 1984, 28). He did not think that the study of philosophy should be encouraged. 'I don't recommend it,' he once said. 'It's for people who cannot leave it alone' (Bouwsma 1986, 68).

He himself tried, again, to leave it alone when his five-year Fellowship at Trinity College was going to expire. In September 1935 he travelled to the Soviet Union with a view to finding some position as a manual worker – but all he was offered there were chairs in philosophy. He also considered training as a psychiatrist, but in the end his fascination with philosophy proved stronger. After his Fellowship ended, he spent some one and a half years living in his hut in Norway. In 1938 Austria was annexed by Nazi Germany. Wittgenstein sought some further employment at Trinity College and applied for British citizenship, which he received in April 1939. He also applied for the Cambridge professorship of philosophy, from which G. E. Moore was due to retire by the end of the academic year, and was duly elected. C. D. Broad, a Cambridge philosopher known to dislike Wittgenstein, felt compelled to say: 'To refuse the chair to Wittgenstein would be like refusing Einstein a chair of physics' (Drury 1984, 141f).

When the Nazis took over Austria, two of Wittgenstein's sisters, Hermine and Helene, were still in Vienna and unwilling to emigrate. But with three Jewish grandparents they would be classified as Jews and be in great danger. Their younger sister, Margaret Stonborough, living in Switzerland at the time, suggested that they offer to the authorities in Berlin a considerable part of their foreign assets in exchange for a reclassification of their racial status. In June and July 1939 Wittgenstein travelled, on a British passport, to Vienna, Berlin and New York, and succeeded in negotiating such a solution. Their paternal grandfather Hermann Christian Wittgenstein, of whose origin no documents seemed to exist, was declared 'Aryan', so that Hermine and Helene could be classified as 'of mixed descent'. After that they were able to survive the Third Reich fairly comfortably.

In 1941 Wittgenstein began to limit his teaching to weekends in order to have time to contribute to the war effort. He became a dispensary porter at Guy's Hospital in London, delivering medicines to the wards – and, apparently, advising patients not to take them. Later he worked there as a pharmacy technician and acquired a reputation for the high quality of the ointments he prepared. He became acquainted with a young doctor carrying out research on the condition of wound shock, took an active interest in that work, and was soon offered a post as laboratory assistant with that research unit. When in April 1943 the unit was transferred to Newcastle, Wittgenstein accompanied them. For a while he gave up his room in Trinity College and stopped all teaching, until autumn 1944, when the wound shock research unit moved to the Italian front, and Wittgenstein returned to Cambridge. He continued as a professor for three more years; then, in 1947, he resigned from 'the absurd job of a prof. of philosophy', which he felt was 'a kind of living death' (LM 98). He wanted to devote all his remaining strength to his philosophical writing.

4
Philosophical Investigations

4.1 Only an Album

Wittgenstein's masterpiece, the *Philosophical Investigations*, is not as artificially compressed as his first book; nor does it contain any formal logic or technical terminology. It is written in beautifully natural and transparent German prose. None the less it is a very difficult book, and egregious misinterpretations abound. The difficulties are owing both to its form and its contents.

Form The book consists of 693 numbered sections,[1] varying in length from a single sentence to one or two pages. The style tends to be somewhat aphoristic. The statements, although not as cryptically short as the propositions of the *Tractatus*, are often laconic; explanations and reasons are given, but rarely elaborated in great detail; indeed, often they are only hinted at or suggested by a rhetorical question. Moreover, the links between sections tend to be rather loose. Sometimes an argument is obviously continued from one section to the next; but

---

[1] Additionally, in the published edition there is a 'Part II' (MS 144) consisting of material that was written later, between 1946 and 1949, and which according to the editors, Elizabeth Anscombe and Rush Rhees, Wittgenstein had intended to be worked into (what they called 'Part I' of) the *Investigations* (*PI* p. vi). If indeed that was at one point his intention, he never carried it out. 'Part I' has remained the final version of his book. Whether and in what way he would have used the material of 'Part II' if he had continued working on his book, we do not know. At any rate, there is no reason to believe that he would have wanted it to be published in this form, as Part II (cf. von Wright 1979, 159f). I shall therefore limit my discussion to what the editors have called, somewhat misleadingly, 'Part I' of the book.

frequently the connection is less clear. The following section may just make a related point, or even move on to quite a different question. Where the same topic is dealt with in a longer sequence of sections, there is rarely a straightforward progression of the argument. Rather, 'The same or almost the same points [are] always being approached afresh from different directions, and new sketches made' (*PI* p. vii). A position that is effectively undermined by an objection in one section may come up again a little later only to be attacked afresh from a different angle. It is usually possible to give a coherent and plausible reconstruction of the arguments in their order of appearance; but then it is equally possible, and sometimes easier and clearer, to present them in a different order, or to join together related points that Wittgenstein placed some 200 sections apart. In short, not too much should be made of the exact order in which the remarks are presented. As Wittgenstein said in the Preface, he had once hoped to present his thoughts in a 'natural and unbroken' progression, but he had abandoned that ambition as unfeasible. Instead, a 'wide field of thought' is traversed 'crisscross in every direction', in a fairly arbitrary order, and the book is 'really only an album'.

The album-like nature of the *Investigations* is also apparent in the way it was composed. Almost all of its sections originated in a somewhat different context. Wittgenstein would write down such remarks in small notebooks, then copy the best ones, with slight modifications, into large manuscript volumes, from which again a selection would be culled and typed up. Then the typescript would be cut up and the best remarks pasted in a new order. This procedure, consisting of selection, possibly some slight stylistic modification, and rearrangement, might yet be repeated a number of times. It is easy to see how such a method is likely to lead to a certain terseness. Often the original context that Wittgenstein preferred to leave out would have provided some further elucidations and made the passage much easier to understand. Again, it is not surprising that the link between two sequential remarks may appear somewhat unclear or less than compelling if originally they were written in different contexts, perhaps in different decades, and have not even been rephrased so as to fit each other.[2]

Another distinctive feature of the *Investigations* is its frequent use of dialogue. Positions to be discussed, questions, objections and replies are presented as if by a different speaker, that is sometimes indicated by inverted commas (e.g., *PI* §347a), but not always (e.g., *PI* §201, first sentence). Thus one must be careful not to attribute to Wittgenstein a position he merely puts forward for criticism; especially as his critical

---

[2] See, e.g., the incoherence of §246 (from MS 180a, 22–4) and §247 (from MS 128, 16).

replies are not always very explicit. A lot of points are made by questions to which the reader is left to find the answer; and they are not always straightforwardly rhetorical questions (e.g., PI §394).

Contents Wittgenstein's later philosophy is by its very nature reactive: a critical response to philosophical misunderstandings. This can produce difficulties for readers in two ways. First, the target of Wittgenstein's criticisms may not always be sufficiently clear. For about the first 100 sections of the book the target is clear enough, thanks partly to the way a certain view of language drawn from St Augustine is explicitly set up for criticism in §1, and partly to an instructive passage in the Preface:

> Four years ago I had occasion to re-read my first book (the *Tractatus Logico-Philosophicus*) and to explain its ideas to someone. It suddenly seemed to me that I should publish those old thoughts and the new ones together: that the latter could be seen in the right light only by contrast with and against the background of my old way of thinking.
> For since beginning to occupy myself with philosophy again, sixteen years ago, I have been forced to recognize grave mistakes in what I wrote in that first book. (*PI* p. viii)

So we should expect an implicit criticism of the *Tractatus* view, especially of language; and that is indeed what we get in roughly §§1–137: not so much of its technical details, but of its general assumptions, which in some form have been shared by a great many thinkers, including St Augustine. Towards the end of those criticisms of the author's earlier views on language are a number of remarks on the nature of philosophy (*PI* §§89–133). The rest of the book is largely devoted to issues that played no, or only a marginal, role in the *Tractatus*, such as understanding, sensations, thinking and intention. There, in some instances, the identification of the target of Wittgenstein's criticisms may pose a real difficulty to the reader.

A second hindrance to understanding the *Investigations* is this: many readers' expectations of finding in a philosophical book some substantial doctrines or theories are so strong that they are virtually self-fulfilling. Such readers are likely to twist and bend Wittgenstein's philosophy to make it fit into more conventional academic patterns. Commonsense observations are spiced up and 'translated' into something like a new philosophical theory, something that doesn't sound at all commonsensical, preferably under the label of some '-ism'. That this is the exact opposite of what Wittgenstein intended becomes clear in the sections on the nature of philosophy (*PI* §§89–133). Philosophy according to the *Investigations* is entirely negative: destructive (*PI* §118). It treats philosophical problems like diseases of the understanding (*PI* §255).

Philosophical doctrines, for Wittgenstein, are invariably the result of conceptual confusion. So his book does not offer any new doctrines to replace the *Tractatus* ones. The only position it adopts is that of common sense (see sect. 4.3 below).

Of course an author cannot be held responsible for misinterpretations that are due to people's prejudices, but the difficulties mentioned earlier could have been avoided. One may well wonder why Wittgenstein did not make matters easier for his readers.

For one thing, much as he would have liked to produce a clearly structured treatise, he found himself unable to do so. He once noted that he was able to *teach* philosophy, but not to write a philosophical book (MS 118, 172). The best he could write were 'philosophical remarks'; his 'thoughts soon went lame' if he 'tried to force them on in any single direction against their natural inclination' (*PI* p. vii). His natural inclination was to 'jump about all round a topic' (*CV* 33); to keep changing his position: 'not to stand too long on one leg, so as not to go stiff' (*CV* 32). Obviously, this natural inclination to jump around is still manifest in the *Investigations*, in spite of the author's attempts to control himself. It was connected with some uncertainty as to what he did and what he did not need to discuss (*CV* 74b). He accused himself of asking 'countless irrelevant questions' (*CV* 77) and of making repetitions that others might find boring (*CV* 3); and in a draft of a preface to the *Investigations*, from 1948, he described the movements of his remarks thus:

> Only every so often does one of the sentences I am writing here make a step forward; the rest are like the snipping of the barber's scissors, which he has to keep in motion so as to be able to make a cut with them at the right moment. (*CV* 76)

In a lecture in 1939, having compared philosophical problems to the difficulty of finding one's way in an unfamiliar town (cf. *PI* §123), and likening his own task to that of a guide, he adds that he is an extremely bad guide: 'apt to be led astray by little places of interest, and to dash down side streets before I have shown you the main streets' (*LFM* 44).

However, the jumping and criss-crossing is also 'connected with the very nature of the investigation' (*PI* p. vii). As noted above, Wittgenstein's philosophy is essentially the disentangling of conceptual confusions. Thus it needs to follow *someone*'s conceptual confusions and someone's inclinations to respond to objections or defend a philosophical picture through further refinements. Therefore the dialogue form is essential to it. But to the extent to which one's interlocutor's worries and responses move, sometimes abruptly, from one issue to another, one needs to follow these movements – even though they may seem confusing to others – if one is to convince one's interlocutor. And the interlocutor in the *Investigations* is not merely an invented straw man, but gives expression to what Wittgenstein himself, at some point, felt inclined to say. He once remarked that he was almost always writing conversations with himself (*CV* 88). In many instances it is views held by Wittgenstein when he wrote the *Tractatus* that are presented and responded to in the *Investigations* (e.g., *PI* §§23, 39ff, 65, 108, 114), but there are also positions he had felt attracted to more recently or objections to his latest views he felt inclined to make or, at least, to take seriously. In any case, Wittgenstein's main aim was to solve *his own* philosophical problems, to achieve clarity for himself.

Thus he would not be particularly concerned to make himself *generally* understood. He certainly hoped to be read and appreciated, but only by a small number of kindred spirits, 'a few friends spread out over the world' (*CV* 9; cf. 12f); those whose style of thinking was sufficiently akin to his own to enable them to understand what must remain obscure to others (*CV* 10d). By no means did he address himself to the community of academic philosophers, the 'philosophical journalists' (*CV* 75), those who wrote for, and enjoyed reading, as 'impotent and bankrupt' a periodical as *Mind* (LM 100; cf. 107). Anyway, Wittgenstein did not think that the study of philosophy should be encouraged. If you were not already puzzled by those problems (– trapped in a fly-bottle, as he put it metaphorically in §309), he would not have wanted to create that puzzlement in you (– to drive you into a fly-bottle). The *Philosophical Investigations* helps the reader to resolve certain problems, but it shows no concern that the reader have those problems in the first place; and if he doesn't, he's not likely to get much out of the book.

Moreover, Wittgenstein was not concerned to make himself *easily* understood. He loathed the idea of giving results to people who had not done any honest work to deserve them. He despised popular science: what he thought of as attempts to give people the impression of understanding something that they did not really understand (Drury 1984, 117). And it is easy to imagine the disgust which he would have suffered at seeing publications like *Wittgenstein in 90 Minutes*. In the Preface to the *Investigations* he announced that he should not like his writings 'to spare other people the trouble of thinking' (*PI* p. viii; cf. *CV* 88; MS 119, 64). Undoubtedly, Wittgenstein did a good job of putting his readers on their mettle.

Finally, (and perhaps most importantly) Wittgenstein believed that a philosopher should be a poet (MS 120, 145r). 'I believe I summed up my attitude towards philosophy by saying: really philosophy should only be written *as poetry*' (*CV* 28).³ This is not to be dismissed as merely a somewhat purple way of saying that philosophy should be presented in a neat and elegant form. That Wittgenstein was serious about the idea of philosophy as a kind of poetry is indicated by the solemn way the remark is prefaced. What exactly does it mean? To begin with, Wittgenstein was obviously concerned about the right flow of language, its quasi-musical aspects. The way he constantly revised his remarks shows that he came as close as probably no other philosopher to enacting Nietzsche's maxim: that one should work on a page of prose as scrupulously and painstakingly as a sculptor works on a statue (1879, §95).⁴ One poetic ideal that appealed strongly to Wittgenstein was *naturalness*, the avoidance of all mannerisms, and false pathos (cf. *CV* 10). On that account he admired the unpretentious prose of Keller, Hebel and Tolstoy, but disliked the preciousness of Rilke (Bouwsma 1986, 72). A mark of great poetry (of the cultural tradition that Wittgenstein appreciated) is the appearance of perfect ease and naturalness in spite of all constraints imposed by form (metre and rhyme). Something analogous, it seems to me, is aimed at and often achieved in the *Philosophical Investigations*: what is difficult and highly complicated is to appear light and effortless.⁵ The constraints that Wittgenstein had to struggle with, while trying to give the impression of a natural succession of seemingly simple observations, were of course not metre and rhyme, but his task of dissolving recalcitrant philosophical problems and tracing their interconnections. But just as the choice of words in a poem should not *appear* to be dictated by metre and rhyme (although largely it is), it seems that Wittgenstein preferred to give the impression that one remark casually led on to the next, while their real purpose – the way they relate to a network of philosophical confusions – was left largely unexplained. 'If this book is written as it should be written,' he once remarked, 'then everything I say must be easily understandable, indeed, trivial, but it should be difficult to understand *why* I say it' (MS 117, 140f). Wittgenstein preferred not to push the point of his remarks under the reader's nose. The light touch he aimed at in his writing precluded him from giving pedantic circumstantial explanations of all his respective targets and their interconnections.

---

[3] Cf. MS 115, 30; MS 146, 32 and 50; MS 133, 13r.

[4] In MS 120, 145r, Wittgenstein compared his aesthetic attitude towards philosophy to Nietzsche's.

[5] In an unintentional tribute to Wittgenstein's success in making his writing appear light and effortless, Russell notoriously commented that in the *Investigations* Wittgenstein seemed to have 'grown tired of serious thinking' (Russell 1959, 216f).

Not only is the point of Wittgenstein's remarks often left unexplained, many of the remarks themselves have the terseness and density that is typical of poetry, and leave so much to say and write to readers and scholars. Often a single paragraph gives the outlines of a thought weighty enough to be spelled out at the length of a substantial journal article (e.g., *PI* §302). It is noteworthy that although Wittgenstein constantly polished and reshuffled his remarks, he never tried to fuse them together by inserting smooth transitions from one to the next. He insisted on emphatic pauses between his remarks, which of course is a formal device closely related to the division of a long poetic text into stanzas.

Finally, Wittgenstein had a poet's taste for striking figures of speech. 'I always take joy in my own good similes' (*D* 144), he once wrote in his diary. Sometimes the same point is made by a whole series of similes: looking up a table in the imagination (*PI* §265), buying several copies of today's paper (*PI* §265), different ways of looking at a clock to determine the time (*PI* §266), testing the stability of a bridge in the imagination (*PI* §267). Are all of them necessary to get the point across, or is it not also artistic enjoyment that accounts for such variations on the same theme?

The peculiarities of Wittgenstein's style that can be annoying from an academic philosopher's point of view are largely those that make his book aesthetically so attractive and that add to Wittgenstein scholarship some of the enjoyment of the interpretation of poetry.

Here is an overview of the topics discussed in the *Philosophical Investigations* (Part I):

Critique of the *Tractatus* view of language	§§1–108, 134–7
The nature of philosophy	§§108–33
Understanding	§§138–242
Sensations	§§243–315
Thinking	§§316–62
Imagining	§§363–97
Personal experience	§§398–411
Consciousness	§§412–27
Intentionality	§§428–65
Induction	§§466–90
Language, grammar, meaning, understanding, negation	§§491–570
Expectation, belief, hope, intention	§§571–94
Feeling	§§595–610
Willing	§§611–32
Remembered intention	§§633–93.

4.2 The Dissolution of Logical Atomism

In 1929 Wittgenstein gave up the *Tractatus* postulate that elementary propositions must be logically independent; since statements which attribute a degree to a quality cannot be further analysed and yet logically exclude other such statements (*RLF* 33; *PR* §76). What is dark blue cannot be light blue, and what is two inches long is not three inches long. At the time this seemed to be a relatively small alteration to the system of logical atomism, although it spoilt the tidiness of the *Tractatus* logic: admitting logical relations that could not be expressed by truth-functions. However, over the next decade Wittgenstein reconsidered the very foundations of logical atomism and found them all unsustainable, at least in their original form and function. In section 2.2 above I identified four basic ideas underlying the *Tractatus* edifice:

Referentialism
Determinacy of sense
Logical analysis
Bipolarity

Two further presuppositions, less explicit in the book, but likewise informing its philosophy and later to be criticized, I shall explicate shortly. They can be labelled:

Essentialism
Meaning through meaning.

Under these six headings I shall now present Wittgenstein's criticisms of logical atomism and its roots.

(a) Referentialism

The *Investigations* opens with a passage from St Augustine's autobiography which describes a child's language learning as essentially a correlation of words and objects. To name an object is assumed to be the function of a word. From this view of language, Wittgenstein suggests, it is but a short step to the philosophical position that 'every word has a meaning. . . . It is the object for which the word stands' (*PI* §1), which comes close to his earlier claim that 'a name means an object. The object is its meaning' (*TLP* 3.203); except that *Tractatus* names are not the words of ordinary language, but the signs that a complete analysis of ordinary language will bring to light (beside logical connectives). This complication, through the concept of analysis, will be considered in section (c).

Against Augustine's picture Wittgenstein first suggests that it may not be equally suitable for all kinds of words. Then he presents this little episode:

> 1. ... Now think of the following use of language: I send someone shopping. I give him a slip marked "five red apples". He takes the slip to the shopkeeper, who opens the drawer marked "apples"; then he looks up the word "red" in a table and finds a colour sample opposite it; then he says the series of cardinal numbers – I assume that he knows them by heart – up to the word "five" and for each number he takes an apple of the same colour as the sample out of the drawer. – It is in this and similar ways that one operates with words.

The crucial point is: one *operates* with words (cf. *PI* §449). We use sentences as instruments to achieve various purposes (*PI* §421): for example, to buy some apples. This is a trivial fact, yet easily neglected in philosophy. Language is not just words and sentences in isolation, but their utterances in particular circumstances where they fulfil particular functions. Language is essentially a form of human *behaviour*. Emphasis of the all-important practical side of language – largely ignored in the *Tractatus* – is the most prominent leitmotiv in the *Investigations*. Wittgenstein repeatedly attempts to disperse the fog of philosophical confusion by presenting 'the phenomena of language in primitive kinds of application in which one can command a clear view of the aim and functioning of the words' (*PI* §5; cf. §122; *BB* 17). Such scenarios of simple linguistic transactions are called *language-games* (*PI* §21), as are verbal exercises used in teaching language (*PI* §7) and also any areas or aspects of language use one may wish to focus on: for instance, the 'language-game' of giving and obeying orders (*PI* §23). This metaphorical use of the word 'game' is meant to indicate not only that language is an activity, something one takes part in, but also that, like a game, it is governed by conventional rules. There are licit and illicit applications of words, as there are licit and illicit moves in chess. (There is, of course, no implication here that like a game language is merely an unimportant leisure pursuit.)

To return to the Augustinian picture of language, Wittgenstein adds this little dialogue to the language-game of buying apples:

> 1. ... But what is the meaning of the word "five"? – No such thing was in question here, only how the word "five" is used.

The meaning asked for here is the referentialist meaning under discussion: that is, an object denoted by the word 'five'.[6] That number words stand for numbers regarded as abstract objects is indeed a widely held

---

[6] That is made clear by Wittgenstein's own translation of this passage in MS 226: 'There was no question of such an entity "meaning" here.'

view in the philosophy of mathematics (e.g., Frege 1884, 49f, 68f), and it is obviously difficult to disprove the existence of anything as elusive as an abstract object. But the point of Wittgenstein's rejoinder is that there is no need to enter into any such recondite ontological discussion here. As far as their everyday use and purpose are concerned, number words are part of the familiar technique of counting objects. What matters is that they are recited in a conventionally fixed order, and that each word of the series is correlated – not with an abstract object, but with one of the objects one wants to count; an apple in this case. That is all a competent user of number words has to know. Hence, as long as our interest in linguistic meaning is an interest in those aspects of words that contribute to the actual workings of language, any postulated abstract number objects – whether they exist or not – are entirely irrelevant to the meaning of number words.

So the view that a word stands for an object (which *is* the meaning, or which is at any rate determined by the meaning) cannot plausibly be extended to all words. Already in the *Tractatus* Wittgenstein had insisted that some words, namely logical constants, must be exempted from referentialism; but now he suggests that the class of words that stand for objects is considerably smaller than philosophers have been prone to believe. To bring out the real scope of Augustine's picture, Wittgenstein presents another language-game:

> 2. . . . Let us imagine a language for which the description given by Augustine is right. The language is meant to serve for communication between a builder A and an assistant B. A is building with building-stones: there are blocks, pillars, slabs and beams. B has to pass the stones, and that in the order in which A needs them. For this purpose they use a language consisting of the words "block", "pillar", "slab", "beam". A calls them out; – B brings the stone which he has learnt to bring at such-and-such a call.

Every one of the four words stands for a kind of object. Setting aside worries about the distinction between *some* block and a *particular* block, in this language-game it can indeed be said that words have meaning due to their correlation with objects. But then, this builders' language is evidently a far cry from a natural language with its far richer and more sophisticated vocabulary and numerous syntactical resources. In this case an invented language-game is meant primarily to elucidate negatively. It is an object of comparison that throws into relief the points in which it differs from a natural language (*PI* §130); or indeed from another, slightly more complicated language-game containing also number words and expressions like 'this' and 'there', used in connection with a pointing gesture (*PI* §8). With number words we have dealt above. Indexicals, like 'this' or 'there', are obviously employed to pick out something; so they would appear to be quite unproblematic from a referentialist point of view. However, the way they can be said to refer to something is markedly different from the way a word like 'block' has a reference. The latter word picks out a kind of building-stone, by its meaning alone, whereas the meaning of 'this' does not determine any type of object as its reference: its reference is entirely fixed by an accompanying gesture, or a suitable context. Again, Wittgenstein does not deny that all, or most, words can be said to stand for something. It is quite correct to say that the word 'five' stands for a number, and not, say, for a building-stone; and that the word 'there' signifies a place, rather than a feeling or a person (*PI* §10). But he denies that to understand a word, to have mastered its use, one only needs to know *what* it stands for (cf. *PI* §264). You may realize on a given occasion which object is picked out by the word 'this' without yet understanding the meaning of the word; and you may understand the use of number words without having any notion that they (might be said to) stand for abstract objects. Hence referentialism fails to identify what is important about words: what a competent speaker needs to understand, and what deserves to be called the meaning of a word.

Even at the first stage of the builders' language-game (*PI* §2), where it is indeed reasonable to say that each word stands for a kind of object and that this correlation is quite essential to the words' linguistic function, referentialism is inadequate. An understanding of the word 'slab', for instance, requires considerably more than a correlation of word and object. B has to understand that he is supposed to *bring* the object in question (cf. *PI* §27). – Here one might demur that it is only due to the paucity of the builders' language that the words need to carry the additional function of conveying an order: to bring the object signified. In a more realistic language it would be expressed by additional words forming the explicit order 'Bring me one slab!', where the word 'slab' can quite plausibly be said to have only the job of denoting a kind of object (Rundle 1990, 37f). But even with the explicit imperative sentence, mere correlation of words with objects will not do the trick. 'Bring', it may be said, stands for the action of bringing; 'me' stands for the speaker, A; 'one' stands for the number one; and 'slab' stands for a slab. Very well, but if that was all the words did – each designate an object – how could the sentence convey what the addressee was supposed to do and indeed *that* he was supposed to do it? The picture theory attempted an answer to part of this problem: To prevent a sentence from being merely a list of names, the word order must be significant too. At least in English, it is surely true that word order is significant: 'Jack loves Jill' says something different from 'Jill loves Jack'. But consider: 'Does Jack love Jill?', and 'Jack, love Jill!'. The difference in sense between this question, the order and the corresponding statement is neither that different objects are mentioned (it's all about Jack, Jill and love), nor that the objects named are in each case represented as being in a different arrangement (they are all concerned with exactly the same state of affairs, viz., Jack's loving of Jill). Hence, whichever way the difference between statement, question and order is indicated in a given language (by word order, word endings, added words or punctuation marks), it goes beyond the resources of the picture theory, which limits the function of language to *stating* 'how things stand' (*TLP* 4.5c); and quite generally, this difference cannot be accounted for in referentialist terms. The force of an order – that the addressee is supposed to act in compliance with it – is by no stretch of the imagination just another object (or a combination of objects) that might be denoted by another name (or combination of names).

The *Tractatus* ontology depended largely on the referentialist corollary that a word has no meaning if nothing corresponds to it. Against this idea Wittgenstein now first remarks that 'the word "meaning" is being used illicitly if it is used to signify the thing that "corresponds" to the word. That is to confound the meaning of a name with the *bearer* of the name' (*PI* §40). After all, a name can be used meaningfully to state that it no longer has a bearer, as in 'Paul is dead'. – This observation, admittedly, is not conclusive. The author of the *Tractatus* would have taken it to show merely that the word 'Paul' cannot be a simple name; analysis must reveal it to contain a description, which would become false after Paul's demise. However, postponing the question of whether such a conception of analysis stands up to scrutiny, it may well be wondered why one should *want* to defend referentialism so tenaciously. What speaks against the idea that words can be meaningful even if they do not stand for any object? Is it more than just a deep-rooted prejudice? To demonstrate that there is no problem in the idea of meaning without reference, Wittgenstein introduces yet another expansion of the builders' language-game. Now there are also proper names for certain tools, among them the word 'N'. But one day N is broken and can no longer be used – we may even imagine that it has been completely destroyed without any residue (to forestall the evasive recourse to analysis). A, who does not know that N no longer exists, gives the order 'N'; B shakes his head in reply (*PI* §41). No one would say that A's order made no sense. B, for one, understood it perfectly well and responded appropriately. – We can even go one step further and imagine that their language contains names that *never* stood for any real object: fictional names, uttered and responded to merely for amusement, to break the monotony of the work (*PI* §42). Again, there can be no doubt that this might be a perfectly regular and understandable use of language. There is no reason to insist that linguistic signs can function only when they stand for an object.

Still, there may be *some* words that would not be meaningful if what they stand for did not exist – colour words for example (*PI* §50). And here one may say that what a colour word like 'red' should be taken to stand for is not particular occurrences of red paint or pigments, but the colour red in the abstract. It is undeniable that any particular red objects (petals, pens or pillar boxes) could easily be destroyed, yet the same could hardly be said of the colour red in the abstract (*PI* §57). Here we have a combination of two considerations that seem to speak in favour of the existence of timeless and indestructible objects. First, even admitting that not all words fit Augustine's picture of language, some surely need something corresponding to them in order to be meaningful. And secondly, with some general terms, like colour words, it is natural to distinguish between the sort of thing in the abstract and its instantiations, and with the former any talk of destruction seems inappropriate. But both reasons are rejected by Wittgenstein.

The fact that a certain language-game requires the existence of a certain kind of object is no guarantee that such an object must exist forever. Tennis cannot be played without rackets; but that does not mean that the world could not at some point be without rackets, and hence without tennis. Suppose the colour word 'sepia' were defined by one canonical sample, the standard sepia, preserved and hermetically sealed in some university laboratory, and judgements that something was of the colour sepia were made only after laying it alongside the standard sepia (suppose that without that direct comparison we could never tell sepia apart from some other, very similar shades of brown). So our use of the word 'sepia' depends on the existence of the sample, which none the less could one day be destroyed in a conflagration (*PI* §50). Of course things are in fact somewhat different with our colour words: there are no such canonical samples involved in their use. Hence no destruction of a single physical object will make the language-game impossible. But we can imagine *all* red objects and phenomena to change colour, and subsequently the disappearance of all memories of red; then even the colour red in the abstract would have gone, and the word 'red' would have lost its meaning for us (*PI* §57).

In the *Tractatus* Wittgenstein (correctly) emphasized the difference between sense and truth. The sense of an empirical proposition has to be ascertainable independently of the question of its truth or falsity. But he went even further: he thought that the sense of a proposition should be ascertainable independently of *any* questions of truth or falsity. In particular, that a given proposition has a sense, or is meaningful, should not presuppose that another proposition is true (*TLP* 2.0211): namely, the proposition that some object mentioned in the former proposition exists. But in fact there is no good reason to take that second step. Our statements frequently rest on presuppositions: they would not be meaningful if certain things were not the case. For the statement 'The house is red' to have the sense it has, the word 'red' must have the meaning it has, which requires the (recent) existence of red things. Thus the meaning of words is based on contingent states of affairs; but there is no need to get nervous about it. After all, there *are* red things in the world, and the word 'red' *has* a meaning, whatever might have been the case, and whatever may be the case in some distant future.

(b) Determinacy of sense

Another preconceived idea behind the atomism of the *Tractatus* is the demand that the sense of a proposition be determinate (*TLP* 3.23; see sect. 2.3 above). Not only is this idea not borne out by our knowledge of natural languages; it seems flatly contradicted by it. Only in exceptional cases can one give a precise definition of a word; most concepts have no sharp boundaries. When exactly does the night end and the day begin? Where do you draw the line between a brook and a river? What height does it take for a man to be tall? As Wittgenstein was well aware even when he wrote the *Tractatus*, no exact rules have been laid down to answer such questions (*NB*, 20 and 22 June 1915). As in the case of referentialism, the author of the *Tractatus* thought that any apparent counter-evidence to his *a priori* ideas could be ignored owing to another *a priori* mainstay of his system: namely, his conception of analysis (combined with the idea that words become meaningful through mental acts of meaning, to be discussed under (f) below). If analysis could excavate what was normally invisible under the surface, then a discrepancy between this subterranean truth and superficial appearances was only to be expected. Again, postponing the scrutiny of this notion of analysis, we should ask why one should want to postulate determinacy of sense in the first place. Wittgenstein explains the attitude behind it: 'it seems clear that where there is sense there must be perfect order. – So there must be perfect order even in the vaguest sentence' (*PI* §98). And further:

> 99. The sense of a sentence – one would like to say – may, of course, leave this or that open, but the sentence must nevertheless have *a* definite sense. An indefinite sense – that would really not be a sense *at all*. – This is like: An indefinite boundary is not really a boundary at all. Here one thinks perhaps: if I say "I have locked the man up fast in the room – there is only one door left open" – then I simply haven't locked him in at all; his being locked in is a sham. One would be inclined to say here: "You haven't done anything at all." An enclosure with a hole in it is as good as *none*. – But is that true?

No. If the man in the room is unlikely to try that unlocked door (because it is very inconspicuous or looks like an airing cupboard), he may still to all intents and purposes be prevented from leaving. Inexact concepts or statements are clearly not useless. If the plumber promises to call on Monday morning, I may not be sure whether I'll have to stay in till 12 o'clock, but it is perfectly clear that he may come at 9.30 a.m. or at 10 a.m., whereas 3 p.m. does not count as morning. Again, the request 'Stay roughly here!', said with a view to finding someone again after a short errand, is somewhat vague, but normally useful enough (*PI* §88). Sauntering just a few yards to the left would clearly be in compliance with the request, taking a bus to the other end of town obviously not. Nipping into the bookshop on the other side of the street may be a borderline case (and give rise to some futile argument afterwards).

Even if an imprecise utterance is not entirely useless, is it not at any rate defective? – Not necessarily. A vague sentence is perfectly appropriate if you do not want to commit yourself, or are in no position to predict the course of events more precisely; or if you want to report a vague impression: 'I noticed that he was tall' may be true, where 'I noticed that he was six foot three' would be false, even if he was six foot three (cf. *PI* §70). (Nor would a precise interval do, say 'between six foot and six foot five'; for no such determinate measurements describe correctly what I noticed.) And even in the example above – 'Stay roughly here!' – the speaker may not in fact be guilty of sloppy language. After all, the existence of borderline cases does not matter as long as it is easy enough to avoid them, and a more precise demarcation would have been either inappropriately arbitrary or absurdly time-consuming, and therefore less advisable.

Note also that Frege's ideal of a perfectly determinate concept (that it be determined for any possible object whether or not it falls under the concept) would require sharp boundaries against an endless number of imaginable cases:

> 80. I say "There is a chair". What if I go up to it, meaning to fetch it, and it suddenly disappears from sight? – "So it wasn't a chair, but some kind of illusion". – But in a few moments we see it again and are able to touch it and so on. – "So the chair was there after all and its disappearance was some kind of illusion". – But suppose that after a time it disappears again – or seems to disappear. What are we to say now? Have you rules ready for such cases – rules saying whether one may use the word "chair" to include this kind of thing? But do we miss them when we use the word "chair"; and are we to say that we do not really attach any meaning to this word, because we are not equipped with rules for every possible application of it?

Of course not. To foresee and accommodate all *conceivable* cases, however bizarre and unlikely, would be virtually impossible and, at any rate, a waste of time: entirely irrelevant to the words' actual applications. Should we really one day be confronted with such strange and unforeseen phenomena for which our concepts are not prepared, there will still be time to refine them as necessary.

Still, it may seem that we use our vague sentences *faute de mieux*; that perfect precision, even if not actually attainable, would be ideal. – Not so. This ideal is an illusion. Where added exactness has no point or function, there is nothing ideal about it. To specify the location where your friend is supposed to meet you in millimetres is not admirable, but ridiculous. Therefore it would not be called 'inexact' *not* to do so. Use of the word 'exact' is relative to a standard that is reasonable in the circumstances. Different standards for an exact measurement of time apply in geology, particle physics and cooking, just as the speed that is called 'fast' depends on whether one is talking of a runner, a Formula One driver or a fighter aircraft. There is no *single* ideal of a good speed (or a big size). Similarly, 'no *single* ideal of exactness has been laid down' (*PI* §88).

(c) Logical analysis

For the author of the *Tractatus* it was the programme of logical analysis that could keep alive the belief that, contrary to appearances, language consisted of names of indestructible objects and that all propositions had a determinate sense. As language was thought to be a reflection of the world, the analysis of its complex expressions into simple names would correspond to the analysis of complex objects into simple particles.[7] In the *Investigations* three objections are levelled at this conception of analysis.

First, a further 'analysed' form of a sentence is not always an appropriate replacement of the original sentence. Wittgenstein considers the following example of a *Tractatus* type analysis:

> 60. When I say: "My broom is in the corner", – . . . that surely means that the stick and brush must be there, and in a particular relation to one another; . . .

Note that this is not yet Wittgenstein's own view, but a presentation of the position under discussion. This section, like may others in the *Investigations*, is a dialogue between the author and his own younger self (or some proponent of philosophical errors). The interlocutor's voice is sometimes marked by inverted commas (see, e.g., *PI* §61), but not always. – Wittgenstein's criticism is indicated a little further down:

> 60. . . . Suppose that, instead of saying "Bring me the broom", you said "Bring me the broomstick and the brush which is fitted on to it"! – Isn't the answer: "Do you want the broom? Why do you put it so oddly?" – Is he going to understand the further analysed sentence better?

---

[7] A similar conception of linguistic analysis was propounded by G. E. Moore (1903, 7f).

No, the further analysed form is odd and less easily understood than the ordinary formulation. Of course it is still easy enough to recognize it as a roundabout request to fetch the broom, as everybody knows that a broom consists of a brush and a broomstick; but imagine that the analysis was carried further, perhaps all the way down to a description of combinations of tiny particles which only a painstaking chemical analysis would disclose to be contained in the broom. Then the 'analysed form' of the request would obviously be extremely long and complicated, and completely incomprehensible to anyone whom you might like to ask for a broom. But quite apart from the problems of deciphering such an 'analysis', even with respect to the information it conveys, it is not obviously superior to the original form (*PI* §63). Although vastly more informative concerning the physical constitution of the object, it leaves out what is likely to be most important to us, and what is clearly conveyed by the word 'broom': that the object is an implement for sweeping the floor.

Secondly, Wittgenstein argues that *the idea of a complete analysis of an object is vacuous as the expression 'simple constituent parts' can mean different things in different contexts*:

> 47. ... What are the simple constituents of a chair? – The bits of wood of which it is made? Or the molecules, or the atoms? – "Simple" means: not composite. And here the point is: in what sense 'composite'? It makes no sense at all to speak absolutely of the 'simple parts of a chair'.

This, however, is unlikely to convince a logical atomist. True, in a given context things may be called 'simple' relative to a certain idea of composition, but why should one not also be able to speak of absolute simplicity, meaning that there are ultimate constituents of matter: atoms, in the original sense deriving from the Greek word 'indivisible'?

The *third* and most fundamental objection to the *Tractatus* conception of logical analysis is implicit, or alluded to, in many passages of the *Investigations*, without being clearly spelt out; for instance, when Wittgenstein remarks lightly: 'what is hidden is of no interest to us' (*PI* §126). He explained this point more fully in conversation with Moritz Schlick in 1930:

> Can only logical analysis explain what we mean by the propositions of ordinary language? Moore is inclined to think so. Are people therefore ignorant of what they mean when they say 'Today the sky is clearer than yesterday'? Do we have to wait for logical analysis here? What a hellish idea! (*WVC* 129f)

Not only G. E. Moore was inclined to this 'hellish idea'; it had been propounded in the *Tractatus*, likewise, that when we use language we do not really know what our words mean (*TLP* 4.002). Indeed, elsewhere Wittgenstein identified as one of the crucial errors in the *Tractatus* his belief that 'logical analysis must bring to light hidden things (like chemical and physical analysis)' (*BT* 101; cf. *EPB* 158). This is an error, because *linguistic meaning is conventional*, accepted among competent speakers. Our verbal sounds have no meaning unless we give them meaning. *So it is nonsense to suggest that (the details of) linguistic meaning may still be completely unknown* and awaiting discovery by logicians (*BB* 27f). One might just as well suggest that prior to scientific investigation nobody knows what the British criminal laws or the rules of football really are. A law or a rule that nobody knows about is obviously not in force. Similarly, if no one takes (uses or understands) a word to have a certain content, or convey a certain idea, then that content or idea is clearly not part of the word's actual meaning.

That disposes of the logical atomist doctrine that every microscopic detail of an object must be registered by its verbal description even if competent speakers have no idea of those details. The error was partly due to the misuse of the word 'meaning' for the object referred to (*TLP* 3.203; *PI* §40). Of course an object named has some atomic constitution, and if you call the object the 'meaning' of its name, then its unknown atomic constitution will be part of that 'meaning'. But then, the investigation of the name's 'meaning', in this sense, will be a physicist's task and nothing to be expected from *logical* analysis. The problem in such a case of a redefinition of a commonly used word arises if one does not stick consistently to the redefinition, but occasionally slips back into the way the word is commonly used. The compounding of two incompatible meanings is a recipe for philosophical confusion. In this case, the author of the *Tractatus* conflated his artificial stipulation that the meaning of a word is the object denoted with the common notion of meaning as what words convey – with the absurd result that our words seem to convey more than anybody knows.

Because a word's meaning is conventional and cannot go beyond what is known by those who are thoroughly familiar with the word's correct application, it is also a confusion to think that analysis can make our concepts more precise than in actual linguistic practice they are. If no sharp boundary between, for example, evening and night is acknowledged among competent speakers, or manifest in their application of the words, then those concepts *have* no sharp boundaries; and no logical analysis could bring such a sharp boundary to light. A sharply defined concept of evening, as lasting, say, from 6 p.m. to 10.30 p.m. sharp, would simply be a different concept from ours (*PI* §76).

(d) Bipolarity

The principle of bipolarity encapsulates an important truth about the difference between empirical and logical propositions. To that extent

Wittgenstein continued to subscribe to it. However, in the *Tractatus*, developed into the picture theory, the principle was used as a criterion of sense: only bipolar propositions were regarded as significant. Lack of bipolarity was the same as lack of sense – with the paradoxically self-refuting consequences discussed in section 2.6e. But as referentialism proved unacceptable as an account of the meanings of words, the picture theory is an equally crude and over-simplified account of the senses of sentences. In both cases the *Investigations* reminds us of the variety in real languages, ignored by many logicians, 'including the author of the *Tractatus Logico-Philosophicus*' (*PI* §23). Depiction is not the only purpose of language, and therefore all sentences need not function as pictures true or false. Wittgenstein realized that the picture analogy was far too narrow to account for linguistic sense in all its varieties. He now preferred to say that the sense of a sentence was its employment (*PI* §421). And although the vast majority of propositions must indeed be bipolar to do their job – an empirical proposition is clearly the paradigm of a meaningful statement – there is (as already argued at the end of sect. 2.6e) occasionally some perfectly reputable employment for mono-polar, or analytic propositions. They serve to express and teach grammatical norms, providing partial definitions of the meanings of our words; for example, when you explain to a child: 'Your father's sister is your aunt'. They also serve to justify the transition from one empirical statement to another one; as do mathematical propositions, whose value needs no demonstration.

(e) Essentialism

The picture theory and the claim that all propositions are truth-functions of elementary propositions were proffered in answer to the big question: what is the general form of a proposition? In the *Investigations* Wittgenstein is less concerned with the flaws of those doctrines as with the rejection of the very question behind them.

> 65. Here we come up against the great question that lies behind all these considerations. – For someone might object against me: "You take the easy way out! You talk about all sorts of language-games, but have nowhere said what the essence of a language-game, and hence of language, is: what is common to all these activities, and what makes them into language or parts of language. So you let yourself off the very part of the investigation that once gave you yourself most headache, the part about the *general form of propositions* and of language."
>
> And this is true. – Instead of producing something common to all that we call language, I am saying that these phenomena have no one thing in common which makes us use the same word for all, – but that they are *related* to one another in many different ways. And it is because of this relationship, or these relationships, that we call them all "language".

We should not assume, as the author of the *Tractatus* did, that language must have an essence; that all significant propositions must be significant in the same way (e.g., as models of how things stand). In general, Wittgenstein now sets his face against the prejudice that whenever things fall under the same concept X, they must do so in virtue of some common feature Y that serves to define X. He illustrates this with the example of the word 'game':

> 66. Consider for example the proceedings that we call "games". I mean board-games, card-games, ball-games, Olympic games, and so on. What is common to them all? – Don't say: "There *must* be something common, or they would not be called 'games'" – but *look and see* whether there is anything common to all. – For if you look at them you will not see something that is common to *all*, but similarities, relationships, and a whole series of them at that. To repeat: don't think, but look!

This slogan epitomizes the dramatic reversal that has taken place in Wittgenstein's approach to language since the *Tractatus*, where his conclusions were based on *a priori* considerations, often in conflict with obvious truths, and where his motto might have been: 'Don't look, but think!' – As a result of his observation of various games Wittgenstein claims that there is no set of defining features of a game; rather, the concept is held together by a network of 'family resemblances' (*PI* §67). We could not teach the word by giving a definition, for none has been laid down. Instead we would describe a few games and add: 'This, *and similar things* are called "games"' (*PI* §69).

But is it really impossible to give a definition of the word 'game'? In response to those passages the following definition has been suggested:

> games are rule-governed activities with an arbitrary and non-serious objective, an objective that is of little or no significance outside the game, but which we set ourselves to attain for the sake of the fun or other satisfaction that is to be derived from participation in the activity and/or attainment of the objective. (Rundle 1990, 48)

But this definition is too inclusive: it is true of a race, karate and competitive ballroom dancing, none of which would be called a 'game'. It seems also too exclusive: when children throw a ball from one to the other in a fairly regular manner, one may well call that a 'game', even though there are no rules (nothing would be sanctioned as an incorrect move), and it is doubtful whether anything can be identified as the game's objective. (It is even more obvious that such activities, without any clear objective and not governed by rules, can be called by the word discussed in Wittgenstein's original German: *Spiel*.) – Of course the incorrectness of that, or any other, definition is no proof that a correct definition may not yet be found. However, that is of little importance to Wittgenstein's position. Admittedly, he claims that there *is* no definition of the word 'game', but that is only by way of giving an example, of no intrinsic interest, to illustrate the crucial point that there *need* not be a definition for every word. In any given case a correct definition *may* in the end be found; Wittgenstein merely warns us not to insist that it *must* be found. We should at any rate be prepared for the possibility that concepts may not be held together by a set of defining features. To use a word that cannot be defined is not to talk nonsense.[8]

In reply, an essentialist may complain that an unspecified set of similarities is not enough to hold a concept together. After all, everything resembles everything else in some respect; so it would appear that on a family resemblance account *everything* must fall under the concept in question (e.g., Davies 2001, 171). – Here it is important to distinguish clearly between the formation of a concept and its use. Accordingly, the essentialist could worry either how a concept could be shaped in a particular way without any defining properties, or how, given a family resemblance concept, it should be possible to apply it. The latter may look like a problem if one is under the impression that each speaker would have to work out the boundaries of the concept for himself, having been shown only one sample (e.g., one game) and being told merely that there was a 'complicated network of similarities overlapping and criss-crossing'. That of course would be impossible. Football can be shown as a sample of a game or a sample of a sport (or many other things); in the first case it will be classed with snakes and ladders, in the second it will be classed with weight lifting. So a family resemblance concept (one might also call it a 'cluster concept') must be taught by giving a sufficiently long list of examples of different types of instances. You have to be taught, or observe, which kinds of things are called 'games', namely: ball-games, board-games, card-games, party games, etc., and you have to be told, or pick up, that certain activities, although quite similar in many respects, are not called 'games' (e.g., steeplechase or fencing). After that, the appreciation of similarities figures just as it does in the application of other concepts. You know that chess, backgammon and draughts are games; now you observe people playing mah-jong, and you understand without being told that that is a game too. Consider how we acquire an understanding of the difference between apples and pears. We are given samples and are told that apples look like this ⇨ . . . and taste like this: . . . , and pears

---

[8] *Pace*, for instance, Clive Bell who declared that 'either all works of visual art have some common quality, or when we speak of "works of art" we gibber' (1913, 17).

look like this ⇨ ... and taste like this: ... Here one could likewise worry that everything was like everything in some respect, and that therefore we would have no reason to deny that anything was an apple or a pear. But of course, in reality, there is no such problem. The fact is that we are able to see which similarities matter, even if we have not been given, and could not give, an exact verbal specification of the range and degree of resemblance required (especially in the case of taste, which is notoriously difficult to describe).

The worry about the formation of a family resemblance concept could be put like this: There are similarities between chess and tennis, between tennis and karate, between chess and karate; then why should chess and tennis be classified as games, but not karate? – Again, there isn't really a problem. Obviously some people at some point have been more impressed by some similarities than by others, and have found some differences noteworthy and others less so. It is just because there is no end of similarities that one could focus on that concept formation is to some extent arbitrary, as illustrated by the different ways in which boundaries are drawn in different languages. Light blue and dark blue are two shades of the same colour in English, but not in Russian, where they are classified as two different colours (*goluboj*, *sinij*). (And why is grey not called 'light black'?) Or compare the word 'science' and its German translation *Wissenschaft*: unlike the former, the latter includes subjects like history and literary criticism, highlighting the obvious similarities between these disciplines and paradigmatic sciences, like physics or chemistry, whereas the English classification highlights their equally obvious differences.

Consider as another example the concept of a work of art (cf. *PI* §77), in the broad sense of the expression covering painting, sculpture, architecture, music, literature, acting, ballet, film and photography (to mention only well-established and uncontroversial domains). To find a definition of art, or at least some common property, has long been a central concern in philosophical aesthetics. Numerous suggestions have been made, such as:

1 Art is imitation (Plato).
2 Art is a representation of eternal forms of nature that induces a silencing of the will (Schopenhauer).
3 Art is the communication of feeling (Tolstoy).
4 Art is the expression of emotion (Croce, Collingwood).
5 Art is significant form (Bell).
6 Art is representation and subject to interpretation (Danto).
7 Art is what is intended to afford an aesthetic experience (Beardsley).
8 Art is what is created to be presented to an artworld public (Dickie).

It would lead us too far afield to discuss any of these definitions in detail,[9] but it is easy to see, and almost generally agreed, that (1)–(6) are inadequate. Either these claims are not true of all works of art, or they are also true of many other things, or both.[10] In (7) 'art' is explained in terms of an aesthetic experience, but it seems unlikely that such an experience should be identifiable independently of what it is an experience of – namely, above all, works of art. In other words, it is doubtful whether a good portrait, a good symphony and a good novel afford the same kind of enjoyment, except in so far as it is all the enjoyment of something called 'art'. Definition (8), the so-called Institutional Theory of Art, is not only problematically indiscriminate in that it means that absolutely anything must be accepted as art if only someone presents it to the artworld; it is also unashamedly circular, and hence useless as an account of our mastery of the concept of art (– you cannot understand the concept of an artworld public unless you have already understood what art is).

To apply Wittgenstein's notion of family resemblance to the concept of art and give up the quest for a definition was first explicitly proposed by Morris Weitz in 1956, and the suggestion is usually discussed (and rejected) with reference to his article. He wrote:

> "Art" . . . is an open concept. . . . its conditions of application can never be exhaustively enumerated since new cases can always be envisaged or created by artists, or even nature, which would call for a decision on someone's part to extend or to close the old or to invent a new concept. . . . the very expansive, adventurous character of art, its ever-present changes and novel creations, makes it logically impossible to ensure any set of defining properties. (Weitz 1956, 32)

This, however, is rather different from what Wittgenstein says about games, and not very convincing. First, the possibility of new cases that would require a decision as to whether or not they should be included exists for virtually all concepts. Wittgenstein gives the example of a strangely vanishing and reappearing chair (*PI* §80; quoted on p. 135 above). In the same vein, you can easily imagine a case where you would be at a loss as to whether to call something a 'puppy'; and yet there is no doubt that a puppy can be *defined* as a young dog. The possibility of unforeseen new cases is no hindrance to a definition of our *current* concept of art; at the worst, we will have to update our definition every now and again. (Think of legal and scientific terminology:

---

[9] As given here, those definitions present the merest outline of their authors' positions, without all the refinements, qualifications and explanations of terms required for a full understanding.

[10] For further discussion see Hanfling 1992.

there you have paradigm cases of sharply defined concepts, and yet they have to be revised frequently due to unforeseen legal conflicts arising from institutional or technological change, or due to new theoretical developments.)

Secondly, it is remarkable that, in order to justify the anti-essentialist move against definition, Weitz makes an essentialist claim: namely, that art is by its nature expansive, adventurous and constantly aiming at radical change. Is it? Well, it is undeniable that artists will always seek to produce something new. You cannot earn much praise for repeating what others have done before you. But that is also true of fashion designers and distinguished chefs, yet neither *haute couture* nor *haute cuisine* seems essentially indefinable. So Weitz's claim must go further: art changes so radically that no main features remain constant. Yet for this stronger claim Weitz offers no convincing reason (cf. Kivy 1997, 35–8); not to mention the fact that he seems to contradict it himself by his insistence on art's essential 'expansiveness'. Of course there has been a lot of dramatic change in the past, but, for one thing, it is not clear how much of the most radical, so-called avant-garde products will stand the test of time, let alone be the vanguard of a new era. Perhaps future generation will regard Duchamp's *Fountain* and John Cage's 4′33″ as jokes (and laugh at a pompous artworld that took them seriously). And even if such notorious pieces become (or remain) part of the canon, one may doubt whether there is much room for development left in those directions. So it is not at all self-evident that future art will be in a permanent state of revolution. (In literature, it is arguable that most novels today, even of the most interesting and sophisticated kind, bear more resemblance to *Barchester Towers* than to *Finnegans Wake*.) Nor is it likely that people will in the long run meekly accept just *anything* as art. There will always be limits to the application of the word – which one might hope to spell out by a definition.

Wittgenstein's remarks on games, by contrast, are based neither on any essentialist claims about the protean nature of the concept, nor on predictions of its unruly future developments. Most importantly, the family resemblance conception does not imply that a definition of the word is logically impossible, as Weitz maintains. The crucial point of a family resemblance concept, as described by Wittgenstein, is that classification under it is based on a sub-classification that is logically prior. If you know that chess and draughts are games, you will recognize backgammon as something of the same kind: a board-game, and therefore clearly a game. Is there a set of properties that board-games have in common with all other games and only with games? We don't know of such a set of properties. And even if it exists, it is irrelevant, as we don't rely on it for our applications of the word 'game'.

It is even more obvious that such is the situation in the case of art. Beethoven's opus 111, for instance, is a most impressive piece of music, and music is one of the fine arts, so opus 111 is a work of art. And similarly for specimens of other art forms. The question, however, as to whether music, architecture, poetry and the rest can be defined *per genus et differentiam* is purely academic and irrelevant to our practice of calling them all 'arts', which stands in no need of such a definition. Each art bears obvious resemblances to some other art (poetry and drama both involve skilful use of language; drama and music are both performance arts; non-abstract painting and drama are both forms of visual representation, and so on); that is enough to explain the use of the same word 'art' (or to make it more than a coincidence as in the case of homonyms, like 'bank').[11] –

In the *Tractatus* Wittgenstein had regarded language as consisting of propositions, propositions as truth-functions of elementary propositions, and elementary propositions as models of reality. It would appear from that account that we use language only to give reports of 'how things stand' (*TLP* 4.5). There was no mention of imperative or interrogative sentences or exclamations, and no awareness that even declarative sentences are used in numerous different ways, such as speculating about an event, forming and testing a hypothesis, making up a story and reading it, play-acting, singing catches, guessing riddles, making a joke, thanking, cursing or greeting (*PI* §23). A belief in the necessity of an essential nature of language made the young Wittgenstein ignore the multifarious ways in which language works. That belief is overcome when one realizes that in fact no common properties are necessary to hold a concept together: family resemblance, a network of similarities, is quite sufficient (cf. *PI* §135). As a motto for the *Investigations* Wittgenstein once considered 'I'll teach you differences' (from *King Lear*, I. iv. 76 (New Cambridge edn); Rhees 1984, 157).

(f) Meaning through meaning

When writing the *Tractatus*, Wittgenstein had conceived of the link between language and the world as psychological, and hence as of no interest to philosophy. It is hardly touched upon in the *Tractatus*, but there are some further remarks in the early notebooks. When using

---

[11] Of course it is possible to present a family resemblance conception *in the form* of a definition. In the case of art, this has been done by Robert Stecker who defines a work of art as what is either of one of the central art forms of the time of its creation and intended to fulfil a function that art has at the time, or some other artefact that achieves excellence in fulfilling such a function (Stecker 1997). This is a disjunctive definition, well in accordance with Wittgenstein's anti-essentialist view, as it does not specify a set of properties common to all and only works of art (cf. *PI* §67c), and even allows for the list of disjuncts to be extended in future (cf. *PI* §68).

language we pin names on to objects by 'thinking the sense of a proposition' (*TLP* 3.11). That is to say, the utterance of a sentence derives its significance from an accompanying act of thinking (mentally representing) what is said. Due to this accompanying thought, words are not just uttered parrot-wise, but *meant* in a particular way. Through such an act of meaning, they have meaning. (This account sounds particularly attractive in English, where both the linguistic significance of words and a speaker's intending his words to be understood in a certain way are called by the same word 'meaning'. In German the former is called *Bedeutung*, the latter *meinen*.)

The young Wittgenstein resorted to that mental act of meaning to defend his idea that sense must be determinate. It is hard to deny that often our *words* are not sharply defined; but then, Wittgenstein insisted, at least what we *mean* by them, our accompanying thoughts, will be precise (*NB*, 20 June 1915). What the *Notebooks* showed to be implicit in the *Tractatus*, the temptation to invoke a mental act of meaning something (*meinen*) as part of a preconceived view of how language works, is repeatedly made explicit in the *Investigations*:

- Augustine described his language learning as correlating words and objects (*PI* §1). Such a correlation may also be performed expressly for a learner's benefit, as an ostensive explanation, like: 'This ⇨ . . . is called "red" '. But such an explanation can be misunderstood. When pointing at a ripe tomato saying 'This is called "red" ', I may be taken to mean this particular object, or this kind of vegetable, or this shape, or something edible, or ripeness, or the number one, or various other things rather than the colour (cf. *PI* §28). The question seems to be whether the speaker *meant* the colour, the shape, the number, the kind of vegetable, or whatever.
- The idea that the meaning of an ostensively defined word depends on what one meant when giving the explanation has interesting consequences when it comes to introducing words for subjective experiences. It appears that what I mean in such a case – say, my idiosyncratic impression of this taste or colour arrangement – is quite definite, but indescribable. I am aware of what I mean – *this* – but I cannot communicate it to anybody else (cf. *PI* §276). It would follow that the meaning of a name I give to any of my specific experiences will be strictly private: incomprehensible to anybody else. The apparent possibility of such a private language is one of the most famous philosophical problems discussed in the *Investigations* (§§243–315). We shall return to it in sect. 4.7.
- Acts of meaning are invoked not only when words are defined or explained for the first time. Any instance of speech, it seems, relies on the speaker's meaning something by his words. Whenever one uses words significantly, one can say: 'I don't just say it, I mean it'.

It feels as if the words were linked with something in us, whereas words we don't mean – say, perfunctorily reproduced nursery rhymes – seem to run in neutral gear (*PI* §507).[12]

- Normally we know what we mean to say before we have said it. Thus from the beginning of our utterance its meaning is present in our mind (*PI* §334).
- When you teach someone to write down the arithmetical series $x_n = 2n$, that is, the series of even numbers, you mean, amongst other things, that after 1,000 he is supposed to write 1,002 (*PI* §187), and so with infinitely many other steps we could not possibly all spell out in our explanation. Thus our meaning an order in a particular way can invest our words with a determinacy stretching to infinity. It appears that:

> 188. ... that act of meaning the order had in its own way already traversed all those steps: that when you meant it your mind as it were flew ahead and took all the steps before you physically arrived at this or that one ... as only the act of meaning can anticipate reality.

Two theses are involved here:

(1) Meaning (*Bedeutung*) is determined, or brought about, through meaning it (*meinen*).

(2) Meaning something (*meinen*) is a mental process.

(1) is based on (2): For linguistic significance to be brought about by meaning something, it must be possible to mean something independently of any already established linguistic content. It must be possible to mean, for example, 'If it doesn't rain I shall go for a walk' by a nonsense word like 'bububu' (*PI*, p. 18); or to mean toothache by 'abracadabra' (cf. *PI* §665). This would appear to be possible if meaning something were like forming sounds, or humming a tune, in one's mind: a psychological process that could occur even if no linguistic practice and conventions existed (cf. *PI* §205). Therefore Wittgenstein's strategy is to show that meaning something is *not* a mental process.

What kind of mental process could meaning something be thought to be? How, for instance, does one mean the colour of a piece of paper, rather than its shape? Perhaps by concentrating one's attention on the colour. But how does one do that?

> 33. ... You sometimes attend to the colour by putting your hand up to keep the outline from view; or by not looking at the outline of the thing; sometimes by staring at the object and trying to remember where you saw that colour before.

---

[12] James 1890, vol. 1, 280f.

... This is the sort of thing that happens *while* one 'directs one's attention to this or that'. But it isn't these things by themselves that make us say someone is attending to the ... colour.

Of someone who pays attention, we also expect that shortly afterwards he will know what it was he paid attention to. Suppose you show someone a series of colour samples, chosen with a view to painting your bedroom, and then ask him: 'Now, which one do you think fits best?' – and he doesn't respond for a second, then starts, looks at you in a disoriented way and ejects: 'Eh ... what?'. Clearly, he hasn't paid any attention; even if all the while he looked at the samples intently, saying to himself: 'This colour ... , or this one? ...'. To pay attention is to try to notice or understand things, not allowing oneself to be distracted. The words 'paying attention', or 'directing one's attention', are expressions of purposiveness: describing a person's state not in terms of what exactly is going on in his mind (or with his body) – very different things can go on in different people paying attention to the same thing – but in terms of his aim: knowledge or understanding. The concept is comparable to that of *looking for something*. Two people may be displaying exactly the same behaviour – say, running their hands through the contents of a drawer – have the same feelings and the same words going through their minds; yet one of them is looking for his keys, the other one isn't. And a third one may behave rather differently: say, walk around nervously, and say very different things to himself, while also looking for his keys. 'Looking for one's keys' does not specify any particular physical or mental behaviour, it describes the *purpose* of one's behaviour. Likewise, 'directing one's attention to the colour' specifies one's purpose, or aim achieved, in doing whatever one does; it is not the name of a specific mental process.

Apart from the fact that paying attention is not a specific mental process, there are further reasons why it cannot be what meaning something consists in. For one thing, inattentiveness does not prevent one from meaning something. One would not say: 'I didn't really mean my pain just now; my mind wasn't on it enough for that' (*PI* §674). For another thing, one may pay attention to something while speaking without meaning it:

> 674. ... Do I ask myself, say: "What did I mean by this word just now? My attention was divided between my pain and the noise..."?

Thirdly, one can mean something to which one cannot pay attention because it does not exist or occurred, or will occur, at some other time:

> 667. Imagine someone simulating pain, and then saying "It'll get better soon". Can't one say he means the pain? and yet he is not concentrating

his attention on any pain. – And what about when I finally say "It's stopped now"?

Finally, one can mean something abstract or general to which one could not in any straightforward sense be said to pay attention, as it is not something one experiences at the time. Consider, for example, the statement 'Whales are mammals'.

A more suitable candidate for the supposed mental process of meaning something is perhaps the presence of a mental image. A version of this view was famously put forward by John Locke (on a plausible interpretation), who observed that significant speech requires more than correctly articulated words and sentences: a parrot can produce those just as well, but a parrot does not talk sense. That is because only in intelligent human beings are words accompanied by ideas in the mind, from which they derive their meaning (Locke 1689, 3.2.2). To understand another's speech, the hearer has to reproduce in his mind the same ideas, or images, with which the speaker backed up his words. Thus meaning and understanding are basically the same mental process, except that one is actively produced and the other passively reproduced.

However, it is easy to convince oneself that understanding a word cannot be the same as having a mental image, for any image can be interpreted, or applied, differently. For instance, the perspectival drawing of a cube may also be taken as a two-dimensional figure consisting of a square and two trapeziums. Again, the image of a dog may be taken to represent a particular golden retriever, or any golden retriever, or any dog, or a mammal, or an upright position, or many other things (cf. *PI* §139). Indeed, one cannot even assume that when an image is produced in one's mind by hearing a word, this image must represent what one takes the word to mean. The word 'winter' may produce in me the image of an old aunt pouring out tea; but I am not for that matter under the strange misapprehension that that is what the word 'winter' means. Thus, two people hearing a word can have the same mental image and yet a different understanding of the word, manifested in the different ways they apply it and the different explanations they give (cf. *PI* §140). And it is also possible that two people have different mental images when hearing the same word, although they are in perfect agreement about its meaning. And these objections are equally applicable to the complementary account of meaning something as having mental images.

> 663. If I say "I meant *him*" very likely a picture comes to my mind, perhaps of how I looked at him, etc.; but the picture is only like an illustration to a story. From it alone it would mostly be impossible to conclude anything at all; only when one knows the story does one know the significance of the picture.

Meaning something is not a mental process.

> 675. "Tell me, what was going on in you when you uttered the words...?" – The answer to this is not: "I was meaning..."!

What goes on in the privacy of my mind is irrelevant to communication (*PI* p. 176h). Meaning something does not consist in anything (*PI* §678): it is not a process of any kind. The inclination to regard it as such is another offspring of the referentialist prejudice, which insists that nouns stand for objects (*BB* 1), and verbs stand for processes. And verbs that take the designation of a person as subject, and are applied to a specific time ('When he shouted, he meant you'), seem to denote an action; and if no physical action can be found, it must be a mental action (*PI* §36). But the referentialist assumption is wrong. The word 'to mean' functions quite differently.

'To mean', said of a person, is a word used to add to an insufficiently specific utterance or to remove misunderstandings. The question 'What do you mean?' arises only when you haven't made yourself sufficiently clear. If in a greengrocer's shop you say 'Five red apples, please' (and there is only one sort of red apple for sale), there is no question of what you mean: you just said it (*BT* 4). In this case the speaker's meaning is obvious, not because his mental processes are so transparent, but because the meaning of those English words in that situation leaves nothing to be explained. Consider an even simpler act of communication: the ringing of a doorbell. The signal of the doorbell means that someone is at the door and wants the door to be opened. Now can there be a further question as to what the person ringing the bell means by that signal? Three possible cases spring to mind. First, the person ringing the bell does not know the meaning of that signal, mistaking it perhaps for a toy. Then one could say that by his ringing he did not mean to call someone to open the door. Secondly, someone may ring the bell inadvertently, mistaking the button for a light switch, or touching it when leaning against the wall. Again, he does not mean to call someone to answer the door. Thirdly, there may be a question as to whom the person wished to call to the door; if, for example, a house with only one doorbell is inhabited by two families. – However, if there is no such ambiguity or lack of specificity about the meaning of a signal, and one can assume that the person using it knows what he is doing, then *what the person means will simply be what the signal means under the circumstances*. Thus, in the normal case, it follows from the meaning of a sign (in a given situation) what a person means by using that sign. Conventional signs, such as words or sentences, have their meaning or sense before any particular utterance; and of course someone who knows that meaning would not use them unless he meant to convey what those signs mean. So, linguistic meaning, far from being produced by a speaker's meaning it, is the primary factor, which guided the speaker's choice of signs in the first place and from which therefore one derives what, presumably, the speaker meant to say. Only when the words are not clear or specific enough (e.g., when the reference of a personal pronoun is not obvious), can one not derive from them what the speaker meant. But then the question 'What do you mean?' does not ask for the uncovering of an inner process, supposed to have given meaning to the utterance – after all, the meaning of the actual words is clear enough; the problem is that that meaning (e.g., of the word 'him') leaves something unsaid. Rather, the question 'What do you mean?' asks for a more explicit utterance to replace or complement the first.

Presupposing that a speaker knows what he is doing, he will seriously utter a sentence that means X only if *he* means (to say) that X. In other words, he will say that X only if he wants to say that X. This is brought out clearly by the French expression for 'to mean something' (said of a person with respect to a verbal utterance): *vouloir dire*, i.e.: 'to want to say'. Bearing in mind that the expression 'to mean something by one's words' is used to spell out one's communicative intentions, it should be clear why Wittgenstein returns a negative answer to the question: 'Can I say "bububu" and mean "If it doesn't rain I shall go for a walk"?' – 'It is only in a language that I can mean something by something' (*PI* p. 18). To mean, that is, to intend to say 'If it doesn't rain . . .' by uttering 'bububu', is like intending to fly through the air on a broomstick. You can have such an intention only if you are under some strange illusion: if indeed you believe that a broomstick can carry you through the air, or that the word 'bububu' means 'If it doesn't rain . . .'. If you know that this is not the case, you may only *wish*, or imagine or pretend, that by uttering 'bububu' you could make that statement, which, however, is quite a different matter. One could of course *stipulate* that from now on the word 'bububu' have the meaning 'If it doesn't rain . . .', and that arbitrary definition could be put like this: 'By "bububu" I mean . . .' (*PI* §665). But in that case, again, meaning something is secondary to what a word means.

4.3 The Nature of Philosophy

It is customary for commentaries on the *Philosophical Investigations* after a chapter on Wittgenstein's criticisms of his earlier position to move on to an account and discussion of the book's positive doctrines. That, however, is a mistake, for the book does not propound any positive philosophical doctrines. Its thrust is entirely negative, aimed at nothing more and nothing less than a demonstration that philosophical doctrine is invariably the result of linguistic confusion (*PI* §119), which needs to be cleared up and removed, somewhat like a disease of the understanding (*PI* §255). The analytic treatment displayed in the *Investigations* is not supposed to produce any new philosophical theses, but merely a clear understanding of the relevant concepts that breaks the spell of philosophical illusion.

Already at the end of the *Tractatus*, Wittgenstein had announced that the correct philosophical method would be to refrain from any philosophical theorizing and limit oneself to denouncing as nonsense others' attempts at such theorizing (*TLP* 6.53); but as we saw, this was not in fact the method practised in the *Tractatus*. Only in 1931 did Wittgenstein begin to take that programme seriously:

> I once wrote, The only correct method of doing philosophy consists in not saying anything and leaving it to another person to make a claim. That is the method I now adhere to. (*WVC* 183)

The only assertions that Wittgenstein means to allow himself in the *Investigations* are trivial reminders of well-known facts, especially of common usage. As he put it in a lecture:

> On all questions we discuss I have no opinion; and if I had, and it disagreed with one of your opinions, I would at once give it up for the sake of argument because it would be of no importance for our discussion. We constantly move in a realm where we all have the same opinions. All I can give you is a method; I cannot teach you any new truths. (*AL* 97; cf. *LFM* 22)

In the light of prevalent academic practice, it may seem astonishing that there could be a philosophy that is not a philosophical doctrine; but perhaps one should rather be astonished that philosophical doctrines have been propounded in the first place. After all, philosophy is not based on any empirical research: philosophers cannot claim to have observed any new facts. So what could their doctrines be about? If they were about empirical matters, specialized scientists would clearly be better qualified to deal with them; philosophy would appear to be but amateurish speculation, hardly a respectable academic discipline. To avoid such hopelessly incompetent rivalry with the sciences, philosophy must not be an empirical discipline; its theories must be *a priori*. But how can there be an *a priori* theory? The problem is that (mathematics apart) what can be known without recourse to experience is likely to be trivial.

It is easy to come up with some examples of truths that are not based on any empirical evidence, but can be known *a priori*: such as 'Bachelors are unmarried' or 'There's ne'er a villain dwelling in all Denmark but he's an arrant knave'. But it takes neither a ghost come from the grave to tell us that, nor a philosophical theory. They are *analytic* statements, true solely in virtue of the meaning, or established use, of the words and their syntactic combination, and thus merely spelling out what any competent speaker of English knows. Of course it is possible to find analytic statements that are less obvious and may need to be worked out in a number of steps: for example, 'The key with five sharps is B major'. Still, to those conversant with the concepts involved, the matter is fairly trivial, and there is certainly no room for any serious research projects (or for the perennial disagreement so typical of philosophy). Of course, mathematics provides examples of *a priori* truths that are not only highly complicated, but also regarded as important and interesting. But for one thing, the awe-inspiring complexity of mathematics results from a calculus of sharply defined symbols, very unlike the words of natural languages in which philosophy is expressed; and for another thing, the importance and dignity of mathematics is due to its usefulness both in everyday life and in the sciences. That is what makes mathematical problems more than just entertaining puzzles: even if not every extension of pure mathematics has an application yet, it is all part of a conceptual system of overwhelming and open-ended usefulness. Obviously, nothing similar could be said of philosophy.

The first philosopher to become alive to the problem of finding a legitimate role for philosophy as a subject that is neither empirical nor mathematical was Immanuel Kant (1724–1804). Accepting that analytic judgements can never express any new insights (unlike their opposites, synthetic judgements), Kant asked: How are synthetic judgements *a priori* possible? His answer was mainly negative: the great metaphysical aspirations, *a priori* theories about God or the immortality of the soul had to be abandoned. Philosophy as systematic knowledge of answers to the Big Questions was impossible. Instead Kant propounded the doctrine of transcendental idealism: It is possible to know *a priori* certain general features of the world (e.g., that it must appear in space and time, and be subject to the law of causality), because those features are the product of our own minds. Thus, Kant insisted against Hume, some *a priori* knowledge of the world – philosophical knowledge – is indeed possible. However, it is highly doubtful whether Kant has succeeded in presenting any genuine examples of synthetic *a priori* judgements: some of his examples can be shown to be analytic, and some may not even be true. Today transcendental idealism has few followers.

More popular with analytic philosophers, from Russell to the present day, is the Socratic conception of philosophy as the search for definitions (e.g., Ayer 1936, 78f). But, as the discussion of essentialism in the previous chapter showed, such a conception is open to two serious objections. First, it is doubtful whether many interesting concepts are susceptible of a precise definition. And, secondly, even if they are, it is far from clear why we should be much interested in their definition. The Platonic Socrates was quite wrong to lament that because his interlocutors were unable to define such concepts as piety, justice or knowledge, they did not really know what piety, justice or knowledge were. Our mastery of such words is not based on definitions, but it is none the worse for that (cf. *BB* 19f). If philosophers finally agreed on a definition of knowledge, they would not thereby achieve a better grasp of the concept of knowledge than we have now. For wherever their definition helped them to decide cases about which we are unclear, it would be incorrect: instead of capturing our existing, somewhat vague, concept, it would yield a new one, more sharply defined than ours. In other words, definitions are either strictly analytic – then they can only be neat summaries of what in our linguistic practice we already know – or, if they go beyond our ordinary linguistic knowledge, they amount to new stipulations, and thus cannot teach us anything about our actual concepts.

Related to modern analytic philosophy's quest for definitions is the idea that logical analysis, like scientific analysis, can lead to new discoveries. Wittgenstein's criticism of this idea was expounded in the previous section (4.2c).

According to the later Wittgenstein, philosophy is all about nonsense (*PI* §119) or patent falsehood (*BT* 412). Either it simply *is* nonsense or patent falsehood, or it is the attempt to understand why some philosophical problems and doctrines really are nonsense or patent falsehood, and thus to dissolve them. So there are two types of philosophers: dogmatic philosophers, who produce nonsense or patent falsehood, and therapeutic philosophers, who analyse and explode nonsense or patent falsehood. Wittgenstein's new, therapeutic philosophy is merely a response to dogmatic philosophy (or its potential sources); it is 'a tool which is useful only against philosophers and against the philosopher in us' (TS 219, 11). Those who are not bothered by meaningless questions have no need for philosophy (MS 183, 65).

Wittgenstein's mature conception of philosophy can be summarized in eight moments.

(i) Philosophical problems are *idle* conundrums. Unlike scientific problems, we do not encounter them in practical life (*BT* 427); they arise 'when language has knocked off' (*PI* §38); when it is 'like an engine idling (in neutral gear), not when it is doing work' (*PI* §132).

(ii) A philosophical problem is a *confusion*, 'expressed in the form of a question that doesn't acknowledge the confusion' (*PG* 193), a question therefore that allows of no answer (*EPB* 156). The question keeps disquieting us until we convince ourselves that it involves a misuse of language and does not make any sense (*PI* §119). 'The first mistake we encounter in a philosophical investigation is . . . always the question itself' (MS 165, 55).

(iii) A major source of philosophical confusion are *analogies* laid down in the forms and idiomatic expressions of our *language* (*PI* §§90, 94, 111, 112, 115; *BT* 408, 409, 427). Philosophers tend to be taken in – 'bewitched' – by those analogies (*PI* §109): they treat as significant what is only an incidental formal feature of grammar, or take metaphorical forms of expression at face value (*EPB* 156).

(iv) In other cases it is not so much language itself that misleads us, but our *idealizing prejudices* about language (*PI* §§98–103): in particular, some unrealistic demands of precision, order and rigour in our concepts.

(v) As a therapy for such confusions, philosophy assembles *trivial reminders* of common usage (and common sense) to clarify how the relevant words are actually used (*PI* §§127f, 599; *WVC* 183; *BT* 412, 419). 'When philosophers use a word . . . one must always ask oneself: is the word ever actually used in this way in the language which is its original home? – What *we* do is to bring words back from their metaphysical to their everyday use' (*PI* §116*).

(vi) When we are confused about some words, it is often useful to consider a *synoptic representation* of their use (*PI* §122): that is, a primitive or simplified linguistic scenario 'in which one can command a clear overview of the aim and functioning of the words' (*PI* §5). Such 'language-games' will remind us of the way in which language is embedded in our lives (*PI* §7), typically neglected in philosophical discussions. Moreover, they can remove the puzzling appearance of certain concepts or applications by showing them to be variants of perfectly familiar language uses (*BT* 416; MS 135, 11; TS 229, §1667).[13]

(vii) Thus *philosophical problems are dissolved* (*BT* 421) as pseudo-problems (MS 140, 10); the disquieting features of language are shown to be unproblematic, often by comparison with other cases (*RPP* I §1000); and apparent philosophical insights are revealed as plain nonsense (*PI* §119) – latent nonsense is transformed into patent nonsense (*PI* §464) – or patent falsehood (*BT* 412).

(viii) As there is nothing more to philosophy than the treatment of such conceptual and ultimately dissolvable problems (*PG* 193), philosophy (if not false or nonsense) is *entirely negative*. Its aim is to destroy illusions (*PI* §118); 'to remove particular misunderstandings; not to produce a real understanding for the first time' (*PG* 115). Contrary to common belief, philosophy does not provide a foundation for other kinds of research: properly understood, it 'only solves, or rather gets rid of, philosophical problems; it does not set our thinking on a more solid basis' (TS 219, 10). We should not expect any new and surprising insights from philosophy (*BT* 419); it only brings us back to the trivi-

---

[13] For a more detailed account of Wittgenstein's concept of a 'synoptic representation' see Schroeder 2004, §§1–2.

alities of common sense (*CV* 50; TS 211, 256; TS 219, 6): 'Our answers, if they are correct, must be commonplace and trivial. – For those answers make, as it were, fun of the questions' (FF §111).

Wittgenstein's philosophy is a defence of common sense against some clever forms of nonsense (or patent falsehood), which, however, requires a good deal more than simply *asserting* common-sense views, in the manner of G. E. Moore (cf. *AL* 108f).

It has been suggested, against this account, that Wittgenstein's later conception of philosophy is not entirely negative, as he also aims at a synoptic representation of grammar to give us a better understanding of the workings of our language (*PI* §122). But for Wittgenstein such an understanding of language is not an end in itself. After all, a philosopher is not a linguist. He investigates and describes only those aspects of language that give rise to philosophical problems (*PI* §109); and the clarity he aims at simply means that the philosophical problems disappear (*PI* §133). As Wittgenstein summarized it in a notebook: 'What we are doing is: clearing away philosophy' (MS 156b, 35r).

Let us consider a few simple examples of philosophical confusions:

1.   Can one step into the same river twice? Of course one can, people often do (FF §111), and yet the pre-Socratic philosopher Heraclitus appears to have denied this (Plato, *Cratylus*, 402a). It is easy to see why. The water in a river is constantly changing. But if the water is different each time, then – as the river consists of its water – the river must be a different one each time. So, it would appear, strictly speaking you never step into the same river on two different occasions. The same line is taken by David Hume, who writes:

> we must attribute a perfect identity to [any] mass [of matter], provided all the parts continue uninterruptedly and invariably the same ... But supposing some very *small* or *inconsiderable* part to be added to the mass, or subtracted from it; ... this absolutely destroys the identity of the whole, strictly speaking ... (Hume 1739, 255f)

However, due to carelessness, we generally 'confound' the notion of identity with that of slow and gradual change (1739, 253), and call 'the same' what are strictly different objects, for instance, a church, a river, a plant, an animal or a man, at different times (1739, 258f). – In fact, it is Heraclitus and Hume who are confused: enthralled by a false ideal of linguistic precision that there should be absolutely no change in what is called by the same word. This idea appeals by its neatness; but it is hopelessly out of touch with the way language really, and usefully, works. Far from being an oversight, it is the very idea behind the concept of a river that there is a constant flow and change of water;

otherwise it wouldn't be a river, but a lake. Likewise, it is quite intentional, perfectly correct and extremely useful that we have a concept of personal identity over time, in spite of a human being's constant change through metabolism, growth and mental development. A little reflection shows that the linguistic ideal behind those philosophical protests against common usage is in fact not at all desirable, indeed entirely unworkable (cf. *PI* §103). Imagine calling a river by a new name whenever there has been an influx of new water: – we could not handle the required number of different names, and they would not allow us to say what we wanted to say about the river.[14]

2. F. H. Bradley, the dominating figure in British philosophy at the end of the nineteenth century, presents the following puzzle:

> We may take the familiar instance of a lump of sugar. This is a thing, and it has properties, adjectives which qualify it. It is, for example, white, and hard, and sweet. The sugar, we say, *is* all that; but what the *is* can really mean seems doubtful. A thing is not any one of its qualities . . . (Bradley 1893, 19)

Obviously, sugar is white; and yet, strictly speaking, one cannot maintain that it *is* white: for it is not identical with white. Thus, it would appear that for a statement to be strictly true, the predicate has to be the same as the subject (e.g., 'Sugar is sugar'); but then it becomes uninformative.

> And we seem unable to clear ourselves from the old dilemma, If you predicate what is different, you ascribe to the subject what it is *not*; and if you predicate what is *not* different, you say nothing at all. (Bradley 1893, 20)

The paradox is easily dissolved by recognizing that a word is used in two different ways: Sometimes 'is' means 'is the same as' ('George Orwell is Eric Blair'), yet more often it does not, but is used to ascribe only a property or a relation to the object (FF §§98f). Bradley's confusion results from his unquestioned prejudice that, really, the word 'is' must always indicate identity.

3. Consider the following passage from Plato's *Theaetetus*:

---

[14] But note that the philosophical misuse of language can have a legitimate use in poetry, as a figurative expression of a feeling or a hyperbolical way of emphasizing a certain aspect of the world (e.g., the prevalence of change in human life; see Goethe's reference to Heraclitus in his poem *Dauer im Wechsel*). The danger is, of course, that the possible figurative use tends to lend an aura of profundity to what in sober-minded philosophy is simply a confusion.

> SOCRATES: . . . while being just this size, without growing or undergoing the opposite, I can within the space of a year be both larger than a young man like you, now, and smaller, later on – not because I've lost any of my size but because you've grown. Because that means I am, later on, what I wasn't before, though I haven't come to be it; because without coming to be it's impossible to have come to be, and since I haven't lost any of my size, I couldn't ever have been coming to be smaller.
> There are thousand more cases of the same sort . . .
> THEAETETUS: . . . it's quite extraordinary what wonder I feel at the question what, exactly, is true about them. Sometimes I get really dizzy looking at them.
> SOCRATES: . . . that experience, the feeling of wonder, is very characteristic of a philosopher: philosophy has no other starting-point . . . (Plato, *Theaetetus* 155b–d)

The feeling of wonder from which philosophy is said to arise here is what Wittgenstein calls a disquiet (*Beunruhigung*; *PI* §111). It is not produced by an insufficient knowledge or understanding of the facts, as one's feeling of wonder at the phenomenon of lightning or a rainbow might be. Rather, it is the bafflement 'arising through a misinterpretation of our forms of language' (*PI* §111). We are prone to construe predicates (like 'is larger than Theaetetus') as designating properties of an object.[15] Hence, if a new predicate becomes applicable to an object, that object must have acquired a new property: it must have changed. '"But *this* isn't how it is!" – we say. "Yet *this* is how it has to *be!*"' (*PI* §112). To dissolve this little puzzle, we need only remind ourselves that *not* all predicates – in particular, not relational predicates – are used to ascribe a property to an object (cf. *PI* §127).

4. St Augustine, in Book XI of his *Confessions*, grapples with some philosophical problems about time. He is particularly disquieted by the following paradox:

> That I measure time, I know; and yet I measure not time to come, for it is not yet; nor present, because it is not protracted by any space; nor past, because it now is not. What then do I measure? (Augustine, XI, xxvi 33)

Wittgenstein comments that here Augustine has stumbled over an apparent contradiction in the grammar of the word 'measure'. There seems to be a conflict between two different uses of the word (*BB* 26). Augustine thinks of the process of measuring a *length*, say, by a tape

---

[15] 'The primitive forms of our language – noun, adjective and verb – show the simple picture to which it tries to make everything conform' (*BT* 434).

measure. In that case the whole object to be measured has to be present: you could not in this way measure the length of a passing train of which only a small part is visible to you at any moment. But such seems to be our stance *vis-à-vis* a period of time. To solve this puzzle, we only need to remind ourselves that *different* procedures are called 'measuring', not all of which require the object measured to be present all at once. Again, one has to overcome the prejudice that what corresponds to the same word must always be exactly the same. This prejudice, as an implicit and unquestioned assumption, can be surprisingly strong. 'It is helpful here to remember,' Wittgenstein remarks, 'that it is sometimes almost impossible for a child to believe that one word can have two meanings' (*BB* 26). When we remind ourselves that even length is sometimes measured while the object is passing by (e.g., by counting the wagons of a railway train), the case of measuring time loses its disquieting uniqueness, its appearance of anomaly, and begins to look once more as common as it is. Thus a philosophical disquiet can be removed 'merely by saying: "*Here* is no more difficulty than *there*"' (*RPP* I §1000; cf. *BT* 416).

5. Furthermore, Augustine wonders about the whereabouts of past and future (XI, xvii–xviii). This provides a particularly clear illustration of what Wittgenstein has in mind when he speaks of pictures or similes that have been absorbed into the forms of our language (*PI* §§112, 115). He spells this out in an earlier version of his main work:

> "Where does the present go when it becomes past, and where is the past?" – Under what circumstances can this question appeal to us? For under certain circumstances it cannot and we should put it aside as nonsense. It is clear that this question most easily arises in our mind if when thinking about time a picture of coming and going, of things flowing by, holds us captive; if primarily we think of occurrences where there really is such a passing by. For example, standing at a river where logs of wood are floating by: the logs pass by us, those that are past are all on our right, those that are still to come are on our left. We then use this situation as a simile for *all* happening. Indeed, the simile is embodied in the expressions of our language, for we say, an illness 'passes by', 'a war comes', etc. We talk about the flow of events, – but also about the flow of time, – of the river on which the logs pass by us. ('The time has come', 'the time is long gone', 'time will come', etc. etc.) And thus with the word 'time' the picture of an ethereal river comes to be indissolubly linked, with the words 'past' and 'future' the picture of regions, from one of which events travel into the other one. ('The land' of the future, of the past.) And yet of course we cannot find any such river or such localities. Our language admits of questions for which there are no answers. And it leads us to ask these questions through the *pictorial character* of the expressions. An analogy captivates our thinking and irresistibly drags us on. (*EPB* 156; cf. *BB* 107f)

6. As one of the problems the picture theory of the *Tractatus* was meant to solve, I mentioned Plato's puzzle about the possibility of false judgements (sect. 2.4): If your judgement is false, then the state of affairs you judge to exist doesn't exist; then there is in fact nothing your judgement is about; so it would appear that you haven't made a judgement at all. It is instructive to see how Socrates leads his interlocutor up to that puzzle:

> SOCRATES: So if someone sees some one thing, he sees something which is.
> THEAETETUS: Evidently.
> SOCRATES: And if someone hears something, he hears some one thing, and a thing which is.
> THEAETETUS: Yes.
> SOCRATES: And if someone touches something, he touches some one thing, and a thing which is, since it's one?
> THEAETETUS: Yes, that's right too.
> SOCRATES: Well now, what if someone judges [thinks]? . . .
> (Plato, *Theaetetus* 188e–189a)

We are invited to consider the verb 'to judge/think' by analogy with some verbs of sense perception: 'to see', 'to hear' and 'to touch'. As they require an existing object, it would appear that the former must require an existing object too – which is paradoxical as we can think of something that doesn't exist. The source of the problem is not hard to find: the analogy between verbs of perception and verbs of thinking (judging, expecting, believing, imagining) is misleading. The two kinds of verbs may look superficially alike – they are both groups of transitive verbs that denote some kind of awareness – but what sets them apart is exactly that what one is aware of in sense perception (as opposed to hallucination) must really be there, whereas the objects of our thoughts may be entirely fictional (cf. *PI* §462). The deceptive grammatical likeness between verbs of perception and verbs of thinking is another 'simile that has been absorbed into the forms of our language', producing 'a false appearance' and a paradox (*PI* §112).

7. In an attempt to solve the paradox above Socrates suggests that in a false judgement one mistakes one thing for another (189c); but that leads to further paradox. The way in which Socrates presents the matter, it seems quite impossible to mistake one thing for another:

> SOCRATES: Well now, try to remember if you've ever said to yourself that beautiful is certainly ugly, or that unjust is just. Or, to put it generally, ask yourself whether you've ever set out to persuade yourself that one of two things is certainly the other . . . And do you think anyone else, sane or mad, has had the face to say to himself in all seriousness, trying

to persuade himself of it, that ox is necessarily horse, or two one? (Plato, *Theaetetus* 190b–c)

What has gone wrong here? Socrates imagines that in mistaking A for B one would say to oneself: 'A is B'; that is, that one would know which of the two was A and which was B, and still think that A was B. But of course, you can mistake A for B only if you don't know that what you take for B is in fact A – that is what 'mistaking A for B' means. What you might say to yourself in such a case is not 'A is B', but rather: 'This (or the so-and-so) is B'; while in fact, unbeknown to you, this (or the so-and-so) is A. For instance, Jones gave you a book for your birthday, Smith gave you a bottle of wine. Later you misremember and thank Jones for the wine. You mistake one donor for the other; yet obviously not by saying to yourself: 'The person who gave me the book is the person who gave me the wine', but rather by thinking 'Jones is the person who gave me the wine'. – Here a philosophical problem arose from an over-simplified account of 'mistaking one thing for another'. It is easily dissolved by considering an example in sufficient detail.

8. Another type of misunderstanding likely to lead to a philosophical question received a famous illustration from Gilbert Ryle:

> A foreigner visiting Oxford or Cambridge for the first time is shown a number of colleges, libraries, playing fields, museums, scientific departments and administrative offices. He then asks 'But where is the University? ...' ... His mistake lay in his innocent assumption that it was correct to speak of Christ Church, the Bodleian Library, the Ashmolean Museum *and* the University, to speak, that is, as if 'the University' stood for an extra member of the class of which these other units are members. He was mistakenly allocating the University to the same category as that to which the other institutions belong. (Ryle 1949, 16)

This is a category-mistake. A word of one category is treated as if it belonged to another category. Typically, a noun is hastily assumed to be the name of a substance, some locatable object, or some datable occurrence (*BB* 1). This is the tendency that was criticized above under the title 'Referentialism' (sect. 4.2a), which takes as the paradigm of linguistic meaning the correlation of a word with some object; and of course the most straightforward kind of object would be something tangible or visible, like a chair or a house. Ryle's famous claim is that Cartesian dualism is the result of such a category-mistake. Misled by the fact that 'body' and 'mind' seem to be a pair of nouns, like 'salt' and 'pepper', apparently standing for two kinds of things or substance, Descartes held that the mind is an independent substance, distinct from the body. And as the mind is not directly visible and has no length and breadth, it must be a rather special kind of thing: an ethereal, unextended substance: 'Where our language suggests a body' – by a noun – 'and there is none: there, we should like to say, is a *spirit*' (*PI* §36). In fact, the word 'mind' functions rather differently. It does not stand for an object; rather, a creature with a mind is a creature with a certain *capacity*: a capacity for various kinds of intelligent behaviour, from opening a door to speaking a language or constructing a computer (Kenny 1989, ch. 2). Consider a car that can go at 140 miles per hour: it would be a similar category-mistake to look for that capacity as for an object beside the engine somewhere underneath the bonnet. However, it would also be bad English: a confusion of categories to say that the engine *is* the capacity (rather than that it *gives* the car the capacity). Hence, those twentieth-century philosophers who in response to Descartes identified the mind with the brain are equally guilty of a category-mistake.

9. Philosophical claims, if they are not incomprehensible, contradict common sense – due to a misapprehension and misuse of language. Sometimes such linguistic aberration is inspired by a scientific discovery, which seems to lend it an incontestable authority:

> We have been told by popular scientists that the floor on which we stand is not solid, as it appears to common sense, as it has been discovered that the wood consists of particles filling space so thinly that it can almost be called empty. This is liable to perplex us, for in a way of course we know that the floor is solid, or that, if it isn't solid, this may be due to the wood being rotten but not to its being composed of electrons. To say, on this latter ground, that the floor is not solid is to misuse language. . . . Our perplexity was based on a misunderstanding; the picture of the thinly filled space had been wrongly *applied*. For this picture of the structure of matter was meant to explain the very phenomenon of solidity. (*BB* 45)

In normal English 'solid' can mean a number of things. A floor could be called solid because it is not liquid or gaseous; because it is firm and able to support weight or resist pressure; or because it is not hollow. A popular scientist claiming that an ordinary floor is not solid would say that it is largely holes and spaces – *on the micro-level*; and that is presumably quite correct. But of course it in no way contradicts the common-sense claim that a given floor is solid in any of the three senses mentioned. For all the scientists' findings, a floor is certainly not a liquid or a gas; it may well be reasonably firm and strong; and *on the macro-level* it may or may not be hollow, depending on the construction. So, the popular scientist uses the word 'solid' in an unconventional way that is likely to mislead us: in that we may wrongly take his claim to be in conflict with common-sense judgements about a floor's solidity. Taken in that way, it is no longer a scientific claim, but a philosophical confusion.

Similar rejections of common sense, allegedly vindicated by science, but in fact only due to an aberrant use of language, abound today. Widely known is the doctrine of secondary qualities (going back to Descartes and propounded in more detail by Locke) which purports, for example, that grass is not really green: that it merely has a surface structure that reflects corpuscles of a certain kind (or electromagnetic radiation of a certain frequency). In all such cases two points should be made. First, a word is used 'in a metaphysical way', that is 'without an antithesis', and therefore idly (*BB* 46). Normal applications of that word have a point because they draw a contrast; they classify: some things are solid, others are liquid (or porous, or fragile); some things are green, others are red, or blue, or transparent. In the metaphysical use, no contrast is drawn: if the floor isn't solid, that's because nothing is; and grass has no colour, because nothing has. But of course no one seriously proposes that we should give up our ordinary classifications in terms of different colours and consistencies. So, after rejecting that classification by a metaphysical claim, the philosopher (or popular scientist) has to reintroduce it somehow: 'Nothing is really solid; but of course some things are firm and, on the macro-level, not porous.' Again: 'Nothing is green; but of course some things look like this ⇨ . . .' But that is exactly *what in English one calls 'solid' and 'green'*, respectively! So the metaphysical rejection of our common-sense classifications turns out to be mere show.

Secondly, one tends to forget in these cases that *to explain is not to explain away*. The scientific accounts, in terms of electrons or electromagnetic radiation, are meant to *explain* how it comes about that some objects are solid and some things are green; not to *deny* it. As Wittgenstein notes, it is a misunderstanding of the scientific model if it is taken to contradict what it is supposed to account for.

10. John Stuart Mill, in his attempt to establish the doctrine of utilitarianism, asserts that 'there is in reality nothing desired except happiness', and 'desiring a thing and finding it pleasant . . . are phenomena entirely inseparable, or rather two parts of the same phenomenon' (1861, ch. 4, pp. 84f). This is at least very close to the view, called 'psychological egoism', that all human actions are motivated by self-interest.[16] The standard argument for psychological egoism goes like this:

> Whenever I do something of my own free will, I do it because I want to do it: because I have a desire to do it. So my action is aimed at the satisfaction of one of my desires; so it is, really, self-interested.

---

[16] Mill does not actually endorse psychological egoism, but it is hard to see how he could plausibly avoid it.

164   *Philosophical Investigations*

Once more, philosophy seems to require that we give up the common use of a word and with it some important distinctions (cf. (9) above). A charitable donation may be motivated by a wish to alleviate suffering, or it may be motivated by a wish to be applauded for one's noble generosity. In ordinary parlance, the latter action is self-interested, the former is not. Yet the defender of psychological egoism wants to persuade us that in fact they are both equally self-interested; that altruism is an illusion (cf. Nietzsche 1881, §334) and that we are mistaken in finding it more praiseworthy than outright selfishness. However, the standard argument for psychological egoism is badly flawed.

First, when I did something of my own free will, it can indeed be said that I wanted to do it, but it does not follow that I did it *because* I wanted to do it. 'I wanted to do it' here simply means 'I did it voluntarily', and that of course is not much of a reason *why* I did something voluntarily. Indeed, the reply 'Because I wanted to' is not really an answer to the question 'Why did you do it?'; it is simply an idiomatic way of saying that one did it for no particular reason, perhaps just following a whim, or because one 'felt like it'. So the claim that every voluntary action is done because one wants to do it would mean that we never have any reason for what we do – which is absurd.

Secondly, when I do something of my own free will, it doesn't follow that I have a *desire* to do it; not when that word is used in its ordinary sense of a strong longing, an earnest wish or craving. Very few of our everyday actions could, in ordinary usage, be said to spring from a desire. Philosophers, however, are prone to use the word in a diluted sense, so that, by definition, every voluntary action – be it shelving a book, adjusting one's tie or calculating 17 times 3 – involves a 'desire'. So far, so good; but we shall see that the argument is calculated to exploit the ambiguity: The word 'desire', though officially used only in a technical sense, is meant to smuggle in something of its ordinary, substantial meaning. Consider the final step:

> My action is aimed at the satisfaction of one of my desires; so it is, really, self-interested.

All the premiss can legitimately mean is that in voluntarily doing something (say, switching on the light) it is my will, or intention, to achieve the result of my action (say, the light being switched on). But in that there is absolutely no implication of self-interest. It remains entirely open whether the result I set out to achieve is in my own interest or not; and if it is, whether that is the reason I pursue it. However, the choice of words 'aimed at the satisfaction of one of my desires' cunningly suggests a different situation. For in the ordinary sense of the word, a desire, unlike an intention, is a strongly felt emotional state;

and, especially as the object of the desire is not even mentioned, the implication is that I am concerned only about my own well-being.

Thirdly, that false impression of self-indulgence is reinforced by misleading connotations of the word 'satisfaction'. One is likely to think of the state of being satisfied, pleased or contented; whereas, in fact, what is at issue is not the satisfaction of a person, but the satisfaction, or fulfilment, of an intention; which may or may not satisfy the person. We are not always satisfied by getting what we asked for, nor do we always expect or intend to derive satisfaction from it. (Think of accepting the offer of an unappetizing-looking piece of cake out of politeness towards your host.) The function of the word 'satisfaction' in this context is that of an internal accusative: that is, the complement to a transitive verb that in combination with it yields an analytic truth. For instance, the verb 'to hear' has the internal accusative 'sound', for whatever one hears (at least in one basic sense of the word) is a sound. In the same way, it is analytic that what one asks (in the main sense of the word) is a question; what one dances is a dance; and the person one is married to is one's spouse. Similarly, to the question 'What does he desire?' one can always give the analytic – and vacuous – answer 'The satisfaction of his desire'; which may easily be confused with the quite different answer 'Satisfaction', where the word signifies a psychological state.

When the *a priori* argument has been dismantled, the proponent of psychological egoism is likely to resort to empirical considerations:

> Good deeds make us feel satisfied with ourselves, whereas after any wrongdoing we tend to be troubled by a bad conscience. And as we cannot fail to be aware of that, we are in acting morally at least partly pursuing our own interest.

But for one thing, the premises are not invariably true. A miser making a charitable donation on an impulse may, predictably, come to regret it bitterly the next moment; and, alas, not everybody's misdemeanours are paid for by the inconvenience of a bad conscience. For another thing, the conclusion does not follow. The fact that I know my action to have a certain effect does not entail that I perform it *because* of that effect. Most of our actions have foreseeable side-effects that do not in the least influence our motivation. Furthermore, to be guided in one's actions by a desire to enjoy the agreeable feeling of a good conscience has a self-defeating tendency; for if one did the right thing only in order to feel good about it – one would find no more virtue in one's behaviour to feel good about. Like true friendship, a good conscience cannot be bought. But of course, this does not rule out the possibility that a good deed may *partly* be motivated in that self-interested way; especially as one can to some extent deceive oneself about the relative importance of one's own past motives. Yet how frequent and serious that kind of hypocrisy is, is a difficult empirical question, well beyond a philosopher's area of competence, which could only be answered by a careful study of individual cases.

In philosophy it is of paramount importance to distinguish sharply between empirical and conceptual issues. And we must guard against a spurious plausibility which some philosophical claims acquire on account of what seems to be an occasional empirical confirmation. Many people are *prima facie* some way inclined towards accepting psychological egoism because they have indeed encountered, in life and in fiction, a number of cases of hypocrisy and self-deception. And they vaguely think that what was found to be the case then may in truth always be so. However, as a philosophical doctrine, psychological egoism is a conceptual, *a priori* claim, which has to be assessed accordingly. The claim that something is *necessarily* true can never be justified on empirical grounds. In fact, our experience of particular cases of egoism under altruistic disguise implicitly contradicts the philosophical thesis of psychological egoism. For the criteria by which we sometimes say that someone's altruistic action had an ulterior motive tell us in other cases that there was no such ulterior motive.

These are some relatively simple examples of the manners in which linguistic misapprehension and prejudice can lead to philosophical problems and 'theories' that are dissolved by a better understanding of the way in which language works in those cases. Typical sources of confusion are the intuitive assumptions that what is called 'the same', or by the same name, should never change in its physical constitution (1); that a word always has the same meaning (2) or is always applied in exactly the same way (4); that predicates always signify properties (3), that nouns must stand for objects or substances (8), and that verbs of thinking must function like verbs of perception (6). Sometimes unanswerable questions are generated by taking idiomatic metaphors literally (5); and an over-simplified description may make the humdrum appear impossible (7). Scientific explanations of the constitution of a familiar phenomenon are sometimes misunderstood as denying the existence of that phenomenon, and as thus disproving the standard use of some common predicates (9). Finally, a philosophical claim may be reached through ambiguous and misleading formulations, and a conflation of empirical and conceptual considerations (10).

As illustrated, philosophical problems are usually the result of a tension between what a form of expression suggests and the humdrum truths of common sense. This perceived tension will produce different responses in different temperaments. Some will not hesitate to cast aside common sense and accept the most bizarre and counter-intuitive philosophical doctrines. The motivation is easily understandable: There is something attractively spectacular and heroic in holding a view in opposition to nearly everybody else, especially if that view is somewhat shocking, like the philosophical 'discovery' that really everybody is an egoist. Another response is to be rather puzzled by that tension, and formulate a 'profound' and tantalizing question to which one despairs of ever finding the answer, especially of the form 'How is it possible . . .?' (TS 303, 2), or 'What is . . .?'. The latter is typically based on the assumption that a noun stands for an object, which then proves difficult to pin-point: e.g., Augustine's puzzlement over 'What is time?' (quoted in *PI* §89). Or it is inspired by the belief that it must be possible to define what is essential to all instances of the thing in question: e.g., Socrates' aporetic quest for a definition of virtue (in *Meno*) or knowledge (in *Theaetetus*). There are no answers to those misbegotten questions, as there is not really any problem (TS 219, 8; MS 114, 18). Yet, given a certain temperament, one may feel compelled to produce some sort of answer or what looks like an explanation. This will be the kind of nonsense that is called a philosophical 'theory', in conflict with common usage and without any clear use; like Bradley's doctrine of absolute idealism which was meant, amongst other things, to settle the problems raised by his misunderstanding of the word 'is'. At this stage again philosophical confusion has become dogmatic.

To avoid misunderstanding when reading the *Philosophical Investigations*, it is vital to bear in mind Wittgenstein's radical account of the nature of philosophy. And it is important to distinguish between what is peculiar in Wittgenstein's philosophy and what is peculiar in his style and presentation. The latter is obviously to a large extent an expression of his aesthetic preferences (see sect. 4.1 above) that need not be shared or emulated by other philosophers, even if they entirely agree with Wittgenstein's observations and conclusions. But there is a danger of conflating this idiosyncratic presentation with the author's equally unconventional views on the subject, and then regarding these also as merely a matter of taste. It is largely a matter of temperament that the *Philosophical Investigations* is not written in a more orderly and systematic manner; so it might appear that Wittgenstein's rejection of philosophical theory is just another manifestation of that aphoristic temperament. Far from it. In a number of case studies, Wittgenstein gives convincing reasons why philosophical theories are not just false and in need of replacement by better theories, but are sheer nonsense or patent falsehood, to be dissolved in favour of common sense. As there is no meaningful question in the first place, there is no occasion for any theory to answer it. This may not amount to a conclusive general proof that philosophical doctrine is impossible, but it is at any rate an extremely well-supported challenge, which has nothing to do with Wittgenstein's literary style. Unfortunately, it is all too common among the academic audience to ignore that challenge or brush it aside lightly, and to treat the book as essentially an ordinary philosophical treatise, containing, at least the sketches of, a number of philosophical theories as controversial as other philosophical theories. In defence of this approach, critics of Wittgenstein's philosophy have been quick to point out that in spite of his protestation not to advance any controversial thesis, all the crucial elements of his philosophy have provoked heated philosophical debates. A little reflection shows that this is not surprising. For one thing, what should not be controversial when fully explained, step by step, may well sound unclear or even paradoxical when only hinted at or condensed to a poignant aphorism (cf. WVC 183). But, more importantly, philosophical theories have always contradicted the most humdrum observations of common sense, so why should we expect Wittgenstein's reminders of common sense to be safe from the onslaughts of philosophical perversity? Philosophers have denied that you can step into the same river twice, that trees continue to exist while unperceived, and that we can know of other people's feelings. So there is nothing extraordinary in the fact that the platitudes to which Wittgenstein draws our attention should not go unchallenged *among philosophers*. It is only to those with no philosophical positions to defend that Wittgenstein's reminders are meant to be uncontroversial.

4.4 Meaning and Use

Against Wittgenstein's startling account of philosophy, in particular his renunciation of all philosophical theories (*PI* §109) and controversial theses (*PI* §128), it has been objected that his own practice involves what he claims to forgo. Does he not early on in the *Philosophical Investigations* propound the theory that meaning is use, which stands opposed to other philosophers' theories of meaning? – What this common view takes to be Wittgenstein's 'theory of meaning' is expressed in the book in a single sentence:

> 43. For a *large* class of cases – though not for all – in which we employ the word "meaning" it can be explained thus: the meaning of a word is its use in the language.

However, this should be taken as a trivial reminder (like the reminder that time is measured by counting events in regular succession: e.g., sunrises), aimed against the impression often evoked by philosophers that linguistic meaning is a mysterious phenomenon which needs to be explained by some sort of theory (as Augustine thought that the measurement of time was a mystery in need of philosophical explanation). There is nothing mysterious about the meaning of a word. Just remember what children learn when they learn what the words 'thanks', 'milk' or 'naughty' mean. They acquire the capacity to handle those words: to say 'thanks' when they've been given something; to ask for 'milk' when they want to drink some of that white stuff; to recognize under what circumstances someone is called 'naughty', and so forth. In short, they learn to understand how those words are used: on what occasions, for what purpose, for what objects, behaviour or people. They also learn how to string words together: how they are used to form sentences, and how those sentences are used: to give orders, ask for help, ask for information, reply to a question, express one's feelings, give a description, make a promise, confirm, contradict, tell a story, etc., etc. To return to Wittgenstein's first example of a language-game, the purchase of five red apples (*PI* §1): the customer and the shopkeeper must know what the words 'five red apples' mean; and what that amounts to is that they know how to use them, which includes how to respond to them. Again, think of dictionaries: how do lexicographers establish the meaning of a word? They study how the word is used, especially by educated and articulate people, and attempt to capture that usage by a definition or paraphrase, and, in a larger dictionary, illustrate it by a few quotations. A dictionary gives the meaning of a word correctly if and only if it accurately represents accepted usage. In short, meaning is use.

As I said, this is not meant to be a discovery, but common sense (for in philosophy one often needs to state the obvious to dispel confusion). However, contradicting common sense is exactly what philosophers do when under the spell of some confusion; so, naturally, philosophers have raised objections to Wittgenstein's observation. Discussing those objections and uncovering some common misunderstandings will shed further light on the concepts of meaning and use.

1. If one ignores Wittgenstein's whole conception of philosophy, or brushes it aside as an irrelevant whim, and stubbornly pursues the idea that philosophers must advance theories, one will naturally assess 'meaning is use' as another 'theory of meaning'. Taken in such a perverse way, as a philosophical theory – just the sort of thing Wittgenstein was intent on debunking – his remark will of course appear far too vague and insubstantial to be satisfactory. One writer insists against Wittgenstein's anti-theory attitude that 'when what is under consideration is a connected and patterned set of practices – whether it is riding a bicycle or speaking a language which is in question – it should be possible to formulate a theoretical representation ... of what is involved' (Grayling 1988, 99). The comparison is revealing: we could indeed produce a detailed account of speaking a language as we could give a detailed account of riding a bicycle. But why should we? Part of

it is trivial, and its circumstantial description in print would be a colossal waste of time: you don't want to read a book that tells you how to hold your arms to reach the handlebars of a bike, and how to move them in order to turn to the right, and how to move them in order to turn to the left, and so on. Part of it is not trivial, but is clearly not within a philosopher's competence: it requires physiological research to describe the role of various muscles and nerves when one rides a bicycle. Similarly for systematic descriptions of speaking a language, except that the familiar and trivial part may be unfamiliar and interesting to foreigners. But, again, the writing of a learners' grammar book of English is hardly a philosophical job. Besides, it is not as tedious as a really comprehensive description of all uses of language would be, for the reader's familiarity with the basic forms and concepts of linguistic communication (ordering, asking for information, thanking, etc.) is presupposed. Just imagine if the kind of description of language use that Wittgenstein gives of the builders' language – with only four different words, one type of utterance and one type of response – were to be provided for the whole of the English language!

People have often wondered why twentieth-century philosophy became so obsessed with language. The question is not unreasonable. After all, there is already a respectable academic discipline that investigates the phenomena of language systematically and in great detail: linguistics. So why should philosophy tread the same ground? It would indeed trespass into linguistics if it offered anything that could be called a theory of linguistic meaning; just as theories of monetary inflation, or gravity, belong to economics, or physics. But philosophy, as presented and practised by Wittgenstein, is not interested in language for its own sake; it concerns itself only with a certain kind of puzzlement or paradox that arises from a misunderstanding of particular words and expressions. Wittgenstein's investigations of language are purely instrumental and limited to what is required to overcome a given conceptual confusion. As it happens, in his early philosophy he had tied himself into knots when thinking about linguistic meaning. In the *Investigations*, to disentangle his own earlier confusions, he needed to clarify the concept of meaning. Naturally the account is highly selective (focusing only on those aspects that have produced confusions or seem likely to do so) and sketchy, as nothing new is to be presented, but we are only to be reminded of what outside philosophy we are perfectly familiar with.

2. Even if it is understood and accepted that no *theory* of meaning is intended by Wittgenstein, one may still complain 'that the term "use" *in vacuo* is too nebulous to be helpful'; that it remains to be worked out in detail 'what aspects of use are relevant to meaning' (Glock 1996a, 209f; cf. Grayling 1988, 99f). – However, in §43 the word 'use' does not

occur *in vacuo*, but in an explanation of the concept of linguistic meaning, thus placing some obvious restrictions on the intended notion of use. Three obvious points need to be borne in mind. Linguistic meaning is determined by:

(i) linguistic conventions;
(ii) what competent speakers are expected to know about words (types);
(iii) what one needs to know about words in order to understand particular utterances.

And so, evidently, is the use that is meaning. It will be seen that some common objections to this identification result from a reading of the term 'use' that is clearly inappropriate, as it neglects those simple truisms about linguistic meaning. Of course a certain amount of vagueness and room for disagreement remain. It may not always be possible to draw sharp boundaries between linguistic convention and stylistic custom, or to ascertain which conventions are relevant to understanding and which are merely ornamental. Such vagueness in our concept of meaning will be reflected by the relevant concept of use.

3. 'Could I not know the use of an expression and fall in with it, mechanically, but without understanding it?' As an example, the author of this objection mentions undergraduates who were adept at picking up and bandying about pieces of academic jargon they had not really understood (Lycan 2000, 94). But how did he know that they had not really understood those words? Obviously by noticing deficiencies in their use of them (cf. VW 464f). To master the use of the word 'metonymy', for example, one needs to learn what to call a 'metonymy' and how it differs from other figures of speech. An undergraduate who spoke glibly of metonymies in Victorian poetry, but when asked to point one out or, perhaps, to explain the difference between metonymy and metaphor proved unable to do so, would not have mastered the use of that expression.

4. How can a rule-governed use of words, something like playing a game, ever generate meaning? After all, chess moves or tennis shots have no meaning; they never *say* anything (Lycan 2000, 95–7). – It is not easy to see the force of this objection: one might as well query how it is possible to score a goal in football, as there are no goals in tennis or chess. However, what the objector appears to have in mind is this: 'no matter how complex the game becomes, the players' utterances do not refer to things external to the game; they are only moves in the game' (Lycan 2000, 96). Now it becomes clear where this writer got hold of the wrong end of the stick. He seems to think that because

Wittgenstein sets his face against referentialism (the idea that meaning is essentially a matter of reference), he can't account for the fact that words can ever refer to anything! In fact, Wittgenstein demonstrates early on, in the language-game of the builders (*PI* §2), how linguistic reference can be brought about: not by some mental act of meaning something, but by a conventional link between the utterance of a certain word by one person and the bringing of a certain object by another. The description of a language-game explains in what way words can be said to refer to objects (*PI* §10). Again, to explain does not mean to explain *away*. The objector appears to have taken the metaphor of a language-*game* all too literally, and he seems to have missed the crucial point that a language-game is not just the uttering of words, but also 'the actions into which it is woven' (*PI* §7): not just A's calling out 'slab', for example, but also B's response of bringing a slab. Hence, where a fully-fledged natural language is concerned, there are no 'things external to the game'.

So how is it possible to *say* something in a language-game? – Well, how is it possible to score a goal in football? Kicking the ball into the net in accordance with the rules *counts* as scoring a goal. And similarly, in the builders' language-game, A's uttering 'slab' counts as saying that B should bring him a slab.

5. It has been objected that two expressions may have the same meaning without having the same use: for example, the pairs 'wireless' and 'radio'; 'pavement' and 'sidewalk'; 'measles' and 'rubeola' (Rundle 1990, 10; 2001, 101). – But they do have the same use – unless we take the word 'use' in an obviously inappropriate sense. The difference in each of these cases is that one word is used by one group of people (elderly, British, laymen), while the other word is used by another group (young or middle-aged, American, medics). But the *way* the word is used – and in particular what things are called by the name – is exactly the same. And that is obviously the sense of 'use' that is at issue here. One wouldn't say that Russian keys are used differently from English keys – because they are used *by Russians*. A difference in the group of users is not normally called a difference in use.

It is different where one of a pair of words has different connotations: for example, 'dog' and 'cur'. Although the words may be applied to the same kind of animals, 'dog' is a neutrally descriptive term, whereas by 'cur' the speaker expresses an attitude of contempt towards the animal in question. This is undoubtedly a difference in the way in which the words are used, but it's equally natural to call it a difference in meaning. Clearly, the meaning of a sentence can be changed considerably by replacing 'dog' by 'cur' (e.g., in 'I see you have a dog'); and any competent speaker must be aware of the pejorative connotation of 'cur' (whereas a monoglot American need not be aware that 'sidewalk' is not used in British English; indeed, he may not even know that there are different varieties of English).

6. Some people have thought that by 'use' Wittgenstein meant mainly the performance of speech acts (such as insulting, cursing, thanking, promising). Thus they took the remark that meaning is use as the claim that word meaning could be explained in terms of speech acts. But that is not at all Wittgenstein's position. Just consider the first section of the *Investigations*, where we are given a simple example of the use of the three words 'five red apples'. They all occur in the same speech act of placing an order in a shop, but their use is evidently different, as brought out by the different responses of the shopkeeper: choosing a kind of fruit, identifying fruit of the right colour, counting up to five. On the other hand, speech acts are of course an important part of what Wittgenstein means to cover by the term 'use' (cf. *PI* §23), and there are indeed words that are closely linked with certain speech acts: for example, 'to thank' or 'to apologize'. To understand their meaning, you have to understand the corresponding speech acts: i.e., the function of uttering expressions like 'Thank you' and 'I apologize'. Yet this point has been denied: 'Suppose I tell you what a given word can be used *for*: if I say it can be used to insult, to appease, to inspire, I ... say nothing about its meaning' (Grayling 1988, 100). – False. If I say that a given word is used to insult: that is, as a term of abuse, I say *something* about its meaning, though probably not everything. That depends on whether beside being a term of abuse the word has any descriptive content, like 'cad', but unlike 'sod'. Consider also the word 'bloody' in its colloquial (if by now somewhat old-fashioned) use as an intensifier: to describe it thus is nearly all one can say about its meaning.[17] That is of course an exception: most words have a use that is far too complicated to be explained fully by saying that they are 'used to ϕ'.

Again, John Searle argued that the meaning of the word 'good' could not be explained by characterizing it as a term of commendation (i.e., as a word used in speech acts of commendation) because not every literal use of the word is a commendation. 'I doubt if this is a good knife', for instance, is not (1969, 136ff). But the argument is unconvincing. It is clear that the understanding of a straightforward predication ('This is F') is a prerequisite for the understanding of the same predicate in more complex sentences ('If this weren't F, I wouldn't tell you') and

---

[17] Wittgenstein was very fond of this queer English expression and used it regularly in his nonsense correspondence with his friend Gilbert Pattison: for example, signing himself 'Yours bloodily' (Monk 1990, 266).

different speech acts ('I promise you that this is *F*'). Hence to learn what speech act is, or can be, performed with an utterance of that straightforward predication will clearly contribute to one's understanding of the predicate in general (cf. Glock 1996a, 211).

7. A standard objection to Wittgenstein is that the use of a word can be fashionable, tactless, accompanied by gestures, effective or uncalled for; none of which can be said about the word's meaning (Grayling 1988, 100; Rundle 1990, 9; Glock 1996a, 378). – This can be discussed together with the next complaint.

8. The use of a word (it has been said) cannot *be* its meaning because it *presupposes* its meaning (Rundle 1990, 13). Only because 'sister' *means* 'female sibling' can the word be used to refer to a female sibling. – Both these objections exploit an ambiguity, and are easily dissolved by spelling it out. By 'the use of a word' one can mean:

(a) a particular application of a word (e.g., your calling Toby a 'chump' last night);
(b) the use of a word in a particular way, or in preference to other expressions (e.g., 'refute' in the original sense of 'disprove'); or
(c) how a word is to be used (correctly).

When Wittgenstein identifies meaning and use, what he means is (c). Learning the use of a word requires more than becoming acquainted with a certain way of using the word; you also have to understand that it is the correct way. The normativity of language is a recurrent theme in the *Investigations*, manifest in the frequently invoked comparison of language to rule-governed games, and also in the extended analogy between understanding language and understanding arithmetical rules (*PI* §§143–242). Thus it should go without saying that Wittgenstein did not intend to identify meaning with use in sense (a) or (b); yet that is exactly how the expression 'use of a word' is taken in the objections under discussion. Your use of the word 'chump' last night when speaking to Toby may have been tactless, accompanied by gestures, effective or uncalled for; but it would be nonsense to say that it is tactless etc. how the word 'chump' is to be used. The way a word is widely used one may call fashionable (b): for example, the use of 'refute' in the sense of 'deny' (and its correct use in the sense of 'disprove' may be said to have gone out of fashion); but how the word 'refute' is to be used is not something one could meaningfully call fashionable or unfashionable. At most one could say that it has become unfashionable *to hold* that this is the correct use. Similarly, it is rather ungrammatical to call a meaning unfashionable; but *regarding* something as the meaning of a certain word may well become unfashionable.

As for objection (8): Any *particular use*, or application, of a word (a) presupposes its meaning and cannot be identified with it; but that does not stand in the way of identifying meaning with how a word is to be used (c). Indeed, it is perfectly true to say that you could use the word 'chump' to insult Toby last night only because it is accepted usage to call a fool a 'chump'. In this respect, the meaning of a word may be compared to the value of a bank note (cf. *PI* §120). You can use a twenty-pound note to buy a book only because the note has a certain value; but what does that value consist in? It is simply the fact that there is a generally accepted use of bank notes as what you give and take in exchange for goods and services. So again, any particular use is dependent on a conventional usage.

9. Many philosophers are inclined to think that the identification of meaning and use is a confusion of areas of linguistics that should be kept separate: namely, semantics and pragmatics. However, that view has no substance unless one can give an account of meaning that is independent of use and an account of use that is independent of meaning. The most natural candidates for the former are referentialism and mentalistic accounts of meaning, both subjected to a devastating critique in the *Investigations* (see sect. 4.2 above). Two more, contemporary philosophical accounts of meaning will be discussed later (sect. 6.2b). As for the latter requirement, an account of use as distinct from linguistic meaning has been put forward by Paul Grice, in an attempt to defend philosophical claims about the meaning of certain words against the so-called linguistic philosophers' protest that those words are not used like that. If we observe that the use of an expression X is inappropriate under conditions C, Grice argues, it doesn't follow that this is part of the meaning of X. For example, it is inappropriate to say that someone *tried* to perform an action unless there was at least a possibility of failure (*PI* §§622f). This is a familiar aspect of the use of the verb 'to try', but not, according to Grice, part of its meaning. Admittedly, by using the verb 'to try' one leads others to expect that there was at least a possibility of failure, but this is merely a matter of what Grice has called 'conversational implicature', not of semantic implication. To illustrate this with an uncontroversial example, by saying of a student, 'NN has good handwriting', a tutor may indirectly convey that NN's academic talents are negligible, yet this is clearly not part of the linguistic meaning of the sentence uttered. To say of an academically *able* student that he has good handwriting may be misleading, but it might well be true. Likewise, Grice would argue, to apply the verb 'to try' to an obviously easy act like raising one's arm under normal circumstances would be misleading, but not incorrect (Grice 1989, ch. 1). Thus use (pragmatics) must be distinguished from meaning (semantics). – However, it is far from clear whether the two cases are really

alike. It would be ludicrous to claim that 'X has good handwriting' implies 'X is academically weak'; but it's not at all implausible to suggest that 'X tried to φ' implies 'either X failed to φ or it seemed possible that he might fail'.[18] Anyway, the phenomenon of indirect insinuation, or 'conversational implicature', is not in doubt, and indeed common enough. Does that contradict Wittgenstein's identification of meaning and use? Not at all. Again, we need to bear in mind that Wittgenstein is concerned with the use of words that is governed by linguistic conventions (cf. (2i) and (8c) above), while Grice reminds us that our aims and effects in using words go beyond what is conventionally fixed; and not only in cases of insinuation. After all, linguistic conventions determine what words mean, but they don't tell you what to say and to what end and what impression your utterance will make (cf. *PI* §498). For example, it is not determined by linguistic conventions when and how one is to amuse one's audience, or surprise them, or impress them with one's knowledge. So there are indeed aspects of language use that cannot be accounted for in terms of linguistic meaning alone. But the apparent contrast between meaning and use is in fact one between different aspects of use: to some extent our use of language can be explained by linguistic conventions, but beyond that it requires psychological explanations in terms of intentions, preferences, beliefs and expectations.

10. Wittgenstein's critics have cited examples of words which they claim have a use, but no meaning, such as 'abracadabra', 'tally-ho' (Rundle 2001, 100), or proper names such as 'Tom' or 'Bert' (Pitcher 1964, 252). Furthermore, there are expressions that have a meaning which, however, is irrelevant to their use and often not known to competent speakers: e.g., 'amen', 'QED', 'Roger' (Pitcher 1964, 252). – To begin with, it should be noted that these objections largely concede Wittgenstein's point: they are based on what we say: on how we use the words 'meaning' and 'use', thus implicitly acknowledging that questions of meaning (as whether, in this context, 'meaning' and 'use' mean the same) boil down to questions of use. However, to assess those objections we need to take a closer look at the concept of the meaning of a word.

The *Concise Oxford Dictionary* defines: '**mean** . . . *v.tr.* . . . (of a word) have as its explanation in the same language or its equivalent in another language'. The normal use of the verb 'to mean' when applied to a word (not a person or an event) is indeed to indicate a paraphrase: 'spruce' means 'neat in dress and appearance'; and the French word *piscine* means 'swimming pool'. Where a word X can be paraphrased,

---

[18] See sect. 4.8 (aii) below.

or translated, as Y, it is always correct to say that X means Y. Following this common usage, we would have to say that the meaning of a word is its paraphrase. – That explains why one hesitates to attribute a meaning to some perfectly common and respectable words: they cannot be paraphrased; no other expression can be used in their place. Proper names are the prime example. If the word 'Arthur' has been chosen as a person's sole first name, then it is unique in this function. As far as this man is concerned, there is no other word in the language – or any other language – that has been given the same role. If you want to call Arthur by his first name, then there is no alternative to 'Arthur': no other way of saying it, hence no expression to complete the sentence 'The English word "Arthur" means . . .'. Similarly, with 'amen', which in English is conventionally uttered at the end of a prayer and in this liturgical role is not replaceable by any other expression. In such cases the request for a paraphrase: 'What does it mean?' is referred to the word's etymology: in Hebrew *'amen'* means 'certainly'. Likewise, the question of what the meaning of a proper name is can be answered etymologically: by giving, say, the meaning of the Greek, Latin or Germanic word from which the English proper name has been derived.

If we were to follow this most common employment of the word 'to mean' in the linguistic sense, we would indeed have to disagree with Wittgenstein. The meaning of a word, it would appear, is not its use, but its paraphrase. However, this is not the end of the story. Consideration of some further aspects of the way we talk about linguistic meaning will lead to a different picture.

First, although it is true that where a word cannot be explained by a paraphrase of the form 'X means Y' we do not normally speak of its meaning (as we cannot *give* it in a few words), we do not for that matter call such words meaningless. After all, it is also correct to say that the linguistic meaning of a word is what is conventionally understood by or about it, and clearly there is something that is conventionally understood about 'amen' or the function of a proper name. – Note that if the explanation is to remain within the same language, even some descriptive predicates do not easily fit the schema 'X means Y'. Colour words, for example, are not explained by paraphrase, but by ostension. The natural answer to the question 'What does "beige" mean?' is not '"Beige" means . . .', but 'Beige is this colour ⇨'. Thus questions for the meaning of a colour word are not answered by calling anything 'the meaning' (or 'what the word means'), yet they are not rejected, or answered in the negative, either. 'Beige is this colour ⇨' does answer the question as to what the word means. Nobody would want to say that colour words have no meaning just because nothing can be easily given as a verbal expression of their meaning.

Secondly, 'grateful' means 'thankful', and so, of course, 'thankful' means 'grateful'. As each has a different paraphrase it would appear that each has a different meaning; but of course both mean the same. (And it is no way out to suggest a third expression, say 'feeling gratitude', as their meaning; for then all three expressions would have the same meaning, and we would need a fourth synonym to *be* that same meaning; but then we would have four expressions with a common meaning which needs to be identified; and so on: we would be launched on an infinite regress.) This shows that meaning and paraphrase cannot be identified after all.

Thirdly, you may learn from a monolingual German dictionary that *bereits* means *schon* – without yet having the foggiest idea *what* they mean. Evidently, a paraphrase gives you the meaning of a word only if you already know the meaning of the paraphrase. And that knowledge of meaning must be more than the ability to provide yet another paraphrase (e.g., *schon* means *déjà* in French). For, again, one may know that paraphrase (from a German–French dictionary) while being entirely ignorant of the words' meaning: unable to use or understand those words in conversation. Clearly, as one cannot go on for ever translating one expression into another, there must be more to knowledge of meaning than the ability to paraphrase (cf. *PI* §201). In short, meaning cannot simply be the same as paraphrase.

Fourthly, not only is the ability to paraphrase not a *sufficient* condition of knowing a word's meaning, it is not even a *necessary* condition. A person may be too simple-minded and have too limited a vocabulary even to understand the request for a synonym or paraphrase, let alone be able to give one. None the less, he may be perfectly competent in handling his limited stock of words – say, to exchange basic reports about the weather and to give and carry out orders to fetch certain objects. There can be no doubt then that he understands, or knows the meaning of, the word 'bread'; for example, he is able to fetch you some bread when you ask for it, ask for it himself when he is hungry, correctly identify something as 'bread', tell you whether there is any bread in the house, and if so where, and so forth. Explanation by paraphrase is one way in which understanding of a word may be manifested, but it's not the only way and not even the most important one. –

So, in summary, as the most common way of explaining a word's linguistic meaning is by paraphrase ('*X* means *Y*'), the word 'meaning' (and its cognates) has come to be idiomatically associated with explanatory paraphrase, and where a word cannot easily be explained by paraphrase, talk of 'meaning' sounds not entirely appropriate. But even with respect to the idiomatic use of 'mean' (and 'meaning') it is not possible simply to identify meaning and paraphrase: knowledge of one does not always coincide with knowledge of the other; a word without paraphrase need not be meaningless; a word and its paraphrase have the same meaning, but different paraphrases. So, on closer inspection, even the idiomatic use of 'mean' refers us back to a more fundamental concept of linguistic meaning.

Linguistic meaning is the internal object of linguistic understanding. Hence, we can say analytically that the linguistic meaning of a word is what is to be understood about a word according to the conventions of the language (cf. (2) above). A paraphrase is merely in most cases the most convenient way of conveying this understanding, provided of course that the addressee has already mastered the meaning of the paraphrase. And what is to be understood about a word according to the conventions of the language? The correct way of using it; and that applies also to words that cannot readily be paraphrased, like 'amen'[19] or proper names.[20] So, going back to this fundamental concept of linguistic meaning, the fact that in some cases we do not give explanations of the form 'X means Y' is no objection to Wittgenstein's identification of meaning and use.

11. It has also been objected that use goes further than meaning: you may know the meaning of a foreign word, but not know how to use it – for example, if you know that the French word *chien* means 'dog', but don't speak French (Pitcher 1964, 252). – But that is not in fact true. You can use it at least as a foreign word in English, of which there are many common examples (*ennui, soupçon, Bildungsroman*). But what if you knew no English either, or any other language, so that you could not use the word *chien* in any sentence: could you not still know its meaning? That is indeed to some extent possible: someone who went in search of a dog whenever the word *chien* was uttered to him could be said to have some (though hardly a full) understanding of the word's meaning. Just as the builders in Wittgenstein's language-game (*PI* §2) have an understanding of the word 'block' etc. But that is precisely because those people show an understanding of the *use* of the word in question: that it is used to order a certain kind of object to be brought.

---

[19] For some of the other examples typically discussed in this context, it is in fact possible to give an explanation by paraphrase. 'Tally-ho' means 'Here's a fox!', and 'abracadabra' means 'hocus-pocus'.

[20] Note that the *linguistic* conventions about a proper name do not attach it to a particular person. It is not a convention of English that my daughter is called 'Monica'. The relevant linguistic conventions in this case are merely that some word is declared to be a person's first name, after which it can be used in certain ways: to attract that person's attention, to label that person's place and belongings, to talk about that person, etc.

12. Part of the use of a word in a language is constituted by its syntactic features. Yet syntactic features, it has been protested, go beyond what we regard as the word's meaning. The words 'but' and 'however', for example, differ in the positions they can take in a sentence, and yet their meaning is the same (Rundle 2001, 102). Similarly, grammatical gender belongs to use, but not to meaning. The French word for moon, for instance, is feminine. Thus:

(*L) Le lune est rond

is incorrect; one says:

(L) La lune est ronde.

That is undeniably an aspect of the correct use of the word *lune*, but one hesitates to regard it as an aspect of the word's meaning (cf. *LW* I §274). – Let us consider once more the restrictions which the concept of linguistic meaning places on the relevant notion of use. The third point noted above (under (2)) was that knowledge of the meaning of words (types) enables one to understand particular utterances of those words. Hence, the use that constitutes linguistic meaning must have the same importance. For the most part, however, grammatical gender (like peculiarities of orthography and pronunciation) is fairly inessential to successful communication. A foreigner who is mistaken about the gender of the French word *lune* will not on that account have any difficulties understanding (L), nor would he fail to make himself understood uttering (*L). Therefore grammatical gender and other relatively unimportant syntactic features of words are not subsumed under word meaning.

About the other example, concerning 'but' and 'however', a little more needs to be said. Consider:

(1) But he's a boy.

(2) He's but a boy.

Does 'but' mean the same as 'however', as Bede Rundle seems to suggest (2001, 102)? Evidently, the most one could maintain is that *in a certain syntactical position* 'but' means the same as 'however' *in a certain syntactical position*. For in (2) 'but' has an entirely different meaning ('only'). Thus, although syntactical aspects of use are not normally regarded as part of a word's meaning, they are inseparably connected with it: You cannot give a full account of a word's meaning (or use in communication) without specifying the word's syntactical use, especially where a word has different meanings in different syntactic positions. For then we cannot even speak of the meaning of *the word*, but only of the meaning of the word in a certain syntactic position. –

In summary, the expression 'the use of a word' can be taken in a number of ways that are obviously unsuited to an explanation of meaning: not every aspect of use is meaning (*LW* I §289). But bearing in mind what we're looking for, it is not difficult to construe the term 'use' in an appropriately restricted way that avoids the commonly rehearsed objections and quibbles.

In order to get clear about the meaning of an expression, one needs to turn to its use (*PI*, p. 220e). This is not a philosophical discovery, or Wittgenstein's theory of meaning, but a platitude. Yet, when in the grip of a misleading picture of meaning, we need to be reminded of our common sense; just as Heraclitus needed to be reminded that it *is* possible to step into the same river twice (*BT* 412). Similarly, the author of the *Tractatus* needed to be reminded that language does not in fact work the way he described it (see sect. 4.2). Yet how does one find out how language works? Words and sentences are not like chemical substances or biological organisms; they are conventional artefacts, and thus their working lies in their conventional role: in the way we conventionally use them.

However, the reminder that meaning is use is required not only to check the growth of philosophical theorizing about language. Linguistic misunderstandings are at the bottom of every philosophical problem. We misconstrue the meaning of a word due to a false analogy, a hidden ambiguity or some other prejudice about what the word *should* mean; thus, to dissolve the problem, we need to remind ourselves what the word does in fact mean. 'Don't think, but look!' is Wittgenstein's advice (*PI* §66). Look at our actual linguistic practice: that is the only way in which questions of meaning and thus philosophical problems can be settled.

4.5 The Philosophical Problem about Mental Processes and States

> How does the philosophical problem about mental processes and states and about behaviourism arise?
>
> *PI* §308

As we saw above (sect. 4.2f), Wittgenstein came to reject the idea that signs are endowed with significance by a mental process of meaning something. Rather, they have meaning because they are used in a regular and understandable way (cf. *PI* §432). However, this is not the end of Wittgenstein's concern with mental occurrences. In fact, mental states and processes, real or postulated, and their apparent importance and efficacy, are the predominant theme of the *Philosophical Investigations*. After the criticisms of the *Tractatus* theory of language (§§1–108), and the sections on the nature of philosophy (§§108–33), almost all the rest of the book is concerned with different kinds of mental phenomena: understanding; sensations; thinking; imagining; consciousness; intentionality; expectation, belief, hope, intention; feeling; willing; and remembered intention (cf. p. 127 above).

Similarly, in what has been published as Part II of the *Philosophical Investigations*: emotions (i); experience of meaning (ii, vi, xi); imagining (iii); behaviour and states of mind (v); dreaming (vii); kinaesthetic feelings (viii); belief (x); seeing aspects (xi); inner speech (xi); and remembering (xiii).

What is Wittgenstein's concern with all those mental phenomena? Not, of course, the construction of any philosophical theory – no such thing is possible. As argued above (sect. 4.3), the only legitimate task for a philosopher is the dissolution of puzzles that are typically due to some linguistic misconceptions. And perhaps the most momentous and most prevalent misconception, which can be encountered in all areas of philosophy, is what I called referentialism: the idea that 'a word has meaning by referring to something' (*PO* 454), and that 'language consists in naming objects, namely: people, species, colours, pains, moods, numbers, etc.' (*BT* 209v). Referentialism applied to the realm of psychological terms results in a philosophical picture which can be called *The Inner-Object Conception*. If words (nouns and verbs, at any rate) stand for objects, then psychological words must presumably stand for inner objects, objects perceived by one's inner sense inside one's mind, which is thought of as a private container to which only its owner has access. Of course the word 'object' must be taken in the broadest sense to cover any objective phenomena, including states, processes and events.

> 308. How does the philosophical problem about mental processes and states and about behaviourism arise? – The first step is the one that altogether escapes notice. We talk of processes and states and leave their nature undecided. Sometime perhaps we shall know more about them – we think. But that is just what commits us to a particular way of looking at the matter. For we have a definite concept of what it means to learn to know a process better. (The decisive movement in the conjuring trick has been made, and it was the very one that we thought quite innocent.)

This Inner-Object Model is at the root of three kinds of puzzle that Wittgenstein found intriguing, and that he kept investigating with respect to various mental phenomena. First, the paradox of the instantaneous experience of complex contents; secondly, the paradox of first-person authority; and thirdly, the problem of other minds. The first paradox is this: Understanding, intention, expectation, remembering and other such mental occurrences can have remarkably rich and complex contents. It may take a very long time to spell out completely what exactly someone understood, intended, expected or remembered on a given occasion. Yet, it appears that the understanding, intending, expecting or remembering can occur instantaneously: in a flash. How is it possible for some incredibly complex contents to be experienced in one moment?

For example, the meaning of a word is its use, which is extended over time; yet it is possible to grasp the meaning of a word in an instant (*PI* §§138f). So it appears that something extended over decades or centuries can be compressed into one moment. How is that possible? – The first mistake in this paradox is an equivocation over the word 'use', already noted above (sect. 4.4). We must distinguish between how a word is to be used and its actually being used that way. The latter may be located in time ('since 1850') and space ('mainly in the South of England and the Midlands'), but not the former; yet it is only use in the former sense that can be equated with meaning. Bearing this distinction in mind, we will no longer be inclined to say that what is sometimes grasped in a moment has been going on for centuries. Even so, the problem remains. What happens in an instant is obviously not the same as what is extended over centuries, but it must be its representation: something from which all those countless applications can be derived. How on earth can that be instantaneously present to one's mind?

> 139. When someone says the word "cube" to me, for example, I know what it means. But can the whole *use* of the word come before my mind, when I *understand* it this way? . . .
> What really comes before our mind when we *understand* a word? – Isn't it something like a picture? . . .

This idea we have already pursued above (sect. 4.2f). We may indeed have a mental image of a cube in our mind when hearing (or uttering) the word 'cube', but that is not what understanding (or meaning) the word consists in, as one can understand without having any mental image, and no mental image guarantees understanding. Still, the idea is there, and persistently recurs in the *Investigations*, that a mental state, possibly instantaneous, can have a determinate content, possibly very extensive and complicated. After all, we do mean, understand, remember or intend complicated processes:

> 151. . . . A writes series of numbers down; B watches him and tries to find a law for the sequence of numbers. If he succeeds he exclaims: "Now

I can go on!" – So this capacity, this understanding, is something that makes its appearance in a moment.

184. I want to remember a tune and it escapes me; suddenly I say "Now I know it" and I sing it. What was it like to suddenly know it? Surely it can't have occurred to me *in its entirety* in that moment! – Perhaps you will say: "It's a particular feeling, as if it were *there*" . . .

197. . . . There is no doubt that I now want to play chess, but chess is the game it is in virtue of all its rules (and so on). Don't I know, then, which game I want to play until I *have* played it? or are all the rules contained in my act of intending?

So this is *the paradox of the instantaneous experience of complex contents*: *The contents must all be there in a flash*, for I can correctly avow that *at a particular moment* I've understood, intend, expect or remember. Yet, of course, *the contents are not all there in a flash*, for I'm not really aware of all the details: all possible uses of the word, all numbers of an arithmetic series, all notes of a melody, all rules of chess – they're not all in front of my mind at the same time. That is particularly obvious in the case of understanding an arithmetical series, where the object of understanding is literally infinite. – ' "But *this* isn't how it is!" – we say. "Yet *this* is how it has to *be*!" ' (*PI* §112).

Another issue is this: Even if we could persuade ourselves that somehow it was possible for a brief mental experience to have indefinitely complex contents – 'mental processes just are remarkable' (*PI* §363) – another problem would remain. As those rich contents must somehow be hidden or implicit in the experience – they're obviously not all spelt out and on the surface – how then do we immediately recognize them, and thus the kind of experience we have? Should it not be necessary, first of all, to run through all its implications before being able to say what it is we've experienced (a desire to play chess, for example, rather than a desire to play a game with similar, but slightly different rules)? In general, how do we identify our mental processes? And how is it to be explained that we're virtually infallible at it, so that usually it doesn't even make sense to consider the possibility of an error? (It would be absurd to ask: 'Are you sure it's your sister you're thinking of: could it not be somebody else looking just like her?') This is the second recurrent theme in Wittgenstein's discussions of mental occurrences: *the puzzle of first-person authority*. The special certainty we seem to have about our own mental states, which concerns all mental occurrences, but which is particularly remarkable in the case of those with complicated contents.

Finally, if we think of mental phenomena as private objects in a person's mind, the question arises as to how we can ever know with certainty what is in another person's mind, or indeed, whether there is anything at all. Might other people not be mindless automata? This is the venerable problem of *scepticism about other minds*.

To summarize, Wittgenstein's investigations of various mental phenomena are largely concerned with three related puzzles, namely:

1 *The paradox of the instantaneous experience of complex contents*: How can brief mental occurrences have indefinitely complex contents?
2 *The puzzle of first-person authority*: How can we so infallibly identify our own conscious states and processes?
3 *The problem of scepticism about other minds*: How can I ever know what others think or feel, or whether they think or feel anything at all?

The underlying linguistic misconception is a corollary of referentialism:

The Inner-Object Conception: psychological terms stand for objects (states or occurrences) in the mind.

We shall now turn to Wittgenstein's discussion of understanding (*PI* §§138–242), which will also lead to further considerations of the complementary concept of meaning something. For in communication, what one person is supposed to understand is what another person means. And of any expression of one's understanding it can again be asked how it is meant. In this discussion we will be concerned mainly with the first of the three puzzles.

4.6 Understanding and Meaning

In some sense it is obviously true that understanding is a mental state: Yesterday I learnt a new word and now I understand it: I am in a 'state of understanding', which ends when I forget the meaning of that word (*PI* p. 59). But it has no 'genuine duration': there is nothing going on in my mind or consciousness all the time I am in that state (*Z* §§81f). It is a capacity, like my capacity to climb over a fence or to recite the alphabet. As a long-term capacity, understanding is obviously not a conscious occurrence; but its first appearance is often experienced as a sudden insight (when the penny drops). Wittgenstein gives this example: *B* tries to understand the series of numbers that *A* is writing down: 1, 5, 11, 19, ... Suddenly *A* realizes that the next number must be 29 (*PI* §151). What, in this case, is the understanding? Different things may happen, none of which seem necessary or sufficient. In particular, saying the formula to oneself is not enough (*PI* §152). So understanding must be hidden behind those accompanying processes, it seems. But if it is hidden, how does one know that one understands? Here we are in a muddle (*PI* §153). To get out of the muddle, we must overcome the idea that understanding is some inner process that stands behind saying the formula. We should rather look at the *circumstances* (*PI* §§154f).

A word that appears to denote a mental process is in fact applied under certain observable circumstances, quite independently of any alleged inner process. To make this clearer, Wittgenstein inserts the discussion of another case, simpler and easier to survey than that of understanding – a 'synoptic representation' (cf. sect. 4.3 (vi)): namely, translating signs into sounds: reading, but without understanding. Consider two people *A* and *B* who appear to 'read' a text: *A* is a competent reader, while *B* only pretends to read, reciting what he memorized earlier. Now what is the difference between real reading and not reading (always taking the word without any implication that one understands what one reads)? It is not the observable behaviour on this occasion: We can assume that they both utter exactly the same words that are written on the page. So we are inclined to say that it must be an inner process of reading that is lacking in the person pretending to read: 'a peculiar conscious mental activity' (*PI* §156e). We are inclined to say: 'A man surely knows whether he is reading or only pretending to read!' (*PI* §159). However, a little reflection shows that there need not be any difference in what the reader and the pretend-reader are conscious of (*PI* §156), and a person's own judgement as to whether he is reading or not may be mistaken:

> 160. But imagine the following case: We give someone who can read fluently a text that he never saw before. He reads it to us – but with the sensation of saying something he has learnt by heart (this might be the effect of some drug). Should we say in such a case that he was not really reading the passage? Should we here allow his sensations to count as the criterion for his reading or not reading?

The answer is obviously no. And we can also imagine the inverse case: someone may be under the impression that he is reading a text although what he is looking at are but rows of meaningless squiggles (*PI* §160). Moreover, the idea of a peculiar experience of reading proves an illusion. It is of course true that saying 'house' while looking at the written word 'house' feels different from saying it while looking at the signs 'غیقگ'. In the former case it is as if 'when one reads, letter and sound form a *unity* . . . I see or hear the sound in the written word' (*PI* §171). However, such an experience is largely the result of *looking* for a peculiar experience of reading, rarely present in normal circumstances of reading:

171. ... But now just read a few sentences in print as you usually do when you are not thinking about the concept of reading; and ask yourself whether you had such experiences of unity, of being influenced and the rest, as you read.

Clearly not. Whatever experience one may come up with, it need not be present in all instances of reading, and it may be present when one is not in fact reading.

Let us return to the puzzle of sudden understanding, exemplified by the case of realizing how to continue an arithmetical series (*PI* §151). We found that no particular experience appears to be present in all cases of understanding how to continue; and it is no way out to posit some *hidden* element, that one might not be aware of, to constitute understanding: for after all one *is* immediately (though not infallibly) aware of one's understanding (*PI* §153) – and it is exactly this awareness that seems puzzling. Taking the case where the right formula suddenly occurs to one, what more is required to make it an instance of understanding? Obviously, it is also required that one *is* in fact able to continue correctly. But how can one be so sure beforehand that having the formula in one's mind will enable one to continue correctly? Is it perhaps a matter of induction, that is, of reasoning from past experience: 'Whenever in such a situation a formula occurred to me I could correctly continue the series. Now a formula has occurred to me. So, I shall be able to continue correctly'? Not exactly. It may indeed be a matter of past experience, but not of *reasoning* from past experience. The utterance 'Now I can go on' is not the expression of such reasoning; nor would one offer such reasoning to justify one's confidence. On the other hand, one's past experience and proficiency in dealing with algebraic formulae may well be a *cause* of one's confidence on this occasion; and it may be a reason for others to trust one's confidence (*PI* §§179, 324). But as far as my current experience in such a situation is concerned, all I can say is that a formula has occurred to me and now I'm confident that I can go on.

In §185 Wittgenstein describes how a pupil is taught to write down (the beginning of) the series of even numbers on being given the order '+2'. Up to 1,000 he does that correctly; we ask him to continue –

185. ... And he writes 1000, 1004, 1008, 1012.
We say to him: "Look what you've done!" – He doesn't understand. We say: "You were meant to add *two*: look how you began the series!" – He answers: "Yes, isn't it right? I thought that was how I was *meant* to do it." – Or suppose he pointed to the series and said: "But I went on in the same way." – It would now be no use to say: "But can't you see . . .?" – and repeat the old examples and explanations.

188   *Philosophical Investigations*

What is the point of this bizarre example and the discussion that ensues for the following fifty sections? Again, we must resist our inclination to look for some philosophical theory in the *Investigations*, some interestingly new and controversial thesis. Wittgenstein is not proffering any philosophical theories – or if he is, it is only to show them up as the result of illusion and misunderstanding. His remarks are aimed at the dissolution of puzzles that spring, for the most part, from false analogies embedded in our language. And the puzzles he is concerned with in this case stem from an analogy of understanding (and meaning) with physical processes. In particular, he is aiming to defuse what I introduced earlier as the first paradox of mental occurrences: How is it possible to have at any one point in time a mental representation of something highly complex or, as in this case, even infinite? The – highly natural – conception of understanding that leads to the problem was described earlier, when the example of a pupil learning to write a series of numbers was first introduced (in §143):

> 146.   . . . Perhaps you will say here: to have got the system (or, again, to understand it) can't consist in continuing the series up to *this* or *that* number: *that* is only applying one's understanding. The understanding itself is a state which is the *source* of the correct use.

One could call this the *Reservoir picture of understanding*.[21] It may partly be inspired by a mathematical analogy: One is 'thinking of the derivation of a series from its algebraic formula' (*PI* §146). My understanding of the infinite series of even numbers is comparable to a formula, such as '$x_n = 2n$', which determines an infinite series. And when asked to explain the mental reservoir of understanding (or meaning), something analogous to the grasp of a formula seems the only plausible candidate. Wittgenstein uses the contrast between the deviant pupil and his teacher (that is, someone like us) to throw the alleged mental reservoir into relief. Obviously, the pupil did not understand the order '+2' in the way his teacher understood it and meant it. The pupil was not meant to write 1004 after 1000. Does that mean that the teacher had thought explicitly of 1002 as the correct number to write after 1000? No, or if he had thought of that particular transition, then not of countless others. He rather thought that the pupil 'should write the next but one number after *every* number that he wrote' (*PI* §186). This is a general rule, or formula, that may have been in the teacher's mind when he gave the shorthand order '+2'. Now the question is whether

---

[21] 'There is a kind of general disease of thinking which always looks for (& finds) what would be called a mental state from which all our acts spring as from a reservoir' (*BB* 143; cf. *EPB* 170).

the presence of such a rule in someone's mind can account for his understanding or meaning an infinite series. Obviously not (cf. *PI* §152). The teacher may give the rule to his pupil (instead of the abbreviated signal '+2'), make him learn it by heart, and yet there is no guarantee that the pupil will continue correctly. It is conceivable that he misunderstands the explicit rule just as he misunderstood the order '+2': taking it as *we* would take the rule: 'Add 2 up to 1000, 4 up to 2000, 6 up to 3000, and so on' (*PI* §185). So, any rule, even the most explicit one, can be misunderstood; and in endless ways, too: whichever way the pupil continues the series, his writing can always be regarded as in accordance with the rule – *on a suitable interpretation* (cf. *PI* §86). And now it is puzzling how it should be at all possible to follow a rule:

> 198. "But how can a rule shew me what I have to do at *this* point? Whatever I do is, on some interpretation, in accord with the rule."

A typical philosophical paradox: something we know to be easy and ordinary, suddenly, looked at in a peculiar way, appears quite impossible! *Of course* a rule can show me what to do; it would be ridiculous to deny that. Wittgenstein's example may be too easy for a rule to have any use; but if you want to know which number to write next in the series:

0, 5, 22, 57 . . .

then, if you're given the rule:

$$x_n = (n^2 + n - 1) \cdot (n - 1)$$

it will instruct you to write: 116. So, something must have gone wrong on the way to the view just quoted from §198. The argument so far can be summed up as follows:

1. A series of numbers can be continued in various ways.
2. The way it is meant to be continued is expressed by a rule (or formula).
3. A rule (or formula) can be interpreted in various ways.
4. Therefore, a rule (or formula) cannot determine a continuation.
5. Therefore, our meaning (as expressed by a rule) cannot determine a continuation.

The final conclusion (5) is partly based on (2): That the teacher *meant* the series to be continued in a particular way, we tried to explain by saying that he had some general rule or formula in mind. So, if that rule cannot fix a standard of correctness, clearly, his meaning that rule cannot do it either.

Before moving on to the dissolution of this paradox, it is worth pausing to say a little more about Wittgenstein's concern with rules. A common view is that he regarded language as essentially a rule-governed activity, so that an exploration of this topic was a natural part of his philosophy of language. But that is not entirely correct. For one thing (as explained earlier) the later Wittgenstein has no philosophy of language in the usual sense: no doctrine that could be developed systematically with 'Rule-following' as one of its chapters. For another thing, the common view overlooks a crucial ambiguity in the notion of following a rule. By 'the rule by which he proceeds' we could mean any of:

> 82. ... [1] The hypothesis that satisfactorily describes his use of words, which we observe; or [2a] the rule which he looks up when he uses signs; or [2b] the one which he gives us in reply if we ask him what his rule is ...

A rule can be present in someone's behaviour either *explicitly* (2) or only *implicitly* (1). If it is explicit, the person is familiar with a formulation of the rule, or at least able to formulate the rule when challenged to explain or justify his behaviour. For example, when you ask a moderately competent chess player why he did not capture his opponent's knight on c5 with his bishop on c1, he should be able to cite the rule that bishops only move diagonally. But now consider the language use of a 6-year-old. The child's utterances are by and large grammatically correct, and he is able to recognize and rectify obvious mistakes in others' utterances. He says, for example, 'I go', 'you go', 'Kate goes', and realizes that there is something wrong with 'Kate go'. A linguist can describe the child's language use by formulating the rule that verbs in the third person of the present tense take the ending '-s'; but the child himself would not be able to cite this rule, which contains concepts a little too abstract for his understanding at that age (cf. *PU* §31b). Still, in some sense the child can be said to follow that rule: implicitly (as I call it).[22] For that it is important that the child's behaviour is not only in agreement with the rule (as a planet's behaviour may be in agreement with an astronomer's predictions), but that it also displays an understanding of *normativity*: of right and wrong: of the fact that

---

[22] Note that what I call 'implicit' rule-following has nothing to do with the confused idea that an unconscious knowledge of rules may somehow be fitted in one's brain.

some forms of behaviour are accepted or even applauded, while others are rejected and rectified (cf. *PI* §54). – And it is not only with little children that we encounter the distinction between, on the one hand, mastery of a normative right and wrong, from case to case, and, on the other, the more advanced ability to cite or formulate rules, as an abstract account, a handy summary of what is right and what is wrong. Even adults' mastery of their mother tongue is largely a matter of an intuitive awareness of right and wrong in any particular case, without any consideration of rules. Of course, in simple cases (such as the third-person '-s' ending) we could easily formulate those rules when challenged; but that rarely happens, and in our everyday use of language such rules are practically irrelevant. They are formulated by grammarians, partly for academic interests, and partly for the benefit of foreign language students. And when it comes to more intricate aspects of grammar, even adults are often quite unable to formulate the rules that would give an accurate description of their native language use (– just think of the question of when to use past perfect and when to use simple past).

So, language can indeed be said to be governed by rules; but those rules are for the most part only implicit in native speakers' common usage. They can be derived from common usage by anyone who pays attention to it, but they are rarely operative in it: we do not normally use rules to work out what is correct. Rather, we have a fairly reliable 'feeling' for what sounds right in a given case. Rules can be formulated to codify our usage, but our usage is not ultimately based on such rules (cf. Rundle 1990, 5–8).

Although language use is essentially normative, it does not necessarily, or even normally, involve *explicit* rule-following. Hence, Wittgenstein's concern with explicit rule-following in §§185ff is not just a natural corollary of his interest in language. Rather, what drives the discussion in those sections is the temptation to invoke explicit rule-following as an explanation of our linguistic and basic mathematical understanding. We are bemused by the fact that one can learn to develop an endless arithmetical series, for instance the series of even numbers – for it would appear that our understanding needs to grasp at once an infinity of steps, which seems impossible. The only way we seem able to imagine such an infinite series to be contained in the mind is by means of a rule, or formula, from which every step can be derived. Thus, knowledge of a general rule suggests itself as an explanation of an elementary mathematical skill (and analogous, though less clear-cut cases could be produced for verbal skills). However, the explanation soon runs into trouble. At closer scrutiny, explicit rule-following itself begins to look paradoxically impossible.

Now let us return to the argument as presented above. The flaw lies in the step from:

192   *Philosophical Investigations*

    (3)   A rule can be interpreted in various ways

– to:

    (4)   Therefore, a rule cannot determine a continuation.

One might as well argue:

    (i)   Your bicycle could always be stolen.

    (ii) Therefore, it can never be used.

The reply is, of course: *if* it is stolen from you, then you cannot use it; but it is well possible, perhaps even likely, that it is not stolen, and then you *can* use it. Similarly: for any given continuation (e.g., 1000, 1002, 1004), a suitable rule (e.g., $x_n = 2n$) can always be interpreted *not* to yield that result – but it need not be so interpreted, and normally it isn't. Roughly speaking, it is fallacious to argue from 'It can go wrong' to 'It can't go right'. Moreover, even if your bicycle is stolen, it can (and probably will) still be used – though not by you. Likewise, if the rule '$x_n = 2n$' is interpreted in a deviant way, it will still determine a continuation of the series, albeit not the one we expected (but perhaps 1000, 1004, 1008).

Perhaps the worry is that the rule needs to be interpreted at all. It cannot *by itself* determine a continuation. To understand it in some way, it seems, you need to give it an interpretation. And once you accept that an interpretation is necessary, you seem to be launched on an infinite regress: for whatever interpretation you give, it is in no better position than the rule itself. It, too, needs to be interpreted in a particular way (cf. *PI* §86) – and so on, and so forth.

Let us first consider the idea that a rule, or formula, cannot by itself determine a continuation. Wittgenstein's reply is that this is a misuse of language that would result in the abolition of an important distinction (*PI* §189). There are formulae (like '$y \neq x^{2}$') that do *not* determine the value of y for a given x; other formulae (such as '$y = x^{2}$') *do* determine the value of y for any x. It would be foolish to ignore this difference. – But this will not satisfy Wittgenstein's interlocutor, who may retort: 'True, one type of formula does, while the other does not determine a value for a given number; but not *by itself*. $y = 3^2$, for instance, yields 9 *only when interpreted in a certain way*. Thus, strictly speaking, it is not the formula that determines the result, but the formula plus a certain interpretation. And now we are back with the infinite regress problem: for the interpretation would itself be in need of an interpretation, and so on.' – Wittgenstein has this reply:

201. ... It can be seen that there is a misunderstanding here from the mere fact that in the course of our argument we give one interpretation after another; as if each one contented us at least for a moment, until we thought of yet another standing behind it. What this shews is that there is a way of grasping a rule which is *not* an *interpretation*, but which is exhibited in what we call "obeying the rule" and "going against it" in actual cases.

For us to think, even for a moment, that on a certain understanding the formula '$y = x^2$' yields 9 for $x = 3$, the infinite regress that seemed to threaten must have been stopped. Our understanding in this case cannot just be an interpretation: that is, another formula to paraphrase the first, of which again it would be an open question how to understand it. Our understanding of a rule need not be mediated by another rule. What it amounts to is simply this: we are able to work out that $x = 3$ yields 9. How? Well, 'I have been trained to react to this sign in a particular way, and now I do so react to it' (*PI* §198). This is the core of the matter: know-how (a skill) cannot, ultimately, be explained in terms of know-that (a piece of information). For any piece of information, for any formula in the mind, we would again need to *know how* to apply it. *Occasionally*, our understanding of a formula may be based on, or mediated by, our understanding of another formula: thus, when we learn to read a new notation, e.g. '$x!2$' as : 'x^2' (*PI* §190). But such a translation of one formula into another cannot be the paradigmatic case of understanding, certainly not the basic case of understanding: or else we would never *begin* to learn the meaning of any formula. Likewise, our basic linguistic understanding cannot be accounted for in terms of translation into another language. This may be appropriate for one's understanding of some *foreign* words or phrases, but obviously not for the initial mastery of one's mother tongue (cf. *PI* §32).

The suggestion under discussion was that a fairly elementary mathematical capacity (such as developing the series of even numbers) could be explained as the result of having grasped a rule; that the ultimate foundation of mathematical competence was explicit rule-following. Now it turns out that it is the other way round. Far from providing a theoretical foundation for basic know-how, explicit rule-following does itself presuppose some know-how for which no further foundation or justification is possible. It is simply the way we continue after some suitable training, 'by means of *examples* and by *practice*' (*PI* §208).

That may sound hard to accept. After all, the examples run through in training and practice are limited, and do not logically entail any particular continuation. One may want to protest:

211. How can he *know* how he is to continue a pattern by himself – whatever instruction you give him? – Well, how do I know? – If that

means "Have I reasons?" the answer is: my reasons will soon give out. And then I shall act, without reasons.

Again and again, we are strongly inclined to insist that somehow all the correct answers must be laid down in advance in the mind, so that each step can be justified by reference to that perfect mental instruction manual. But that perfect mental instruction manual is an illusion and (as explained) a logical impossibility. Our basic skills must stand on their own. They are engendered by training, but what they enable us to do is open-ended and cannot be exhaustively listed in training, nor could there be such an exhaustive list in the mind or anywhere else.

> With the words '*this* number is the right continuation of this series' I may bring it about that in the future someone calls such-and-such the 'right continuation'. What 'such-and-such' is I can only show in examples. That is, I teach him to continue a series (basic series), without using any expression of the 'law of the series' . . .
> He must go on like this *without a reason*. Not, however, because he cannot yet grasp the reason but because – in *this* system – there is no reason. ('The chain of reasons comes to an end.')
> . . . For at *this* level the expression of the rule is explained by the value, not the value by the rule. . . . (Z §§300–1)

In this manner Wittgenstein dissolves the first of the three paradoxes listed in section 4.5: the paradox of the immediate experience of complex, or even infinite, contents. It resulted from a misguided – and yet highly natural, almost unavoidable – idea of a mental process or occurrence. We are prone to envisage mental occurrences as comprehensive representations, that must somehow *contain* everything the mental representation is about or directed at. That kind of mental representation would be astonishing enough where what we have in mind is fairly complex – as with the rules of chess, which appear to be represented in our momentary desire to play chess (*PI* §197); but it becomes patently impossible when we mean or understand an infinite arithmetical series. At first glance it seemed that such infinity could be represented conveniently by a short formula, but then it became clear that our meaning or understanding the formula would have to contain how the formula was to be applied in an infinity of instances (to forestall an infinity of possible misunderstandings) – which again appears to make such meaning (or understanding) a mind-boggling feat. So, how can the mind perform such a feat? It cannot. The truth is that no such marvellously rich representation occurs; and it is an error to think that it needs to occur for meaning (or understanding) to be possible. But then: if meaning one thing rather than another is not brought about by a comprehensive and infallible mental representation of that thing, how *is* it brought about?

No spectacular answer should be expected. ('One of the greatest impediments for philosophy is the expectation of new, unheard of disclosures' (*BT* 419).) Wittgenstein offers no original doctrine of meaning; he merely invites us to remember under what circumstances it is correct to say that somebody meant something. There is no such thing as an intricate mental mechanism of meaning that could be investigated and explained (*PI* §689). There is no process of meaning: 'For no *process* could have the consequences of meaning' (*PI* p. 218). Any process you might think of can occur without your meaning the thing in question. 'I meant Mary' should not be construed as similar to: 'I kissed Mary'; it is better understood on the analogy of 'I got engaged to Mary'. This is not made true by any bodily or mental process – any such process would be compatible with my getting engaged to somebody else. Rather, for the link of an engagement to be forged, I must be in a suitable situation: characterized not only by what happens at the time, but also by its antecedents and consequences, and by a certain social background involving the institution of marriage. What makes it true that when I say 'Let's play a game of chess' I mean the game of chess with all its rules, and not some other game? Again, the link is not made by some miraculous mental mechanism, but by the circumstances in which the utterance is made: In English 'chess' is the name of a particular game the rules of which have been listed and widely published; there are clubs and organizations that insist on those rules, and people are taught those rules at home or at school. So when a competent and normally educated English speaker speaks of 'chess' he can be taken to mean what we all call 'chess' (cf. *PI* §197). In other words, there is no doubt that when he speaks of 'chess', he speaks of chess (cf. *PI* §687).

'Of course,' Wittgenstein's interlocutor might reply, 'that is what we naturally assume under the circumstances. But is not *what* we assume something more than those circumstances? Is not Wittgenstein confusing the evidence that someone means something with what it is evidence for?' – Admittedly, it is conceivable that someone uses the word 'chess', but means draughts; either because his knowledge of English is less than perfect, or simply through a slip of the tongue. But how would such a person differ from someone who uses the word 'chess' correctly? There need not be any difference in what went through their heads at the time of the utterance: If God had looked into their minds, he might not have been able to see *there* which game they wanted to play (*PI* p. 217). Rather, the difference will be manifest in their responses when the chess-men are set up in front of them. One of them will start to play, the other is likely to look surprised and demur: 'No, I didn't mean *that* game!' – But what if he is too polite or too shy to say anything? Or if the proposal to play is declined in the first place? – Then the difference between them is only a conditional one. To say that they meant different games amounts to saying that they would have said or done different things had the matter been pursued further (*PI* §§187, 684).

Here it might be helpful to remember that 'to mean' belongs to the family of conative verbs together with 'to want', 'to intend', 'to desire', 'to prefer'. (This is more obvious in French where for 'to mean' one says *vouloir dire*: 'to want to say'.) It is easy to see that in order to want or intend something it is not always necessary to be thinking of it, to represent it in one's mind:

> Someone says to me: "Shew the children a game." I teach them gaming with dice, and the other says "I didn't mean that sort of game." Must the exclusion of the game with dice have come before his mind when he gave me the order? (*PI* p. 33)

Of course not. The kind of game he meant is the kind of game he wanted the other one to teach the children. But, normally, it is true to say that someone does not want what he regards as bad or harmful, even when he is not consciously thinking of it. Thus, even at a moment when my mind is blank, indeed even when I am asleep, it is true to say that I do not want anyone dear to me to come to any harm. To have such a want is not a mental process, it is more like an attitude. Similarly, for me not to want an utterance of mine (e.g., 'Develop the series of even numbers!') to be misconstrued in a bizarre way, I do not have to think in advance of all the bizarre ways in which my utterance could possibly be misunderstood; nor do I have to spell out in advance all the obvious implications I would want, and can expect, others to draw from it.

When you mean something, how is the connection brought about? The question sends us in search of some specific connecting mechanism in the mind, which cannot be found. All that can be said is that under certain circumstances, which in practice we are all familiar with, it is correct to apply the expression 'he means . . .'. That sounds disappointing – but only as long as we haven't freed ourselves from the misguided assumption that there must be something more to be discovered. 'The difficulty here is: to stop' (*Z* §314):

> Here we come up against a remarkable and characteristic phenomenon in philosophical investigation: the difficulty – I might say – is not that of finding the solution but rather that of recognizing as the solution something that looks as if it were only a preliminary to it. (*Z* §314)

Namely: a clarification of the way some words are in fact used, where we were misled by some analogy to expect a rather different use. In this case, the misleading analogy is between the word 'to mean' and words for mental activities, like 'to concentrate on' or 'to imagine' (*PI*

§693). To construe the former on the model of the latter sends us in search of a chimera.

An instructive misinterpretation

The gist of Wittgenstein's argument is that meaning something is not a mental process minutely and comprehensively representing its object. Now imagine a reader whose prejudice to the contrary is so strong that Wittgenstein's reminders of how the word 'to mean' is in fact used fall on deaf ears. At the same time this reader is deeply impressed by Wittgenstein's observation that by itself no mental process can absolutely determine a particular continuation of a series, say, or the future use of a word. The conclusion to which this reader will jump is truly alarming: 'There can be no such thing as meaning anything by any word'! Such a reader was S. A. Kripke (1982, 55), and unfortunately his bizarre interpretation has become one of the most widely read books on Wittgenstein. Partly for this reason, but mainly because Kripke's reading affords a nice illustration of exactly the kind of view that Wittgenstein is trying to undermine, I shall insert some comments on it.

Inspired by the deviant pupil of *PI* §185, Kripke poses a 'sceptical' challenge: How can I be certain that I am right when rejecting the pupil's continuation, 1004, 1008, 1012, and insisting on my own, 1002, 1004, 1006? Is there any fact about my past history – mental or behavioural – that would establish that I meant the latter rather than the former (Kripke 1982, 8ff)? There isn't. The sceptical challenge remains unanswered (1982, 55); so 'the entire idea of meaning vanishes into thin air' (1982, 22). In the end, however, Kripke comes up (still in Wittgenstein's name)[23] with a solution of sorts: a 'sceptical solution', that is – somewhat paradoxically – a solution 'conceding that the sceptic's negative assertions are unanswerable' (1982, 66): Although it is never *true* to say that someone means something by a word or sign, yet there are conditions when it is *acceptable to say so*, namely: when the word is used in agreement with common usage (Kripke 1982, 108f).

The first thing to note is that Kripke misapplies the word 'sceptical'. Scepticism is the view that certain things cannot be known; and that must not be confused with the view that there is nothing to be known. For instance, I am not sceptical about the birthday of Father Christmas. Where there is no fact of the matter, there is nothing to be ignorant or sceptical about. And that is exactly what Kripke claims about meaning. As he holds on to the naïve presumption that meaning something

---

[23] Kripke shows some awareness that the views he attributes to Wittgenstein may not, after all, be Wittgenstein's (1982, 5).

requires an occurrence in the person's mind which infallibly determines what is meant, yet accepts Wittgenstein's point that nothing could possibly fit the bill, his position is not scepticism about meaning, but simply (and absurdly) the denial of meaning. So the problem is not (as Kripke's own examples suggest) how to establish that I mean one thing rather than another: e.g., the series with the continuation 1002, 1004, 1006, rather than the series with the continuation 1004, 1008, 1012. If Kripke were right, there could be no question of what I meant. It would simply be impossible to mean anything at all.

Secondly, it is difficult to make sense of the idea (involved in Kripke's 'sceptical solution') that although it is never *true* to say that somebody means something, it is none the less acceptable to say so. For if it is acceptable to say that p, it is also acceptable to say: 'It is true that p' (which is simply an emphatic or concessive way of saying 'p'); and then it must also be acceptable to reject anybody's denial of the truth of 'p' – for instance, Kripke's denial of the truth of any attributions of speakers' meaning.

Thirdly, if Kripke is indeed serious about his denial of meaning (as he seems to be), then his subsequent attempt to patch things up by invoking the agreement among a community of speakers is a non-starter. For the concept of agreement cannot be separated from those of meaning, regularity and rules, and so cannot provide a foundation for them (*PI* §§214, 224ff). Remember that two people can disagree by using exactly the same words, e.g.:

A: I am taller than you.

B: I am taller than you.

And they can agree by using different words:

C: I am taller than you.

D: You are taller than me.

And sometimes it is not clear whether we should say that their statements agree (cf. *PI* §226):

E: We shall go to London tomorrow.

F: We shall go to London tomorrow.

Whether two speakers can be said to agree depends on what they *mean* by their words, and on what we *mean* by 'agree' (*PI* §§214f).

Fourthly: It is widely agreed that Kripke's interpretation is perverse in attributing to Wittgenstein the view that meaning something is impossible. In particular, it has often been pointed out that Kripke makes a lot of the first paragraph of §201 ('This was our paradox . . .'), but completely ignores that immediately afterwards, in §201b, this apparent paradox is brushed away as a 'misunderstanding'. However, the thesis that rule-following and meaning require a community of speakers (henceforth: the community thesis) has been widely applauded, both as an interpretation of Wittgenstein's remarks and in its own right.[24] To begin with the exegetical question: – There is no textual support for the community thesis in the *Philosophical Investigations*. In §199 Wittgenstein makes the point that rule-governed forms of behaviour must be a recurrent practice or custom: 'It is not possible that there should have been only one occasion on which someone obeyed a rule. It is not possible that there should have been only one occasion on which a report was made, an order given or understood; and so on' (*PI* §199). There is no implication that a solitary person could not have a practice of following a rule. Of course that would be an exceptional case. For, as a matter of fact, human beings do not live in complete isolation, and our most important and sophisticated normative practices (language, mathematics) have developed from social interaction and are often forms of social interaction (making a report, giving an order). Hence the most natural examples of rule-governed forms of behaviour, taken from our everyday life, will of course tend to have a social background and involve more than one person. Shared rules are what we are mostly interested in, but they are not the only ones that are possible.

The most likely passage to be cited from the *Investigations* in support of the view that Wittgenstein propounded the community thesis is this:

> 202*. And hence [because there is a way of grasping a rule which is exhibited in correct applications] 'following a rule' is a practice. And to *think* one is following a rule is not to follow a rule. Hence it is not possible to follow a rule 'privately': otherwise thinking one was following a rule would be the same thing as following it.

However, the word 'privately' occurs in inverted commas. That is because it does not simply mean: in private, as is made clear by the final clause: '"Privately"' means: in a way that there can be no distinction between following a rule correctly and only believing to follow a rule. Yet even in the privacy of my study, apart from any community, I can draw that distinction: I can, for example, write a diary in a secret

---

[24] E.g., Malcolm 1986, ch. 9; Fogelin 1987, ch. 12 and 241–6 (Fogelin seems to have propounded the community thesis even before Kripke); von Savigny 1996, 94–125.

code (as Samuel Pepys did) and from time to time consult a table to check if what I think is the sign for a given letter is in fact the correct sign. So this passage does not exclude solitary rule-following. Rather, the 'privacy' that is ruled out here (because it does not allow for the distinction between appearance and reality) is the 'privacy' of one's mind where no independent check of one's impressions is possible. That is confirmed in §256, where Wittgenstein calls a language '"private"' (in inverted commas) only if nobody else could *possibly* understand it. Hence something like Pepys's secret code would not be a 'private' rule, in Wittgenstein's sense, as even if nobody else happens to know it, it is well possible for others to learn to understand it and then to check if it was applied correctly.

It is also worth noting that the community thesis is exactly the sort of thing we should *not* expect to find in the *Philosophical Investigations*, as Wittgenstein emphatically renounced all controversial theses (*PI* §128). At the same time, it is exactly the kind of thesis, or 'theory', that academic philosophers feel comfortable with – much more comfortable than with Wittgenstein's subversive conception of philosophy – and would naturally try to excavate from Wittgenstein's writings.

The closest Wittgenstein gets to the community thesis is in MS 164, a first draft notebook, later published as Part VI of *Remarks on the Foundations of Mathematics*. There is in particular one pertinent passage where Wittgenstein *raises the question* of whether a solitary person could calculate or follow a rule, or whether, like trade, any rule-following requires at least two people (*RFM* 349) – but no answer is given, and the matter is not pursued any further. In other manuscript remarks the question is answered in no uncertain terms: even a completely isolated individual, like Robinson Crusoe, could use a language if his behaviour was sufficiently complex (MS 124, 213 and 221; MS 116, 117). Anyway, none of this found its way into the *Investigations*. Obviously, Wittgenstein did not in the end attach all that much importance to the matter.

Admittedly, rule-following or the application of predicates requires some standard of correctness. But, as noted above, such a standard need not be supplied by other people, it can also consist in a written table which I consult when in doubt. (And if now you want to object that the written table can be misunderstood, the answer is: so can other people.) Indeed, even independent applications of the same sign or rule by a single speaker can confirm each other, and thus allow for a distinction between right and wrong (cf. Schroeder 2001c, 189–91). Imagine a desert islander. Is there any reason why he should not be able to carve some symbolic notches into the wall of his hut to indicate the number of coconuts he has in store? In this case the standard of correctness is particularly straightforward: he can always check if for every notch there is indeed a coconut. – Even defenders of the community thesis tend to shrink from the implausible consequence that a Robinson Crusoe could not be said to follow a rule. 'I do not see that this follows,' writes Kripke: 'What does follow is that *if* we think of Crusoe as following rules, we are taking him into our community and applying our criteria for rule following to him' (1982, 110).[25] But then the community thesis becomes quite vacuous, as now there does not seem to be anything that it rules out. What it boils down to is that if *we* judge or imagine somebody to follow a rule, then we apply *our* criteria for rule-following. Well, obviously. That is true of all predications: if we call something a tree, then we apply our criteria for something's being a tree; but it does not follow that there could not be any tree in our absence. –

To return to the main point: Kripke's problem is that he cannot divest himself of the philosophical theory of meaning that Wittgenstein is attacking: the myth of a mental process that of itself determines once and for all the meaning of a sign. Kripke seems unable to conceive of meaning as anything other than such a process. So when he is compelled to admit the force of Wittgenstein's objections to such a process, he takes that to show that there is no such thing as meaning anything; and that even if our common talk of meaning must somehow be acceptable, it cannot be taken to be true. That is: Wittgenstein's rejection of a philosophical explanation (or pseudo-explanation) of a common fact is mistaken by Kripke for the denial of that fact (the trivial fact that words and formulae are meant and understood in one way rather than another). This is as if someone who denied the existence of phlogiston (a hypothetical substance postulated by eighteenth-century chemists to explain the process of burning) was taken to deny that things ever burn.

4.7 The Inner-Object Conception of Sensations

In §243 Wittgenstein asks:

> 243. ... could we ... imagine a language in which a person could write down or give vocal expression to his inner experiences – his feelings, moods, and the rest – for his private use? – Well, can't we do so in our ordinary language? – But that is not what I mean. The individual words of this language are to refer to what can only be known to the person speaking; to his immediate private sensations. So another person cannot understand the language.

Why should Wittgenstein be interested in such a private sensation language? Again, his concern is with what I called the inner-object

---

[25] In a similar vein: Peacocke 1981, 93; von Savigny 1996, 122.

model: the view that psychological terms stand for objects, or states or occurrences, in a person's mind. His procedure in §§243–315 is to develop the consequences of that view with respect to words for bodily sensations and feelings, and then to show how those consequences lead to absurdity or contradiction. Most important among those consequences is this: as an inner object, a bodily sensation – and indeed, the mind on the whole – is logically independent of any behavioural manifestations; just as the contents of a box are logically independent of the label on the box.[26] This leads straight to the problem of other minds. If minds are independent of behaviour, how can we ever know for certain what others think or feel, or indeed, whether they think or feel anything at all? There is always the possibility of deception: people can hide their feelings and simulate feelings they do not have. But there is also the deeper worry that the contents of our minds may be, to some extent, incommunicable. How do you know whether what you call your 'pain' is at all like the private experience *I* call 'pain'? When I give names to my feelings, the meanings of these names are, strictly speaking, as inaccessible to you as those private feelings of mine. You may guess what I feel, and hence what my words mean, but you can never be certain about it. Thus the inner-object model of sensations leads to the idea of a private language.[27] Box 4.1 is a synoptic arrangement of the view that Wittgenstein is attacking with some of its implications.

(a) The Ascribability Argument

At the core of Wittgenstein's criticisms of this view is a response first expressed in the following dialogue:

> 246. In what sense are my sensations *private*? – Well, only I can know whether I am really in pain; another person can only surmise it. – In one way this is wrong, and in another nonsense. If we are using the word "to

---

[26] In the classical form of dualism, propounded by René Descartes in his *Meditations* (1641), body and mind are described as two distinct substances ('substance dualism'): matter and immaterial spirit. It is rarely held today. Most philosophers now are materialists, inclined to believe that the mind is just a (somewhat mysterious) aspect of some part of the body (the brain). But the dualist separation of the inner and the outer, the idea that mind and behaviour are logically independent, is still popular among contemporary philosophers. It has been explicitly argued for in a well-known paper by H. Putnam, 'Brains and Behaviour' (1965). See sect. 6.2c below.

[27] Although it is not stated explicitly at the outset of the discussion, there is good evidence that Wittgenstein regarded the inner-object model, i.e., referentialism applied to sensation words, as the ultimate source of the private language confusions:

Box 4.1 The inner-object conception of sensations

> (R) The meaning of a word is due to its reference and independent of its use.
> §1
>
> (S) The meaning of sensation words is due to their standing for sensations and independent of their use.
> §§263f
>
> (S*) A sensation is an occurrence in a person's mind, logically independent of expressive behaviour.
> §§243, 257
>
> (1) I *perceive* my sensations directly.
>
> (2) Others can learn of my sensations only *indirectly*.
>
> (3) I cannot describe my sensations to others.
> §§257f
>
> (1a) I *know* what sensations I have.
>
> (2a) Others can never *know* what sensations I have.
>
> §§243, 246
>
> (2&3) For all we know, different people may attach different meanings to the same sensation word (private sensation language).
> §§243, 256–8

(i) The reader is reminded of referentialism in *PI* §264; and its application to sensation language is rejected in §§293 and 304 (cf. §374).

(ii) The text of §257, right at the core of the private-language discussion, was originally (in MS 115, 91) a continuation of the first paragraph of §27, where Wittgenstein lists some one-word exclamations and then asks rhetorically: 'Are you inclined still to call these words "names of objects"?'

(iii) In *BT*, pains and moods figure in a list of what one is naïvely inclined to regard as objects designated by names: 'Language consists in naming objects, namely: people, species, colours, pains, moods, numbers, etc.' (*BT* 209v).

know" as it is normally used (and how else are we to use it?), then other people very often know when I am in pain. – Yes, but all the same not with the certainty with which I know it myself! – It can't be said of me at all (except perhaps as a joke) that I *know* I am in pain.

There is no denying that by ordinary standards we often do know when others are in pain, so in order to make scepticism about other minds appear at all plausible, some more demanding standard needs to be invoked; and that is (what seems to be) the infallible knowledge one has of one's own sensations. By comparison with this paradigm of 'real knowledge', it would indeed appear that not much else can be 'known'. Wittgenstein's rejoinder swiftly turns the tables: Far from being a paradigm of knowledge, this is not really a case of knowledge at all!

To that point I shall return presently. First, let us consider another objection to the view that one cannot know, but only surmise what others feel (2) and (2a). Although apparently a consequence of the inner-object assumption (S*), that assumption is in fact inconsistent with it. The claim that I know sensations only from inner experience is incompatible with my attributing sensations, though precariously, to others. It does not even make sense to assume that something like one's private experience might also be had by somebody else. This objection may be called the Ascribability Argument. It is developed in the following passage:

> 302. If one has to imagine someone else's pain on the model of one's own, this is none too easy a thing to do: for I have to imagine pain which I *do not feel* on the model of the pain which I *do feel*. That is, what I have to do is not simply to make a transition in imagination from one place of pain to another. As, from pain in the hand to pain in the arm. For I am not to imagine that I feel pain in some region of his body. (Which would also be possible.)

The inner-object view is that one learns what pain is by *having* pain. Suppose I have hurt myself, and now I concentrate on the feeling and impress it upon myself that *this* is what one calls 'pain'. But, Wittgenstein objects, even *if* that procedure allowed me henceforth to

---

(iv) MS 166, entitled 'Notes for the Philosophical Lecture', contains three drafts of a lecture on the private-language problems; each one begins with the referentialist assumption:

Meaning consisting of the word referring to an object. . . .
As introduction: / Word referring to an object. . . .
Common idea: a word has meaning by referring to something. . . .
(*PO* 447, 451, 454)

identify my own pains correctly, it would not enable me to understand statements of the form 'NN is in pain'. We may assume for the moment that introspection is good enough to provide me with a notion of a specific occurrence as long as I stay, solipsistically, within the precincts of my own mind; but *introspection can never teach me how to ascribe a sensation to a particular person.* Not even to myself. For, as Hume famously discovered, the self does not occur as an object of introspection (1739, 634). I feel pain, but I do not feel my self having the pain. Hence, the difficulty Wittgenstein points out (in §302) is not how to make the transition from 'I am in pain' to 'He is in pain', but from 'There is pain' to 'He is in pain'.[28] For 'He is in pain' does not mean that what I named 'pain' is now occurring in another place, viz. another person's body. What I, according to the inner-object view, named 'pain' was something observable through introspection only; whereas another person's pain would, analytically, be something I could *not* observe through introspection. Hence the supposition that someone else might have what I, through introspection, defined as 'pain' amounts to a contradiction in terms.

What is required to make sense of the assumption that someone else is in pain is not having experienced pain oneself. It is not the pain one needs, but the *concept* of pain (cf. Z §§547f). And a grasp of this concept includes an understanding of what it means to ascribe pain to a particular person. One must know, in brief, that 'the subject of pain is the person who gives it expression' (*PI* §302). Of course, a pain need not be expressed: one can in many cases keep one's sensations to oneself. Still, it is part of our concept of pain that certain patterns of behaviour (crying, moaning, sighing, gnashing one's teeth, holding or protecting the aching part of one's body, etc.) are natural expressions of pain (cf. *PI* §244). By analogy, it might be said to be part of our concept of a violin that it is a musical instrument that produces a certain kind of sound, although it produces that sound only when in good condition, well tuned and competently handled. Similarly, pain (of a moderate degree) is expressed by such typical forms of behaviour only when the person suffering is unrestrained and willing to show his feelings. And as typical pain-behaviour is not always accompanied by pain (simulation, play-acting), so the sound of a violin may also be produced by something else, electronically.

To repeat, attending to his own experience the proponent of the inner-object model says: 'If I suppose that someone has a pain, then I am simply supposing that he has just the same as *this*' (cf. *PI* §350). Wittgenstein's reply (the Ascribability Argument) is that the proponent

---

[28] Or, indeed, 'I am in pain', for the concepts expressed by those personal pronouns can be acquired only together; as an understanding of 'today' presupposes a notion of other days.

of the inner-object model has not got the conceptual resources for this transition from introspection to talk about others. For even if some inchoate notion of pain could be culled from introspection, it would not allow the ascription of pain to a particular person (cf. Strawson 1974; 1959, ch. 3).

(b) The Idle-Wheel Argument

Wittgenstein's reminder about the way we speak of others' pains (*PI* §246) can be developed into another objection, directed specifically at (2&3) the idea of a private sensation language.

In §272 Wittgenstein sets out another well-known sceptical consequence of the inner-object picture:

> 272. The essential thing about private experience is . . . that nobody knows whether other people also have *this* or something else. The assumption would thus be possible – though unverifiable – that one section of mankind had one sensation of red and another section another.

The *locus classicus* of this marginally worrying consideration is a passage in John Locke's *Essay Concerning Human Understanding* (2.32.15). There Locke discusses the possibility that some people's sense-organs might be set up in such a way that blue objects produce sensations of yellow in their minds, and vice versa. Like Wittgenstein, Locke notes that this speculation of inverted colour perception can never be verified or falsified. And he anticipates another of Wittgenstein's points: namely, that such discrepancies between different people's colour perceptions *would not matter anyway*. No error or confusion would ensue. People would still agree in calling the same colours by the same names, even though the 'appearances or ideas in their minds' were different. However, what Locke fails to notice is that this observation effectively undermines his philosophy of language. Locke's philosophy of language rests on the assumption that what gives meaning to words is their association with 'ideas in the mind of him that uses them' (3.2.2). And 'unless a man's words excite the same ideas in the hearer which he makes them stand for in speaking, he does not speak intelligibly' (3.2.8). But exactly that view is neatly refuted by the thought experiment of the inverted spectrum. Under the envisaged circumstances, there would be no disagreement between different people about what should be called 'yellow' and what should be called 'blue'; hence no disagreement about the meanings of those words in public use. But different people's private experiences of those colours are *ex hypothesi* different. It follows that those private experiences cannot be what determine the meanings of those words in public conversation.

The temptation to explain linguistic meaning in terms of private experiences is relatively easy to resist in the case of colour words. For after all, colours are for the most part objective features of material objects, and not (*pace* Locke) sensations. Pain, by contrast, undoubtedly is a sensation. So it is quite tempting to regard pain as private, in the sense that nobody who had not experienced pain himself could know what the word 'pain' means – the inner-object model. Against this view Wittgenstein employs a manoeuvre like the one above. He gives the following analogy:

> 293. ... Suppose everyone had a box with something in it: we call it a "beetle". No one can look into anyone else's box, and everyone says that he know what a beetle is only by looking at *his* beetle. – Here it would be quite possible for everyone to have something different in his box. One might even imagine such a thing constantly changing. – But suppose the word 'beetle' had a use in these people's language? – If so it would not be used as the name of a thing. The thing in the box has no place in the language-game at all; not even as a *something*: for the box might even be empty. – No, one can 'divide through' by the thing in the box; it cancels out, whatever it is.

'Suppose the word "beetle" had a use in these people's language' – what use could that be? They cannot give descriptions of their respective beetles ('My beetle is a crawling animal, two inches long and red with black dots'), for in that case the thing in the box would no longer be *private* in the required sense. People might learn what a beetle is not only from looking into their own box, but also from what others tell them about *their* beetles; differences between different exemplars would be noticed; and so would a constantly changing beetle or an empty box. – Perhaps a suitable use of the word 'beetle' would be the following: where we say 'I am bored', 'You are cheerful' or 'He is annoyed', those people use the expressions: 'My beetle is boring me', 'Your beetle is pleasing you' and 'His beetle is annoying him'. Now, although they like to picture some of their moods and emotions as being brought about by some concealed creature, the characteristics of that creature – apart from its alleged effects – are entirely irrelevant. They may differ from person to person; they may be constantly changing; indeed, what is said to be pleasing, boring or annoying someone when that person is pleased, bored or annoyed, may as a matter of fact even be a void, an empty box. As far as the meaning of those expressions containing the word 'beetle' is concerned, the actual contents of the boxes are completely irrelevant.

Likewise in the case of sensation talk. Suppose that when people complain about pains, they have *private* experiences that vary dramatically from person to person. Yet, due to their insuperable privacy, these differences can never be ascertained. Then, by the same token, these differences can never affect the *public* use of the word 'pain'. For example, someone complains about a pain in his left knee, and the doctor applies a treatment that cures the pain. This kind of successful communication is quite independent of whether what occurs in the inviolable privacy of the sufferer's mind is of type x, y or z. Hence, where the meaning of our public word 'pain' is concerned, any entirely private occurrence that might accompany the use of that word 'drops out of consideration as irrelevant' (*PI* §293). As Wittgenstein puts it in §271: 'a wheel that can be turned though nothing else moves with it, is not part of the mechanism.'

The Idle-Wheel Argument can be summarized as follows:

1   When other people complain about pain, *we cannot know* whether any *private* experiences they might have are ever of the same kind as our experiences. Perhaps they are completely different.
2   Still, the word 'pain' has a common use. We manage to talk about each other's pains without difficulty.

Therefore

C1   The identity of such private experiences is immaterial to our public talk about pain.
C2   The meaning of the word 'pain' is not determined by the identity of a private experience. In short: pain is not a private experience.

(c)   Knowledge of other minds

Back to §246: Against the sceptic's claim that we cannot know of others' pain with the same certainty with which we know of our own pain, Wittgenstein remonstrates: 'It can't be said of me at all (except perhaps as a joke) that I *know* I am in pain.' Why not? The crucial point is that knowledge (at least in the ordinary sense of the word) presupposes the logical possibility of error and ignorance. You can be said to know something only where it would also have been conceivable for you not to know it. Just as you cannot meaningfully be said to be the winner of a game in which nobody can lose, there is no sense in speaking of knowledge where there is, logically, no possibility of ignorance, doubt or error (*PI* p. 221). But one cannot be mistaken or in doubt about one's own sensations (*PI* §288). Again, where there is knowledge (in the ordinary sense of the word) there is an answer to the question 'How do you know?' (*OC* §550): Either one can cite some evidence, or one can describe one's way of finding out or learning (e.g., by calculating, or simply by looking).²⁹ I can find out from somebody else's behaviour that he is in pain, but I could not find out that *I* am in pain: because it is impossible for me not to be aware of it. Therefore my finding out about others' pain cannot be denigrated as only an indirect and unsatisfactory way of finding out; as ways of finding out, and thus of knowing, about sensations go, there *is* nothing more direct (*PI* §246). Thus scepticism about other minds is stopped in its tracks. By ordinary standards it is undeniably possible often to know what others feel; and the attempt to argue that the first-person case provides a better standard of knowledge fails, for it isn't a case of knowledge at all (not in the same sense of the word).³⁰

The Ascribability Argument (*PI* §302) shows that in order to ascribe a sensation to a particular person, we need a criterion by which to identify sensations in others. And there is indeed such a criterion: namely, appropriate expressive behaviour, which forms an integral part of the grammar of sensation words.³¹ But with that criterion in place, the inner-object picture collapses. As there is a *conceptual* link between pain, for example, and certain forms of expressive behaviour, the idea that in spite of that behaviour – by reference to which the word 'pain' has been given its meaning (*PI* §244) – there might never be any pain becomes inconsistent. Admittedly, the criterial link between the inner and the outer is not a neat one-to-one correlation. There is the possibility of deception. First, we learn that a certain behaviour is called an expression of pain; later we learn that there are exceptions: people may pretend to be in pain (*NfL* 254de; *RPP* I §142); their pain-behaviour may be insincere. However, this qualification is limited. First, deceit too is a form of behaviour (*NfL* 241d): there are criteria by which to tell whether someone is sincere or deceitful; otherwise we could not meaningfully speak of sincerity and deception (*LW* II, 42g). Although we may not always be able to satisfy ourselves as to whether someone is sincere or not, we can normally say what kind of further evidence

---

[29] One may of course have forgotten how exactly one acquired a piece of information (e.g., that Madrid is the capital of Spain); still, there was a way one learnt it.

[30] That is not to deny that one can use the expression 'I know I am in pain' in a meaningful way; but then the word 'know' will function rather differently from its ordinary employment. It may be used to indicate that, unlike an animal, I possess the concept of pain; or it may be a peevish request not to be told what one doesn't need to be told; or to convey that in this case doubt is logically impossible (*PI* §247). At any rate, that it has this latter feature sets it categorially apart from other uses of the word 'know' (*PI* p. 221d) and makes it unreasonable to invoke it as an ideal for those other uses to which the logical possibility of doubt and error is of the essence (as the logical possibility of losing is of the essence in a competitive game).

[31] Wittgenstein introduced a useful distinction between two types of evidence: *criteria* and *symptoms*. If it is part of the very meaning of a term '*F*' that some phenomenon is

would settle the matter. Secondly, deceit is a rather complicated form of behaviour that can be attributed only to creatures whose behavioural repertoire displays a good deal of intelligence. It requires a motive, an understanding of what is to be gained by simulation (*RPP* I §824). Thus the idea that an unweaned infant may be dishonest doesn't make sense (*PI* §249; cf. Z §570). Thirdly, although for any isolated utterance or piece of behaviour one could imagine a setting that would expose it as mere pretence, this is not true of sufficiently long sequences of circumstances and behaviour. Someone may appear to be writhing in agony – but in the next moment get up laughing and show pride in his skills as an actor. But if over months you observe someone suffering from an obvious injury that may even prove fatal in the end, it would be plain ridiculous to insist that this might have been just a pretence. Finally, there is a general objection to all forms of philosophical scepticism. That it is logically possible for a proposition to be false, far from providing a reason to doubt its truth, is merely a trivial grammatical feature of *any* empirical proposition: namely, that it is only *contingently* true or false (cf. Hanfling 1987; Glock 1990).

(d) The No-Criterion Argument

To shed further light on the matter, Wittgenstein sketches a simplified language-game (like that of the builders in §2): a 'synoptic representation' (cf. §122) of the use of sensation words. However, the language-game is given in two instalments: To begin with (in §258) we are given only a reduced version of it, stripped of anything that might make the language understandable to others. That is the way sensation language is envisaged by the proponent of the inner-object picture. Wittgenstein uses this incomplete, private version of the language-game to demonstrate shortcomings of the inner-object model, before he adds the second instalment (in §270) that makes it possible to regard the scenario as one of sensation language. Here is the first instalment:

> 256. ...suppose I didn't have any natural expression for [a given] sensation, but only had the sensation? And now...
>
> 258. ...I want to keep a diary about the recurrence of [that] sensation. To this end I associate it with the sign "S" and write this sign in a calendar for every day on which I have the sensation. – I will remark first of

---

(good, though not infallible) evidence for the presence of F, then that phenomenon is a criterion of F. If, however, we have only discovered through experience that F is usually accompanied by a certain phenomenon, then that phenomenon is only a symptom of F (*BB* 24f; cf. *PI* §354). Thus, pain-behaviour (like crying or moaning) is not just a symptom, but a criterion of pain.

all that a definition of the sign cannot be formulated. – But still I can give myself a kind of ostensive definition. – How? Can I point to the sensation? Not in the ordinary sense. But I speak, or write the sign down, and at the same time I concentrate my attention on the sensation – and so, as it were, point to it inwardly.

Wittgenstein's first critical comment I call: The No-Criterion Argument. It is presented in the same section, immediately after the quoted passage:

> 258. ... But what is this ceremony for? for that is all it seems to be! A definition surely serves to establish the meaning of a sign. – Well, that is done precisely by the concentration of my attention; for in this way I impress on myself the connexion between the sign and the sensation. – But "I impress it on myself" can only mean: this process brings it about that I remember the connexion *right* in the future. [1] But in the present case I have no criterion of correctness. [2] One would like to say: whatever is going to seem right to me is right. [3] And that only means that here we can't talk about 'right'.

In keeping a private sensation diary I have no criterion of correctness (1). But does it really follow that (2) whatever is going to seem right to me is right? And does that entail that (3) here we can't talk about 'right'? – To take the second question first, the answer is: no, that verdict is a little too harsh. (2) 'Whatever is going to seem right to me is right' is not the same as 'Anything is right'. It would still be *wrong* for me to write down 'S' on a day when none of my sensations seemed to be of the same kind as the one I initially called 'S'. Hence, according to (2), one can very well speak of a right or correct application of 'S'. As Wittgenstein remarked in a different place, truth can coincide with truthfulness (*PI*, p. 222). There is no distinction between seeming right and being right in the domain of sensations and feelings. The conclusion that is warranted by (2), the lack of a distinction between appearance and reality, in §258 is rather: (3*) 'And that only means that here we can't talk about an *error*.' Which is exactly what Wittgenstein says about reporting one's pain:[32] 'But I can't be in error here; it means nothing to doubt whether I am in pain!' (*PI* §288).

---

[32] And in the case of pain, too, Wittgenstein once used that slightly exaggerated expression ('no "right"' instead of 'no error'): 'One cannot "be right (or wrong)" in saying: "I am in pain"' (MS 121, 5). Cf. MS 159, 11v: '"You are immediately aware" makes one think you are *right* about something, that you can be shown to be wrong about; whereas the point is that there is no *right* (or wrong) about it. (And of course no one would say: I'm sure I'm right that I have pain.)'

Now to the first question: given that there is no criterion to check whether truthful 'S' inscriptions are *objectively* true or false,[33] is it not possible none the less to wonder whether they are? After all, there are other cases of unverifiable propositions that must nevertheless be objectively true or false. Here is an example: Assuming that Queen Victoria during the last hour of her life did not express any thoughts or memories (and assuming also that there is no life after death), we may still *imagine* (as Lytton Strachey does) or even *believe* that during that hour she remembered Prince Albert in his smart uniform on their wedding day. But we can never know whether this was really so (cf. *RPP* I §366; *LPP* 32). So, 'Immediately before her death Queen Victoria remembered her wedding day' is a proposition that is either true or false, although, as it happens, it can never be confirmed or disconfirmed. The question arises whether the private diarist's 'S' inscriptions might not be of the same character: they are not susceptible of confirmation or disconfirmation, but could they not be objectively true or false for all that?

No. There is a difference between those cases. In the case of Lytton Strachey's conjectures about Queen Victoria we may insist on truth or falsity because we know perfectly well what it means to say that someone remembers Prince Albert, etc. That is to say, although baffled under those special circumstances, we are able in countless other cases to ascertain whether that predicate applies or not. Whereas with 'S' the problem is precisely that we cannot draw a distinction between a generally unproblematic predicate and its baffling application in only some particular cases. We cannot refer back to other applications of 'S' under more straightforward circumstances. The diarist's entries are, and will remain, the only applications of 'S' available. Nor is the case as with some complex predicates (like 'seems to me to be a blackbird') which leave no room for a distinction between appearance and reality, but can be analysed to contain a predicate which does ('is a blackbird'). The sign 'S' is semantically simple and doesn't involve any other predicate. – In conclusion, the attempt to construe the sign 'S' as the name of objective mental occurrences fails: there is no room in this case for a notion of truth that would not coincide

---

[33] Why is there no criterion of correctness? Wittgenstein remarks that the private ostensive definition fails to provide one, which is correct. But it would be rash to think that in order to be respectable or useful an ostensive explanation must provide a standard of correctness. After all, one can teach colour words by pointing at ephemeral samples, like flowers or birds. But then the complexity and regularity of our experiences of physical objects provide us indirectly with standards of correctness which are absent in the case of private sensations. For a discussion of this issue, see Schroeder 2001c, 185–91.

with sincerity; not simply because 'S' inscriptions are found to be uncheckable, but because (unlike in the Lytton Strachey case) there is no predicate involved whose applications would be checkable under *any* circumstances.[34]

This is a powerful argument directed at the very core of the inner-object picture. If a sensation were an inner object perceived and identified through introspection, it would be conceivable that one might misperceive and misidentify it. It would be possible to be mistaken in one's belief that one was in pain. That sounds absurd, and §§258 and 290 go some way towards explaining why: we do not identify our sensations by criteria. And where there is no criterion, there is no possibility of error. But how *do* we identify the sensation of pain? We don't –

> 244. How do words *refer* to sensations? ... how does a human being learn the meaning of the names of sensations? – of the word "pain" for example. Here is one possibility: words are connected with the primitive, the natural, expressions of the sensation and used in their place. A child has hurt himself and he cries; and then adults talk to him and teach him exclamations and, later, sentences. They teach the child new pain-behaviour.

Natural responses to pain are not the result of an identification. The sensation of pain *makes* you cry. But verbal expressions are grafted on to natural ones: we are trained until when it hurts, the word 'ouch', and later 'it hurts', etc. spring automatically to our lips (although, to be sure, we may stop ourselves from saying them aloud).[35] It is part of the very concept of pain that certain forms of behaviour are natural expressions of pain. That means, if someone behaves in such a way, and is truthful – that is what we call 'being in pain'. In other words, the concept of pain is shaped in such a way that the question of whether

---

[34] Note that this conclusion is not based on the controversial doctrine of verificationism: the view that the sense of a proposition is its method of verification or falsification, and that therefore any un(dis)confirmable statement must be meaningless. For one thing, the issue is about simple *predicates*, not about statements. The possibility of unverifiable statements was explicitly acknowledged. For another thing, the claim is not that because 'S' inscriptions are unverifiable they are meaningless (otherwise much of our ordinary sensation talk would have to be dismissed as meaningless too); the claim is merely that 'S' inscriptions cannot be construed as descriptions of inner objects. – For Wittgenstein's mature views on verificationism see *PI* §353; *Z* §437; Malcolm 1984, 55.

[35] Wittgenstein calls this 'one possibility'. What other possibility is there? We could also learn what pain is without ever feeling pain ourselves, by being shown someone who is visibly in pain.

someone is in pain or not is decided by that person's sincere behaviour – originally natural behaviour, later also verbal behaviour. It follows that the philosophical query as to whether someone's sincere avowals of pain are correct – whether he is *really* in pain when he truthfully says he is – does not make sense. They are correct 'by definition'; their correctness is built into our concept of pain. – That, as far as sensations are concerned, is the solution of the puzzle about first-person authority. Our virtual infallibility (linguistic mistakes apart) in expressing our own feelings is not due to our eagle-eyed gaze of introspection (Hume), but simply to linguistic meaning. Whatever you find painful *is* painful to you. That is what we mean by 'painful'.

We might have had a different concept of pain:

> One could imagine that a kind of thermometer is used to ascertain whether someone is in 'pain'. If someone screams or groans, then they insert the thermometer and only when the gauge reaches this or that point do they begin to feel sorry for the suffering person, and treat him as we do someone who 'obviously is in pain'. (*LW* II, 93)

But it is easy to see why such a concept of an objectively identifiable occurrence would be less useful given our normal sympathetic interest in our fellow human beings. Primarily we want to know what they feel: what it feels like to them. The state of their body interests us only indirectly, in so far as it is likely to affect the way they feel, now or in future. But where the two data contradict each other, it is the felt state that matters.

The 'no-criterion' objection of §258 is not an objection to the private sensation diary described in this section, but an objection to a misconstrual of this or indeed any other sensation language: namely, the inner-object conception and its immediate consequence that one *perceives* one's own sensations. It is directed at (1) in box 4.1 (p. 203), and hence also at (2): the view that others can have only an indirect perception of my sensations (for if I don't *perceive* my sensations, others cannot be said to perceive them only indirectly). But the argument is not supposed to show that one cannot keep a record of sensations without a natural expression. The point concerns ordinary sensations, like pain, just as much as the 'private', fictitious scenario without the distraction of natural expressions or a familiar use of the sensation word.

The scenario of §258 itself – and not just a misconstrual of it – is criticized in §§260 and 261; not as irremediably flawed, but as incomplete. Once the inner-object account of sensations has been discredited, we have to turn back to what that account made appear irrelevant: namely, the behavioural environment of sensations, including the use of sensation words.

(e) An understandable use

Wittgenstein remarks:

> 260. ... Don't consider it as a matter of course that a person is making a note of something when he makes a mark – say in a calendar. For a note has a function; and this 'S' so far has none.

As it stands, this is a little exaggerated: not every meaningful note has a function. Train-spotters' records do not seem to serve any purpose, but it is undeniable that each entry has a meaning, designating a certain locomotive. A word that has been applied usefully (e.g., the name or number of a locomotive) will not lose its meaning when on other occasions it is used in a pointless or playful way. Further, even the pointless use of newly invented names (e.g., for individual ladybirds) will be regarded as meaningful if it is sufficiently similar to some well-established language use. Moreover, for an action not to be utterly pointless and incomprehensible, it need not be useful or a means to an end. Train-spotting, bird-watching or stamp-collecting can hardly be called useful activities, they serve no further purpose; but they are not for that matter unintelligible as leisure pursuits. It is not surprising that people take an interest in trains, birds or even stamps, or that they often show a tendency to collect things, to strive for complete sets.

We should not insist, then, that in order to be meaningful, every 'S' inscription must fulfil a function. It would suffice if the sign 'S' was sometimes employed usefully, or if it was used similarly to some useful sign, or if its use was at least an understandable form of behaviour (cf. MS 119, 275 and 285).

Assuming that a regular correspondence between 'S' and a kind of occurrence obtains, the private diarist of §258 resembles a person who regularly reacts to the appearance of something green by making the sound 'dong'. Not by saying 'green'; for 'green' – unlike 'S' – has a well-established status as a word. Therefore, we would accept saying 'green' whenever one sees something green as verbal behaviour of sorts, although a rather eccentric one. But 'S' is supposed to earn its credentials as a word entirely from the diarist's so far quite incomprehensible behaviour; and that does not work. As Wittgenstein has been arguing from the very beginning of the book, reference alone cannot account for meaning.

However, the 'so far' (in 'so far ... incomprehensible') should be stressed.[36] This line of criticism is drawing attention to an incomplete-

---

[36] And it is actually underlined in a manuscript version of §260: 'a note has a function, and this "S" *so far* has none' (MS 129, 44).

ness, rather than an incorrigible flaw in the set-up of the private diary. Wittgenstein himself proceeds in §270 to fill in some details to make that alleged linguistic behaviour understandable as such and to complete this model of sensation language:

> 270. Let us now imagine a use for the entry of the sign "S" in my diary. I discover that whenever I have a particular sensation a manometer shows that my blood-pressure rises. So I shall be able to say that my blood-pressure is rising without any apparatus. This is a useful result.

But any such further information that can make the use of the sign 'S' understandable, and thus meaningful, will diminish its original privacy. As soon as we can see the point of registering certain occurrences, we will have some notion of what kind of occurrences they are (e.g., possible symptoms of high blood pressure). So the meaning of 'S' will no longer be entirely incommunicable.

(f) *The grammar of a sensation word*

In §261 Wittgenstein raises the question: 'What reason have we for calling "S" the sign for a *sensation*?' To be sure, the diarist *says* that it's a sensation that he intends to name. But that, for Wittgenstein, is not good enough:

> 261. ... For "sensation" is a word of our common language, not of one intelligible to me alone. So the use of this word stands in need of a justification which everybody understands.

What kind of justification is he asking for?

Some have taken him to demand that for every sensation there must be outward criteria in the form of natural expressive behaviour. Only natural expressive behaviour could give meaning to a sensation term. – But there is no textual evidence for this interpretation, and it is an extremely implausible view.[37] Almost every painless contact between my body and a piece of clothing or furniture produces a light sensation, but I would be hard put to express that kind of sensation non-verbally.

---

[37] In §580 Wittgenstein remarks: 'An "inner process" stands in need of outer criteria.' But there is no reason why all outer criteria should be natural, i.e. non-verbal. The acquisition of language does not only add to our means of expression, it enables us to have entirely new thoughts and feelings. Many nuances of and distinctions among our bodily sensations we would never become aware of without the intelligence that is bound up with linguistic competence.

Dissatisfied with this far too stringent requirement for sensation terms, one might make the following suggestion: Some sensations, like pain, have natural expressions. If someone has a proven record of using words for sensations of this kind correctly, i.e., in conformity with observable natural expressions, we say that he has mastered sensation language. And henceforth we accept that he has whatever sensation he sincerely claims to have (cf. Kripke 1982, 103). Obviously, such a *bona fide* account of sensation terms would suit the private linguist: provided he has a proven record of having used sensation terms and the word 'sensation' correctly in the past, no further questions will be asked about his calling S a sensation. But we should not let him off the hook so easily. The word 'sensation' is a generic term. It applies to various particular kinds of sensations; and where something is correctly called a 'sensation', it should be possible to specify what kind of sensation it is. To give an analogy, 'colour' too is essentially a generic term, covering the hues and shades of the spectrum, black and white, and all their possible intermediates and mixtures. Hence, a colour that could not be at least roughly specified according to those parameters in relation to other colours would be like one of the four seasons, but neither spring, nor summer, nor autumn, nor winter. Similarly, there can be no such thing as an indeterminable sensation. But the private diarist must claim that his sensation S *is* indeterminable. We must bear in mind that the privacy we are interested in is supposed to be a necessary and insuperable privacy. Of course, I can write an 'X' in my diary whenever I have heartburn. But then I could easily explain that 'X' stands for heartburn, and thus lift the veil of privacy. By contrast, the sign 'S' is to stand for an occurrence in the privacy of someone's mind, and is therefore not to be translatable into English. The idea is that the private linguist should find it impossible to give others an explanation of what 'S' means: 'a definition of the sign cannot be formulated' (*PI* §258). Yet, if at the same time we want to insist that 'S' stands for a sensation, we must assume that it is an indeterminable sensation; a sensation that cannot be further specified.

In §270 the scenario of the private diary is enriched in order to make it a veritable (if highly stylized) sensation language-game, and the absolute privacy of 'S' is broken. 'S' entries are found to be correlated with rising blood pressure, and now the diarist is able to say correctly that his blood pressure is rising without using any apparatus. We ask, 'How do you know?', and get the reply, 'There's S again'. An awareness of S is understood to be informative about one's bodily state; – so the use of 'S' displays an important and typical feature of bodily sensation language-games. Now we have some reason for calling 'S' the sign for a sensation – though, it must be said, not a very compelling one. It seems to me that a good deal more needs to be added to make S anything like an ordinary sensation.

What kinds of sensations are there? We can quickly tick off sensations with a propositional content, that involve some thought: e.g., a sensation of being watched, a sensation that time passes slowly, or a sensation that one's fingers are bent. Those are specifications that swiftly do away with any semblance of privacy. More promising candidates for S are plain bodily sensations, such as pains, aches, tickles, tingles, twinges, itches, prickles, nausea, giddiness, fatigue, butterflies in one's stomach, or a dry throat. But even such elementary cases bear out that the concept of a sensation implies the possibility of further specification.

1   A bodily sensation either has a *location* in the body (toothache, butterflies in one's stomach), or in what feels to be part of one's body (phantom pains); or if they are diffuse, they have at least localized symptoms (tiredness: limbs feel heavy, eyelids tend to close, tendency to yawn; giddiness involves the head and nausea the stomach and the area underneath one's throat, but not one's knees or fingers; hunger: empty stomach, feeble limbs).
2   A sensation has a *degree of intensity* that can vary according to a pattern (a pain can wax and wane, or pulsate).
3   Sensations have *phenomenal qualities* (pains may be sharp and piercing or dull and throbbing).
4   A sensation is more or less *pleasant*, neutral, or more or less *unpleasant*.
5   A sensation can be characterized by the *bodily movements* it tends to produce (as an itch is a sensation that makes one want to scratch oneself).
6   A sensation can be characterized by the way it can be *influenced by one's behaviour* (some pain gets worse with movement, some pain can be more easily endured while one is moving about).

Now, for S to be anything like an ordinary bodily sensation, it should be possible to characterize it according to at least some of those parameters (to say, for example, that S is a slightly irritating throbbing sensation in my left knee that makes it difficult to sit still and concentrate) – in which case its claim to absolute privacy is clearly relinquished. No such details are given in §270; but then the tentative wording suggests that it is not meant to be a *paradigmatic*, or fully-fledged, case of a sensation word:

> 270. ... And what is our reason for calling "S" the name of a sensation here? Perhaps the kind of way this sign is employed in this language-game.

The crucial point is that the use of 'S' links it with bodily states in a way rather like a sensation word. Thus we have some reason to expect

S to be something like a sensation. But for it really to fit into that category, it must be possible to say a little more about it along the lines sketched above.

To sum up, if the possibility of some such further characterization of S is taken as read, §§258 and 270, together, provide us with a simplified, hence easily surveyable, representation of a segment of sensation language. In two steps we are given a scenario that fulfils the minimum requirements of a language-game of naming and referring to a comparatively (but not strictly) private sensation:

(i) Every now and again, in response to certain sensations that have no other expression, someone enters the sign 'S' into a diary.
(ii) After a while he is able to say correctly when his blood pressure is rising, citing S as evidence.

(i) alone does not suffice to endow the sign with meaning. Correlation of a sign with some phenomenon is not enough for the sign to become a *name* of that phenomenon. The sign must have an understandable use (*PI* §260), and its grammar must show some typical features of the use of sensation words (*PI* §261). The description of (i) affords Wittgenstein a good opportunity to show, once more, that sensations are not inner objects perceived through introspection (the 'no-criterion' objection) (see box 4.2 on p. 220).

4.8 Actions and Reasons

(a) Voluntary action

Of the things that happen in the world, some are mere events, and some are voluntary actions. What is the difference between the two? Obviously, a voluntary action requires a conscious agent, someone with a will, but that is not enough to characterize voluntariness, for conscious agents can also be passively involved in a mere event. I can jump off a bridge, but I can also inadvertently fall off it or be pushed off it against my will. The bodily movements in these cases are likely to be somewhat different, but they *need* not be different. Suppose in a given pair of instances they are exactly the same, how are we then to distinguish between the voluntary action and the mere event? It seems that the voluntary action must contain *more* than the mere event: there must be an extra element of willing or intention. And that voluntary element it should be possible to isolate by a thought experiment of subtraction:

> 621. ... what is left over if I subtract the fact that my arm goes up from the fact that I raise my arm?

Box 4.2 Wittgenstein's attacks on the inner-object conception of sensations

> (R) The meaning of a word is due to its reference and independent of its use.
> [e] §260 Words require understandable use.
>
> (S) **The meaning of sensation words is due to their standing for sensations and independent of their use.**
> [f] §270 Sensation words require suitable use.
>
> (S*) **A sensation is an occurrence in a person's mind, logically independent of expressive behaviour.**
> [a] §302 Ascribability Argument
>
> | (1) I *perceive* my sensations directly. | (2) Others can learn of my sensations only *indirectly*. | (3) I cannot describe my sensations to others. |
> |---|---|---|
> | | [d] §258 No-Criterion Argument | [f] §261 Sensations must be describable in certain ways. |
> | (1a) I *know* what sensations I have. | (2a) Others can never *know* what sensations I have. | |
> | | [c] §246 Awareness of one's own sensations is not knowledge. | |
> | | | (2&3) For all we know, different people may attach different meanings to the same sensation word (private sensation language). [b] §293 Idle-Wheel Argument |

Wittgenstein raises this question not in order to answer it, but to show that it is misguided – as philosophical questions usually are (MS 165, 55). It is another instance of referentialism leading us to the construction of some spurious inner object (event, process or state). Words used to characterize an action as voluntary (like 'will' and its cognates)[38] are uncritically taken to denote some mental occurrence,

---

[38] The misconstrual is perhaps somewhat less tempting in English where the verb 'to will' is rarely used outside philosophy; but in German the verb derived from the noun

some phenomenon that added to the mere bodily movement makes it voluntary. This is the inner-object conception of voluntary action. According to its classical version, going back to Descartes and the British Empiricists, 'what is left over if I subtract the fact that my arm goes up from the fact that I raise my arm' is an *act of will*, or (as Hume called it) a *volition*. For a bodily movement to be voluntary, it must be *caused* by an act of will; without such a cause the same movement would be involuntary. Wittgenstein was familiar with similar views held by Russell and William James. It was Russell's 'main thesis' in *The Analysis of Mind* 'that all psychic phenomena are built up out of sensations and images alone', and so he also believed that 'sensations and images, with their causal laws, yield all that seems to be wanted for the analysis of will' (Russell 1921, 279 and 285). According to James's 'ideo-motor theory', for a bodily movement to be voluntary, it must be caused by an image of the kinaesthetic sensations of such a movement (James 1890, vol. 2, 492f).

(i) The first problem with any account of willing as a mental event causing a bodily movement is the *elusiveness* – not to say non-existence – of suitable mental events. This is obscured if the discussion is focused on only a few especially favourable examples, such as this one: 'I deliberate whether to lift a certain heavyish weight, decide to do it, I then apply my force to it and lift it' (*BB* 150). Here we have some occurrences that could, without absurdity, be thought to constitute willing: some anticipatory thinking of the action, an act of resolve, a sensation of bodily effort. And now: 'One takes one's ideas, and one's language, about volition from this kind of example and thinks that they must apply – if not in such an obvious way – to all cases which one can properly call cases of willing' (*BB* 150; cf. *EPB* 234; *Z* §444). But of course not all cases are like that. We frequently do things without any such preliminaries. Just think of ordinary speech, which is often entirely unpremeditated and effortless, yet not for that matter involuntary. Moreover, with respect to the idea that willing must involve some sensations of effort or movement, one should remember that sitting still, too, can be intentional (*Z* §597).

(ii) More recently it has been suggested that voluntary action is to be characterized by an element of *trying*. For the rising of my arm to be the result of a voluntary action, it has to be brought about by my trying to raise my arm. Wittgenstein's response is simple:

622. When I raise my arm I do not usually *try* to raise it.

Wille (the will), viz. *wollen*, can quite naturally be applied to most voluntary actions. It is roughly equivalent to the English 'to want'.

We would not use the word 'try' unless, for all we knew (or wanted to suggest), there was at least a possibility of failure. However, this recourse to common usage has not gone unchallenged. The standard reply is due to Grice (1989, chs 1–3), who agrees that it is often *inappropriate* in describing an action to use the word 'try', but not because it would be false to do so, but merely because it would be *misleading* – though none the less (trivially) true. To say 'I tried to raise my arm' suggests that there was (likely to be) some difficulty, not because that is part of the meaning of the word 'try', but because otherwise the utterance would flout some 'general principle of discourse' (Grice 1989, 20). On Grice's construal, the verb 'to try' is comparable to the verb 'to begin'. Every action extended in time has a beginning; so whenever it is true that someone carried out an action, it will also be true that he 'carried out the beginning' of that action. If it's true to say 'N φ-ed [for some time]', it must also be true to say: 'N began to φ'. However, saying the latter, although true, would often be misleading: giving the wrong impression that N did not, or not yet, finish φ-ing. – Is Grice correct in giving the same kind of account for the verb 'to try'? – No. For one thing, Grice's diagnosis of 'conversational implicature' (see sect. 4.4, (9) above) is plausible to the extent to which it is obvious that the suggestion conveyed is not implicit in the meaning of the words. It would, for example, be ludicrous to claim that part of the meaning of 'to begin' is 'to leave unfinished', or (to take one of Grice's own examples) that the English words 'N has good handwriting' mean, amongst other things, 'N is academically weak'; but it's not at all implausible to suggest that 'N tried to φ' implies 'either N failed to φ or it seemed possible that he might fail'.

For another thing, whereas it is indeed analytic that every action (extended in time) has a beginning, so that it goes without saying that whoever did it must also have carried out the beginning, it is not at all analytic that every voluntary action involves trying. If you ask someone who under normal circumstances has just raised his arm whether in doing so he first *began* to raise his arm, the question may be brushed aside as stupid, because the answer is so pointlessly obvious. If, however, you ask the same person whether in raising his arm he *tried* to raise it, you're not just being tiresome, you're incomprehensible. The question is as odd as this one: 'When you raised your arm, did you *perhaps* raise your arm?' In either case the response might be: 'What do you mean? Do you mean whether I expected any difficulties in raising my arm? No, of course not.'

Thirdly, it is essential to conversational implicature that unless we attribute to the speaker an intention to convey something more than his words mean, his utterance would flout some general maxim of discourse (Grice 1989, 31). Thus, the utterance 'N has good handwrit-

Philosophical Investigations 223

ing' in answer to a question about *N*'s academic talents would flout the maxim 'Be relevant' (Grice 1989, 27) unless it was taken as an indirect disparagement of *N*'s academic abilities. But which maxim would be flouted by saying 'He tried to ϕ' rather than 'He ϕ-ed'? One might suggest the rule:

> Don't give a less informative statement when you could just as conveniently give a more informative one.

But Grice was quite right not to list this as one of the general maxims operative in conversation, for it is very often perfectly appropriate to say less than you know (for example, if you don't expect your further knowledge to be of much interest to your interlocutor). Thus a more plausible suggestion is Grice's rule:

> 'Make your contribution as informative as is required' (Grice 1989, 26).

But this won't do. For there are frequently situations in which all that matters to the conversation is whether an agent had an *intention* to do something, while the success of the action is quite irrelevant. If Grice were right, in such a situation it should meet the case to say that the agent *tried* to act – whatever one's knowledge or expectations about the outcome. But in fact that would still carry the (possibly inappropriate) implication that failure seemed to be on the cards. (For example, to settle the question of whether Mary is a vegetarian, it is quite enough to report her intention of buying meat; whether she did so or whether she failed, because she forgot to take her wallet, is immaterial. Even so, it would be inappropriate for you to report that you saw her *trying* to buy some meat unless you want to convey that there appeared to be a problem.)

Finally, in cases where Grice's analysis is plausible (where what is conveyed is not part of the meaning of the words), the suggestion in question can easily be cancelled (Grice 1989, 44). When the sentence '*N* began to ϕ' is followed by the words 'and ten minutes later he had finished' there is obviously no longer any implication that the action remained unfinished. Again, although on its own, in a suitable situation, the utterance '*N* has good handwriting' can be used to insinuate that not much else can be said in *N*'s praise, that 'implicature' can easily be cancelled by adding some commendation of *N*'s other talents. But no such smooth cancellation is possible when the word 'try' is used to suggest that failure was on the cards. Consider: 'Sam tried to close the door. But I don't mean to suggest that there was any possibility of failure.' The effect is slightly comical – as with: 'You're a silly fool. But

I don't mean to be disrespectful.' For in either case, if we were to take the disclaimer seriously, we could no longer make sense of the initial utterance. The fact is that if you *don't* want to suggest any possibility of failure, you don't qualify your statement by putting in the word 'tried' in the first place. The word's function is comparable to that of adverbs like 'perhaps' or 'possibly', which are not used to add to the description of an action (unlike other adverbs, such as 'quickly' or 'hesitatingly'), but to indicate that the speaker cannot guarantee the truth of the description. Similarly, by saying 'He's *trying* to ring his solicitor', rather than 'He's ringing his solicitor', one does not add anything to the description of the action, one simply enters a *caveat*: 'for all I know (or care to say) he may not be successful'.

The philosophical idea that the word 'try' denotes some particular mental phenomenon that could be invoked to explain voluntary action is just another instance of the referentialist mistake to assume naïvely that words must stand for things. Thus, Brian O'Shaughnessy, the main proponent of the doctrine that voluntary action is to be explained as the result of trying, simply takes it for granted, against all linguistic evidence to the contrary, that a word like 'try' must always stand for the same 'true *sui generis* element of animal psychology life', '*some single something*' that would occur, like a headache, independently of what people might know or say about an action (O'Shaughnessy 1980, 55, 45). The possibility that the concept of trying might *not* be that of a uniform phenomenon, that the word's function might rather be to express the speaker's attitude towards an action – this possibility O'Shaughnessy dismisses lightly as 'unacceptable' (1980, 45). Such is the force of a philosophical prejudice, which is usually just an oversimplified picture of some aspects of language.[39]

(iii) Let us now return to the general idea of willing as a mental event. It gives rise to a *dilemma*. If willing is a mental phenomenon, we may ask whether (like other mental phenomena) it is subject to the will. But no answer to this question is satisfactory. If the phenomenon of willing is itself subject to the will, in order to be proper, willing it would have to be willed. But then we are launched on an infinite regress. For the event of willing to be voluntary, it has to be caused by an earlier event of willing; but that earlier event, too, in order to be voluntary, would have to be caused by yet an earlier event of willing, and so on *ad infinitum* – which is absurd (Ryle 1949, 67). So it seems more promising to deny that willing itself could be subject to the will: 'I can't will willing'

---

[39] For a more detailed discussion of the concept of trying, including criticisms of arguments given by O'Shaughnessy and Jennifer Hornsby (proponents of the view that all voluntary action involves trying), see Schroeder 2001b.

(*PI* §613). But that sounds odd as well. So it would appear that 'willing too is merely an experience . . . It comes when it comes, and I cannot bring it about' (*PI* §611). But now the whole idea of voluntariness, of being in control of one's actions, seems to be lost. That must be wrong too. 'I should not say of the movement of my arm, for example: it comes when it comes, etc. . . . "I don't need to wait for my arm to go up – I can raise it"' (*PI* §612). The dilemma shows that the whole question (whether or not willing can be willed) is misbegotten. Willing is not the sort of thing of which it makes sense to ask whether it is voluntary or involuntary. 'Willing' is not the name of an action (*PI* §613; cf. §619), nor of course of a passive experience. It is not the name of any kind of mental occurrence.

(iv) Contrary to the philosophical model of voluntary action as bodily movement caused by a mental act, raising one's arm is not *bringing it about* that the arm rises (*PI* §614). I don't do anything else as a means to effect the rising of my arm. The contracting of the right muscles is not such a means; for I don't even know which muscles need to be contracted for the arm to go up. (It is rather the other way round: I could raise my arm in order to bring about the contraction of whatever muscles are involved in the process.) Nor do I bring about bodily movements by acts of wishing or deciding. Wishing that something may happen is indeed incompatible with doing it voluntarily (*PI* §616). The word 'wish', like 'hope', implies that one is not fully in control of what will happen. If I wish my arm to rise and, lo! it does – it wouldn't be my own action and I'd be very surprised (*Z* §586b). A decision to raise my arm, on the other hand, is of course likely to lead to my raising my arm; but it does not just cause my arm to go up. Again, I'd be rather surprised if it did. It would not be my own doing (*PI* §627). A decision to act is likely to lead to a voluntary action, but it is not itself part of that action and therefore cannot be used to analyse it. –

The inner-object conception of voluntary action is untenable. Words like 'voluntary' or 'willing' do not stand for some distinctive mental occurrence that must precede or accompany a movement for it to be voluntary. How, then, is the word 'voluntary' used? Again, the answer should not be a revelation, but merely a reminder of what in practice we are all familiar with. 'Voluntary movement is marked by the absence of surprise' (*PI* §628). One is not a third-person observer to one's own behaviour: one cannot look on with interest to see what will happen next, and then perhaps be surprised by it. That is related to the observation that one's actions being voluntary is incompatible with one's wishing for it to happen (*PI* §616). For you can only have wishes about what is not entirely under your control, and where something is not under your control, you can doubt whether it will happen (or never have thought of it), and hence be surprised if it does. Of course, that is not to say that all things that happen to us come as a surprise; but with mere events and involuntary actions surprise is at least always logically *possible*, whereas to the extent to which an action is voluntary, surprise is logically excluded.[40]

Wittgenstein adds: 'And now I do not mean you to ask "But *why* isn't one surprised here?"' (*PI* §628). It is tempting to think that one is not surprised here because one knows so reliably of one's own voluntary movements. Then the question is of course *how* does one know, and the almost unavoidable answer is that one *feels* one's own voluntary movements, perhaps in one's muscles and joints' (*PI* §625; Z §595). But feelings can be deceptive. Whatever sensations may be characteristic of, say, raising one's arm, it is surely conceivable that in a laboratory they might be produced artificially, by drugs or electric currents. So when now I raise my arm with my eyes shut, whatever sensations I have in my muscles and joints, it should be conceivable that *they* are deceptive. Hence, if my awareness of my voluntary movements were based on such sensations, I should be able in this situation to consider it possible that I am *not* moving my arm (*PI* §624). But I find myself unable to do so; for my certainty that I am moving my arm is not based on the evidence of such sensations. Furthermore, if I knew of my bodily movements from recognizing the accompanying sensations, it should be possible occasionally to misidentify those sensations: e.g., to mistake the sensation of raising my arm for that of lowering it, which sounds absurd. And a little reflection shows that this is the wrong picture. My awareness of having raised my arm is not indirect, mediated by the recognition of a peculiar feeling. I am just certain that I have raised my arm, and there is no evidence on which my certainty is based (*PI* §625). The puzzle of first-person authority about one's own agency is not unlike that about one's sensations, and can be dissolved in a similar way. The puzzle is generated by treating the case as one of *knowledge*: which, first, makes it appear strange that there shouldn't be any possibility of error, and which, secondly, makes us look (in vain) for some grounds or evidence on which this extraordinary knowledge could be based. To remove the puzzle, we need only realize that the certainty is the result of our grammar. It is built into our very concept of a voluntary action that the agent is aware of it (cf. Z §600) – which is therefore as unsurprising as the fact that bachelors are without exception unmarried. – Here it is also illuminating to think of expressions of intention

---

[40] It might be suggested that sometimes even our voluntary behaviour can be surprising to us, but what in such cases takes us by surprise is always an aspect of our behaviour that was not entirely under our control. Thus one can find one's own remarks surprisingly witty or courageous; for wit and courage are assets one cannot simply decide to have (cf. *PI* §616).

(cf. *PI* §629). When you say 'I will go for a walk', the question 'How do you know?' makes no sense (or could only be understood as asking: 'How do you know that you will not be prevented?'). An expression of intention is not based on any evidence and cannot be erroneous. This is the same kind of grammatical certainty that attaches to one's expression that one acted voluntarily.

(b) Acting for reasons

Often when asked why we did something, we can give a reason. What is a reason? Again, a referentialist prejudice will make us expect a reason to be some sort of mental occurrence (– the inner-object picture of reasons). Moreover, there is a strong temptation to regard the reason why an action was performed as its cause. After all, reasons are cited in answer to why-questions ('Why did you do it?'), and why-questions typically ask for a cause ('Why did the bridge collapse?').[41]

The view that reasons are mental occurrences causing actions may have some plausibility in the case of premeditated actions. An agent first considers and accepts a reason, and then acts accordingly. But for the greater part our intentional behaviour is not preceded by practical reasoning. We act habitually when we handle knife and fork, drive on the left side of the road, or pass the time of day. We act spontaneously when we take a pear rather than an apple from a bowl of fruit or take a closer look at a particular volume in a bookshop. An action might not be the upshot of any practical reasoning or previously felt desire, and yet be performed for a reason. The reason was not brought to consciousness before or during the action, but only given afterwards.

When asked why we did something, we are likely to mention some of our wants or beliefs. But, in general, there is no need for wants and beliefs to have an independent mental existence behind their behavioural manifestations (*PI* §330; *OC* §431; cf. Rundle 1997, 12–13, 142, 164ff, 216, and *passim*). There are countless things I believe without ever wasting a thought on them: for instance, that the chair I'm sitting on is sufficiently stable to support me (*PI* §575), that bread is edible, that grass isn't dangerous to tread on. Again, there are countless things which I can be said to have wanted only on the strength of my doing them. For there need not be a mental event that might be cited to testify to my want when, for example, I whistle a tune, keep quiet, tell a joke, or write orthographically (cf. *PI* §616; *Z* §§579, 586). Verbal behaviour affords a particularly clear example of manifested wants and beliefs

---

[41] A currently influential proponent of this causal inner-object account of reasons is Donald Davidson (1963). For a critical discussion of his position see Schroeder 2001a.

that do not exist apart from that manifestation. Expressing one's thoughts or will is in many cases not reporting what has gone through one's mind before (cf. *PI* §§317, 335). Nor is the utterance accompanied by a simultaneous process of thinking or meaning it (*PI* §329).

Now the question arises as to how it is possible for an agent to be absolutely certain about the reason for which he acted although at the time of acting no thought about that reason had crossed his mind. On the one hand, it seems undeniable that there is a difference between correctly reporting the reason for which one acted and deciding afterwards what would have been a good reason. Giving one's reason after the event is not a performative utterance: saying so does not make it true. It is rather a matter of reporting more or less accurately what was the case. On the other hand, as far as we can actually remember the contents of our mind, in many instances nothing much was the case; nothing that could be remembered as the reason for which we acted. Still, when stating that reason afterwards, we are normally granted first-person authority. How is this puzzle to be solved?

One common kind of reason is an intention. ('Why did you buy flour?' – 'Because I wanted to make a cake'.) Towards the end of the *Investigations*, Part I (§§633–63), Wittgenstein looks at the remarkable certainty with which we are able to remember our past intentions, in particular what one meant to express by one's words or what one was going to say. The following points emerge.

(i) One knows what one was going to say or wanted to say, and yet one does not read it off from some mental process which took place then and which one remembers (*PI* §637). One may be helped by remembering various details from the situation (*PI* §635), mental images (*PI* §663), a wider context (*PI* §638); but often none of these would really provide sufficient evidence to justify one's statement:

> 635. ... It is as if a snapshot of a scene had been taken, but only a few scattered details of it were to be seen: here a hand, there a bit of a face, or a hat – the rest is dark. And now it is as if I knew quite certainly what the whole picture represented. As if I could read the darkness.

Even if I had at the time formulated my intention *in foro interno*, the puzzle would resurface in the form of the question: How can I be sure that I meant it seriously? (*PI* §641).

(ii) My words do not report what happened on that occasion, they are a *conditional* statement about the past. 'They say, for example, that I *should have* given a particular answer then, if I had been asked' (*PI* §684). But how do I know what I *would* have said?

(iii) My utterance is a *reaction* to what I remember of the situation (*PI* §§648, 657, 659). That is to say, remembering the context, the situation and a certain amount of details, I will now say: 'I wanted to φ'; or,

'I did it because *p*'. Moreover, '*I am now inclined to say* "I read the intention of acting thus in certain states of mind which I remember"' (*PI* §653) – although there is not really anything from which the intention *could* be read off.

(iv) Wittgenstein's main point, however, is that the apparent groundlessness of some of our utterances should not worry us:

> 655. The question is not one of explaining a language-game by means of our experiences, but of noting a language-game.

> 656. What is the purpose of telling someone that a time ago I had such-and-such a wish? – Look on the language-game as the *primary* thing. And look on the feelings, etc., as you look on a way of regarding the language-game, as interpretation.
> It might be asked: how did human beings ever come to make the verbal utterances which we call reports of past wishes or past intentions?

We ask people for their reasons, and the explanations they give, even if retrospective, enjoy a privileged status. This is what Wittgenstein wants us to regard as the '*primary* thing': primary, that is, relative to feelings and other mental occurrences which one might be prone to invoke as a justification for such explanations. Our having acted, or intended to act, for a certain reason was not an event we can recall and report. Where the agent's reasons were not displayed by the action itself (or some other behaviour at the time), his confident claim that such-and-such was his reason must stand on its own. Not even to his own mind may he be able to justify it by citing any circumstances he remembers.

In this respect the language-game is primary: it cannot really be supported by evidence of the details one remembers. But that is not to say that it is an inexplicable brute fact. It can be elucidated – and this is a typical Wittgensteinian move – in terms of the interest which such an unsupported utterance of the agent's may have to us (cf. *PI* §108). Why do we take so seriously what people are inclined to say about their past actions? Let us first work out just *how* seriously we take it. How far does first-person authority extend in such cases?

The agent's authority retrospectively to explain his actions is restricted by the following factors:

(i) The action must not be too transparent for the agent's explanation to have any function. Having called someone an idiot, I'm not free to declare that I meant to pay a compliment. Similarly, having punched someone on the nose, I wouldn't get away with saying that I did it to make him feel better. If an action *obviously* manifests a certain intention, the agent's saying so would be superfluous, but his explanation to the contrary would not be accepted.

(ii) The agent's claim as to his reason must be sincere and not conflict with what he expressed (by words or deeds) at other times.

(iii) The reason cannot have been a fact of which the agent was not aware, nor a supposed fact which the agent did not believe to (or knew not to) obtain.

If these three conditions are taken to be fulfilled, an agent's avowed reasons will be accepted.[42] More than that, they will, as a matter of fact, *be* the agent's reasons, for the concept of an agent's reason is the precipitate of this language-game together with the considerations given by those conditions. That is the force of Wittgenstein's remark that the language-game is the *primary* thing, not to be measured against an underlying mental reality. Yet how can this be: What is supposed to be the point of the concept if not to register actual occurrences informing the action?

Before sketching an answer to this question, let us first complete our efforts to break the spell of the idea that giving one's reasons must be to report what occurrences led to one's behaviour. It has already been argued that in many cases suitable occurrences cannot be found. Wittgenstein emphasizes that whether or not there are any suitable mental occurrences, it is an illusion to think that our statements of past reasons have to be based on our remembering them.

To explain one's action is typically to perform another action, manifesting the same want and belief as the original action. To explain one's verbal utterance is normally a matter of paraphrasing or supplementing it. 'It's a disgrace!' – ? – 'I mean: it's very unfair that he got sacked

---

[42] Do cases of self-deception make an exception to the rule that an agent's avowed reasons will be accepted if conditions (i)–(iii) are fulfilled? I think not. What is properly called self-deception involves some kind of disingenuity, some kind of purposive refusal to face the truth (cf. Gardiner 1970). But in that case, condition (ii) will not be fulfilled. The agent, when giving his reasons, prevents himself from considering some relevant aspects, for he feels that might lead to unpleasant discoveries.

Perhaps more of a challenge to my account are cases of delusion or selective attention, where the agent in giving his reasons conveniently, but quite sincerely, overlooks some embarrassing circumstances. When Jeff made some tactless and unpleasant remarks, Sam told him off in no uncertain terms. Sam got angry with Jeff, he said, because Jeff wouldn't behave himself. But then, Sam is not normally given to such strong reactions; and on that evening Jeff attracted a lot of attention from Sam's girlfriend. Shall we say that the real reason why Sam lashed out at Jeff was that he was jealous? We may indeed say that. But if we accept that Sam was really completely unaware of that 'real reason', and had not just managed to avert his attention from it, then we are using the term 'reason' here in a different way. To make that clearer, let us modify the example. Suppose that what made Sam so irritable was not jealousy but a few glasses of cocktail. What then would we call the reason why Sam upbraided Jeff? We may say that he did it because he was drunk. But that was clearly not his *reason*, it is simply a *cause* of his outburst. In other

after all he has done for the firm.' In this case the philosophical question as to the virtual infallibility of an agent's explanation of his action is easily answered. Action and explanation are on the same footing. In both cases the person speaks his mind; and there is no puzzle about our ability to say repeatedly what we think about a subject, being a little more explicit the second time.

There are similar pairs of actions in the non-verbal sphere. Suppose you see Fanny Robin throwing a snowball against a wall, and ask yourself: 'What on earth did she do that for?' Then you see her throwing another snowball against a first-floor window, and you understand that that was what she was trying to do the first time: hit the window to attract someone's attention. The second action explains the first by pursuing the same purpose more expediently, and thus more evidently.

Now consider the case where, being asked for her reason after the first throw, she explains: 'I want to hit that window to attract Sergeant Troy's attention.' Her ability correctly to give her reasons ceases to look puzzling if we see this kind of case as a variation upon the preceding ones. Action and explanation both express the same want (e.g., to attract someone's attention) and the same belief (e.g., that it can be done by throwing a snowball against a window). Given that she can speak, her ability to say for what reason she acted is not more surprising than her ability to repeat the action.

---

words, by saying that Sam's reaction should be explained not so much by Jeff's misbehaviour as by Sam's intoxication, we are not replacing one reason by another reason; rather, we suggest that Sam's behaviour shouldn't be explained in terms of his reasons, but primarily in causal terms. To borrow an expression from P. F. Strawson, we adopt an *objective attitude* towards Sam. The outburst is seen not so much as an intentional human action, but rather as an unfortunate event (cf. Strawson 1962). Similarly, in the original example, if we say 'Never mind Jeff's misbehaving; Sam's outburst was really just a manifestation of his jealousy,' we dismiss a reason-giving explanation in favour of a dispositional explanation. As far as the agent's reasons are concerned, that dispositional explanation has nothing new to offer; for we assumed that Sam was not aware of that disposition, and the fact that someone has a disposition of which he is unaware can't possibly figure among his reasons. Therefore, to the extent to which we are interested in Sam's *reasons*, there is no alternative to his sincere statement. It's only that this interest in an agent's reasons will diminish if we find that his behaviour was largely due to factors of which he was unaware. However, such a pair of explanations need not be incompatible; they can complement each other. Jeff did behave disgracefully, and that's why Sam quite rightly rebuked him (he wouldn't have done it otherwise); still, if it hadn't been for his bad mood (or those cocktails), he wouldn't have had the guts to speak out.

Here we have an illustration of how giving one's reason need not be a matter of describing what happened in one's mind. One only has to express truthfully what one wants and believes (or knows) in the matter. Of course, things are a little different if one's wants or beliefs are no longer the same. Once Fanny Robin has succeeded in hitting the window and thus attracted Sergeant Troy's attention, she will no longer have a want to do so. Hence explaining her own behaviour will no longer be merely a matter of expressing a *current* want and belief. But even then no more is required of her than a sincere expression of her inclinations, only in a conditional form: 'If I hadn't yet succeeded in hitting the window, what would I want to do?' Again, the answer that will explain her action need not draw on any mental events she might remember; she only has to express truthfully her present inclinations to say what under such circumstances she *would* want to achieve and believe to be achievable by the behaviour in question.

Imagine a somewhat abnormal chess-player whose mind during a game is a complete blank. He plays almost as if in a trance. Nevertheless he plays well, and when asked afterwards why he made a particular move, he thinks for a moment and then unfailingly comes up with a perfectly reasonable explanation. Clearly his answers are not reports of his quiet musings at the time, but does that detract in any way from their interest? When we do not understand the point of a move, will we be less inclined to inquire afterwards because we know that the explanation will only be produced then and was not already present as a silent commentary when the move was made? He can tell us why he would make such a move in such a position. Isn't that what we want to know?

One might object that what we really want to know is not why he *would* make such a move, but why he *did* make such a move. But how is this past tense to be cashed out? If it is to be a matter of what happened at the time, then by hypothesis we draw a blank. We would have to say that the move was done for no reason at all. And not only in this artificial example. A normal chess-player's moves will frequently not be the result of any explicit calculating or reasoning, especially when time is running out. And life in this respect isn't any different. Construing an agent's subsequent rationalizations as reports of past reasoning would immensely diminish the class of actions done for a reason. But reasons are also given and accepted where no past reasoning can be reported. So that construal must be wrong.

Still the past tense is not vacuous. 'Why did you do it?' often means: 'What reason would you have given *at the time*?' So how can we be satisfied with what the agent is inclined to say *now*? Surely the two need not always coincide. – To the extent to which such a discrepancy could be probable, it is covered by the limitations on first-person authority listed above. It is true that even where there is absolutely no evidence on which to suspect such a discrepancy, it is still theoretically conceivable. The fact remains that the agent's retrospective explanations will, in such a case, be accepted. This language-game is played. And it partly defines the concept of the reason for which one acted. – The point of such a concept is easy to see. A reason, thus defined, may give us an insight into the agent's character. It tells us what considerations he regards as justifying a given action. And assuming (what could never be known) that there is a discrepancy between the reason as subsequently given by the agent and what he *would* have said at the time, holding on to the former has the advantage of making the concept actually applicable and not merely a matter of idle speculation; moreover, what a reason thus expressed teaches us about the agent's character will be more up to date. That may not always be our main interest. Occasionally we ask for a person's reasons in the past out of a purely historiographical curiosity. But at least as often we are concerned about people's actions and reasons to find out more about their character; to learn what to expect of them henceforth.

Finally, it should be remembered that very frequently the justificatory aspect of explanations in terms of reasons is of paramount importance to us. Asking a person to give a reason for his behaviour, we challenge him to justify it, to tell us (if he can) why it wasn't a bad thing. Here the question of when this justification was (or would have been) thought of for the first time may be quite irrelevant. We will be satisfied to learn that the action was sensible as an attempt to pursue some respectable goal, and make no further inquiries as to what extent the agent acted with that goal in mind; just as when asking someone to justify one of his beliefs, we will usually content ourselves with hearing that the agent *can* rationally defend it, without worrying whether those convincing grounds did actually occur to the person when he first adopted that belief. We don't normally censure people for adopting beliefs 'instinctively' or 'intuitively', as long as they *can* support them when pressed. Likewise, we are happy for people to act according to their gut feelings as long as they will eventually be able to justify their behaviour.

Thus our interests shape our concept of a reason, and take it, at least in some of its applications, a considerable distance away from questions of the causation of events, which seem all-important to many contemporary philosophers. By a reason we mean what an agent could in honesty say in explanation of his action. So, again, first-person authority is not a remarkable epistemic feat, but is, by definition, at the core of our concept of a reason.

5
The Final Years

In 1947, when Wittgenstein resigned from his professorship and left Cambridge, he became homeless. For the remaining three and a half years of his life he had no place of his own, but lived as a lodger or guest in other people's houses: in a hotel in Dublin, in a guesthouse in Wicklow, in a friend's cottage on the Irish west coast, in his sister's house in Vienna, as a guest of G. H. von Wright in Cambridge, with Ben Richards in Uxbridge, with Norman Malcolm in Ithaca, with Rush Rhees's wife in London, with Elizabeth Anscombe in Oxford, in a friend's farmhouse in Norway, and finally as a guest of his doctor, Edward Bevan, in Cambridge. He was constantly looking for some quiet place where he could work; on the other hand, he also felt the need to see a friendly face around him every now and again, and his increasing health problems made it impractical for him to spend the winter time in complete isolation. His main worry was that he was losing his ability to do any work in philosophy, as repeatedly he felt he was: 'When a person has only one thing in the world – namely a certain talent – what is he to do when he begins to lose that talent?' (Malcolm 1984, 76). For considerable periods he was unable to write anything and, of course, became very depressed about it. When staying with former pupils, he was eager at least to have philosophical discussions with them and their colleagues, which he found less demanding than writing, although his interlocutors would very much feel the strain of Wittgenstein's unremitting intensity. John Nelson later remembered such a discussion as

> probably the most philosophically strenuous two hours I have ever spent. Under the relentless probing and pushing of his enquiry my head felt almost as if it were ready to burst . . . There was no quarter given – no sliding off the topic when it became difficult. I was absolutely exhausted when we concluded the discussion. (Quoted in Monk 1990, 553f)

Between 1946 and 1949 Wittgenstein worked on topics in the philosophy of psychology. A topic that he found particularly intriguing was the perception of aspects: for example, seeing a puzzle picture now as a duck and a moment later as a rabbit (cf. *PI* p. 194). For some time he probably intended to work this material into his book, but he never did: it remained a separate piece of work. Its most polished version was finished in 1949 and was later published, somewhat misleadingly, as 'Part II' of the *Philosophical Investigations*.[1]

By the summer of 1949 Wittgenstein had resigned himself to the fact that his book would never reach a completely finished state (Malcolm 1984, 75), and that he would leave it to his literary executors to publish its final version after his death. He continued working on some of the issues in the philosophy of psychology, but he also began writing down thoughts in two new areas: the grammar of colour words (now published as *Remarks on Colour*) and the concepts of doubt, knowledge and certainty (now published as *On Certainty*). The former remarks were inspired by his reading Goethe's *Theory of Colour* in 1950; his interest in the latter topic was raised by discussions he had with Norman Malcolm about G. E. Moore's essays 'Proof of an External World' and 'A Defence of Common Sense'.

In October 1949 Wittgenstein was diagnosed with cancer of the prostate. By February 1951 his state had deteriorated so much that he needed constant medical care. As he was horrified at the prospect of dying in hospital, he gratefully accepted his doctor's remarkable offer that he could spend the last weeks of his life in the doctor's house in Cambridge, appropriately called 'Storeys End'. He had abandoned the thought of doing any more philosophical work, and just hoped that life in this miserable state wouldn't continue for much longer (LM 132). When soon afterwards all treatment was given up as pointless, he was relieved. But then, in March he felt much better. 'It's the first time after more than 2 years that the curtain in my brain has gone up,' he wrote to Malcolm (LM 134). Unexpectedly, he was able to do some good work again. The spell lasted for about two months, almost to the very end of his life. His last philosophical remarks (of what is now *On Certainty*) were written on 27 April 1951. He died on 29 April. His last words, spoken to his doctor's wife, were: 'Tell them I've had a wonderful life!' (Malcolm 1984, 81).

A wonderful life for Wittgenstein was certainly not the same as a happy life. For the most part, it seems, his life was fiercely unhappy. But it was a life lived with great seriousness and intensity. He would do nothing in a casual, half-hearted manner: whatever he did, he would

---

[1] The typescript volumes from which that text was drawn have also been published: under the titles *Remarks on the Philosophy of Psychology* (2 vols) and *Last Writings on the Philosophy of Psychology*.

apply himself to with unsparing dedication. That, paired with the great force of his intellect, is obviously the reason why he accomplished so much in philosophy. But at least as important to him was the moral seriousness which as a young man he had learnt from Weininger (see sect. 1.3): an abhorrence of all forms of affectation and an uncompromising insistence on truthfulness. Neither his moral nor his philosophical accomplishments were lightly won. They had to be fought for in a constant struggle that would frequently make him miserable. But perhaps it was the very fact that what he had done had cost him so dear that allowed him to review his life with some satisfaction. He had attempted to do what he thought right, even at the price of his happiness. That, in a sense, was wonderful. It was certainly what, by all accounts, made Wittgenstein a uniquely impressive personality.

6
After Wittgenstein

6.1 Oxford Philosophy and American Philosophy

In 1959 Russell wrote: 'During the period since 1914 three philosophies have successively dominated the British philosophical world: first that of Wittgenstein's *Tractatus*, second that of the Logical Positivists' – heavily influenced, one might add, by Wittgenstein's *Tractatus* – 'and third that of Wittgenstein's *Philosophical Investigations*' (Russell 1959, 216). Strictly speaking, that third era could begin only in 1953 when the *Investigations* where published, but in fact the influence of Wittgenstein's later philosophy began to make itself felt immediately after the war, especially in Oxford. That was due partly to the circulation of the *Blue Book* and the *Brown Book*, partly to the transmission of Wittgenstein's thoughts through his Cambridge students, and partly to Friedrich Waismann, whom in the early 1930s Wittgenstein had entrusted with giving a systematic account of his philosophy at the time, and who from 1940 until his death in 1959 held teaching posts in Oxford. Between 1945 and 1970 Oxford was the centre of analytic philosophy not only in Britain, but worldwide. Many well-known academics taught there, beside Waismann, such as Gilbert Ryle, J. L. Austin, Elizabeth Anscombe, Stephen Toulmin, A. J. Ayer, Isaiah Berlin, H. L. A. Hart, J. O. Urmson, H. P. Grice, P. F. Strawson, R. M. Hare, D. F. Pears, Stuart Hampshire, G. J. Warnock, J. L. Mackie, A. M. Quinton and A. J. P. Kenny. Soon it became common to speak of 'Oxford Philosophy' or 'Oxford Ordinary Language Philosophy', seen by many as the 'school' based on Wittgenstein's *Philosophical Investigations*. However, the label is misleading, for the views of those philosophers were far too varied for them to be classed as members of the same school, and some of them (e.g., Austin, Ayer and Grice) were in many respects highly critical of the later Wittgenstein. However, on a number of points crucial to Wittgenstein's later thinking they would all have agreed:

> There was a general belief in clarity of expression and perspicuity of argument ... there was an aversion to the introduction of unnecessary or ill-defined technical terminology. There was general consensus that formal logic is not an 'ideal language', or even the bare syntax of an 'ideal language' ... There was a broad consensus that philosophy is not continuous with the empirical sciences, and that its methods and goals differ from those of science. And there was general agreement that the predicate calculus is not a representation of the depth structure of any possible language. Hence most philosophers writing in Oxford eschewed appeal to the calculus as a key to philosophical analysis. (Hacker 1996b, 159)

The glorious days of Oxford philosophy and the time when Wittgenstein's ideas were at the forefront of academic debate came to an end in the 1970s. They were brushed aside as outmoded 'ordinary language philosophy' in the name of a more systematic and scientific approach to the subject that was first flourishing in American universities and soon came to dominate Britain as well. Its most prominent proponents were Willard Van Orman Quine and Donald Davidson. Davidson in a series of carefully written and technically sophisticated articles set up and pursued the programme of a 'theory of meaning' for natural languages in terms of truth-conditions. From a set of axioms and rules, using only the resources of the predicate calculus, the theory was supposed to yield for every sentence 'ϕ' in the language a statement of the form:

'ϕ' is true if and only if ψ.

The way in which a potential infinity of such statements of truth-conditions would be derivable from a limited set of axioms and rules was supposed to explain how, on the basis of a finite vocabulary and mastery of a finite set of rules, we are able to understand any of a potential infinity of sentences (Davidson 1967, 17). – This ought to sound vaguely familiar. The *Tractatus* proposed to explain our ability to understand propositions we have never heard before on the basis of our knowledge of a finite set of names and rules of syntax (see sect. 2.4). In the *Tractatus* our understanding of (non-elementary) propositions was explained in terms of truth-conditions. The predicate calculus was deemed sufficient to represent the logical form of any proposition. But most importantly, the logical form was thought to be disguised by natural language and needed to be excavated by sophisticated logical analysis, so that an ordinary speaker, although perfectly conversant with the use of the language, was not able to spell out exactly what his sentences meant. Similarly, Davidson's analyses of specific types of sentences go well beyond the explanations that a competent speaker would be able to give, and nobody as yet had been able to provide the envisaged theory of meaning.

In short, the philosophical view of language that in the 1970s began to oust the influence of Wittgenstein's later work was, ironically, in many ways a variant of the position that the *Investigations* had reacted against: a reversion to some of the 'grave mistakes' Wittgenstein had been forced to recognize in what he wrote in his first book (cf. *PI* p. viii). This reversion was not coincidental. The *Tractatus* had made an immense impression on the logical positivists of the Vienna Circle and also on kindred spirits in other continental universities, most notably Berlin. The rise of the Nazis in the 1930s drove many of them into exile, and a considerable number of them emigrated to the United States, including Herbert Feigl, Rudolf Carnap, Philipp Frank, Kurt Gödel, Carl Hempel, Hans Reichenbach and Alfred Tarski. Their impact upon American philosophy was considerable. Carnap, especially, became extremely influential, not least with his student Quine, the pre-eminent American philosopher of the 1950s and 1960s (cf. Quine 1970, 464). And Quine had an equally formative impact on his outstanding student Davidson, who was also considerably influenced by reading Feigl, Hempel and Tarski.

In the philosophy of mind too Wittgenstein's influence was waning in the 1970s. His views were labelled 'logical behaviourism' and dismissed glibly. Again, Davidson's work (his account of reasons as causes and his theory of 'anomalous monism') was a factor in this development, as was Noam Chomsky's idea of grammatical principles innately encoded in the brain. But mainly it seems to have been the recent progress both in neurophysiological psychology and computer science ('artificial intelligence') that spurred philosophers on to give their treatment of the mind a more scientific appearance. They produced theories of the mind that tried to incorporate some of the latest scientific findings, so that philosophy could appear involved in the excitement of new discoveries about the workings of our minds or the new successes in computer science. Occasionally, in this area too, philosophers unwittingly reverted to some of Wittgenstein's immature views, blissfully ignorant of the reasons why Wittgenstein had later discarded them. John Searle (1983), for example, defended the *Tractatus* view of intentionality as unaccountably intrinsic to thinking, and only through thinking bestowed on language; and Wittgenstein's naïve idea of an innate language of thought has more recently been propounded by J. A. Fodor (1976).[1] George Santayana once remarked that those who

---

[1] For an account of these ideas in the *Tractatus* see sect. 2.4 above. For criticism see Malcolm 1986, chs 4, 5, 10; Hacker 1990, 313–34; Hacker 1992; Ammereller 2001.

don't know the history of philosophy are likely to repeat it. Justly discarded philosophical views can be expected to get a new lease of life when criticisms of them are neglected or ignored.[2]

6.2 Challenges to Wittgenstein's Philosophy

Wittgenstein's philosophy, when expounded in sufficient detail, contains controversial theses only for those who have philosophical commitments – that is, of course, the majority of his readers. As illustrated earlier (sect. 4.3), philosophical theorizing is prone to contradict virtually everything; so it is not surprising that even fairly straightforward observations in Wittgenstein's work have been treated by other philosophers as on a par with their own controversial doctrines. Three fundamental points, in particular, have been attacked: first, that there is a distinction between empirical statements and conceptual statements; secondly, that linguistic meaning is known to competent speakers; thirdly, that there is a conceptual link between feelings and thoughts, on the one hand, and expressive behaviour, on the other hand. I shall, in this final chapter, briefly consider some influential attempts to undermine those three observations.

(a) Attacks on the distinction between conceptual and empirical statements

An *analytic* statement is usually defined as true simply in virtue of the meanings of the ingredient words. It is therefore *a priori*: that is, its truth can be ascertained without recourse to experience. Its opposite is a *synthetic* statement. To find out whether a synthetic statement is true or false, it is not sufficient to be entirely clear about the words' meanings: one needs to draw on experience. Synthetic statements are *a posteriori*.[3] Wittgenstein hardly used any of these terms (he tried to avoid technical jargon as far as possible), but the distinction they are used to draw is crucial to his philosophy.[4] Effectual philosophical inves-

---

[2] A more detailed account of Wittgenstein's place in post-war analytic philosophy, to which this section is much indebted, is given in Hacker 1996b, chs 6–8.

[3] Kant attempted to show that there are also synthetic *a priori* judgements, allowing for metaphysics as a respectable science. But it is widely agreed that his attempt failed.

[4] It has been argued that Wittgenstein abandoned the concept of an analytic truth and instead introduced the rather different concept of a *grammatical proposition*, characterized not as an *a priori* truth, but as a norm of representation (Baker and Hacker 1985, 267–9; Glock 1996c, 201f). It is true that he used the latter concept rather than the former, but there is no reason to see the two as mutually exclusive. Moreover, the concept of

tigations are conceptual investigations, while misguided philosophical theory, metaphysics, is typically the result of overlooking the distinction between factual and conceptual questions (Z §458).

The analytic/synthetic distinction was famously attacked by Quine in his article 'Two Dogmas of Empiricism' (1953). Quine observed that the notion of analyticity could not be defined 'extensionally' – that is, in terms of 'truth' or 'reference' – but only in terms of a cluster of other 'intensional' words (such as 'synonymous', 'self-contradiction' or 'necessity') – that is, words that, again, cannot be defined in terms of 'truth' or 'reference' alone. He regarded such definitions as viciously circular and dismissed the analytic/synthetic distinction as ill-founded. – The weakness of this line of argument has been well exposed by Paul Grice and P. F. Strawson (1956), and further by H.-J. Glock (1996c, §1; 2003, ch. 3), who concluded that:

> Quine's circularity-charge comes down to the rather odd complaint that 'analytic' can be explained only via notions with which it is synonymous, and not via notions with which it is not synonymous.... The idea that legitimate concepts must be translatable into a purely extensional language presupposes that intensional notions have been discredited, which is what the circularity-charge set out to do. (Glock 2003, 75)

Another line of argument in Quine's paper is based on his *holism*, the view that our statements do not admit of confirmation or disconfirmation individually, but face the tribunal of experience only as a whole (1953, 41). Thus, when a scientific prediction turns out to be false, it is really the whole web of our beliefs, including mathematics and logic, that is in conflict with experience. We could resolve the conflict in numerous ways, even by abandoning some of our logical or mathematical statements. Hence no statement is *a priori* and immune from revision in the light of new experience, not even the axioms of logic and mathematics (Quine 1953, 42f). – Apart from the fact that this holistic picture appears to exaggerate the extent to which our beliefs are logically interrelated, it seems hard to imagine how we might possibly give up our ordinary logical thinking without undermining the whole idea of a web of interrelated beliefs and, indeed, the very idea of confirmation or disconfirmation by experience. But the most telling weakness in Quine's argument is this: The fact that any sentence, even '2 + 3 = 5' or '~(p . ~p)', may in future be rejected as false, does not show that they do not *now* express an *a priori* (mathematical, logical or analytic) truth. Rather, if future generations decide that '2 + 3 = 5' is

---

a grammatical proposition does not make that of an analytic statement superfluous: for there are derivative analytic statements whose conceptual credentials are so unobvious that they could not be used as grammatical norms (e.g.: 'In the position White: Kc3, Qa8, Be4; Black: Ka1, Ba2, White can mate in three moves').

false, we know that at least one of these signs must have *changed its meaning* (cf. Grice and Strawson 1956, 211; Glock 1996c, 211f). For the current meaning of those signs is such that '2 + 3 = 5' *is* an *a priori* truth, a norm of representation which we do not regard as subject to empirical confirmation or disconfirmation.

Although it is widely acknowledged that Quine's attack on the analytic/synthetic distinction was unsuccessful, many philosophers have misgivings about the idea that some statements are true in virtue of meanings or conventions. Such qualms have been expressed as follows:

> What could it possibly mean to say that the truth of a statement is fixed exclusively by its meaning and not by the facts? Isn't it in general true – indeed, isn't it in general a truism – that for any statement **S**,
>
> **S** is true iff for some **p**, **S** means that **p** and **p**?
>
> How could the *mere fact that* **S** *means that* **p** *make it the case that* **S** *is true?* (Boghossian 1996, 364)

In a similar vein Plato asked how one could possibly mistake one thing for another (*Theaetetus* 190b–c). The answer is that this seems impossible only as long as one has an overly simplified idea of what it is to mistake one thing for another. As soon as one describes a real case in sufficient detail, the problem dissolves (see sect. 4.3 (7) above). Likewise, as soon as one considers actual examples of suitable statements – rather than just sentence letters of formal logic, which effectively hide from view the crucial differences between different types of sentences and statements – it is not that difficult to see how truth can be due to meaning alone. Consider:

(1) 'A tandem' means: a bicycle with two seats.

This is true because the word 'tandem' *does* mean a bicycle with two seats. And so (1) is true in virtue of the meaning of the word 'tandem'. But (1) functions in the same way as an analytic statement in its usual form:

(2) A tandem is a bicycle with two seats.

This too can be verified simply by looking up the meaning of the word 'tandem' in a dictionary. Thus there should be no qualms about truth in virtue of meaning. But of course the truth of (2) is dependent not only on the meaning of the word 'tandem', but also on the meanings of its other words. If, for example, the word 'two' meant a different number, the statement would be false. So (2) is true in virtue of the meaning of the whole sentence.

Another philosophical worry might be that since meaning is due to convention, statements of meaning would appear to be just stipulations, and therefore – like decrees – neither true nor false. – But this overlooks the crucial distinction between the original stipulation and later reports of what has been stipulated. When, for example, the game of chess was being invented, an utterance of the sentence:

(3)   The bishop moves diagonally

(or its Persian equivalent) would have been a stipulation, and therefore neither true nor false. But when I describe to someone the game of chess (rather than invent a new game), my utterance of (3) is a true statement; and what makes it true is the fact that among chess-players there is indeed a convention that the bishop moves diagonally. Similarly with linguistic conventions: since there is a convention in English to use the word 'tandem' for a two-seater bicycle, my utterance of:

(2)   A tandem is a bicycle with two seats

is perfectly true: I do not *give* a meaning to the word 'tandem' myself, I *report* correctly what meaning it has in English.[5] And in the sense in which my report that Fiddleworth arrived at Totleigh Towers is rendered true by Fiddleworth's arrival at Totleigh Towers, my utterance of (2) is rendered true by the conventional use of the English word 'tandem'. That is the way a convention too can be said to create a truth.

More interesting is the way in which a *combination* of conventions can create a truth; for instance:

(4)   The white king's bishop can never move on a black square.

This is not simply the report of a rule of chess, but it follows from the combination of three rules: first, that bishops move only diagonally; secondly, that a chess-board is chequered black and white; and thirdly, that the white king's bishop is placed on a white square at the beginning of the game.

---

[5] Therefore it is quite inappropriate to say of such a 'grammatical statement' (as Wittgenstein called statements such as (2)) that it 'partly *determines* or *constitutes* the meanings' of the words involved (e.g., Glock 2003, 84). The meaning of the English word 'tandem' is completely independent of what I may say. What 'partly constitutes' the meaning of the word 'tandem' is not the statement (2), but the linguistic convention that such a statement reflects.

The concept of analyticity explains how it is possible to verify or falsify statements without recourse to experience, just on the basis of one's linguistic understanding; and thus, how philosophical – non-empirical – investigations are possible. It also explains the phenomenon of *necessary* truth: If the statement

(2)   A tandem is a bicycle with two seats

is true simply in virtue of the meanings of the ingredient words, then, given those meanings, its truth is not just a contingent matter of fact. It could not possibly be false, for, as long as we take the words to be understood in their established meanings, its negation makes no sense.[6] Analytic truths are necessary truths.

At this point an objection may be raised. I said above that the analytic statement (2) functions like

(1)   'A tandem' means: a bicycle with two seats

– that is, as an explanation of meaning. However, it would appear that such explanations of meaning, unlike analytic statements, are not necessary truths, for it is easily imaginable that the word 'tandem' might have had a different meaning in English. – Here it needs to be remembered that the necessity in question is conditional on our holding on to the established meanings of the words involved. Considering the possibility that our words have different meanings, we can of course imagine (1) to be false; but the same applies to (2). One might, for example, speculate that if the bicycle had not been invented and people used scooters instead, then today a tandem would perhaps be a scooter for two people. That is how under such circumstances we might possibly use the word 'tandem'. – Just as in our talk of necessary truths we set word meanings aside as given and stable, so when we speak of *a priori* truths we regard knowledge of meanings as given. That is, when analytic statements are called *a priori* – i.e., knowable independently of experience – this must not

---

[6] However, where the meaning of the relevant words cannot be presupposed, but is to be explained, a failed attempt at an analytic statement will be taken as false, not as nonsense. Consider:

(Z)   A tantrum is a bicycle with two seats.

Given the actual meanings of the words, this is nonsense. But the speaker presents it as a claim about the meaning of the word 'tantrum', and as such it is false.

be taken to include linguistic experience. Of course you wouldn't know that (2) is true if you hadn't first learnt the meanings of the English words.

Thus three distinctions run neatly parallel:

a priori	*a posteriori*
analytic	synthetic
necessary	contingent

This, however, has been denied by S. A. Kripke in his influential lectures *Naming and Necessity* (1972), where he tries to establish the existence of both necessary *a posteriori* truths and contingent *a priori* truths. The latter claim, in particular, contradicts Wittgenstein's views, as it seems to open the way for substantial philosophical theories: If *a priori* reasoning were able to establish contingent truths, it would appear that philosophy might be able to reach more positive results than Wittgenstein allows for. Kripke's argument for the existence of contingent *a priori* truths is of further interest to us because it is based on an example drawn from the *Philosophical Investigations*, namely:

> 50. ... There is *one* thing of which one can say neither that it is one metre long, nor that it is not one metre long, and that is the standard metre in Paris. – But this is, of course, not to ascribe any extraordinary property to it, but only to mark its peculiar role in the language-game of measuring with a metre-rule.

Kripke is puzzled by this remark. He stubbornly insists that Wittgenstein *is* ascribing an extraordinary property to the standard metre, and swiftly concludes that 'he must be wrong' (1972, 54). He then presents his own view that the statement

(5) S (the standard metre in Paris) is 1 metre long at t_0 (when it was declared to be the standard metre).

is a contingent *a priori* truth (1972, 54–6). Kripke's use of the term '*a priori*' is rather sloppy. As it stands, (5) is certainly not an *a priori* truth: for all we know, it may not even be true: there may not *be* a standard metre in Paris. All one could claim to be an *a priori* truth is the conditional statement

(5a) If S is the defining sample of '1 metre', S is 1 metre long.

However, Kripke observes that

(5b) It would have been possible for S to be the defining sample of
'1 metre' and not to be 1 metre long.

This is supposed to show that (5a), although *a priori*, is only *contingently* true. It might have been false: the length called '1 metre' might have been fixed by a stick of a different length. (In that case we would of course use the expression 'metre' differently today from the way we do use it.)

A typical philosopher's argument: a conceptual sleight of hand, exploiting an ambiguity. Ironically, the ambiguity on which it hinges is exactly what Wittgenstein's example was meant bring to the reader's attention. The point is that the copula 'is' can be used in a factual and in (what one might call) an 'analytic' sense. 'S is 1 metre long' can mean either:

(F5) S is *as a matter of fact* 1 metre long.

or:

(A5) S is *by definition* (called) '1 metre long'.

In denying that the standard metre in Paris is or is not one metre long, Wittgenstein takes the copula in its factual sense. The denial sounds paradoxical because there is also the analytic sense, in which it is perfectly correct to say that the standard metre is (by definition called) one metre long. To present a statement that is clearly true in one sense and false in another sense is of course a way of drawing attention to the distinction (though it may be too subtle for some readers).

For (5a), in Kripke's argument, to be *a priori*, the copula in the consequent has to be taken in the analytic sense:

(5a*) If S is the defining sample of '1 metre', S is *by definition* (called) '1 metre long'.

But the second clause of (5b) is about the length that a certain stick might *as a matter of fact* have, so the copula needs to be taken in the factual sense:

(5b*) It would have been possible for S to be the defining sample of '1 metre' and not *in fact* to be 1 metre long.

Once the equivocation has been removed, it becomes clear that what is *a priori* and what is contingent are not the same statement: The *a priori* truth (5a) contains an analytic 'is' in the consequent, while the statement to demonstrate its contingency (5b) contains a factual 'is' instead. What (5b) shows to be a contingent truth is not (5a). Had stick S been stretched to a different length (say, 1.07 metres) before becoming the defining sample of '1 metre', (5a) would still have been true: It would still have been true that S was *by definition called* '1 metre' (although, to be sure – from the point of view of our actual definition of '1 metre' – S would not *in fact* have been 1 metre long). The *a priori* truth (5a) is, after all, a necessary truth: its negation is self-contradictory:

(N5a) S is the defining sample of '1 metre', and it is not the case that S is defined as '1 metre'.

Kripke produces the opposite impression by conflating the two different sense of 'is' and switching from one to the other.[7]

(b) Attacks on the common-sense view of linguistic meaning

After his return to philosophy in 1929 Wittgenstein came to reject the idea that the meaning of ordinary words or statements was hidden beneath the surface of language awaiting excavation by highly skilled logicians. Languages are made, mastered and regulated by us. Our words have meaning only by convention: that is, because we agree in our use and understanding of what they mean. Hence the idea that beyond what we commonly take our words to mean there might be yet another, 'deeper' meaning doesn't make sense.

---

[7] Note incidentally that Kripke is also wrong in thinking that this (specious) appearance of a contingent *a priori* truth is due to the alleged phenomenon of 'rigid designation' (that a word stands for the same object 'in all possible worlds'). By conflating the analytic and the factual sense of the copula, one can produce the same paradox with a sentence that does not involve any term Kripke would call a 'rigid designator', e.g.:

1 The Prime Minister is the Head of Government.
2 Tony Blair is the Prime Minister.
3 Tony Blair is the Head of Government.
4 Tony Blair might not have been Head of Government.
5 The Prime Minister might not have been Head of Government.

Again, through equivocation (5) *seems* to show that (1) is a contingent *a priori* truth, but in fact (1) claims that by convention the two titles always apply to the same incumbent, and *that* is not said to be contingent by (5), which makes the entirely different point that Tony Blair's career might have taken a different turn.

Opposed to the common-sense view of meaning is the doctrine of *scientific realism*, propounded by Kripke (1972) and Hilary Putnam (1973). They denied that the meaning of a 'natural kind' term (such as 'water', 'gold' or 'tiger') is constituted by the way we apply it: by the criteria we use to tell whether anything falls under the term or not. Rather, they held, the meanings of such terms are determined by the real nature or essence of the kinds in question, which scientific investigation strives to discover.[8] Natural kind terms are introduced through a sample and a declaration that everything that has the same underlying essence as the sample is to fall under the term, even though that essence may as yet be unknown. A paradoxical consequence of this view is that two words may be used in exactly the same way, according to exactly the same criteria, yet differ in meaning because they happen to be applied to things or substances with different essences. For example, people on a different planet may use a word exactly as we use the word 'water': to denote a transparent, tasteless, drinkable liquid that occurs in rivers, lakes and as rain, but their word would have a different meaning if 'water' on their planet was not constituted of H_2O. Conversely, if water was discovered to have the same molecular structure as tar, then the words 'water' and 'tar', in spite of their markedly different use, would have the same meaning.

This account is implausible for a number of reasons. First, the assumed definition involving a sample and a declaration that the term is to apply to everything that shares the sample's underlying essence is pure fiction. This is very obvious in the case of concepts that, like 'water' or 'bird', are much older than the scientific idea of an underlying essence. But even today when we are familiar with the idea of molecular structure, atomic number and DNA, nothing forces us to make use of any such hidden features when classifying things for non-scientific, everyday-life purposes. In fact, with many of our common or garden concepts we happily ignore scientific taxonomy. We group plants as trees, bushes or flowers, although biological classification cuts right across these concepts. From a scientific point of view, oak trees and daisies belong to the same class, whereas oak trees and pine trees do not. The difference between a tree and a bush is important to a gardener, but non-existent to biological taxonomy.

Secondly, Putnam's thought experiments are unconvincing. He claims that if in some lakes or rivers we discovered a substance that was indistinguishable from water except that it was not H_2O, but of a different molecular structure, we would not call it 'water'. But it seems much more likely that we would speak of the discovery of a new type of water. And even if scientists refused to call that new substance

---

[8] There are obvious similarities between scientific realism and the *Tractatus* account of meaning. Cf. sects 2.3 and 4.2.

'water', that would not show that classification must be decided by the underlying essence; it would only show that where we know what micro-structure a substance has, it may, obviously, be used as a criterion for identifying the substance. As for the converse scenario, where a stuff very unlike water (say, black, viscous, smelly, poisonous) was discovered to have the molecular structure H_2O, we could not seriously regard such a substance as identical with water. For whatever special interest scientists have in micro-structure, there is no denying that macroscopic features are just as objective and real. Indeed, scientific interest in micro-features is largely due to the role they play in explanations of the macro-features we experience in everyday life.

One may well wonder why Putnam and Kripke went as far as attributing their scientific essence concepts even to the most simple-minded people and even to societies with neither science nor a notion of underlying essences. For a twentieth-century chemist water may be H_2O, but the idea that in the mouth of a Babylonian washer-woman the Babylonian word for water had exactly the same meaning sounds bizarre. The reason why Putnam was so averse to acknowledging any change of meaning, or difference in meaning between different words for roughly the same sort of thing, appears to be that he thought it incompatible with the idea of scientific progress. To say, for example, that the term 'water' has changed its meaning over the last 500 years 'obscures just what we want to stress: that the changes in the accepted criteria reflect the fact that we have more and more knowledge concerning' the same thing: water (Putnam 1962, 219f). – The point is feeble. There is no good reason to think that change in concepts must amount to a change of topic; that, for example, the patient who complains of *something that gives him pain in the stomach* and the doctor who diagnoses that pain to be caused by an *appendicitis* must be at cross-purposes because they use different concepts to describe the case. This is just what manifests cognitive progress: that we are able to describe the same phenomena by increasingly sophisticated concepts.

Thirdly, it is naïve to believe that by picking out some object or stuff and referring facilely to its essence – 'whatever that may be' – one can define a concept. As Locke pointed out in a similar debate some 300 years ago, to an individual object (or amount of stuff) all its properties are equally essential (1689, 3.6.5). The concept of an essence is relative to a given classification, and therefore cannot be invoked as the basis of classification. Imagine someone pointing at an Alsatian and inviting us to group together everything that shares its essence. We don't know what to do as long as we are not told whether to regard the object as an animal, as a carnivore, as a mammal, as a dog, as an Alsatian, as a bitch, as a well-trained guide-dog or, say, as a black and fawn coloured animal. Objects in nature have myriads of different features, and it is up to us which ones to select as criteria for classification. Putnam and

Kripke believe that on the micro-level nature herself takes the decision for us. But apart from the fact that it is still our decision to take into account anything on the micro-level (and for many purposes we don't), down there we are just as much overwhelmed with data and still have to decide which ones (which genes, for example) are to be relevant to classification. Words and their meanings are man-made, and humans have to take responsibility for them.[9]

Another aspect of Wittgenstein's common-sense view of meaning is that although philosophers may have occasion to clarify certain facets of it, it does not stand in need of a systematic theoretical explanation. In answer to a request for such an explanation, Wittgenstein would simply remind us of our ordinary understanding of the term: 'but don't you understand it? Well, if you do, what is there left to explain, what is there left for an explanation to do?' (*BT* 418). Unless there is some particular philosophical puzzle about a concept, the request for a philosophical explanation of that concept is quite pointless.

Sometimes the cry for a theory of meaning does indeed seem to spring from nothing more than a vague feeling that it would be nice to have a theory about everything – 'whether it is riding a bicycle or speaking a language' (Grayling 1988, 99). But life is too short to give elaborate descriptions that serve no explanatory need (cf. sect. 4.4 (1) above). Davidson's theoretical account of meaning, however, is presented in answer to the philosophical puzzle of 'linguistic creativity' (cf. *TLP* 4.03). It is meant to explain 'the fact that, on mastering a finite vocabulary and a finitely stated set of rules, we are prepared to produce and to understand any of a potential infinitude of sentences' (Davidson 1967, 17). But what is the problem here? Our ability to form and understand an indefinite number of sentences could appear puzzling only to those who expect all sentences to be learnt in foreign tourists' phrase-book fashion, as indivisible units. But nobody does. We all know that children learn individual words and the ways they are strung together, or, when they learn full sentences ('Tommy wants milk'), they also learn how those sentences can be modified in open-ended ways ('Monica wants milk', 'Archie wants milk', 'Tommy wants chocolate', etc.). So what is there to be explained through the construction of a theory of meaning? By equipping us with axioms, rules and definitions to derive the truth-conditions of an indefinite number of sentences, Davidson's 'theory' is supposed to figure in an explanation of 'compositionality' (the way in which sentences are composed out of words). But in fact,

---

[9] For further criticisms of scientific realism see Hanfling 2000, ch. 12; Hacker 1996b, 250–3.

what the proposed theoretical project could offer is not *explanation* – as there is nothing to be explained – but merely *logical formalization*, the point of which remains obscure.

Davidson promises that from his proposed theory we could learn 'what is necessary and sufficient for [linguistic] understanding' (1994, 112); but it is easy to see that he cannot keep this promise. At best his 'theory' would amount to a translation manual which for every sentence in a given language yields a truth-functional equivalent in the language of the theory (e.g.: '"*Schnee ist weiß*" is true if and only if snow is white'). Hence it could at most be regarded as a model of how we might understand a second language by translating it into our first language. But with respect to our first language, and thus the basic case of linguistic understanding, Davidson's account is a non-starter: Our understanding of a first language cannot possibly be accounted for by a 'theory' which effectively translates that language into another language. The monolingual child has no other language in which to theorize about his mother tongue (cf. *PI* §32). So the construction of such a theory cannot explain the child's linguistic capacities, just as the construction of a helicopter cannot explain how birds fly.[10]

(c) Putnam's criticism of 'logical behaviourism'

Against the Cartesian claim that mind and body are entirely distinct, and linked only contingently, Wittgenstein insisted that there is a *conceptual* link between mental phenomena and expressive behaviour. That view has often been labelled dismissively as 'logical behaviourism', and it is sometimes said that in the early 1960s logical behaviourism was effectively refuted by Hilary Putnam (e.g., Stegmüller 1979, 410–12). Putnam admits that when we introduce and explain our terms for psychological phenomena, in the absence of science, we depend upon their links with characteristic patterns of expressive behaviour. But he denies that such a link between the inner and the outer is in any way necessary or analytic. Expressions like 'dream' or 'pain' denote physiological occurrences which *normally* cause a certain expressive behaviour; but it would be perfectly possible for them to occur without their normal behavioural effects and to be detectable only through neurophysiological investigation: 'there is nothing self-contradictory . . . in talking of hypothetical worlds in which there are pains but no pain behaviour' (Putnam 1965, 7). He attempts to support this claim by a thought experiment:

---

[10] For further and more detailed criticisms of Davidson's project, see Mulhall 1990, ch. 4; Glock 1993; Schroeder 1998, 207–16.

Imagine a community of 'super-spartans' or 'super-stoics' – a community in which the adults have the ability to successfully suppress all involuntary pain behaviour. They may, on occasion, admit that they feel pain, but always in pleasant well-modulated voices – even if they are undergoing the agonies of the damned. They do not wince, scream, flinch, sob, grit their teeth, clench their fists, exhibit beads of sweat, or otherwise act like people in pain or people suppressing the unconditioned responses associated with pain. However, they do feel pain, and they dislike it (just as we do). They even admit that it takes a great effort of will to behave as they do. It is only that they have what they regard as important ideological reasons for behaving as they do, and they have, through years of training, learned to live up to their own exacting standards. (Putnam 1965, 9)

Does this scenario bear out Putnam's claim? Clearly not. For even the world of the super-spartans contains not only pain but also pain-behaviour. For one thing, it is only the *adults* who are said to have the ability to successfully suppress all involuntary pain-behaviour; children would presumably cry and moan, just as in our world. For another thing, even adult super-spartans express their pain verbally. True, in a continuation of the thought experiment, making those people into 'super-super-spartans', Putnam proceeds to abolish even their verbal pain-behaviour. However, it is then furtively reintroduced in the form of 'brain waves which can be decoded into English'; so that the situation remains on the whole unchanged (1965, 11–17).

Setting aside those still uninhibited children (possibly an oversight on Putnam's part), we might well wonder why in the absence of any natural pain-behaviour we should ascribe pain to super-spartans. Of course, they *say* that occasionally they feel 'pain'. But how do we know what they mean by 'pain'? Suppose we were to confront them with paradigmatic examples of natural pain-behaviour, would they be able to recognize it as such? If not, we would have no reason to say that by 'pain' they mean the same as we do. Hence, only if they could recognize pain-behaviour as such could the scenario be said to present a world of unexpressed pain. But that confirms the very view that Putnam is trying to attack: that one cannot have the concept of pain without having a grasp on what counts as an expression of pain (cf. Kenny 1971, 281 n. 12).

Furthermore, the super-spartans are said to 'have what they regard as important ideological reasons for behaving as they do'. So what kind of ideology do they have? Presumably one that forbids them to show any natural pain-behaviour – which again implies that they must have a clear notion as to what natural pain-behaviour is.

Finally, the claim that the super-spartans are 'undergoing the agonies of the damned' makes rather doubtful sense. For the degree of someone's suffering is partly determined by his ability or inability to suppress any signs of it. A light headache can easily be kept entirely secret. Not letting on that one is suffering from a severe migraine is a good deal more difficult. For it is not only a matter of keeping quiet, but of being as sprightly, active and clear-headed as ever. There are also behavioural signs of making a 'great effort' not to show one's pain. And extremely severe pains are characterized by the very fact that they manifest themselves even against a person's will. In short, we might believe the super-spartans when they say that they are feeling a little under the weather, but 'the agonies of the damned' – surely not.

Science is naturally interested in causes. Scientific concepts tend to classify phenomena not by their appearances but by their underlying causes or micro-structure. The examples discussed by Putnam are usually drawn from the sciences: multiple sclerosis, polio, acid, H_2O, aluminium. So it is not surprising that he is inclined to regard the concept of pain likewise as a causal concept. To begin with, he maintains, we characterize pains as causes of certain behavioural patterns, yet science will strive to identify them directly, in terms of what they are physiologically. Is this an appropriate account of our common or garden concept of pain?

The physiological basis of pain is:

(Φ) an excitation of free nerve endings, which is transmitted through Aδ- and C-fibres to the spinal cord and is projected via the lateral spinothalamic tract to the parafasciculare and intralaminare thalamic nuclei. (Arnold, Eysenck, Meili 1980, 1995f)

Does (Φ) spell out what the word 'pain' means and has meant all along? Surely not, for (Φ) does not have the same extension as the concept of pain. In the case of phantom pains, for instance, there is a pain in a place in which no (Φ)-excitation could occur. And when the (Φ)-excitation responsible for the cramps in my leg has reached the thalamic tract, the cramps in my leg have not thereby moved to the forebrain. But even if the concepts of pain and (Φ) were coextensional, they would still be different. It would still remain *conceivable* that someone might suffer pain without having any (Φ)-excitations, or vice versa.

This result may not worry Putnam too much. Of course scientifically informed judgements about what is F may differ from our pre-scientific views. What looked like multiple sclerosis, going by the symptoms, and thus was called 'multiple sclerosis', turns out to have a different aetiology and therefore not to be counted as multiple sclerosis at all. Even if we are not convinced by Putnam's bold claim that in these cases there has been no change of meaning, that today's sophisticated concepts have really been current all along (cf. (b) above); – it is at any rate true that they have carried the day. With regard to diseases or chemical substances, we readily defer to the latest scientific classifications. Even if for me iron pyrites were absolutely indistinguishable from gold, I would not insist on calling it 'gold' after scientists told me that, not having seventy-nine protons, it was not really gold. Our traditional concept of pain, however, is not in the same way in competition with concepts that, like (Φ), classify the same phenomena in terms of their underlying conditions. No physiologist could convince me that what in my own case I call 'pain' may not in fact be pain when not accompanied by (Φ)-excitations, or that my pain was in truth not where I felt it but in the brain. Why is that so?

Concepts are an expression of our interests. We group things together and call them by a common name according to those resemblances we find striking or important. And in different contexts we may be interested in different aspects of things. To classify phenomena scientifically, by their underlying structures or causes, is not always what we want. For instance, when taking an aesthetic attitude towards things, we are concerned entirely with their appearances. Invisible micro-structures become wholly irrelevant. And another area in which the scientifc urge to leave behind the surface for underlying causes is often out of place is the realm of feeling: where our primary interest is in people's conscious experience. Their suffering and well-being is important to us in its own right, and not merely as an indication of some underlying physiological conditions. Therefore physiological concepts like 'lesion of tissue' or '(Φ)-excitation' – whatever their importance for diagnosis and therapy – can never be in competition with, or act as substitutes for, our traditional concepts of feelings and emotions that are taught and understood through their links with natural expressive behaviour and characterized by the special authority we have in their first-person use (see sect. 4.7 above).

Further Reading

Reliable and highly readable biographies are:

- Brian McGuinness, *Wittgenstein: A Life*, vol. 1: *Young Ludwig 1889–1921*, London: Duckworth, 1988.
- Ray Monk, *Wittgenstein: The Duty of Genius*, London: Cape, 1990.

A useful tool for Wittgenstein students is:

- Hans-Johann Glock, *A Wittgenstein Dictionary*, Oxford: Blackwell, 1996.

It contains, in alphabetical order, clear accounts and brief discussions of all the major topics and key terms of Wittgenstein's philosophy, with valuable references to the most relevant passages.

Those who wish to make a close study of the *Philosophical Investigations* will find an extremely helpful companion in the analytical commentary by G. P. Baker and P. M. S. Hacker, which contains both detailed exegesis of all 693 sections and illuminating essays on all the book's major topics:

- G. P. Baker and P. M. S. Hacker, *Wittgenstein: Understanding and Meaning*, Volume 1 of *An Analytical Commentary on the Philosophical Investigations*.

    Part I: *Essays*, rev. edn, Oxford: Blackwell, 2004.
    Part II: *Exegesis §§1–184*, rev. edn, Oxford: Blackwell, 2004.

- G. P. Baker and P. M. S. Hacker, *Wittgenstein: Rules, Grammar and Necessity*, Volume 2 of *An Analytical Commentary on the Philosophical Investigations*. Oxford: Blackwell, 1988.

- P. M. S. Hacker, *Wittgenstein: Meaning and Mind, Volume 3 of An Analytical Commentary on the Philosophical Investigations*, Oxford: Blackwell, 1990.
- P. M. S. Hacker, *Wittgenstein: Mind and Will, Volume 4 of An Analytical Commentary on the Philosophical Investigations*, Oxford: Blackwell, 1996.

Bibliography

Ammereller, Erich (2001), 'Wittgenstein on Intentionality'. In Glock 2001, 59–93.
Anscombe, G. E. M. (1959), *An Introduction to Wittgenstein's Tractatus*. London: Hutchinson.
Arnold, Wilhelm, Eysenck, Hans Jürgen and Meili, Richard (eds) (1980), *Lexikon der Psychologie*, 3 vols. Freiburg im Breisgau: Herder.
St Augustine, *Confessions*, tr. E. B. Pusey. London: Dent, 1907.
Ayer, A. J. (1936), *Language, Truth and Logic*. Harmondsworth: Penguin, 1971.
Bell, Clive (1913), *Art*. New York: Capricorn Books, 1958.
Baker, Gordon (1988), *Wittgenstein, Frege and the Vienna Circle*. Oxford: Blackwell.
Baker, G. P. and Hacker, P. M. S. (1985), *Wittgenstein: Rules, Grammar and Necessity, Volume 2 of An Analytical Commentary on the Philosophical Investigations*. Oxford: Blackwell.
Baker, G. P. and Hacker, P. M. S. (2004a), *Wittgenstein: Understanding and Meaning, Volume 1 of An Analytical Commentary on the Philosophical Investigations*. Part I: *Essays*, rev. edn. Oxford: Blackwell.
Baker, G. P. and Hacker, P. M. S. (2004b), *Wittgenstein: Understanding and Meaning, Volume 1 of An Analytical Commentary on the Philosophical Investigations*. Part II: *Exegesis §§1–184*, rev. edn. Oxford: Blackwell.
Black, Max (1964), *A Companion to Wittgenstein's 'Tractatus'*. Cambridge: Cambridge University Press.
Boghossian, Paul Artin (1996), 'Analyticity'. *Noûs*, 30, 360–91.
Bouwsma, O. K. (1986), *Wittgenstein: Conversations 1949–1951*, ed. J. L. Craft and R. E. Hustwit. Indianapolis: Hackett.
Bradley, F. H. (1893), *Appearance and Reality: A Metaphysical Essay*. London: Allen & Unwin.

Britton, Karl (1955), 'Portrait of a Philosopher'. Repr. in Fann 1967, 56–63.
Broad, C. D. (1925), *The Mind and its Place in Nature*. London: Routledge.
Broch, Hermann (1955), *Hofmannsthal und seine Zeit*. Frankfurt/Main: Suhrkamp, 2001.
Cioffi, Frank (1998), *Wittgenstein on Freud and Frazer*. Cambridge: Cambridge University Press.
Clark, Ronald W. (1975), *The Life of Bertrand Russell*. London: Cape and Weidenfeld & Nicolson.
Conant, James (2000), 'Elucidation and Nonsense in Frege and Early Wittgenstein'. In Crary and Read 2000, 174–217.
Crary, Alice and Read, Rupert (eds) (2000), *The New Wittgenstein*. London: Routledge.
Davidson, Donald (1963), 'Actions, Reasons and Causes'. In his *Essays on Actions and Events*, Oxford: Clarendon Press, 1980, 3–19.
Davidson, Donald (1967), 'Truth and Meaning'. In his *Inquiries into Truth and Interpretation*, Oxford: Clarendon Press, 1984, 17–36.
Davidson, Donald (1994), 'The Social Aspect of Language'. Repr. in his *Truth, Language, and History*, Oxford: Clarendon Press, 2005, 109–25.
Davies, S. (2001), 'Definitions of Art'. In B. Gaut and D. McIver Lopes (eds), *The Routledge Companion to Aesthetics*, London: Routledge, 169–79.
Descartes, René (1641), *Meditations on First Philosophy*, tr. J. Cottingham. Cambridge: Cambridge University Press, 1986.
Diamond, Cora (1988), 'Throwing Away the Ladder: How to Read the *Tractatus*'. In her *The Realistic Spirit*, Cambridge, Mass.: MIT Press, 1991, 179–204.
Drury, M. O'C. (1984), 'Some Notes on Conversations with Wittgenstein'; 'Conversations with Wittgenstein'. In Rhees 1984, 76–171.
Engelmann, Paul (1967), *Letters from Ludwig Wittgenstein: With a Memoir*. Oxford: Blackwell.
Fann, K. T. (ed.) (1967), *Ludwig Wittgenstein: The Man and his Philosophy*. Hassocks, Sussex: Harvester Press.
Fodor, J. A. (1976), *The Language of Thought*. Hassocks, Sussex: Harvester Press.
Fogelin, Robert J. (1987), *Wittgenstein*, 2nd edn. London: Routledge.
Frascolla, Pasquale (2001), 'Philosophy of Mathematics'. In Glock 2001, 268–88.
Frege, Gottlob (1879), *Conceptual Notation and Related Articles*, tr. T. W. Bynum. Oxford: Oxford University Press, 1972.
Frege, Gottlob (1884), *The Foundations of Arithmetic*, tr. J. L. Austin. Oxford: Blackwell, 1968.
Frege, Gottlob (1892), 'On Sense and Meaning'. In P. Geach and M.

Black (eds and trs), *Translations from the Philosophical Writings of Gottlob Frege*, Oxford: Blackwell, 1952, 56–78.

Frege, Gottlob (1903), *The Basic Laws of Arithmetic*, vol. 2, tr. and ed. M. Furth. Berkeley: University of California Press, 1964.

Gardiner, P. (1970), 'Error, Faith and Self-Deception'. Repr. in J. Glover (ed.), *The Philosophy of Mind*, Oxford: Oxford University Press, 1976, 35–52.

Gasking, D. A. T. and Jackson, A. C. (1951), 'Wittgenstein as a Teacher'. Repr. in Fann 1967, 49–55.

Geach, P. (1981), 'Wittgenstein's Operator N'. *Analysis*, 41 (4), 168–71.

Glock, Hans-Johann (1990), 'Stroud's Defence of Cartesian Scepticism – A "Linguistic Response"'. *Philosophical Investigations*, 13, 44–64.

Glock, Hans-Johann (1993), 'The Indispensability of Translation in Quine and Davidson'. *Philosophical Quarterly*, 43, 194–209.

Glock, Hans-Johann (1996a), *A Wittgenstein Dictionary*. Oxford: Blackwell.

Glock, Hans-Johann (1996b), 'Abusing Use'. *Dialectica*, 50 (3), 205–23.

Glock, Hans-Johann (1996c), 'Necessity and Normativity'. In H. Sluga and D. G. Stern (eds), *The Cambridge Companion to Wittgenstein*, Cambridge: Cambridge University Press, 198–225.

Glock, Hans-Johann (ed.) (2001), *Wittgenstein: A Critical Reader*. Oxford: Blackwell.

Glock, Hans-Johann (2003), *Quine and Davidson on Language, Thought and Reality*. Cambridge: Cambridge University Press.

Graßhoff, Gerd (2004), 'On the Origin of Wittgenstein's *Tractatus*'. In M. Siebel and M. Textor (eds), *Semantik und Ontologie*, Frankfurt/Main: Ontos Verlag, 419–45.

Grayling, A. C. (1988), *Wittgenstein*. Oxford: Oxford University Press.

Grice, Paul (1989), *Studies in the Way of Words*. Cambridge/Mass.: Harvard University Press.

Grice, P. and Strawson, P. F. (1956), 'In Defense of a Dogma'. In Grice 1989, 196–212.

Griffin, James (1964), *Wittgenstein's Logical Atomism*. Repr. Bristol: Thoemmes, 1997.

Hacker, P. M. S. (1986), *Insight and Illusion: Themes in the Philosophy of Wittgenstein*, rev. edn. Oxford: Clarendon Press, (1st edn 1972); repr. Bristol: Thoemmes, 1997.

Hacker, P. M. S. (1990), *Wittgenstein: Meaning and Mind, Volume 3 of An Analytical Commentary on the Philosophical Investigations*. Oxford: Blackwell.

Hacker, P. M. S. (1992), 'Malcolm and Searle on "Intentional Mental States"'. *Philosophical Investigations*, 15, 245–75.

Hacker, P. M. S. (1996a), *Wittgenstein: Mind and Will, Volume 4 of An Analytical Commentary on the Philosophical Investigations*. Oxford: Blackwell.

Hacker, P. M. S. (1996b), *Wittgenstein's Place in Twentieth-Century Analytic Philosophy.* Oxford: Blackwell.
Hacker, P. M. S. (2000), 'Was he Trying to Whistle it?'. In his 2001, 98–140.
Hacker, P. M. S. (2001), *Wittgenstein: Connections and Controversies.* Oxford: Clarendon Press.
Hacker, P. M. S. (2003), 'Wittgenstein, Carnap and the New American Wittgensteinians'. *Philosophical Quarterly*, 53 (210), 1–23.
Hanfling, Oswald (1987), 'How is Scepticism Possible?'. *Philosophy*, 62, 435–53.
Hanfling, Oswald (1992), 'The Problem of Definition'. In Hanfling (ed.), *Philosophical Aesthetics: An Introduction*, Oxford: Blackwell, 1–40.
Hanfling, Oswald (2000), *Philosophy and Ordinary Language.* London: Routledge.
Hanfling, Oswald (2002), *Wittgenstein and the Human Form of Life.* London: Routledge.
Hornsby, Jennifer (1980), *Actions.* London: Routledge.
Hume, David (1739), *A Treatise of Human Nature*, ed. L. A. Selby-Bigge. Oxford: Oxford University Press, 1888.
Hume, David (1748), *Enquiry Concerning Human Understanding*, ed. L. A. Selby-Bigge and P. H. Nidditch. Oxford: Oxford University Press, 1975.
Hylton, Peter (1990), *Russell, Idealism and the Emergence of Analytic Philosophy.* Oxford: Clarendon Press.
James, William (1890), *The Principles of Psychology*, 2 vols. Repr. New York: Dover, 1950.
James, William (1902), *The Varieties of Religious Experience: A Study in Human Nature.* London: Longmans.
Janik, Allan and Toulmin, Stephen (1973), *Wittgenstein's Vienna.* New York: Simon & Schuster.
Johnston, William M. (1972), *The Austrian Mind: An Intellectual and Social History 1848–1938.* Berkeley: University of California Press.
Kant, Immanuel (1785), *Groundwork of the Metaphysics of Morals*, tr. M. Gregor. Cambridge: Cambridge University Press, 1998.
Kenny, Anthony (1971), 'The Verification Principle and the Private Language Argument (ii)'. In O. R. Jones (ed.), *The Private Language Argument*, London: Macmillan, 204–28, 280–2.
Kenny, Anthony (1973), *Wittgenstein.* Harmondsworth: Penguin.
Kenny, Anthony (1989), *The Metaphysics of Mind.* Oxford: Clarendon Press.
Kivy, Peter (1997), *Philosophies of Arts: An Essay in Differences.* Cambridge: Cambridge University Press.
Kraus, Karl (1899–1936), *Die Fackel.* Repr. Munich: Kösel Verlag, 1968–76.

Kripke, Saul A. (1972), *Naming and Necessity*. Cambridge, Mass.: Harvard University Press.
Kripke, Saul A. (1982), *Wittgenstein on Rules and Private Language*. Cambridge, Mass.: Harvard University Press.
Leavis, F. R. (1973), 'Memories of Wittgenstein'. Repr. in Rhees 1984, 50–67.
Lewy, C. (1967), 'A Note on the Text of the *Tractatus*'. *Mind*, 76, 417–23.
Locke, John (1689), *An Essay Concerning Human Understanding*, ed. P. H. Nidditch. Oxford: Oxford University Press, 1975.
Loos, Adolf (1931), *Trotzdem*. Repr. Vienna: Prachner, 1982.
Luckhardt, C. G. (ed.) (1979), *Wittgenstein: Sources and Perspectives*. Hassocks, Sussex: Harvester Press.
Lycan, W. G. (2000), *Philosophy of Language*. London: Routledge.
Malcolm, Norman (1984), *Ludwig Wittgenstein: A Memoir*. Oxford: Oxford University Press.
Malcolm, Norman (1986), *Wittgenstein: Nothing is Hidden*. Oxford: Blackwell.
Mays, Wolfe (1967), 'Recollections of Wittgenstein'. In Fann 1967, 79–88.
McGuinness, B. (1988), *Wittgenstein: A Life*, vol. 1: *Young Ludwig 1889–1921*. London: Duckworth.
McGuinness, B. (1999), 'The Idea of Jewishness'. In his 2002, 27–42.
McGuinness, B. (2002), *Approaches to Wittgenstein: Collected Papers*. London: Routledge.
Mill, J. S. (1861), *Utilitarianism*, ed. R. Crisp. Oxford: Oxford University Press, 1998.
Monk, R. (1990), *Wittgenstein: The Duty of Genius*. London: Cape.
Moore, G. E. (1903), *Principia Ethica*. Cambridge: Cambridge University Press.
Morton, Frederic (1980), *A Nervous Splendor: Vienna 1888/1889*. London: Weidenfeld & Nicolson.
Mulhall, Stephen (1990), *On Being in the World: Wittgenstein and Heidegger on Seeing Aspects*. London: Routledge.
Musil, Robert (1931), *The Man without Qualities [Der Mann ohne Eigenschaften]*, tr. S. Wilkins and B. Pike. London: Picador, 1997.
Nedo, M. (1993), *Ludwig Wittgenstein, Wiener Ausgabe: Einführung/Introduction*, Vienna: Springer.
Nedo, M. and Ranchetti, M. (eds) (1983), *Wittgenstein: Sein Leben in Bildern und Texten*. Frankfurt/Main: Suhrkamp.
Nietzsche, Friedrich (1873), 'On Truth and Lying in a Non-Moral Sense'. In his *The Birth of Tragedy and Other Writings*, ed. R. Geuss and R. Speirs, Cambridge: Cambridge University Press, 1999, 141–53.
Nietzsche, Friedrich (1879), *Human, All Too Human*, vol. 2, tr. R. J. Hollingdale. Cambridge: Cambridge University Press, 1986.

Bibliography

Nietzsche, Friedrich (1881), *Daybreak*, tr. R. J. Hollingdale. Cambridge: Cambridge University Press, 1997.

O'Shaughnessy, Brian (1980), *The Will*, vol. 2. Cambridge: Cambridge University Press.

Pascal, Fania (1973), 'Wittgenstein: A Personal Memoir'. Repr. in Rhees 1984, 12–49.

Peacocke, C. (1981), 'Reply: Rule-following: The Nature of Wittgenstein's Arguments'. In S. Holtzman and C. Leich (eds), *Wittgenstein: To Follow a Rule*, London: Routledge, 72–95.

Pears, David (1987), *The False Prison: A Study of the Development of Wittgenstein's Philosophy*, vol. 1. Oxford: Oxford University Press.

Pitcher, George (1964), *The Philosophy of Wittgenstein*. Englewood Cliffs, NJ: Prentice-Hall.

Plato, *Cratylus*. In *The Dialogues of Plato*, vol. 3, tr. B. Jowett, Oxford: Oxford University Press, 1953, 41–106.

Plato, *Meno*, tr. G. M. A. Grube. Indianapolis: Hackett, 1976.

Plato, *Theaetetus*, tr. J. McDowell. Oxford: Clarendon Press, 1973.

Prokop, Ursula (2003), *Margaret Stonborough-Wittgenstein: Bauherrin, Intellektuelle, Mäzenin*. Vienna: Böhlau Verlag.

Proops, Ian (2001), 'The New Wittgenstein: A Critique'. *European Journal of Philosophy*, 9 (3), 375–404.

Putnam, Hilary (1962), 'Dreaming and "Depth Grammar"'. In R. J. Butler (ed.), *Analytical Philosophy*, Oxford: Blackwell, 211–35.

Putnam, Hilary (1965), 'Brains and Behaviour'. In R. J. Butler (ed.), *Analytical Philosophy*, 2nd series, Oxford: Blackwell, 1–19.

Putnam, Hilary (1973), 'Meaning and Reference'. *Journal of Philosophy*, 70, 699–711. Repr. in S. P. Schwartz (ed.), *Naming, Necessity, and Natural Kinds*, Ithaca, NY: Cornell University Press, 119–32.

Quine, W. V. O. (1953), 'Two Dogmas of Empiricism'. In his *From a Logical Point of View*, Cambridge, Mass.: Harvard University Press, 20–46.

Quine, W. V. O. (1970), 'Homage to Carnap'. Repr. in R. Creath (ed.), *Dear Carnap, Dear Van*, Berkeley: University of California Press, 1990, 463–6.

Ramsey, F. P. (1923), 'Review of *Tractatus Logico-Philosophicus*'. *Mind*, 32, 465–78.

Rhees, R. (ed.) (1984), *Recollections of Wittgenstein*, rev. edn. Oxford: Oxford University Press.

Rundle, B. (1990), *Wittgenstein and Contemporary Philosophy of Language*. Oxford: Blackwell.

Rundle, B. (1997), *Mind in Action*. Oxford: Clarendon Press.

Rundle, B. (2001), 'Meaning and Understanding'. In Glock 2001, 94–118.

Russell, Bertrand (1903), *The Principles of Mathematics*, 2nd edn. London: George Allen & Unwin, 1937.

Russell, Bertrand (1905), 'On Denoting'. In his 1956a, 41–56.
Russell, Bertrand (1910), 'On the Nature of Truth and Falsehood'. In his *Philosophical Essays*, London: Allen & Unwin, 147–59.
Russell, Bertrand (1912), *The Problems of Philosophy*. London: Oxford University Press, 1964.
Russell, Bertrand (1913), *Theory of Knowledge: The 1913 Manuscript*. In *The Collected Papers of Bertrand Russell*, vol. 7, ed. E. A. Eames, London: Allen & Unwin, 1984.
Russell, Bertrand (1919a), *Introduction to Mathematical Philosophy*. London: George Allen & Unwin.
Russell, Bertrand (1919b), 'On Propositions: What They Are and How They Mean'. In his 1956a, 285–320.
Russell, Bertrand (1920), 'Introduction' to *TLP*, pp. ix–xxii.
Russell, Bertrand (1921), *The Analysis of Mind*. London: George Allen & Unwin.
Russell, Bertrand (1956a), *Logic and Knowledge*. London: Routledge.
Russell, Bertrand (1956b), *Portraits from Memory*. London: George Allen & Unwin.
Russell, Bertrand (1959), *My Philosophical Development*. London: George Allen & Unwin.
Russell, Bertrand (1968), *The Autobiography of Bertrand Russell*, vol. 2: *1914–44*. London: Allen & Unwin.
Russell, Bertrand, with A. N. Whitehead (1927), *Principia Mathematica*, 2nd edn (1st edn 1910), Cambridge: Cambridge University Press.
Ryle, Gilbert (1949), *The Concept of Mind*. London: Hutchinson.
Savigny, Eike von (1996), *Der Mensch als Mitmensch: Wittgensteins 'Philosophische Untersuchungen'*. Munich: Deutscher Taschenbuch Verlag.
Schopenhauer, Arthur (1840), *On the Basis of Morality*, tr. E. F. J. Payne. Indianapolis: Hackett, 1995.
Schopenhauer, Arthur (1859), *The World as Will and Representation*, 2 vols, tr. E. F. J. Payne. Indian Hills, Colo.: The Falcon's Wing Press, 1958.
Schorske, Carl E. (1981), *Fin-de-siècle Vienna: Politics and Culture*. New York: Vintage.
Schroeder, Severin (1998), *Das Privatsprachen-Argument: Wittgenstein über Empfindung und Ausdruck*. Paderborn: Schöningh.
Schroeder, Severin (2001a), 'Are Reasons Causes? A Wittgensteinian Response to Davidson'. In S. Schroeder (ed.), *Wittgenstein and Contemporary Philosophy of Mind*, Basingstoke: Palgrave, 150–70.
Schroeder, Severin (2001b), 'The Concept of Trying'. *Philosophical Investigations*, 24 (3), 213–27.
Schroeder, Severin (2001c), 'Private Language and Private Experience'. In Glock 2001, 174–98.
Schroeder, Severin (2004), 'The Demand for Synoptic Representations

and the Private Language Discussion – *PI* 243–315'. In E. Ammereller and E. Fischer (eds), *Wittgenstein at Work: Method in the 'Philosophical Investigations'*, London: Routledge, 147–69.

Searle, John (1969), *Speech Acts*. Cambridge: Cambridge University Press.

Searle, John (1983), *Intentionality*. Cambridge: Cambridge University Press.

Spiel, Hilde (1987), *Vienna's Golden Autumn 1866–1938*. London: Weidenfeld & Nicolson.

Stecker, Robert (1997), *Art Works: Definition, Meaning, Value*. University Park, Pa.: Pennsylvania State University Press.

Steed, Henry Wickham (1913), *The Hapsburg Monarchy*. London: Constable, 4th edn 1919.

Stegmüller, Wolfgang (1979), *Hauptströmungen der Gegenwartsphilosophie: eine kritische Einführung*, Band II, 6. Auflage. Stuttgart: Kröner.

Stone, Norman (1999), *Europe Transformed: 1878–1919*, Oxford: Blackwell.

Strawson, P. F. (1959), *Individuals*. London: Methuen.

Strawson, P. F. (1962), 'Freedom and Resentment'. In his *Freedom and Resentment and Other Essays*, London: Methuen, 1974, 1–25.

Strawson, P. F. (1974), 'Self, Mind and Body'. In his *Freedom and Resentment and Other Essays*, London: Methuen, 169–77.

Sullivan, P. M. (1996), 'The "Truth" in Solipsism, and Wittgenstein's Rejection of the A Priori'. *European Journal of Philosophy*, 4/2, 195–219.

Timms, Edward (1986), *Karl Kraus: Apocalyptic Satirist. Culture and Catastrophe in Habsburg Vienna*. New Haven: Yale University Press.

Waismann, Friedrich (1965), *The Principles of Linguistic Philosophy*, ed. R. Harré. London: Macmillan.

Weininger, Otto (1903), *Geschlecht und Charakter: eine prinzipielle Untersuchung*. Repr. Munich: Matthes & Seitz, 1997.

Weininger, Otto (1904), *Über die letzten Dinge*. Repr. Munich: Matthes & Seitz, 1997.

Weitz, Morris (1956), 'The Role of Theory in Aesthetics'. *Journal of Aesthetics and Art Criticism*, 15, 27–35.

Wijdeveld, Paul (1993), *Ludwig Wittgenstein: Architect*. Amsterdam: The Pepin Press.

Wittgenstein, Hermine (1949), 'My Brother Ludwig'. Extract from an unpublished MS, 'Familienerinnerungen', tr. M. Clark, in Rhees 1984, 1–11.

Wright, Georg Henrik von (1979), 'The Origin and Composition of Wittgenstein's *Investigations*'. In Luckhardt 1979, 138–60.

Wright, Georg Henrik von (1982), 'The Wittgenstein Papers'. In his *Wittgenstein*, Oxford: Blackwell, 35–62.

Zweig, Stefan (1941), *Die Welt von gestern*. Stockholm: Bermann Fischer-Verlag.

Index

action 219–33
  see also reason(s); voluntary action
Adrianople, battle at 10
aeronautics 14–16, 20
aesthetics 5, 9–10, 99, 101, 104,
  126–7, 142–3, 167, 254
Alexander, Samuel 15
ambiguity 33, 35–6, 157, 166, 246
analysis, logical 32–6, 37, 38–40,
  42–52, 58–9, 62, 69, 70, 75–80, 85,
  86, 87, 92, 94, 98, 100, 115, 128,
  132, 134, 136–8, 154, 238–9
analytic statement(s) 109, 111, 139,
  152–3, 165, 222, 240–5
anomalous monism 239
Anscombe, Elizabeth 234, 237
appearance *v.* reality 199–200,
  211–12
a priori 37, 62, 64, 75, 97–8, 105, 112,
  115, 134, 140, 152–3, 165, 166,
  240, 241, 242, 244–7
  contingent truths 245–7
architecture 7, 9, 114, 145
argument (of a function) 63, 70–1, 79
arithmetic 16, 19–20, 65, 72, 110–11,
  112, 174
arrow 55
art 141 n.8, 142–3
artificial intelligence 239
art nouveau 9
Ascribability Argument 202–6, 209
aspects, perception of 235

attitude 196, 224
  objective 231 n.42
Augustine, St 13 n.4
  on time 158–9, 167, 168
  picture of language 123, 128–30,
    133, 146
Aurelius, Marcus 104 n.44
Austin, J. L. 237–8
automata 185
Ayer, A. J. 237–8

Bahr, Hermann 8
bathroom 93 n.37
Beardsley, Monroe C. 142
beetle in the box 207
behaviourism, logical 99, 181, 239,
  251–4
  see also semi-behaviourism
belief 127, 227–8, 230–2, 233, 241
Bell, Clive 141 n.8, 142
Berchtold, Count 8
Berkeley, George 95
Berlin, Isaiah 237
Bevan, Edward 234, 235
Big Typescript 116, 117
bipolarity 37–8, 53–5, 59, 62, 64, 66,
  69, 75, 88, 91, 92, 98, 99, 105,
  109–10, 111, 112, 128, 138–9
Black, Max 43
blood pressure 216, 217, 219
'bloody' 173
Blue Book 116, 117, 237

Index

Boghossian, P. A. 242
Boltzmann, Ludwig 14–15
Bradley, F. H. 157, 167
Brahms, Johannes 4, 5
British Empiricists 221
Britten, Benjamin 3
Broad, C. D. 24 n.1, 119
Brouwer, L. E. J. 115
Brown Book 116, 117, 237

Cage, John 144
Campbell, Mrs Patrick 16
capacity 162, 184, 185, 193, 231, 251
Carnap, Rudolf 108 n.49, 239
categorical imperative 100
category-mistake 161–2
cause(s) 96, 207, 213, 218, 221, 224, 225, 227, 230–1 n.42, 233, 253–4
 see also reason(s)
certainty 184, 226–7, 229, 235
chess 49, 58, 129, 190, 194, 232, 241 n.4, 243
Chicago School 9
Chomsky, Noam 239
class(es) 19–20, 88–9
classification 163, 248–50, 253–4
coffee-house 7–8
Collingwood, R. G. 142
colour exclusion problem 51–2, 115
colour words 132–4, 142, 177, 206–7, 212 n.33, 217, 235
common sense 96, 123–4, 155–6, 162–3, 166, 167, 168, 169, 181, 235, 247–8, 250
community agreement (community thesis) 197, 198, 199–201
compositionality 47, 250
computer science 239
Conant, James 106 n.45, 107 n.48, 107–8 n.49
concept formation 141, 142
conceptual *v.* empirical questions (statements) 36–8, 152, 166, 240–7
conditional 63, 79, 100, 228, 232–3, 245
confirmation *see* verification
confusion, philosophical 108, 124–5, 126, 129, 138, 151–2, 154–5, 156–67, 169, 170

conjunction 62–3, 67–8, 73–4, 75, 79–80, 81, 115
consciousness 127
Constable, John 56
contradiction 19–20, 64, 108, 115, 202
convention 53–4, 60, 138, 147, 150, 171, 172, 175, 176, 177, 179, 181, 242, 243, 247
conversational implicature 175–6, 222–4
criterion 201, 209–10, 211, 212, 213, 216, 248, 249
 v. symptom 209–10 n.31
Croce, Benedetto 142
Crusoe, Robinson 200–1

Danto, Arthur C. 142
Davidson, Donald 227 n.41, 238–9, 250–1
deception 202, 209–10
decision 225
decision procedure 78, 81–2
definition 40–1, 63, 65, 67–8, 134, 138, 139, 140–1, 142–5, 146, 151, 153–4, 167, 169, 211, 246, 250
 defining sample 245–7, 248
 see also ostensive explanation
denoting phrases 34
Descartes, René 161–2, 163, 202 n.26, 221, 251
description 43, 44, 45, 132
 v. prescription 99–100
descriptions, theory of 34–5, 38, 40, 42, 62
desert islander *see* Crusoe, Robinson
desire (want) 163–5, 227–8, 230–2
destruction 41, 44, 45, 132, 133
deviant pupil 187–9, 197
Diamond, Cora 106 n.47, 109
Dickie, George 142
disinterestedness 104
disjunction 67–9, 80, 81
disposition(s) 99, 231 n.42
disquiet (*Beunruhigung*) 154, 155, 158, 159
doorbell 150
doubt 235
dualism (of mind and body) 96, 161–2, 202 n.26, 251

Index

Duchamp, Marcel 144
duel 7

Eine philosophische Betrachtung 116, 117
empiricism 40, 221
Engelmann, Paul 113, 114
entailment 76, 78–80, 88
entropy 44
error 160–1, 206, 208, 211, 213, 226
essence 248–50
essentialism 128, 139–45
ethics 5, 9–10, 11–14, 26–7, 29–30, 88, 99–104, 105, 111, 236
etymology 177
Excalibur 45
expectation 127
experience 37, 54, 94–5, 97–8, 103, 127
explanation 22, 24, 27–8, 111, 147, 149, 163, 168–9, 172, 176–8, 250, 251
 of action 227–33
 of meaning 140–2, 144–5, 244, 250
 see also saying *v.* showing
expression 71
expressive behaviour (behavioural manifestation) 98–9, 202, 203, 205, 209–10, 213–14, 216–17, 227–8, 230–2, 240, 251
extensional *v.* intensional terms 241

fact(s) 38–40, 53, 55, 57, 59, 84, 90, 95, 100, 101, 103, 152
false judgements *see* error; proposition(s): false
family resemblance concepts 140–5
feeling 127, 254
Feigl, Herbert 239
feuilleton 8, 10
first-person authority (paradox) 183, 184, 185, 214, 226–7, 228–33, 254
Fodor, J. A. 239
Fogelin, Robert J. 81 n.29, 199 n.24
formal concepts 88, 90
formalization, logical 17–19, 33 n.5, 34–5, 251
Ficker, Ludwig von 21, 27, 29
Frank, Philipp 239
Franz Ferdinand, Crown Prince of Austria 21

Franz Joseph, Emperor of Austria 5–7
Frege, Gottlob 15, 17, 19–20, 22, 23, 30, 31, 32, 34, 35, 36, 38, 46, 52, 70–1, 78, 82, 86, 104, 113, 135
function (material) 70–2, 80
 (purpose; interest) of a word; of language 129, 130–2, 139, 150–1, 155, 162, 177, 209 n.30, 215, 224, 229, 233, 254

game 140–1, 143, 144, 171, 174, 196
general principle (maxim) of discourse 222–3
generic term 217
genuine duration 185
Glock, Hans-Johann 170–1, 174, 241
Gödel, Kurt 239
Goethe, Johann Wolfgang von 5, 56 n.15, 157 n.14, 235
gold 254
'good' 173–4
Grayling, A. C. 169–70, 173, 174, 250
Grice, Paul 175–6, 222, 237–8, 241
Grillparzer, Franz 5
groundlessness 229

Hacker, P. M. S. 106, 108, 238, 240 n.4
Hampshire, Stuart 237
happiness 101, 103–4, 163, 235, 236
Hare, R. M. 237
Hart, H. L. A. 237
Haydn, Franz Joseph 5
Hebel, Johann Peter 5, 126
Hempel, Carl 239
Heraclitus 156, 157 n.14, 181
Hertz, Heinrich 15 n.7
Hindemith, Paul 3
holism 241
hope 127, 225
Hornsby, Jennifer 224 n.39
Housman, A. E. 93
Hume, David 85 n.32, 97, 98, 100, 153, 156, 205, 214, 221

Ibsen, Henrik 12, 101
idealism 4, 95–6, 167
 transcendental 96, 153
ideo-motor theory 221

identity 19, 32, 33, 35, 82–3, 91, 110 n.50, 156–7
  personal identity 157
Idle-Wheel Argument 206–8
indexicals 130–1
individualism 13–14, 101
induction 127, 187
ineffable *see* saying *v.* showing
inference *see* entailment
infinity, axiom of 20, 90 n.36
inner-object conception 182–3, 185, 201–2
  of reasons 227
  of sensations 201–19, 220
  of voluntary action 220–5
inner process *see* mental process
instantaneous experience of complex contents (paradox) 182–5, 188–90, 191–4
Institutional Theory of Art 142–3
intention 123, 127, 151, 164–5, 196, 219, 222, 223
  expression of 226–7, 228
  to play chess 184, 194, 195–6
  remembering past 228–32
  to say *see* meaning (*meinen*)
intentionality 60–1, 127, 239
internal accusative (object) 165, 179
internal properties (relations) 39, 47, 62, 76, 88, 90
interpretation 189, 192–3, 229
  infinite regress 192–3
introspection 204–6, 213, 214, 219
inverted colour perception 206
'is' 33, 157, 167
  factual *v.* analytic sense 246–7

James, William 13, 221
jealousy 230–1 n.42
Jews and Jewishness 2, 3, 11, 119–20
Joachim, Joseph 4
joint negation 68, 74–5, 75–8 n.27, 80–1, 83 n.31
Jourdain, Philip 20
Joyce, James 144

Kant, Immanuel 12, 96, 100, 153, 240 n.3

Keller, Gottfried 5, 126
Kenny, Anthony 49, 51, 237
kinaesthetic sensations 221, 226
King Lear 145
know-how *v.* know-that 193–4
knowledge 27–8, 153, 208–9, 226–7, 235
Kokoschka, Oskar 21
Königgrätz, battle of 5
Kraus, Karl 2, 9–10, 11, 104
Kripke, S. A.
  on contingent *a priori* truth 245–7
  on meaning of natural kind terms 248–50
  on rule-following 197–201

ladder, throwing away 105, 107
language 9–10, 26–7, 29, 30, 35–6, 46, 52–61, 76, 89, 91–2, 93–5, 96, 105, 109, 112, 116, 123, 127, 129, 132, 134, 139–40, 145, 155, 156, 158, 170, 203 n.27, 238–9, 247
  ideal 35–6, 46, 238
  illogical 91–2, 94
  misleading forms of 155, 158, 159, 160, 161–2, 166, 196
  misuse of 154, 162–3, 192
  normativity of 174, 190–1
  philosophy of 31, 168, 170, 239
  private 94, 146, 200, 201–4, 206
language-game(s) 129, 133, 139, 155, 172, 207, 233, 245
  builders 130–2, 170, 172, 179, 210
  buying apples 129–30, 169, 173
  as primary 229–30
  sensation diary 210–19
Last Writings on the Philosophy of Psychology 235 n.1
Leavis, F. R. 14
lectures 118
Lee, Desmond 50 n.11
linguistics 156, 170
literature 5, 10, 93 n.37
Locke, John 43, 149, 163, 206–7, 249
logic 16–20, 21, 26–7, 29, 30, 36, 62–87, 89, 90 n.36, 92, 94, 96, 105, 109, 111 n.50, 112, 238, 241, 251
logical atomism 28, 38–52, 75, 83, 115
  dissolution of 128–51

Index

logical form 27–8, 32–6, 37, 38, 58–9, 76, 88, 89–90, 91–2, 116, 238
  of an object 39, 92
logical objects 37, 69
logical picture 60
logical positivists 237, 239
logical symbols (connectives, constants, signs) 18, 35, 47, 63–9, 71–5, 85–7, 128, 130
logical syntax 88–90
logical truth (proposition) 29, 37, 48, 69–70, 76–8, 81–2, 83, 88, 92, 97, 138
logicism 17, 19–20
looking for 148
Loos, Adolf 9, 10, 11, 21, 104, 114
Lycan, W. G. 171, 171–2

Mackie, J. L. 237
Malcolm, Norman 234, 235
mathematics 15, 16–17, 19–20, 29, 105, 110–11, 112, 116, 139, 152, 153, 241
  philosophy of 16–17, 105, 114, 116–17, 129–30
meaning (*Bedeutung*) 30–5, 37, 41, 42, 43, 46–8, 53–4, 76, 82, 87, 91, 92, 105, 127, 128, 129–30, 138, 145–51, 153, 171, 240, 245
  change of 242, 249, 253
  common-sense view of 168–9, 247–8, 250
  explanation of 140–2, 144–5, 244, 250; *see also* definition; ostensive explanation
  hidden 33, 137–8, 247–8
  of natural kind terms 248–50
  as object named *see* referentialism
  and paraphrase 176–9
  of sensation terms 206–8, 213–14, 215–19
  theory of 169–70, 181, 238–9, 250–1
  through ideas in the mind 206
  through meaning (*meinen*) 47, 60–1, 145–51, 175, 181
  truth in virtue of 109, 153, 240–4
  and use 110–11, 116, 129–33, 134–6, 155, 168–81, 183, 203, 207–8, 210, 214–17, 218–19, 225, 238–9, 248

meaning (*meinen*; acts of) 46–7, 60–1, 95, 98, 128, 134, 145–51, 185–201
  circumstances 195–6
  explanation of 231
  Kripke's denial of 197–8, 201
  and meaning (*Bedeutung*) 47, 60–1, 145–51, 175, 181
  as mental process 147–50, 151, 172, 195, 197–8, 201, 228; as mental images 149; as paying attention 147–9
  see also intention; understanding
measuring 158–9, 245
memory 127, 133, 184, 228–32
mental image(s) 149, 183, 221, 228
mental instruction manual 194
mental mechanism 195, 196
mental occurrences (activities; events; phenomena; processes; states) 99, 165, 181–5, 185–9, 194, 196–7, 201, 216 n.37, 220–1, 224–5, 227, 228–30, 232, 251
mental representation 194, 196, 197
metaphysics 27–8, 100–1, 105, 106, 155, 163, 240 n.3
micro-structure 162–3, 248–50, 253–4
military 7
Mill, John Stuart 163
mind 85, 161–2, 195, 202
  philosophy of 182, 239
  see also dualism; other minds
model(s) 56–60, 145
modus ponens 79
Moore, G. E. 16, 91, 115, 119, 136 n.7, 137, 156, 235
morality *see* ethics
Mörike, Eduard 5
multiple sclerosis 253
music 3–5, 144–5

N (operator) *see* joint negation
name(s) 17, 30–2, 34, 35, 39, 40, 42, 45, 52, 53, 55, 60, 65–70, 82–3, 86–7, 91, 92, 94, 105, 128, 132, 146, 176, 177, 179, 202, 203 n.27, 207, 219
  as simple sign(s) 45, 46, 60, 68–9, 128, 132, 136
  see also referentialism

nationalism 6
natural kinds 248–50
necessity (necessary truth) 37–8, 40, 47, 62, 69–70, 75–6, 82, 83, 85, 88, 89, 94, 99, 105, 109, 111–12, 166, 244–7
  a posteriori 245
negation 63, 66–9, 71, 73–4, 75, 86–7, 127, 244
Nelson, John 234
Nietzsche, Friedrich 14, 54, 126
No-Criterion Argument 210–14, 219
non-cognitivism 13
nonsense 15 n.7, 26, 27, 33, 42, 45, 65, 72, 83, 84, 88–112, 115, 138, 140, 152, 154, 155, 156, 159, 167, 173 n.17, 174, 244
Nonsense Interpretation 26 n.3, 105–10, 112
norm of representation 240–1 n.4, 242
Notebooks 1914–1916 29, 46–8, 50 n.11, 86, 87, 96, 100, 104, 145, 146
'Notes for the Philosophical Lecture' 204 n.27
'Notes on Logic' 27
number(s) 19, 83, 90–1, 129–30, 131
  writing arithmetical series 147, 183–4, 185–6, 187–90, 191–4, 196

object(s) 65–71, 72, 83, 84, 86, 87, 88–9, 90–1, 92, 94–5, 97
  abstract 129–30, 133
  as meaning of a name *see* referentialism
  simple 39–48, 49–52, 85, 87, 92, 94, 105, 136–7
Ogden, C. K. 1, 22
On Certainty 235
ontology 29, 30, 39–52, 92, 130, 132
operation(s), logical 20, 64, 70–2, 77–80
order 130–2, 147
O'Shaughnessy, Brian 224
ostensive explanation (definition) 146, 177, 211, 212 n.33
  private 212 n.33
Ostwald, Wilhelm 22

other minds (problem; scepticism) 93, 95–9, 183, 185, 202–6, 208–10

pain 97–9, 202–6, 207–10, 211, 213–14, 217, 218, 251–4
  ascription of 204–6
  and expressive behaviour 98–9, 205, 208–10, 213–14, 251–4
  thermometer 214
paradox (puzzle) 19–29, 52, 54, 88–90, 104–5 156–66, 168, 170, 182–5, 188–90, 191, 194, 199, 247 n.7, 248, 250
Pattison, Gilbert 118–19, 173 n.17
Pears, D. F. 94, 237
Pepys, Samuel 199–200
performative utterance 228
Philosophical Grammar 116, 117
Philosophical Investigations 5, 44–5, 116, 117, 121–233, 237, 239, 245
  form and composition of 121–3, 124–7, 167
  overview 127
  'Part II' 182, 235
Philosophical Remarks 98, 116–17
philosophy
  American 238–9
  difficulty to stop 196
  of language 31, 53, 170, 239
  of mathematics 16–17, 105, 114, 116–17, 129–30
  of mind 182, 239
  nature of (method in) 15 n.7, 27–9, 105, 106–7, 115, 123–4, 125–6, 127, 151–68, 182, 195, 244
  Oxford (ordinary language) 237–8
  as search for definitions 153–4
  theory (doctrine; theses) 27–8, 53, 106, 107, 123–4, 151–3, 166, 167–8, 169, 182, 188, 190, 200, 240, 241, 245
phlogiston 201
pictorial form 57–8
pictorial relationship 57–60
picture theory of language 55–61, 62, 64, 75, 86–7, 91, 100, 105, 110, 111, 116, 131–2, 139, 160

Pinsent, David 21, 102
Pitcher, George 176, 179
Plato 52–3, 142, 154, 157–8, 160, 242
Platonism, logical 37
poetry 125–7, 145, 157 n.14
predicate 17–19, 89–90, 157, 158, 166, 212–13
predicate calculus 82, 238
private mental occurrences (experiences) 184–5, 199–200, 201–2, 206–8, 216, 217–18
private sensation diary *see* language-game: sensation diary
Prokofiev, Sergei Sergeyevich 3
Proops, Ian 106, 108
proposition(s) 27–8, 52–61, 64, 71–2, 76, 77, 84, 86–7, 88, 89, 92, 100, 105, 107, 116, 133
  elementary 38–9, 49–51, 62, 63–5, 66, 69, 71, 74–5, 80, 83, 87, 92, 115, 128, 139, 145
  false 52–4, 160
  general 80–2
  general form of 75, 139
  grammatical 111, 139, 240–1 n.4, 243 n.5
  as models 55–60
  v. names 52–5, 71
  as names of truth-values 70–1
  understanding new propositions 52, 54–5, 59, 238, 250
propositional attitudes 83–5
propositional calculus 78, 82
propositional function 71
propositional sign 60, 89
propositional variable 71–2, 80–1
pseudo-propositions 107, 110 n.50
psychological egoism 163–6, 167
psychological state(s) *see* mental occurrences
psychology 61, 85, 100, 176, 239
  philosophy of 235
Putnam, Hilary
  on logical behaviourism 202 n.26, 251–4
  on meaning of natural kind terms 248–50

quantifier 18, 19, 82, 83
Queen Victoria 212
Quine, Willard Van Orman 238, 239, 241–2
Quinton, A. M. 237

Ramsey, Frank 114–15, 116
Ravel, Maurice 3
reaction 228
reading 186–7
  peculiar experience of 186–7
Realschule 4
reason(s) 164, 194, 227–33
  v. cause(s) 187, 227, 230–1 n.42, 233, 239
reference 30–2, 34, 42–8, 52–3
referentialism 30–5, 37, 38, 42–8, 52–3, 65, 69 n.22, 128–34, 138, 139, 150, 161, 172, 175, 182, 185, 202–4 n.27, 215, 220, 224, 227
  of sensation words *see* inner-object conception: of sensations
Reichenbach, Hans 239
religion 4, 12–14, 102, 103
Remarks on Colour 235
Remarks on the Foundations of Mathematics 117, 200
Remarks on the Philosophy of Psychology 235 n.1
remembering a tune 184
Rhees, Rush 234
Richards, Ben 234
right *v.* wrong *see* appearance *v.* reality
rigid designator 247 n.7
Rilke, Rainer Maria 21, 126
Ringstraße 7, 9, 11
river 156–7
rules 140, 174, 188–9, 243
  and community (solitary rule-following) 199–201
  can be misunderstood 189, 192–3, 200
  explicit *v.* implicit 190–1
  of language 129, 134, 135, 171, 190–1, 250
  standard of correctness 200
  syntactical 89, 115, 238
Rundle, Bede 140, 172, 174, 176, 180

Russell, Bertrand 1, 12, 13, 14, 15–16, 17, 19–20, 21–2, 23, 25–6, 30, 31–6, 37, 38, 40, 42, 45, 46, 52, 61, 62, 64, 69, 71, 77, 78, 82–3, 84, 86, 88, 90 n.36, 91, 102, 104, 113, 115, 126 n.5, 153, 221, 237
Russell's paradox 19–20, 88–90
Ryle, Gilbert 161, 237

Salzer, Helene (née Wittgenstein) 118, 119–20
Santayana, George 239–40
satisfaction 164–5
saying *v.* showing 26, 59, 62, 76–80, 81–2, 83, 85, 88–112, 107 n.48, 110, 111 n.50
scepticism 93, 96, 185, 197–8, 206, 208–9, 210
Schiller, Friedrich 5
Schlick, Moritz 108 n.49, 115, 137
Schopenhauer, Arthur 4, 13, 95–6, 100–1, 103 n.43, 104, 142
science 27–8, 105, 115, 125, 142, 143–4, 152, 162–3, 166, 238, 239, 241, 248–50, 251, 253–4
scientific progress 249
scientific realism 248–50
Searle, John 173–4, 239
secondary qualities 163
self-deception 165–6, 230 n.42
self-interest 163–6
semantics *v.* pragmatics 175–6
semi-behaviourism 98–9
sensations 123, 127, 186, 201–19, 220, 221
  knowledge of 202–4, 208–9
  perception of 214
  see also pain
sense 26, 31, 32, 36, 38, 41–8, 55, 59–60, 62, 64, 75–6, 85, 86–7, 88–90, 92, 105, 107, 110–11, 131, 133, 139
  autonomy of 41–8
  determinacy of 36, 38, 46–8, 128, 134–6, 146
senseless 65, 77, 83, 105, 110
sense-data 40
sense perception 160
sentence *see* proposition

Shaw, G. B. 16
Sheffer, H. 74 n.26
simple sign(s) *see* name(s)
Socrates 153, 154, 160–1, 167
solidity 162–3
solipsism 88, 92–9, 100–1, 105, 109, 112, 205
  moral 10–14, 101
'Some Remarks on Logical Form' 115–16
soul 85, 101
speech acts 173–4
Spinoza, Baruch 104
Sraffa, Piero 116
standard of correctness *see* criterion
standard metre 245–7
state(s) of affairs 38–9, 44, 48–53, 57, 63, 91, 92, 100, 105, 160
Stecker, Robert 145 n.11
stipulation 54, 154, 243
stoicism 103–4, 252–4
Stonborough, Jerome 114
Stonborough, Margaret (née Wittgenstein) 13, 114, 119
Strachey, Lytton 212–13
Strauss, Richard 3
Strawson, P. F. 231 n.42, 237, 241
structure 57, 60 n.16
subject (I; person; self) 85, 95 n.42, 96–8, 100–1, 205
sub specie aeternitatis 104
substance of the world 39, 41–8, 51
suicide 3, 11, 15 n.7, 26 n.2, 102, 111, 113
super-spartans 252–4
surprise 155, 225–6
synoptic representation 155, 156, 186, 210
synthetic *a priori* judgements 153, 240 n.3

tableau vivant 56, 57
tandem 242–4
Tarski, Alfred 239
tautology 48, 64, 69, 76–9, 82, 83, 92, 103, 105, 110, 111
theatre 7–9
theory *see* philosophy: theory
therapy 106, 123, 152, 154, 155, 254

thinking (thoughts) 51–2, 60–1, 84–5, 106, 107, 123, 127, 146, 160, 166, 184, 228, 239
  language of thought 61, 239
time 158–9
Tolstoy, Lev Nikolayevich 12–13, 14, 126, 142
Toulmin, Stephen 237
Tractatus Logico-Philosophicus 4, 10, 14 n.5, 15 n.7, 17 n.8, 20, 21–2, 24–112, 113, 115, 116, 152, 237, 238, 239, 248 n.8
  criticisms of 123–4, 125, 127, 128–51, 182
  form of 24–5
  table of contents 25
Tractatus paradox 27, 104–12
train-spotting 215
Trakl, Georg 21
translation 33, 55 n.14, 251
Trollope, Anthony 144
Trotsky, Leon (Bronstein, L. D.) 8
truth 27, 41–3, 54, 93, 106, 112, 133, 211, 212–13
  in virtue of meaning 109, 153, 240–4
truth-conditions 64, 87, 238, 250
truthfulness (sincerity) 9–10, 11–14, 101–2, 211, 212–14, 230–2, 236
truth-function(s) 49 n.9, 62–87, 128, 139, 145
truth-grounds 79–80
truth-operation(s) *see* operation(s)
truth-possibilities 63, 79–80
truth-table(s) 62–5, 67–8, 77–80, 82, 87
truth-value 62–5, 67–8, 70
trying 175–6, 221–4
types, theory of 20, 88–9

understanding 36–7, 41, 53, 54–5, 66, 82, 94, 105, 107, 112, 123, 127, 131, 149, 171, 179, 185–201, 251
  circumstances of 186
  as having mental images 149, 183
  reservoir picture of 188

sudden 183–4, 185, 187
  see also meaning (*meinen*)
Urmson, J. O. 237
use *see* meaning: and use
utilitarianism 163

value (of a function) 70
vanity 11–12, 101–2, 113
variable 18, 70, 71, 83, 90
variable proposition 71 n.24
verification 116, 212–13, 241–2, 244
Vienna 2, 5–10, 11
Vienna Circle 108 n.49, 109, 115, 117, 239
volitions *see* will: acts of
voluntary action 164, 219–27

Waismann, Friedrich 115, 117, 237
war 21, 29, 101, 102–3, 120
Warnock, G. J. 237
water 248–9
Weininger, Otto 11–13, 236
Weitz, Morris 143–4
Whitehead, A. N. 16, 17
will 100–1, 103–4, 127, 163–4, 219, 220–1, 228, 253
  acts of (willing) 100, 221, 224
  see also voluntary action
wish(ing) 225–6, 229
Wittgenstein, Hans 3
Wittgenstein, Helene *see* Salzer
Wittgenstein, Hermann Christian 2, 119–20
Wittgenstein, Hermine 3, 16, 114, 119–20
Wittgenstein, Karl 2–3
Wittgenstein, Kurt 3
Wittgenstein, Leopoldine (née Kalmus) 2–3
Wittgenstein, Margaret *see* Stonborough
Wittgenstein, Paul 3–4
Wittgenstein, Rudolf 3
world 39, 41–2, 50–1, 91–2, 93–8, 100, 103, 104, 105, 107, 108, 111 n.50, 112
Wright, G. H. von 234

Printed in Great Britain
by Amazon